CONSTITUTIONS, RELIGION AND POLITICS IN ASIA

As religious polarization in society deepens, political actors and policymakers have begun to struggle with questions about the role of the dominant religion and how religion influences constitutional commitments and development. By focusing on Indonesia, Malaysia and Sri Lanka, *Constitutions, Religion and Politics in Asia* demonstrates how constitution-making and the operation of constitutional arrangements involving religion cannot be separated from the broader political dynamics of society. Although constitutions establish legal and political structures of government institutions and provide tools for rights protection, they do not operate in a vacuum divorced from the games of power and the political realities surrounding them. Here, Shah sets out how constitutions operate and evolve and demonstrates how constitutional provisions can produce unintended consequences over time. This book stands to be a vital new source of scholarship for students and scholars of law and religion and of comparative constitutional law, and those interested in issues of constitutionalism and legal and political history in Asia.

Dian A. H. Shah is a Research Fellow at the Centre for Asian Legal Studies, National University of Singapore. She previously taught at the Faculty of Law, University of Malaya, where she remains a faculty appointee. Her research interests span the fields of constitutional history, comparative constitutional law and human rights, focusing on issues arising from the interaction between constitutional law, religion and politics in selected Asian jurisdictions.

Comparative Constitutional Law and Policy

Series Editors

Tom Ginsburg
University of Chicago
Zachary Elkins
University of Texas at Austin
Ran Hirschl
University of Toronto

Comparative constitutional law is an intellectually vibrant field that encompasses an increasingly broad array of approaches and methodologies. This series collects analytically innovative and empirically grounded work from scholars of comparative constitutionalism across academic disciplines. Books in the series include theoretically informed studies of single constitutional jurisdictions, comparative studies of constitutional law and institutions, and edited collections of original essays that respond to challenging theoretical and empirical questions in the field.

Books in the Series

Constitutions, Religion and Politics in Asia: Indonesia, Malaysia and Sri Lanka Dian A. H. Shah

Proportionality: New Frontiers, New Challenges edited by Vicki Jackson and Mark Tushnet

Constituents Before Assembly: Participation, Deliberation, and Representation in the Crafting of New Constitutions Todd A. Eisenstadt, A. Carl LeVan, and Tofigh Maboudi

Assessing Constitutional Performance Tom Ginsburg and Aziz Huq

Buddhism, Politics and the Limits of Law: The Pyrrhic Constitutionalism of Sri Lanka Benjamin Schonthal

Engaging with Social Rights Brian Ray

Constitutional Courts as Mediators Julio Ríos-Figueroa

Perils of Judicial Self-Government in Transitional Societies David Kosař

Making We the People Chaihark Hahm and Sung Ho Kim

Radical Deprivation on Trial Cesar Rodríguez-Garavito and Diana Rodríguez-Franco

Unstable Constitutionalism edited by Mark Tushnet and Madhav Khosla

Magna Carta and Its Modern Legacy edited by Robert Hazell and James Melton

Constitutions and Religious Freedom Frank Cross

International Courts and the Performance of International Agreements: A General Theory with Evidence from the European Union Clifford Carrubba and Matthew Gabel

Reputation and Judicial Tactics: A Theory of National and International Courts Shai Dothan

Constitutions, Religion and Politics in Asia

INDONESIA, MALAYSIA AND SRI LANKA

DIAN A. H. SHAH

Research Fellow, Centre for Asian Legal Studies,
National University of Singapore
Senior Lecturer, Faculty of Law, University of Malaya

CAMBRIDGE
UNIVERSITY PRESS

CAMBRIDGE
UNIVERSITY PRESS

University Printing House, Cambridge CB2 8BS, United Kingdom

One Liberty Plaza, 20th Floor, New York, NY 10006, USA

477 Williamstown Road, Port Melbourne, VIC 3207, Australia

4843/24, 2nd Floor, Ansari Road, Daryaganj, Delhi – 110002, India

79 Anson Road, #06–04/06, Singapore 079906

Cambridge University Press is part of the University of Cambridge.

It furthers the University's mission by disseminating knowledge in the pursuit of education, learning, and research at the highest international levels of excellence.

www.cambridge.org
Information on this title: www.cambridge.org/9781107183346
DOI: 10.1017/9781316869635

First published 2017

Printed in the United Kingdom by Clays, St Ives plc

A catalogue record for this publication is available from the British Library.

Library of Congress Cataloging-in-Publication Data
NAMES: Shah, Dian Abdul Hamed author.
TITLE: Constitutions, religion and politics in Asia : Indonesia, Malaysia and Sri Lanka / Dian A. H. Shah, Research Fellow, Centre for Asian Legal Studies, National University of Singapore Senior Lecturer, Faculty of Law, University of Malaya.
DESCRIPTION: Cambridge; United Kingdom ; New York, NY, USA : Cambridge University Press, 2017. | Series: Comparative constitutional law and policy
IDENTIFIERS: LCCN 2017023166 | ISBN 9781107183346 (hardback)
SUBJECTS: LCSH: Religion and state–Indonesia. | Religion and state–Malaysia. | Religion and state–Sri Lanka. | Freedom of religion–Indonesia. | Freedom of religion–Malaysia. | Freedom of religion–Sri Lanka. | Religious minorities–Legal status, laws, etc.–Indonesia. | Religious minorities–Legal status, laws, etc.–Malaysia. | Religious minorities–Legal status, laws, etc.–Sri Lanka.
CLASSIFICATION: LCC KNC615 .S524 2017 | DDC 342.508/52–DC23 LC record available at https://lccn.loc.gov/2017023166

ISBN 978-1-107-18334-6 Hardback

Contents

Tables

Tables

Acknowledgements

It was at Duke University – where I spent five years and two months as a Master's and Doctoral student – that this book had its foundations. There, I had the privilege of being mentored by Donald Horowitz, Laurence Helfer and Ralf Michaels. Don Horowitz's decades of work on constitutional design and severely divided societies has stimulated my interest and thinking in these areas. Ralf Michaels has been a great source of wisdom, and Larry Helfer has never failed to enlighten me with his ideas and knowledge. His ability to bring the best out of his students is truly inspirational. I owe a lot to them for guiding me through legal academe, even after I left Duke, and their discipline and intellectual enthusiasm are traits that I hope to emulate in my career.

In those years at Duke, my studies and research were made possible by financial and institutional support from the University of Malaya (UM), Duke Law School (especially the International Studies Office) and the Duke Asian Pacific Studies Institute. In the course of developing and completing this book project, in particular, I have been afforded a substantial grant from the Centre for Asian Legal Studies (CALS) and Ministry of Law, Singapore. The current and former administrative staff at CALS (Margaret Ang, Haikel Rino and Regana Mydin) and the Faculty of Law, National University of Singapore (NUS) have provided remarkable support to facilitate my research in Singapore and abroad. I am also greatly indebted to Andrew Harding and Dan Puchniak (Director of CALS) for their unwavering encouragement, patience and understanding as I completed the monograph.

Various aspects of this book have trotted the globe with me. They have been presented and written at various institutions, and during those times I have been humbled by the kindness of many individuals. I am unable to list and thank all of them here, but I am forever grateful for the resources, support and hospitality.

My first step into Sri Lanka was made possible through a generous grant from the American Institute for Sri Lankan Studies (AISLS). The idea of spending months in a country one has never visited before was daunting, but I have come to appreciate the beautiful country, thanks to the warmth and generosity of those I have encountered during my travels. John Rogers and Ira Unamboowe from AISLS helped get my feet off the ground; The Amerasinghes were not only hospitable hosts; they also helped facilitate my research in some ways, and conversations with Asanga Welikala (whom – quite incredibly – I have not met in person to this very day) have been particularly enlightening. I benefitted tremendously from Mario Gomez and his team at the International Centre for Ethnic Studies (ICES), whose support and network of intellectuals, lawyers, researchers and policy-makers have made my work in Sri Lanka possible. I would also like to thank the staff at the N. M. Perera Centre and Harshani Connel from the Law and Society Trust for her help with my repeated requests for documents and materials. Benjamin Schonthal, who has come to be my 'partner-in-crime' for research and discussions on constitutional law, religion and politics in Sri Lanka, deserves special mention. The Sri Lanka portion of this book owes a lot to him – it would not come close to the state it is in today were it not for his generous counsel and intellectual camaraderie.

In Indonesia, my special thanks go to Luthfi Widagdo Eddyono. I would not have been able to access the Indonesian Constitutional Court with great ease, nor would I have been able to obtain a wealth of materials on constitutional reforms in Indonesia, if it were not for his resourcefulness. Over time, Luthfi has become a dependable *teman bicara* on Indonesian constitutional law issues. In the later stages of my research in Jakarta, Bisariyadi (also from the Indonesian Constitutional Court) provided important support. Conversations with Nadirsyah Hosen and Arskal Salim in the earlier days of my research in Jakarta helped develop some of my thoughts and ideas on religion and law in Indonesia. M. Syafii Anwar was also instrumental, at the very beginning, for his assistance in connecting me to various legal, political and academic personalities in Indonesia. Some of the relationships forged then have continued to this day, and I remain grateful for the thought-provoking exchanges and discussions that inspired some of the ideas in this book. I am also indebted to Rizal Mallarangeng and his team at the Freedom Institute, who since 2012 have always welcomed me and provided a 'home' for my research and writing expeditions in Jakarta. I will never forget an occasion in early 2014, when Pak Rizal offered me the opportunity to experience the workings of political campaigns from the front lines. It turned out to be one of the highlights of my many field trips to Indonesia. Conversations with him and with many others – scholars, analysts, activists and political actors alike – have, over the years, piqued my (healthy) obsession with Indonesian law and politics. *Terima kasih sedalam-dalamnya!*

In Malaysia, I am grateful for the incredible support from Johan Shamsuddin Sabaruddin (Dean of the Faculty of Law, UM), with whom I have also enjoyed stimulating conversations on constitutional law and politics. Azmi Sharom, in his own unique ways, has been a trusted adviser, confidant and partner-in-crime, providing respite from the travails of writing. Shad Saleem Faruqi has been an instrumental teacher – I have never had the privilege of formally studying Malaysian constitutional law with him, but his writings and our many discussions together have profoundly shaped my knowledge on the subject. Discussions with Mohd Azizuddin Mohd Sani and K. Shanmuga have also taught me a lot about politics and law in my country. I am also thankful to Ong Kian Ming – a fellow Dukie – for his insights and for diligently providing various data and information. The ideas and thought processes in this book were also provoked by conversations with Kevin Tan, Jaclyn Neo, Sharon Kaur, Tamir Moustafa, Melissa Crouch, Herlambang Wiratraman, Al Khanif, Haidar Adam, Fritz Siregar, Feri Amsari, Pranoto Iskandar, Kikue Hamayotsu, R. William Liddle, Matthew Nelson, Sumanasiri Liyanage, Tom Ginsburg and others, especially those working in the fields of Comparative Constitutional Law and Law and Religion.

Every aspiring author needs a great acquisitions editor, and in that respect I am very fortunate to have been able to work with Joe Ng at Cambridge University Press. He has made what seemed like a long, arduous process a very smooth one. In relation to that I would like to take this opportunity to thank the three peer reviewers whose critical feedback helped significantly improve this book as a whole. Four other individuals also helped bring this book to up its current form. KarLuis Quek, Nisha Rajoo and Chai Duwei provided tremendous assistance, reading every chapter carefully and making sure that no stone is left unturned. Alan Tan inspired the cover images of this book. Alan reminded me that 'people always judge the book by its cover', which is of course true, but I do hope that readers will appreciate this book by the information and intellectual contribution nestled within its many pages.

Last but certainly not least is my family, to whom I have incurred a great debt over the years. I have missed a great many birthday celebrations, *Hari Raya* festivities and significant family events, but they have always been there for me, providing a source of joy and laughter, particularly through the dark days of meeting deadlines. I dedicate this book to my mother – my best friend and ever-loyal supporter. She has 'travelled' around the globe with me in this academic endeavour, patiently listening to the random rants and stories from my journeys. In her own special way, she has also shown me what it means to persevere through challenging times.

Cases

Aktas v. France, Application No. 14308/08, Court (Fifth Section), European
Court of Human Rights (30 June 2009)

Bayrak v. France, Application No. 43563/08, Court (Fifth Section), European
Court of Human Rights (30 June 2009)

Che Omar bin Che Soh v. Public Prosecutor [1988] 2 Malayan Law Journal 55
Constitutional Court of Indonesia, Decision No. 19/PUU-VI/2008,
Concerning the Examination of Law No. 7, Year 1989 on the Religious
Courts as amended by Law No. 3, Year 2006 (12 August 2008)
Constitutional Court of Indonesia, Decision No. 10-17-23/PUU-VII/2009,
Concerning the Examination of Law No. 44, Year 2008 on Pornography
(30 December 2009)
Constitutional Court of Indonesia, Decision No. 140/PUU-VII/2009,
Examination of Law No. 1, Year 1965 on the Prevention from Abuse of
and/or Desecration of Religion (Arts. 1, 2(1), 2(2), 3 and 4(a)) (19 April 2010)
Constitutional Court of Indonesia, Decision No. 84/PUU-X/2012,
Examination of Law No. 1, Year 1965 on the Prevention from Abuse of
and/or Desecration of Religion (Arts. 1, 2(1), 2(2), 3 and 4(a)) (9 April 2013)

*Haji Raimi bin Abdullah v. Siti Hasnah Vangarama binti Abdullah and
Another* [2014] 4 Current Law Journal 253

Jasvir Singh v. France, Application No. 25463/08, Court (Fifth Section),
European Court of Human Rights (30 June 2009)
J.P. Berthelsen v. Director General of Immigration [1987] 1 Malayan Law
Journal 134

*Kamariah bte Ali & Others v. Governments of the State of Kelantan, Malaysia
& Another* [2002] 3 Malayan Law Journal 657
Kapuwatta Mohideen Jumma Mosque v. OIC Weligama, S.C. Application
No. 38/2005 (FR); S.C. Minute of 9/11/2007

Leyla Şahin v. Turkey, Application No. 44774/98, Grand Chamber, European
  Court of Human Rights (10 November 2005)
Lina Joy v. Majlis Agama Islam Wilayah Persekutuan [2004] 2 Malayan
  Law Journal 119
Lina Joy v. Majlis Agama Islam Wilayah Persekutuan & Another [2007]
  4 Malayan Law Journal 585

Mamat bin Daud & Others v. Government of Malaysia [1988] 1 Malayan
  Law Journal 119
Meor Atiqulrahman Ishak & Others v. Fatimah Sihi & Others [2000]
  5 Malayan Law Journal 375
Meor Atiqulrahman bin Ishak v. Fatimah bte Sihi [2006] 4 Malayan Law
  Journal 605
*Menteri Dalam Negeri & Others v. Titular Roman Catholic Archbishop of
  Kuala Lumpur* [2013] 6 Malayan Law Journal 468
Mohd Noor Bin Othman v. Mohd Yusof Jaafar [1988] 2 Malayan Law
  Journal 129

Persatuan Aliran v. Minister for Home Affairs [1988] 1 Malayan Law
  Journal 440
Premalal Perera v. Weerasuriya [1985] 2 Sri Lanka Law Report 177
Prohibition of Forcible Conversion of Religion Bill, Supreme Court Special
  Determination, S.C. Nos. 02–22/2004 (12 August 2004)

*A Bill Titled 'Provincial of the Teaching of the Holy Cross of the Third Order of
  Saint Francis in Menzingen of Sri Lanka (Incorporation)'*, Supreme Court
  of Sri Lanka Special Determination, S.C.S.D. No. 19/2003 (25 July 2003)

Ranjit Singh v. France, Application No. 27561/08, Court (Fifth Section),
  European Court of Human Rights (30 June 2009)
Rev. Stanislas v. State of Madhya Pradesh (1977) All Indian Rep. S.C. 908

Subashini A/P Rajasingham v. Saravanan Thangathoray & Other Appeals
  [2008] 2 Malayan Law Journal 147
*Sulaiman bin Takrib v. Kerajaan Negeri Terengganu (Kerajaan Malaysia,
  intervener) & other applications* [2009] 6 Malayan Law Journal 354

The Christian Sahanaye Doratuwa Prayer Center (Incorporation) Bill,
  Supreme Court of Sri Lanka Special Determination, S.C.S.D No. 2/2001
  (24 May 2001)
The New Wine Harvest Ministries (Incorporation) Bill, Supreme Court of
  Sri Lanka Special Determination, S.C.S.D No. 2 /2003 (16 January 2003)
*Titular Roman Catholic Archbishop of Kuala Lumpur v. Menteri Dalam
  Negeri & Another* [2009] 2 Malayan Law Journal 78
*Titular Roman Catholic Archbishop of Kuala Lumpur v. Menteri Dalam
  Negeri & Others* [2014] 6 Current Law Journal 541

ZI Publications Sdn Bhd & Another v. Kerajaan Negeri Selangor [2016]
  1 Malayan Law Journal 153

Regulations, Legislation and Statutes

Administration of Islamic Law (Federal Territories) Act 1993

Control and Restriction of the Propagation of Non-Islamic Religions (Johor)
Enactment 1991
Control and Restriction of the Propagation of Non-Islamic Religions (Kedah)
Enactment 1988
Control and Restriction of the Propagation of Non-Islamic Religions
(Kelantan) Enactment 1981
Control and Restriction (Propagation of Non-Islamic Religions among
Muslims) (Negeri Sembilan) Enactment 1991
Control and Restriction of the Propagation of Non-Islamic Religions to
Muslims (Malacca) Enactment 1988
Control and Restriction of the Propagation of Non-Islamic Religions (Pahang)
Enactment 1989
Control and Restriction of the Propagation of Non-Islamic Religions
(Terengganu) Enactment 1980

Elucidation on Law No. 1 of 1965 on the Prevention on Abuse and/or
Desecration of Religion

Firearms (Increased Penalties) Act 1971

Internal Security Act 1960

*Keputusan Bersama Menteri Agama, Jaksa Agung dan Menteri Dalam
Negeri Republik Indonesia* (Joint Decision of the Minister of Religion,
the Attorney General and the Minister of Home Affairs of the Republic
of Indonesia), No. 3 Year 2008, KEP-033/A/JA/6/2008, No. 1999 Year 2008
(9 June 2008)
*Ketetapan Majelis Permusyarawatan Rakyat Republik Indonesia Nomor
WVII/MPR/1998 Tentang Hak Asasi Manusia* (MPR Decree No.
WVII/MPR/1998 on Human Rights)

Law No. 1 of 1965 on the Prevention from Abuse of and/or Desecration
   of Religion
Law No. 24 of 2003 on the Constitutional Court
Law No. 10 of 2004 on Rules on Establishing Legislation
Law No. 32 of 2004 on Regional Government
Law No. 44 of 2008 on Pornography
Law No. 8 of 2011 on the Amendment of Law No. 24 of 2003 on the
   Constitutional Court

Non-Islamic Religions (Control of Propagations among Muslims) (Selangor)
   Enactment 1988
Nineteenth Amendment to the Constitution (Private Member's Bill),
   Gazette of the Democratic Socialist Republic of Sri Lanka (1 November
   2004)

*Peraturan Bersama Menteri Agama dan Menteri Dalam Negeri Nomor 9
   dan 8 Tahun 2006* (Joint Regulations of the Ministers of Religion and
   Home Affairs Number 9 and 8 Year 2006)
Prohibition of Forcible Conversion of Religion (Private Member's Bill),
   Gazette of the Democratic Socialist Republic of Sri Lanka (28 May 2004)

Selangor Islamic Religious Administration Enactment 2003
Syariah Criminal Offences (Selangor) Enactment 1995
Syariah Criminal Offences (Federal Territories) Act 1997

Abbreviations

ABIM	Angkatan Belia Islam Malaysia
ACBC	All-Ceylon Buddhist Congress
BBS	Bodu Bala Sena
BN	Barisan Nasional
BPUPKI	Badan Penyelidik Usaha Persiapan Kemerdekaan Indonesia
DPR	Dewan Perwakilan Rakyat
ECtHR	European Court of Human Rights
EPDP	Eelam People's Democratic Party
FPI	Front Pembela Islam (Islamic Defenders' Front)
FUI	Forum Umat Islam
GARIS	Gerakan Reformis Islam (Islamic Reformist Movement)
Gerindra	Gerakan Indonesia Raya
Golkar	Golongan Karya
HTI	Hizbut Tahrir Indonesia
ICCPR	International Covenant on Civil and Political Rights
JAI	Jemaat Ahmadiyah Indonesia
JAIS	Jabatan Agama Islam Selangor
JAKIM	Jabatan Kemajuan Islam Malaysia
KB	Kebangkitan Bangsa
LSSP	Lanka Sama Samaja Party
MCA	Malaysian Chinese Association
MIC	Malaysian Indian Congress
MORA	Ministry of Religious Affairs
MPR	Majelis Permusyawaratan Rakyat
MUI	Majelis Ulama Indonesia
NU	Nahdlatul Ulama
PAH I	*Panitia Ad Hoc I*

PAN	Partai Amanat Negara
Parkindo	Partai Kristen Indonesia
PBB	Partai Bulan Bintang
PDI-P	Partai Demokrasi Indonesia – Perjuangan
PDKB	Partai Demokrasi Kasih Bangsa
PDS	Partai Damai Sejahtera
PDU	Partai Daulatul Ummah
PK	Partai Keadilan
PKI	Partai Komunis Indonesia
PKS	Partai Keadilan Sejahtera
PNI	Partai Nasional Indonesia
PPP	Partai Persatuan Pembangunan
PSII	Partai Sarekat Islam Indonesia
SBY	Susilo Bambang Yudhoyono
SLFP	Sri Lanka Freedom Party
SLMC	Sri Lanka Muslim Congress
SU	Sinhala Urumaya
TNI-Polri	Indonesian National Army and Police
UDHR	Universal Declaration of Human Rights
UMNO	United National Malays Organization
UNP	United National Party
YDPA	*Yang di-Pertuan Agong*

1

Introduction

Shortly after Soeharto's resignation in 1998, the Indonesian legislature embarked on a series of constitutional reforms to advance democratic norms and practices in the country. There were twenty-one chapters of revisions and additions on the agenda, but two were particularly important: article 29 on religion and the bill of rights. These items stood out because the proposals for change were considered quite revolutionary at the time. The proposal to amend article 29 involved incorporating a provision that would constitutional-ize the implementation of *Shariah* law for Muslims alongside the existing provision which states that the state shall be based on 'the belief in the one and only God'. On the other hand, with wounds still fresh from decades of human rights violations under Soeharto's authoritarian rule, the inclusion of a bill of rights was a matter of great urgency, receiving widespread support both in public and in the constituent assembly. Today, article 29 survives in its original form, and the constitution boasts impressive rights guarantees comparable to international human rights instruments. One important concession, however, was the approval of a last-minute proposal to include 'religious values' as one of the grounds for restricting fundamental rights. The deliberations led to serious disagreements within the constituent assembly, to the point of an imminent deadlock, proving how contentious religious issues are in Indones-ian politics.

The outcome of the debates on the constitutional arrangements on religion and religious freedom is unique in the context of a country with the largest Muslim population in the world. This distinctiveness becomes more marked and interesting when we consider the paths that were taken by the two other case studies in this book: Malaysia and Sri Lanka. In Malaysia, the estab-lishment of Islam as the religion of the state is balanced by the guarantee that 'other religions may be practiced in peace and harmony' and that such establishment will not supersede the constitution's fundamental rights guarantees. As in the Indonesian experience, the process of reaching this settlement stretched over countless debates and negotiations among those involved in the constitution-making exercise, not least because they deeply disagreed on whether a state religion should be constitutionalized at all. In Sri Lanka, the 1972 constitutional reforms introduced a provision obligating the state to 'protect and foster Buddhism', but the same provision also provides that other religions are guaranteed the rights expressed in the constitution's bill of rights. The inclusion of the bill of rights and the religion clause was a significant departure from Sri Lanka's 1948 independence constitution, which contained neither an establishment clause nor comprehensive fundamental rights guarantees.

Having identified these three distinct arrangements, the next obvious questions are: What are the effects of these different provisions? How do they influence state policies and practices on religion and religious freedom? These questions, which implicate the divergence between theory and practice, are often asked in religious freedom discourses. Indeed, they constitute part of the central inquiries in this book. These questions are not only of interest to practitioners and scholars; they are also relevant for constitution-makers or policymakers contemplating constitutional reforms.

Scholarship on religion-state relations, religious freedom and fundamental rights more generally is extensive. Scholars have written on the philosophical underpinnings and justifications for religious freedom, developed models of religion-state relations and studied their impact on religious freedom and demonstrated the importance of bills of rights in national constitutions. A study by Fox and Flores[1] on constitutional clauses protecting religious freedom and state-religion relations, for instance, focuses on the very question of how practice diverges from theory. In particular, Fox and Flores find that even with the existence of provisions on the separation of religion and state, freedom of worship and prohibition of religious discrimination, most countries inevitably engage in some form of religious discrimination and administer some form of religious regulation. More recently, Cross's examination of the consequences of state-religion provisions establishes several important findings that are relevant to the analysis in this book: formal constitutional recognition of a state religion leads to less religious freedom, and the existence of provisions guaranteeing religious freedom generally serves to promote religious freedom.[2]

---

[1] Jonathan Fox and Deborah Flores, 'Religion, Constitutions, and the State: A Cross-National Study' (2009) 71(4) *The Journal of Politics* 1499.
[2] Frank B. Cross, *Constitutions and Religious Freedom* (Cambridge: Cambridge University Press, 2015).

Despite these studies, the puzzle of how constitutional commitments operate in societies divided along ethnic, religious, regional, linguistic and/or
economic lines, where such divisions are highly salient, and where there is
deep conflict over the character of the state has received inadequate scholarly
attention, particularly from a comparative perspective.[3] Even less has been
said comparatively about how constitutional arrangements on religion were
adopted and how they operate over time. In Indonesia, Malaysia and Sri
Lanka, ethnic and/or religious fault lines are socially and politically salient,
rendering societal consensus on the core values and character of the nation
difficult (or sometimes even impossible). In these countries, religious beliefs
are not only deeply held as a matter of personal conviction; they are also
powerful forces for social and political mobilization.

In the realms of constitutional law and politics, the challenges faced by the
three countries are remarkably similar. The constitution-makers were confronted with the question of striking an appropriate balance for the role of
religion in the state against a largely secular constitutional setup. The disagreements were intense, pitting – broadly speaking – those who demanded a more
prominent constitutional role for the dominant religion in the respective
countries against those who pursued a secular state. These conflicts did not
dissipate over time; in fact, under conditions of growing polarization along
religious lines, political actors and policymakers have continued to struggle
with questions about the appropriate role of the dominant religion in the
state – questions that also implicate commitments to protecting and enforcing
religious freedom rights, particularly for minorities. The divergences and
convergences in how religion factored into constitution-making processes
and outcomes and influenced public policy choices in the three countries
present important comparative lessons for similarly situated countries elsewhere. In short, this book seeks to fill the scholarly gap by illuminating an
understanding of the evolving interaction between constitutional law, religion
and politics in a manner sensitive to the contextual intricacies of these three
deeply divided societies.

By focusing on the experiences of Indonesia, Malaysia and Sri Lanka, this
book demonstrates that constitution-making and the operation and implementation of constitutional commitments on questions implicating religion are
shaped by the politics of wider society. Under conditions of weak rule of law

---

[3]   Hanna Lerner has produced a comparative study on the process of constitution-making in
Israel, India and Ireland. These three countries are what Lerner calls 'deeply divided societies',
that is, societies in which there are deep divisions and conflicts about the foundational
norms and values of the state, particularly on issues of national and/or religious identity.
See Hanna Lerner, *Making Constitutions in Deeply Divided Societies* (Cambridge: Cambridge
University Press, 2011), p. 6.

and intense politicization of religion, constitutional provisions may prove to be malleable and yield unintended (sometimes even perverse) consequences on rights guarantees.

THE SIGNIFICANCE OF CONSTITUTIONAL HISTORY

A noticeable void in the aforementioned studies about constitutions and religion is that they do not tell us much about what the examined constitutional clauses on state-religion relations mean. Asking how and why particular provisions on religion and religious freedom were adopted are crucial because, as Chen argues, the substance of modern constitutions is linked to the drafters' choices on the constitutional solutions that would best serve the objectives of the state.[4] Without this information, there is a danger – both as a matter of scholarly inquiry and as a matter of practical, policymaking consideration – that we might draw inaccurate conclusions about the role of constitutional provisions vis-à-vis the protection of religious freedom. For example, the constitutions of Malaysia and Sri Lanka provide privileged positions for Islam and Buddhism, respectively. If these provisions are taken at face value, one might argue that religious freedom violations (particularly against adherents of religions other than the constitutionally recognized religion) are expected – that they are the inevitable consequence of the privileging of one religion over others. Indeed, as this book illustrates and as I shall explain later in this chapter, the constitutional recognition of Islam in Malaysia and Buddhism in Sri Lanka have often been used as a justification to restrict religious freedom. Constitutional history, however, will tell us why such justification is flawed.

This book proceeds on the idea that reliance on the formal legal text alone is not enough to aid our understanding on how constitutional provisions operate or how to contextualize the problems in protecting and enforcing religious freedom. The turn to constitutional history is important to facilitate such understanding, and to that end, this book delves into the issue of constitution-making. There is, to be sure, a burgeoning literature on constitution-making both generally and in deeply divided societies.[5]

---

[4] Albert H. Y. Chen, 'The Achievement of Constitutionalism in Asia: Moving Beyond "Constitutions without Constitutionalism"' (2015) University of Hong Kong Faculty of Law Research Paper No. 2015/002, p. 5.

[5] See Cass R. Sunstein, *Designing Democracy: What Constitutions Do* (New York: Oxford University Press, 2001); Yash Ghai, 'A Journey around Constitution: Reflections on Contemporary Constitutions' (2005) *African Law Journal* 122; Andrew Reynolds (ed.), *The Architecture of Democracy: Constitutional Design, Conflict Management, and Democracy*

For instance, Elster argues that constitution-making involves a complex web of constraints, diverging interests and goals on the part of constitutional framers and aggregating choices and preferences amongst constitution-makers.[6] Delegating constitution-making to a special body or commission rather than the legislators is thought to be preferable,[7] as is ensuring that the process is transparent and participatory.[8] Horowitz's study of constitutional change in Indonesia tells a story of the distinct processes and choices of reform and constitution-writing in Indonesia's transition to democracy and the resulting institutions that emerged from those processes and choices.[9] Lerner's seminal study of constitution-making in three deeply divided societies – Israel, India and Ireland – illustrates how democratic constitutions can emerge even where societal consensus regarding the fundamental nature and norms of the state is absent.[10] She argues that this was made possible by the drafters' pursuing three different constitutional strategies, which could be formulated as the 'incrementalist approach' to constitution-making.[11]

It is beyond the scope of this book, however, to develop a grand theory about the constitution-making experiences in Indonesia, Malaysia and Sri Lanka. Instead, the goal is to explicate the extent to which religion influences the socio-political dynamics in the countries under study and clarify the role and meaning of the religion provisions in relation to the framers' broader visions of protecting religious freedom and maintaining pluralism in nation-building. Is the constitutional recognition of Islam and Buddhism a mere symbolic and psychological exercise, or are these provisions intended to have practical effect on state practices and policies? With respect to

(New York: Oxford University Press, 2002); Arend Ljiphart, 'Constitutional Design in Divided Societies' (2004) 2 *Journal of Democracy* 15; Benjamin Reilly, *Democracy in Divided Societies: Electoral Engineering for Conflict Management* (Cambridge: Cambridge University Press, 2001); Donald L. Horowitz, 'Democracy in Divided Societies' (1993) 4 *Journal of Democracy* 18; and Haider Ala Hamoudi, *Negotiating in Civil Conflict: Constitutional Construction and Imperfect Bargaining in Iraq* (Chicago: Chicago University Press, 2013).

6 Jon Elster, 'Forces and Mechanisms in the Constitution-Making Process' (1995) 45 *Duke Law Journal* 364–96. See also Justin Blount, Zachary Elkins and Tom Ginsburg, 'Does the Process of Constitution-Making Matter?' in Tom Ginsburg (ed.), *Comparative Constitutional Design* (Cambridge: Cambridge University Press, 2012), pp. 31–66.

7 See Elster, 'Forces and Mechanisms', ibid.

8 See Vivien Hart, 'Democratic Constitution Making', *United States Institute of Peace (USIP) Special Report No. 107* (Washington, DC, July 2003) and Jill Cottrell and Yash Ghai, 'Constitution Making and Democratization in Kenya' (February 2007) 14 (1) *Democratization* 1.

9 Donald L. Horowitz, *Constitutional Change and Democracy in Indonesia* (Cambridge: Cambridge University Press, 2013).

10 Lerner, *Making Constitutions*.   11 Ibid., pp. 6–11.

Indonesia, what does 'the belief in the one and only God' mean? Why were these provisions enacted?

This book answers these questions by drawing on archival documents, parliamentary records, as well as memoranda and letters exchanged among individuals and bodies involved in the constitution-making process. Its analysis differs, to some extent, from the exercise of describing the processes and debates that led to the current constitutional arrangements implicating religion and religious freedom. The works of Hosen, Fernando and Schonthal are instrumental in explaining the origins and formulation of the religion clauses in the Indonesian, Malaysian and Sri Lankan constitutions, respectively.[12] This book draws on these studies and goes into more detail: it teases out and compares the social contexts and political compromises that shaped those arrangements. Given the deep ideational conflicts and competing visions about the state in deeply divided societies, the process of constitution-making becomes a risky affair: it can exacerbate conflicts, trigger political instability and, in worst-case scenarios, lead to territorial partition.[13] This book illustrates how constitution-makers responded to competing demands from different groups in the society. It also discusses the ways in which the roles and ideologies of key political figures involved in the constitution-making process influenced the outcomes. The historical approach, therefore, uncovers not just the framers' intentions and the purpose for which the provisions were enacted but also the principles and negotiations underpinning those provisions.

The Malaysian experience provides an instructive example. The constitutional commission (Reid Commission) tasked to draft the independence constitution had, at the beginning of the constitution-making process, rejected the idea of establishing Islam as the state religion. The proposal was instead advanced by the Alliance – a coalition consisting of political parties representing the Malay, Indian and Chinese communities. Yet, despite the Commission's resistance, the provision was included in the final draft of the constitution. Why did the Alliance make the proposal, and what did the leaders want to achieve from this? More importantly, why did the Commission eventually agree? The book provides answers to these questions and gives similarly detailed treatment to the Indonesian and Sri Lankan provisions.

[12] Nadirsyah Hosen, *Shari'a & Constitutional Reform in Indonesia* (Singapore: Institute of Southeast Asian Studies, 2007), Joseph M. Fernando, *The Making of the Malayan Constitution* (Kuala Lumpur: Malaysian Branch of the Royal Asiatic Society, 2001) and Benjamin Schonthal, *Buddhism, Politics, and the Limits of Law* (Cambridge: Cambridge University Press, 2016).

[13] Lerner, *Making Constitutions*, pp. 33–4.

The comparative approach adopted in this study of Indonesia, Malaysia and Sri Lanka also illustrates that despite the existence of comparable demands, constraints and conditions in the constitution-making process, the constitution-makers settled for three different formulations of the religion clause. (Indeed, the three countries were selected precisely for this reason.) Against this background, a comparison of the direction that each state has taken in relation to the protection of religious freedom – both on paper and in practice – produces valuable food for thought. The problems and trajectories that are carefully elaborated in this book will also be instructive for other countries grappling with the challenges in managing religious pluralism.

CONSTITUTIONS AND RELIGIOUS FREEDOM: UNPREDICTABILITY, EVOLUTION AND PERVERSION

A comprehensive understanding of the constitutional deliberations and settlements that underlie the founding of the three countries provides a departure point for analysing the unfolding trajectories of religious freedom protection. Here, this book asks: What are the different forms of religious freedom violations? What are the common justifications for such violations? To what extent are courts willing to uphold the constitutional settlements and protect religious freedom? With the origins and formulations of the constitutional provisions in mind, this book reveals how the provisions might operate to protect or curtail religious freedom and how, in some cases, the effects of such provisions are unpredictable. In doing so, it provides detailed insights into how religious freedom is conceived and contested within the social and political contexts of the three countries.

We know at this point that the Indonesian, Malaysian and Sri Lankan constitutions provide three distinct religion-state arrangements. These arrangements are also important guarantees of religious freedom, which exist alongside other religious freedom provisions in the bills of rights of the three constitutions. Yet, state-enforced religious freedom violations (manifested, for instance, in the form of limitations on the right to worship, proselytizing and public preaching) have been growing in recent years. Ironically, among the three countries, Indonesia – whose constitution lacks any formal recognition of a state religion – has consistently recorded very high levels of government restrictions on religion, compared to Malaysia and Sri Lanka.[14] The situation becomes more perplexing when we consider other indicators of

---

[14] This is based on the scores provided by the Pew Forum's Government Restrictions on Religion Index between 2007 and 2012.

the state of religious freedom as a whole, such as the prevalence of religious violence in the society. Social persecution against religious minorities includes acts of intimidation, physical attacks (occasionally resulting in death or serious injuries) and attacks on places of worship. Sometimes these violations are not adequately investigated and punished. This has been particularly serious in Indonesia and Sri Lanka, where vigilante violence against minorities is worsened not only by government inaction but also by alleged state complicity with the perpetrators of violence.

The recognition that constitutions may not always protect the rights contained therein is not new. Sartori developed the term 'façade constitution' to refer to constitutions that take the form of a 'true constitution' but whose essential guarantees are nevertheless disregarded.[15] In a similar vein, Howard argues that in many countries, constitutions are worthless scraps of paper.[16] Nonetheless, the studies by Fox, Flores and Cross remind us that the value of constitutional guarantees in ensuring religious freedom should not be completely dismissed. This book may contribute to the wider – albeit inconclusive – debate on whether constitutions matter, but its specific significance lies in the illustration of how violations of religious freedom may actually find their roots in the constitutional arrangements of the three countries. In other words, contrary to popular belief, religious freedom violations are not always grounded in any distinctly anti–human rights propaganda; instead, empirical evidence suggests that they are predicated on the clauses that were enacted to safeguard religious freedom in these three plural societies. In other cases, religious freedom restrictions are justified based on the public order limitation or a perverse interpretation of the right to religious freedom.

There are a few instructive examples. In Malaysia, Christians are prohibited from using the word 'Allah' as a reference to God in their Malay-language bibles. It is argued that such prohibition protects the sanctity and special constitutional position of Islam spelled out in article 3. Yet, as this book demonstrates, the constitutional provision on Islam was neither formulated nor intended to supersede fundamental rights guarantees in the constitution. In Indonesia, support for the Blasphemy Law, which has been used to curtail non-mainstream Muslim groups like the Ahmadiyah and other religious minorities, is deemed consistent with the principle of the 'belief in the one

---

[15] Giovanni Sartori, 'Constitutionalism: A Preliminary Discussion' (1962) 56 *American Political Science Review* 853.

[16] A. E. Dick Howard, 'The Essence of Constitutionalism' in Kenneth W. Thompson and Rett T. Ludwikowski (eds.), *Constitutionalism and Human Rights: America, Poland, and France* (Lanham, MD: University Press of America, 1991).

and only God'. In both these examples, the right to religious freedom is also construed as the right of the majority Muslims to be 'free' from acts that may offend their religious sensitivities. Similarly, in Sri Lanka, objections against Christian organizations and their proselytizing activities are justified on the belief that religious freedom encompasses the right to be 'free' from the influences of other religions. All these arguments have found favour with the highest courts exercising constitutional jurisdiction in these countries.

One might argue that cases like these are not unique – that they are merely part of the broader, ongoing process of constitutional interpretation to shape the dominant norms governing a country. However, while these cases reflect the inevitability of competing interpretations of religious freedom in a plural society or the evolving interpretation of constitutional arrangements over time, they are also part of a growing pattern of utilizing constitutional arrangements in ways that are radically different from their original purpose. Such a pattern becomes especially worrying when they indicate that constitutional guarantees and the exercise of rights are made to yield to majoritarian demands and/or state prerogatives, especially in cases in which an issue or dispute involves – directly or indirectly – a 'contest' between majority and minority interests. All this raises troubling questions about the commitment to principles of constitutionalism and the pluralist visions of the founding fathers. The perverse interpretation and manipulation of the constitutional arrangements has not only served to undermine religious freedom; it also reinforces the hegemony of the religious majority and legitimizes government repression of rights. This book formulates this emergent pattern as a 'constitutional perversion'.

The focus on the three countries facilitates a nuanced evaluation of religious freedom issues that large-*n* studies are, by design, unable to provide. This book does not purport to describe every conceivable type of religious freedom violation that has emerged in these countries. Instead, it focuses on state-enforced violations of the freedom to express, manifest and practice one's religion. These aspects of religious freedom deserve special attention because they are rights that can be qualified. This sets the stage for an evaluation of how governments justify the restrictions on those rights and, as a threshold matter, whether the justifications are warranted. Throughout the book, emphasis will be given to leading cases that highlight both the value and the unique challenges in securing religious freedom in the countries under study: the Blasphemy Law case (Indonesia), the right of Christians to use 'Allah' to refer to God (Malaysia) and the incorporation of Christian organizations (Sri Lanka). These constitutional contests demonstrate the different ways in which the religion clause can adversely affect religious freedom.

More importantly, they illustrate how such courtroom battles may turn into high-stakes, zero-sum games between majority and minority groups.

To provide a more comprehensive picture of the overall state of religious freedom in the three countries, this book devotes a chapter on societal abuses of religious freedom and the role of the state apparatus therein. Admittedly, this falls outside the scope of the conventional understanding of religious freedom as a negative right – that is, the government simply must not encroach on the exercise of religious liberties. Constitutional claims for the right to religious freedom extend only insofar as the government, through its actions, represses such rights. However, an exposé of societal abuses of religious freedom raises several important issues as we evaluate the interaction between constitutions and religious freedom in Indonesia, Malaysia and Sri Lanka.

First, the history of interethnic hostility and the continuing symptoms of socio-political polarization along religious lines in these countries cannot be ignored. In Malaysia and Sri Lanka, this is further complicated by overlapping divisions across ethnic lines. In issues implicating religion, the survival of a religious and/or ethnic group is seen to be at stake. In Indonesia and Malaysia, for instance, hostilities against Christians or minority Muslims (i.e., non-Sunni Muslims) emerge out of the fear that the dominant position of Islam (or Sunni Islam) is threatened by the growing influence of Christianity or other Muslim denominations. Likewise, in Sri Lanka, the spate of violence against Christians and Muslims is fuelled by deep insecurities about the position of Sinhalese-Buddhists and Buddhism in the 'promised land'. Religious hostilities may inevitably affect the ability of individuals to practice their religion in the public and private spheres.

Maintaining public order is thus an important concern, especially when competing rights claims between hostile groups may trigger conflict. How, then, does the state and the courts balance the right to religious freedom against the protection of public order? Rights limitations are not problematic *per se*. Indeed, many national constitutions and international human rights documents allow restrictions of religious freedom on several specified grounds. One can also expect that the exercise of balancing rights against other interests is inevitably a subjective one. Aside from the proportionality principle, there is no clear and uniform balancing mechanism that applies across all countries. However, what becomes alarming, as this book illustrates, is the abuse of the public order limitation in ways that disregard standards of proportionality.

The second important point concerns religious persecution at the societal level. The government may prevent religious freedom violations by non-state actors, mediate interreligious contests on rights and strike a resolution through political compromise. However, as this book highlights, government inaction – manifested in the failure to prevent, investigate and prosecute religious violence – have hampered the right to religious freedom. For example, in the attacks against the Ahmadiyah community in Cikeusik, West Java, the police stood by as several Ahmadis were beaten to death. Similar incidents have been observed in attacks against minorities' places of worship in Sri Lanka. All this signals to the instigators of violence that the government may well tolerate anti-minority hostility, especially if such actions could serve its political interests and agenda.

In any case, private abuses of religious freedom or societal violence do not occur in a vacuum. While it is plausible that they are symptoms of growing religious fundamentalism, it will become apparent, through an elaboration of the cases in this book, that constitutional clauses on religion may become a source of empowerment for intolerant forces in the society. This leads to the third point: the perversion of constitutional meanings also occurs at the societal level. Non-state actors involved in spreading anti-minority propaganda have utilized such clauses to support their cause, demanding the prioritization of the religious majority's interests. In some cases, they have invoked the clauses to justify attacks against religious minorities, on the premise that they are merely 'enforcing' the constitutional order. This book also explains the ways in which violence and state responses thereof relate to governance problems ranging from corruption to the lack of executive accountability. Some political leaders, for instance, have provided explicit political patronage to individuals or groups engaged in spreading anti-minority rhetoric, while others have reportedly engaged in tit-for-tat arrangements with hard-line organizations during election campaigns. It will become apparent, therefore, that state and non-state actors work in a symbiotic but mutually corrupting relationship that reinforces the perversion of constitutional arrangements.

CONSTITUTIONAL DEMOCRACY, RULE OF LAW AND THE POLITICS OF RELIGION

An analysis of the different forms of religious freedom violations and the constitutional contests implicating religion helps bring attention to the social and political forces shaping religious freedom protection in the three countries. In this regard, identifying the emerging perversion of constitutional provisions is important because it also highlights the reactive nature of constitutional law and interpretation. Depending on various conditions and contexts, these reactive processes may either facilitate or undermine the overall protection of religious freedom.

Over the years, scholars have theorized the conditions that might positively or adversely affect religious freedom. For instance, Cross finds generally positive correlations between democracy and the rule of law and the protection of religious freedom.[17] This resonates with earlier empirical studies, all of which largely confirm the positive effect of democracy on human rights protection. Indeed, democratic governance – or liberal democratic governance, as Zakaria notes – entails not just free and fair elections but also the protection of basic fundamental liberties and the rule of law.[18] The latter requires accountability to laws that are independently adjudicated. The existence of and interaction among these elements are also central to constitutionalism. There are, of course, different views on what constitutes the core components of constitutionalism, but a survey of the literature suggests that the rule of law, judicial independence and human rights protection are key features. For British jurist A. V. Dicey, the rule of law encompasses three main aspects: (1) the supremacy of law over arbitrary exercises of power; (2) the equality of every person before the law and that every person is subject to the jurisdiction of the courts; and (3) the guarantees of the rights of individuals derived from ordinary laws of the land as defined and enforced by the courts.[19] Today, drawing on Dicey's definition, several basic elements have been identified and included within the concept of the rule of law: the protection of human rights, separation of powers, participatory decision-making and accountability to laws that are equally enforced and independently adjudicated. The latter not only implies the existence of effective judicial review of governmental action, but it also means that the government must actually enforce and uphold the law across the board.[20]

Against this background, the view that constitutionalism involves fostering democratic institutions and commitments is instructive. If governmental actions are accountable to laws, procedures and other institutions (the

---

[17] Cross, *Constitutions and Religious Freedom*, p. 93. However, Cross noted that a country's laws might restrict religious freedom. In such case, if one adopts the thin (procedural) conception of the rule of law, then the enforcement of such restrictive laws (according to the rule of law) would be counter-productive to religious freedom. Ibid., pp. 90–1.

[18] Fareed Zakaria, 'The Rise of Illiberal Democracy' (1997) 76(6) *Foreign Affairs* 22.

[19] A. V. Dicey, *Introduction to the Study of the Law of the Constitution*, 5th ed. (London: Macmillan, 1897).

[20] The judiciary forms one of three main institutions central to the building and strengthening of the rule of law according to the United Nation (UN)'s Rule of Law Indicators. See Department of Peacekeeping Operations and the Office of the High Commissioner for Human Rights, *The United Nations Rule of Law Indicators: Implementation Guide and Project Tools* 4 (1st ed., 2011), online: www.un.org/en/events/peacekeepersday/2011/publications/un_rule_of_law_indicators.pdf.

legislature and judiciary), such checks and balances mechanisms may operate to curtail the tyranny of the majority. The rule of law may thus limit the arbitrary exercise of a state's coercive powers vis-à-vis a person's religious choices and practices. The principles of equality and non-discrimination may foster a marketplace of ideas and beliefs that ought to be conducive to the promotion of religious tolerance. One can thus expect that adherence to principles of democracy and constitutionalism will secure religious freedom, which presupposes the protection of minorities from the will of the majority. This is assuming, however, that the institutions and procedures will function to curb majority tyranny and discrimination of minorities.

This book concretizes the nature and dynamics of the relationship between rule of law and democracy and the constitutional protection of religious freedom. In this respect, it emphasizes the role of courts and the mechanics of electoral politics in shaping the protection of religious freedom by focusing on two fundamental questions: (1) What explains the judicial approaches to questions implicating religion and religious freedom?; and (2) What explains government policies and practices on religious freedom? By doing so, my hope is that this book provides important insights on the conditions that might facilitate or undermine the operation and effectiveness of constitutional commitments on religion and religious freedom.

Electoral processes are majoritarian in nature. Elected representatives tend to be driven by populist concerns that may conflict with pluralistic values and the protection of rights, especially for minorities. The role of the judiciary as a counter-majoritarian institution entrusted to protect rights is thus important. The judiciary is expected to fulfil its function as the last bastion for rights protection when policymakers, the executive or the elected representatives are unwilling or unable to do so. The case studies in this book, however, reveal how and why institutions and democratic procedures (i.e., elections) may facilitate violations – as opposed to the protection – of religious freedom. The preceding section indicates that courts appear to be willing to restrict religious freedom by ceding (intentionally or otherwise) to majoritarian demands and anti-minority fervour, or by following the preferences of the government of the day. While free and fair elections are a defining feature of a healthy democracy, this book also demonstrates how policymakers and elected representatives can be enticed into prioritizing the dominant religious fervour and restricting religious liberties to meet their immediate electoral goals. This, in effect, challenges the view that democracy (albeit in its procedural form) is always conducive for stronger protection of religious freedom.

All this raises a set of broader issues that this book attempts to address. Why do politicians foment majority religious passions or formulate policies that violate religious freedom, especially in cases involving minorities? Why do governments fail to tackle religious violence and, in some cases, condone such violence? With regard to the judiciary, do particular features of institutional design promote particular judicial attitudes in resolving issues implicating religion and religious freedom? Do judges' ideological or political preferences affect their choices and responses? How far do public reaction and threats of sanctions affect judicial decision-making? This book attests that there is a degree of variation across the three countries in terms of how electoral politics and judicial institutions and behaviour influence religious freedom protection. Nonetheless, taken together, this comparative analysis offers rich and fresh perspectives on understanding the relationship between constitutions, religion and politics.

The importance of the electoral incentives available to politicians and the nature of interparty competition for votes within the majority electorate (i.e., the mainstream Sunni Muslims in Indonesia, the Malay-Muslims in Malaysia and the Sinhalese-Buddhists in Sri Lanka) are part of the highlights of this study. In Indonesia, political parties compete at the centre to appeal to a broader base of the Muslim electorate, while in Malaysia and Sri Lanka the ruling coalitions have turned to the strategy of maximizing Malay-Muslim and Sinhalese-Buddhist votes, respectively. This has also led parties vying for Malay-Muslim and Sinhalese-Buddhist support to co-opt right-wing organizations in the society. Although the exact strategies vary, they nevertheless disincentivize politicians to tackle sensitive, religious issues implicating the minorities. The situation is complicated by the rising tide of religious nationalism, which is fuelled both by the politicization of religion and by the propaganda that the dominant religious communities are faced with an existential threat. Influential religious movements continue to campaign on sectarian platforms, and the practice of politicians seeking electoral endorsements or 'blessings' from religious figures or organizations is seen as symbolically significant. In a climate where the majorities feel increasingly insecure about their interests and see minorities as a threat, politicians may not see the electoral benefits of supporting minority interests, as they do not want to risk losing votes from the majority group. In fact, in some cases, fomenting majority religious passions and demonizing the minorities may well be the key winning strategy.

With regard to courts, the first point of departure for my analysis is the institutional independence of the judiciary. Here, independence is defined in terms of the judiciary's ability to insulate itself from political interference – be it direct or indirect – by the government of the day. The analysis builds on existing theories that highlight the importance of judicial appointment and removal mechanisms in ensuring judicial independence.[21] Certain modes of appointment may determine the types of judges who comprise the courts (for example, whether they are politically compliant or share similar ideologies with their appointers). Selection and removal mechanisms may shape judges' behaviour (for instance, whether their decisions are influenced by the anticipated responses from other political actors). Institutional design may thus dictate the incentives and constraints surrounding judicial decision-making.

A look at the history across the three countries highlights the profound influence of the mechanics and politics of judicial appointment and removal on the image and independence of the judiciary (and, by extension, the rule of law). Once a highly respected institution, the Malaysian judiciary is increasingly viewed with suspicion after Prime Minister Mahathir removed three Supreme Court judges in 1988 and engineered a constitutional amendment to place judicial power under the purview of the legislature. Similarly, in Sri Lanka, threats against the judiciary are not unheard of. In 2013, the chief justice was impeached in what many commentators saw as a politically motivated response to an unfavourable judgment against the government. Indonesia, on the other hand, has had to grapple with the legacy of a weak and corrupted judiciary that was subordinated to the government. The post-Soeharto reforms led to the establishment of the Constitutional Court, which has since developed a solid reputation for independence and integrity. However, corruption scandals involving the chief justice in 2013 and a sitting judge in 2017 raised questions as to whether the judiciary can overcome its troubled history.

Each of the three countries tells a unique story about the significance of institutional design in determining the willingness of judges to produce rights-enforcing decisions. The Malaysian and Sri Lankan experiences remind us of the perils of unchecked appointment and removal powers that are virtually concentrated in a single political actor. Yet, as we shall see, an evaluation of institutional design is only the starting point; design alone cannot fully explain the rigour with which judges protect religious freedom. The Indonesian case

---

[21] See Tom Ginsburg, *Judicial Review in New Democracies: Constitutional Courts in Asian Cases* (Cambridge: Cambridge University Press, 2003); Gretchen Helmke and Julio Rios-Figueroa, (eds.), *Courts in Latin America* (Cambridge: Cambridge University Press, 2011); Linda Camp Keith, 'Judicial Independence and Human Rights Protection around the World' (2000) 85 *Judicature* 195; and James Madison, 'The Structure of the Government Must Furnish the Proper Checks and Balances between the Different Departments', *The Federalist Papers*, No. 51, (6 February 1788). See also J. Mark Ramseyer, 'The Puzzling (In)dependence of Courts: A Comparative Approach' (1994) *The Journal of Legal Studies* 721. Ramseyer demonstrates the relationship between judicial independence and electoral considerations of politicians.

shows that even though design mechanisms produced a largely independent institution, the court was unwilling to uphold religious freedom in the Blasphemy Law case. To complicate matters further, an overview of other cases that have come before the highest courts exercising constitutional jurisdiction in the three countries suggests that courts have, at times, been willing to uphold other human rights protections such as free speech.

What exactly motivates judicial decision-making is, therefore, mystifying, and this study is careful not to overemphasize any single explanation across the board. Instead, this book seizes the opportunity to broaden the understanding of the factors that drive judicial choices in cases implicating religion and religious freedom. Here, theoretical debates about judicial behaviour provide a useful analytical framework.[22] For one, judges – regardless of the institutional settings that they operate in – may simply interpret and apply the law or follow precedent. They may also read their own political or ideological preferences into their decisions, and such preferences may not be any different from those of the political actors. In this respect, the salience of religion in the social and political spheres, which I have explained previously, is relevant. Ideological biases are, of course, not explicitly stated or made apparent in written decisions. However, there is some likelihood that judges' choices could be affected by the ideological blinkering derived from the wider political propaganda that minorities are threatening the survival and interests of the country's dominant religious identity. Judges might also decide in accordance with their personal religious beliefs. Alternatively, it is possible that judges' strategic motivations are not only shaped by the responses of other political actors, but also by concerns about public reaction to their decisions.

The ways in which judges reason their decisions might help us decipher why judges decided the way they did, but in this book I also emphasize the contexts and environments in which particular cases were decided. Aided by information obtained through structured interviews and extrajudicial writings, this study traces some evidence of ideological and political biases that shape judges' attitudes. A close reading of the Indonesian Constitutional Court's decision on the constitutionality of the Blasphemy Law and the Malaysian Federal Court's decision in the 'Allah' case also reveals the courts' anxiety about public reaction against enforcing religious freedom in favour of the

---

[22] See Ginsburg, *Judicial Review*, Chapter 3; Keith E. Whittington, 'Legislative Sanctions and the Strategic Environment of Judicial Review' (2003) 1 *International Journal of Constitutional Law* 446; and Gretchen Helmke and Julio Rios-Figueroa, 'Introduction: Courts in Latin America' in Gretchen Helmke and Julio Rios-Figueroa (eds.), *Courts in Latin America* (Cambridge: Cambridge University Press, 2011), pp. 13–14. See also Richard A. Posner, *How Judges Think* (Cambridge, MA: Harvard University Press, 2010).

minority groups implicated in those cases. The Indonesian court feared that declaring the law unconstitutional would breed more violence against non-mainstream Muslims, whereas the Malaysian court stressed that any 'threats' to the sanctity of Islam is a public order concern because offended Muslims might be provoked to retaliate against the Christians. Overall, this book presents ample evidence for substantiating and evaluating the theoretical debates on judicial behaviour.

ORGANIZATION OF THE BOOK

As a device to investigate the relationship between constitutions, religion and politics in the context of the protection of religious freedom, this book is divided into three main parts. The first part – essentially Chapter 2 – sets the foundation for subsequent analyses. Given the overall aims and objectives of the book, the chapter is deliberately designed to be descriptive. It focuses on a historical analysis of the constitutional provisions on religion and religious freedom in Indonesia, Malaysia and Sri Lanka. I discuss, in particular, the constitution-making processes, debates and outcomes in the three countries. In doing so, the chapter highlights the parallels and differences in the political compromises, as well as the forces and counterforces, which shaped existing constitutional arrangements. Among them is the popular sentiment in all three countries that the majority religion deserves special constitutional recognition and that it ought to shape the countries' cultural and political outlooks. Political bargaining emerged as one of the most significant features of all three constitution-making experiences. It helped overcome the deep ideological divide between the nationalists and religionists in Indonesia's pre-independence constitution-making process; the competing political interests between the multiethnic political elites and the traditional Malay rulers in Malaysia; and the divisions between members of Sri Lanka's constituent assembly on the constitutional recognition of Buddhism. Yet, as I mentioned earlier and as we shall see in greater detail, the constitution-makers in the three countries opted for distinct arrangements to constitutionalize religion.

The second part of the book is devoted to demonstrating how constitutional provisions and guarantees on religion operate in practice. Three chapters shall focus on unearthing the forms and sources of religious freedom violations, as well as how and why various actors respond to or justify such violations. The primary goal is to discern and theorize the dominant patterns across all three countries, as well as the extent to which policies and practices comport with the underlying spirit and intentions of the constitutional provisions.

To that end, Chapter 3 evaluates state policies and practices implicating religion and religious freedom; Chapter 4 documents and analyses the prevalence of religious tensions in the society, how they evolve into violence and the nuances in government responses to violence and societal abuses of religious freedom; and Chapter 5 focuses on judicial reaction to, and resolution of, constitutional contestations involving religion and religious freedom. The latter also presents an account of both the vertical (between the ruling elites and the society) and the horizontal (between different groups in the society) competing visions on what the constitutional arrangements mean and how they should be enforced. In line with the book's overarching aim of examining the interaction between constitutional law, politics and religious freedom, Chapter 3 explains the understandings and interpretation of constitutional arrangements in the political spheres. For example, Soeharto invoked the principle of the 'belief in the one and only God' to compel every citizen to adopt one of the five officially recognized religions. In Malaysia, Prime Minister Mahathir declared, in 2001, that Malaysia is an Islamic state. An evaluation of such use (or misuse, as the case may be) of constitutional arrangements helps us understand why particular policies, which are deemed restrictive of religious freedom, are in place today.

The analysis presented in all three chapters raises questions about the role and effect of constitutional provisions on religion and religious freedom. They highlight the extent to which the conception and interpretation of those arrangements have evolved over time. What becomes obvious is that the provisions, well-intended though they might be, cannot always constrain government exercises of power in religious matters or ensure the enjoyment of religious freedom. Instead, constitutional provisions may be interpreted and applied in perverse ways to undermine religious freedom. Put differently, constitutional arrangements may become proxies for government control over religion and for majority tyranny.

Finally, the analytical significance of this book rests in the third part, comprising Chapters 6 and 7. They articulate the institutional and political conditions that may shape the enforcement of constitutional commitments on religion and religious freedom. In Chapter 6, I emphasize that while institutional design is important to ensure judicial independence, its causal effects on decisions implicating religion and religious freedom are not always clear-cut. Executive attacks against the judiciary in Malaysia and Sri Lanka, triggered by a series of unfavourable decisions against the government, indicate that there are serious consequences for judges going against government interests or policies. The lack of oversight in judicial appointments may also enable the executive to appoint judges who share or are willing to be subservient to its political agenda. One caveat here is that my analysis on Sri Lanka does not take into account the constitutional amendment in 2015, which introduced a set of institutional reforms, including additional checks and balances on judicial appointments. Nonetheless, the Indonesian case demonstrates that institutional independence does not always correlate with judicial willingness to uphold religious freedom. To build the story on the judiciary's role and responses in constitutional contests on religion, this chapter also draws attention to how judges' behaviour in such cases can be understood as a product of their strategic considerations, their underlying ideological preferences and/or their adherence to strict legalism.

Chapter 7 chronicles the politicization of religion in the three countries and examines the ways in which electoral politics can facilitate or undermine the constitutional protection of religious freedom. By extension, it also demonstrates how politics shapes the state's changing conceptions and interpretation of the state-religion provisions over time. The two main issues driving this inquiry are the electoral incentives available to politicians and the workings of interparty competition for majority support. This chapter builds on and recalibrates Wilkinson's seminal study on how electoral incentives determine states' responses to anti-minority violence and how the extent of politicians' reliance on minority support may motivate them to either prevent or provoke violence against minorities.[23] The core lesson that the chapter stresses is that the structuring of electoral competition around the majority electorate may dictate how politicians respond to issues implicating religion and religious freedom. While Wilkinson argues that strong political competition for majority support will incentivize politicians to appeal to minority voters and their interests, Chapter 7's analysis reveals the opposite, owing to the nuances of electoral politics across all three countries.

Chapter 8 concludes with a brief summary of the key arguments in the book and raises questions that could inform future studies on the relationship between constitutions, religious freedom and politics. The comparative analysis that this study pursues – both in terms of the countries and in terms of the range of issues that it examines – is relatively under-explored in the literature on constitutional law, comparative constitutional law and human rights.

The constitutionalization of religion has been considered most prominently in Hirschl's *Constitutional Theocracy*.[24] The discussion in this book (particularly Chapter 2's analysis of constitution-making) validates, to some extent,

---

[23] Steven I. Wilkinson, *Votes and Violence: Electoral Competition and Ethnic Riots in India* (Cambridge: Cambridge University Press, 2006).

[24] Ran Hirschl, *Constitutional Theocracy* (Cambridge, MA: Harvard University Press, 2010).

Hirschl's argument about the merits of adopting constitutional theocracies or the formal constitutionalization of religion. However, it also analyses the dangers of such approaches, especially when the state and its apparatus utilize religion to maintain or enhance political control, or when they begin ceding to pressures from religious authorities as a means of shoring up political support. The literature on Indonesia – its constitution-making and constitutional reform process,[25] its judiciary[26] and its religious freedom practices[27] – is extensive. However, much less has been published on these issues in Malaysia and Sri Lanka. Yet, their experience, whether individually or jointly, may offer compelling insights for contemporary debates on constitution-making and constitutional practices implicating religion and/or religious identities, particularly in divided societies. They may also provide meaningful content to the question of why the protection of religious freedom is valuable in such societies.

In light of the increasing salience of religion and religious identities in the social and political spheres, a comparison of these three plural societies is apt and timely. As a practical matter, my hope is that the book will offer useful lessons for efforts to strengthen the protection of religious freedom and inter-ethnic relations in the context of deeply engrained institutional and political challenges, as well as an increasingly fervent anti-minority environment.

---

[25] See Denny Indrayana, *Indonesian Constitutional Law Reform 1999–2002: An Evaluation of Constitution-Making in Transition* (Jakarta: Kompas, 2008) and Horowitz, *Constitutional Change*.

[26] For example, Sebastiaan Pompe, *The Indonesian Supreme Court: A Study of Institutional Collapse* (Ithaca, NY: Cornell Southeast Asia Program Publications, 2005); Simon Butt, *The Constitutional Court and Democracy in Indonesia* (Leiden: Brill Njihoff, 2015); and Simon Butt, 'Islam, the State, and the Constitutional Court in Indonesia' (2010) 19 *Pacific Rim Law & Policy Journal* 279.

[27] For example, Ahmad Suaedy et al., *Islam, the Constitution, and Human Rights: The Problematics of Religious Freedom in Indonesia* (Jakarta: Wahid Institute, 2010); Melissa Crouch, *Law and Religion in Indonesia: Conflict and the Courts in West Java* (Oxon: Routledge, 2014); and Tim Lindsey and Helen Pausacker (eds.), *Religion, Law and Intolerance in Indonesia* (Oxon: Routledge, 2016).

2

Three Constitutional Arrangements on Religion

A constitution cannot be understood merely by looking at its texts, but one has to learn how those texts came about ... understand their explanation and the context in which they were formulated. Only then we can understand the meaning of the constitution, and the ideas behind it. *Professor Dr. Soepomo, 15 July 1945, speech before the Indonesian Investigating Committee for Preparatory Work for Indonesian Independence.*

Constitutional provisions are often the first point of reference in assessing the extent to which fundamental rights are protected and enforced. In countries with deep societal divisions, a constitution and the bill of rights therein are seen as important guarantees against government excesses of power and as restraints on the will of the majority. They also act as an expression of national unity[1] – as an aspirational document to bind a multicultural, multiethnic polity by providing shared commitments and securing rights of different groups. But how far do constitutions actually reflect these ideals? If a constitution explicitly recognizes, for example, a special position for the religion of the majority, does it mean that other minority religions (and their respective adherents) assume a second-class status in the constitutional order? While a reading of the plain text might tempt one to answer in the affirmative, an examination of the origins and process of formulating such provisions might point to an opposite conclusion.

These considerations lie at the heart of this chapter. It examines two distinct but interrelated constitutional arrangements involving religion, which may shape religious freedom outcomes: (1) provisions on religion or the state-religion relationship and (2) provisions on the fundamental right to religious

---

[1]   Mark Tushnet, 'Constitution-Making: An Introduction' (2013) 91 *Texas Law Review* 1983, 1984.

freedom. The primary aim here is not to describe what those provisions are or to theorize constitutional models of state-religion relations based on a study of the three countries. Rather, this chapter assesses how and why those arrangements were incorporated into the three constitutions. In doing so, it uncovers the understandings behind such arrangements, the purposes for which they were adopted and the political contexts and bargains that drove their enactment. In short, the discussion illuminates the *strategies* that constitutional drafters in Indonesia, Malaysia and Sri Lanka have adopted to resolve the ingrained divisions in the social and political spheres over the place and role of religion in the constitutional order.

Central to this chapter, therefore, is an analysis of constitutional design and constitution-making processes and outcomes. Several elements may shape and define these exercises. For one, constitution-makers may face particular procedural and substantive limitations. They may face different contextual and practical circumstances; they may each have distinct goals, visions and motivations; and they may choose to take an uncompromising attitude on certain issues but may be willing to bargain on others. As we shall see in later sections, the intricate dynamics between these aspects of constitution-making may have some bearing on constitution-making outcomes. Indeed, as Elster argues, constitution-making 'involves making choices under constraints'.[2] These constraints may be imposed by 'upstream actors' other than the constitution-makers themselves or they may arise internally from the decision-making process, particularly at the ratification stage.[3] The case studies, however, illustrate that constitution-makers may face a larger breadth of constraints, especially in resolving salient and sensitive issues that implicate ethnicity and religion. The realization of the need to appease populist demands – even those that might be contrary to the constitution-makers' objectives and motivations – is one striking example that this chapter will expound.

Then, there is a question of making choices, which will inevitably influence constitutional *design*. For Elster, these choices are the collective choices that constitution-framers must make, having regard to individual goals and motivations, as well as assumptions on the outcomes that particular arrangements will bring.[4] In divided societies like Indonesia, Malaysia and Sri Lanka, the framers faced different – yet to some extent, similar – circumstances which necessitated hard choices and hard bargains, especially on questions where

---

[2]   Jon Elster, 'Forces and Mechanisms in the Constitution-Making Process' (1995) 45 *Duke Law Journal* 364, 365.
[3]   Ibid., p. 374.   [4]   Ibid.

societal consensus is lacking or absent. While constitutions should reflect common norms and values of the population, it should also promote equality and contain provisions designed to protect against the perils of majoritarian passions and tyranny.[5] However, in divided societies, constitution-makers may not be fully insulated from the majoritarian passions that surround the constitution-making exercise.

The following sections will show just how constitutional decision-making became mired in various competing demands, interests and choices. These issues are appealing for their historical and academic value, but more importantly, current trends necessitate an understanding of the then-prevailing forces and counterforces that shaped present-day constitutional settlements. This shall inform, in subsequent chapters, our assessment of how far current interpretation, policies and practices on religion and religious freedom conform to the provisions and limitations of the constitution. All of this becomes even more pertinent, given the extent and manner in which judges, politicians and policymakers are increasingly turning to historical records to understand what the provisions on religion mean and to justify the policy choices that they make. It is thus important to bear three points in mind as we explore this chapter: (1) the salience of religion in the social and political life of the three countries; (2) the ways in which the constitution-makers sought to address the competing (and divisive) interests implicating questions on religion; and (3) the extent to which the contexts, debates and controversies surrounding the constitution-making processes still persists today.

An examination of the three constitution-making experiences in Indonesia, Malaysia and Sri Lanka reveals that constitutionalizing state-religion relations may take different forms and may follow different paths. The point that this chapter makes is that these outcomes are products of a difficult process of political bargaining and compromise – so difficult that threats of deadlock were imminent at various points of the constitution-making process. This was made even more challenging by the historical importance and socio-political salience of religion in the three countries. There were, to be sure, crucial nuances in the constitution-making experiences of the three countries, but one feature shared by all of them was the demands for explicit constitutional recognition of the religion of the majority. The constitution-makers in all three countries, however, settled for three distinct arrangements.

---

5   See, e.g., Cass R. Sunstein, 'Constitutionalism, Prosperity, Democracy: Transition in Eastern Europe' (1991) 2 *Constitutional Political Economy* 371, 385.

CONSTITUTIONALIZING RELIGION AND RELIGIOUS
FREEDOM: THREE ARRANGEMENTS

In Indonesia, where at least 85 per cent of the population are Muslim, the founding fathers and constitution-makers rejected any express reference to or prioritization of Islam. Instead, the preamble and article 29(1) of the constitution firmly entrenches the pan-religious principle of 'the belief in the one and only God'. This is one of the five key philosophical foundations (*Pancasila*) upon which the state was founded, and it was kept intact by the People's Consultative Assembly (MPR) in the post-Soeharto constitutional reforms exercise. Although there is no textual preference for or endorsement of a single religion, the constitution appears to endorse a theistic worldview as one of the state's foundations. The establishment of the Ministry of Religious Affairs (MORA) in 1946 was a manifestation of the purported 'religious character' of the nation and a realization of the ideology underlying the *Pancasila* and the constitution. Reinforcing this pan-religious principle is article 29(2), which guarantees 'all persons the freedom of worship, each according to his/her own religion or belief'. There are currently six officially recognized religions in Indonesia – Islam, Protestantism, Catholicism, Buddhism, Hinduism and Confucianism.

The Malaysian arrangement, by contrast, establishes Islam as the state religion in article 3(1) of the Federal Constitution. There are two qualifications to this provision. First, article 3(1) also states that 'other religions may be practiced in peace and harmony'. This is thus the first indication of a religious freedom guarantee in the constitution. Second, article 3(4) provides that the establishment of Islam 'shall not derogate from other provisions in the Constitution'. In the context of fundamental rights, this means that the establishment of Islam cannot be the basis for abolishing or restricting rights. It is worth noting, however, that while the general law in Malaysia remains secular, a separate *Shariah* jurisdiction is carved out to address personal status matters for persons professing the religion of Islam. As a result of a constitutional amendment in 1988, article 121(1A) of the Federal Constitution strips the civil courts of jurisdiction in matters that are exclusively within the *Shariah* jurisdiction.[6] The consequence is that the relationship among Islam as the state religion, religious freedom and *Shariah* jurisdictional autonomy is often an uneasy one.

---

[6]   See Schedule 9, List II, Federal Constitution of Malaysia for details on such matters.
      They include, but are not limited to, matters involving succession, testate and intestate,
      marriage, divorce and creation and punishment of offences by persons professing the
      religion of Islam against precepts of that religion.

In Sri Lanka, a constitutional reform in 1972 led to the enactment of article 9, which accords Buddhism the 'foremost place' in the state. Although this falls just short of expressly establishing Buddhism as the state religion, the provision states that the state bears the duty to 'protect and foster the Buddha Sasana'. This does not only establish state patronage of Buddhism as a religion; the duty extends to Buddhist institutions, practices, principles, clergy and so on.[7] The same provision, however, emphasizes that the state's obligation to 'protect and foster' is to be carried out *while assuring* the rights and freedoms accorded to other religions in the fundamental rights chapter of the constitution. For some scholars, the two prongs of the provision must be read together so that the protection afforded to Buddhism does not supersede the religious rights of others.[8]

In addition to the guarantees that accompany constitutional provisions on religion, specific provisions in the bills of rights of the three constitutions guarantee the right to religious freedom. Under article 28E(1) of the Indonesian Constitution, 'every person shall be free to choose and to practice the religion of his/her choice', while article 28E(2) guarantees 'the right to the freedom to believe his/her faith, and to express his/her views and thoughts, in accordance with his/her conscience'. In a similar vein, article 10 of the Sri Lankan Constitution provides that 'every person is entitled to freedom of thought, conscience and religion, including the freedom to have or to adopt a religion or belief of his choice'. The Sri Lankan arrangement also guarantees, by virtue of article 14(1)(e), a person's right to manifest his or her religion through worship, observance, practice and teaching.

---

[7] The Report of the Buddha Sasana Presidential Commission in 2002 defines the Buddha Sasana as 'the Buddha, the nine super-mundane (*navalokuttara*) Dhamma, the Sangha, the Buddhist temples (*viharas*) with their ancillary structures, forest hermitages (*aranya senasana*) and meditation centres, Bo trees, stupas, image houses, relic chambers, *dhamma* books and libraries, designated buildings for performance of vinaya acts by the sangha (*uposathagara*), fields, gardens and properties belonging to the Buddhist temples, Buddhist education, *devalas*, nuns and nunneries, the laity who had taken refuge in the Triple Gem, Buddhist literature, culture and civilisation, Buddhist festivals and processions (*peraharas*), Buddhist customs and traditions, Buddhist principles and values and all that are required for its perpetuity.' See 'Report of the Buddha Sasana Presidential Commission: Summary of conclusions and recommendations', *Lankaweb* (1 May 2012), online: www.lankaweb.com/news/items/2012/05/01/report-of-the-buddha-sasana-presidential-commission-2002-summary-of-conclusions-and-recommendations.

[8] Interview with Dr. Jayampathy Wickramaratne in Colombo, Sri Lanka (10 June 2013) and a president's counsel in Colombo, Sri Lanka (11 June 2013). See also Benjamin Schonthal, 'Constitutionalizing Religion: The Pyrrhic Success of Religious Rights in Post-Colonial Sri Lanka' (2014) 29 *Journal of Law and Religion* 470, 472.

In the Malaysia Federal Constitution, article 11 guarantees the right to profess, practice and propagate one's religion, but the right to propagate is qualified by clause (4). Clause (4) basically allows state legislatures to restrict the propagation of any religious doctrine or belief among Muslims. This limitation clause sets the Malaysian arrangement apart from the religious freedom provisions in the Indonesian and Sri Lankan constitutions. Following this provision, at least nine state legislatures in Malaysia have passed laws that criminalize acts to persuade, incite or influence a Muslim to be a follower of another religion, or to distribute certain religious publications to Muslims. This restriction also covers unauthorized proselytizing activities within the Muslim community in order to control the spread of doctrines deemed heretical or those that fall outside the mainstream Sunni Islam doctrine.

There are, however, three other important differences among the three constitutions. First, Malaysia's article 11 also guarantees the rights of religious *communities* to manage their own affairs. Second, the Malaysia Federal Constitution carefully omits the explicit right to *choose* one's own religion. Although scholars suggest that article 11 can be construed broadly to include one's freedom to change his or her religious belief or to renounce a religion, whether this is possible in practice, especially for Muslims, is a different question altogether. Third, while all three constitutions provide that the exercise of religious freedom may be restricted on the grounds of public order and morality, the Indonesian Constitution goes a step further. During the post-Soeharto constitutional reforms, the constituent assembly inserted an additional restriction in the form of 'religious values'.

In short, there are important variations in the constitutionalization of religion and religious freedom in Indonesia, Malaysia and Sri Lanka. There are various degrees of formal separation of religion and state affairs in these countries, but each arrangement is also supported by constitutional guarantees of religious freedom. Nevertheless, the relationship between the establishment of religion and the protection and enforcement of religious freedom in practice is inherently tricky. Where express preference or special position is given to a particular religion, one would expect more robust restrictions on religious freedom because one religion (and hence, its adherents) may be singled out for particular privileges (or burdens, as the case may be) over other religions.[9] Conversely, the non-establishment of a religion is expected to yield positive outcomes for religious freedom since it purportedly advances neutrality and facilitates equal treatment of different religious groups.

---

[9] Ran Hirschl, *Constitutional Theocracy* (Cambridge, MA: Harvard University Press, 2010), p. 28.

However, as subsequent chapters illustrate, the dichotomous assumption on the relationship between religious establishment and religious freedom may not be so straightforward. There are also specific intentions or meanings accompanying certain arrangements on religion, which may or may not yield the expected or intended effect on religious freedom.

RELIGION AND CONSTITUTION-MAKING: CONTEXTS, CONSTRAINTS AND CONDITIONS

Religion holds great historical and socio-political significance in Indonesia, Malaysia and Sri Lanka. In Indonesia, Hinduism and Buddhism shaped the cultural and religious life of the Indonesian islands for centuries before the arrival of Islam. Islam then played an important role in driving nationalist consciousness in the lead up to independence. Similarly, in Malaysia and Sri Lanka, Islam and Buddhism, respectively, significantly influenced the social and political spheres. The Malay state constitutions of the nineteenth and early twentieth centuries, for example, stipulated that the ruler of the state (the sultan) must be a Muslim and become the head of Islam in his state. The sultanate and elements of Islamic governance in the Malay states are thus important as far as the traditional identity of the polity is concerned. Aspects of this system were retained even when the British colonialists set foot on Malaya: the British Residential System provided a British Resident as an adviser to the ruler (sultan), but the latter retained control over matters pertaining to Islam and Malay customs.[10] In Sri Lanka, the *Mahavamsa* chronicle – regarded as the most comprehensive and definitive work on the island's history[11] – emphasizes, among others, the inseparable link between Buddhism, Sri Lanka and the Sinhalese people and portrays Sri Lanka as the *Dhammadeepa*: the chosen land in which Buddhism will flourish for 5,000 years.[12] For proponents of the Sinhalese-Buddhist nationalist ideology, the *Mahavamsa* is sacrosanct and indisputable.

The constitution-making processes in all three countries reflect how constitution-makers sought to accommodate religion in various ways, especially since religion became intimately tied to nationalist sentiments. These efforts, however, were challenging and complicated due to various factors

---

[10] Andrew Harding, *Law, Government and the Constitution in Malaysia* (The Hague and London: Kluwer Law International, 1996), p. 13.

[11] K. M. De Silva, *A History of Sri Lanka*, rev. ed. (London: Penguin Books, 2005), p. 28.

[12] *Mahavamsa* is translated into English as the 'Great Chronicle'. See also Neil DeVotta, *Sinhalese Buddhist Nationalist Ideology: Implications for Politics and Conflict Resolution in Sri Lanka*, Policy Studies, No. 40 (Washington, DC: East-West Center, 2007), p. 6.

such as differing ideologies among the constitution-makers, time constraints and the need to cater for the interests of different groups that were divided not just along religious lines, but also along ethnic, regional and linguistic cleavages. With regard to the question of religion, as we shall see, the constitution-makers in all three countries faced strong demands by sections of the majority community and the political elite to establish a state that is closely identified with the dominant religion in the country.

In Indonesia, there were demands for the establishment of an Islamic state during the promulgation of the country's independence constitution in 1945. One of the reasons for this was the strong sense that Muslim figures and organizations had played a central role in resisting colonial occupation. We must remember, however, that Indonesian Muslims at the time did not speak with a united voice, nor did they subscribe to identical ideological leanings and religious practices. The Javanese Muslims were categorized as either *abangan* or *santri*: the *abangans* were regarded as nominal Muslims who were less committed to Islamic rituals and practices, while the *santris* were the more pious Muslims.[13] The more observant Muslims were further divided into different streams, such as modernist and orthodox. Political affiliations among them also varied. Nonetheless, during the post-Soeharto constitutional reforms almost sixty years later, the call for the entrenchment of *Shariah* into the constitution emerged again, although public and political support for the proposal was notably weaker than it was during the first two decades of independence.

In Malaya, various Malay-Muslim groups sought a special recognition for Islam in the constitution. They were driven, in part, by concerns that 'their' country's history, culture and traditions were under threat due to the growing population of the non-Malays (that is, the Chinese and Indians who had migrated to or whose ancestors had settled in Malaya during the British occupation) and the emergence of citizenship proposals for the non-Malays that were deemed too generous. Chinese groups, in particular, had demanded that *jus soli* citizenship be granted retrospectively and that the Chinese language would be made one of the official languages.[14] In the case of Sri Lanka, the rise of Sinhalese nationalism was intertwined with the Buddhist revivalist movement that emerged in the late nineteenth century.

---

[13] M. C. Ricklefs, *A History of Modern Indonesia since C. 1200*, 4th ed. (Stanford: Stanford University Press, 2008), pp. 158–60. The Javanese were predominantly *abangan*. See ibid., p. 217. However, the *abangan-santri* distinction is almost irrelevant today.

[14] Shad Saleem Faruqi, *Document of Destiny: The Constitution of the Federation of Malaysia* (Petaling Jaya: Star Publications, 2008), p. 13.

The movement assumed a strongly anti-colonialist and anti-Christian tone due to the deep resentment toward British policies that severed the traditional link between Buddhism and the state, as well as evangelical activities by missionary organizations that were seen to be supported by the colonial power.[15] One of the most prominent leaders of the revivalist movement, Anagarika Dharmapala, was a fierce advocate of Sinhalese-Buddhist domination in Sri Lanka.

Nationalist-Religionist Divide in Indonesia

A key distinguishing feature of the Indonesian constitution-making experience – as compared to its Muslim-majority neighbour, Malaysia – was the way in which the founding fathers' ideological division and debates drove the process of constitutionalizing state-religion relations. During the pre-independence constitution-making process in 1945, the Investigating Committee for Preparatory Work for Indonesian Independence (BPUPKI) was primarily split into two factions: the nationalists (*golongan nasionalis*) and the religionists (*golongan agama*).[16] A large section of the BPUPKI comprised those favouring religious neutrality as the foundation of the state, while Islamic-oriented figures comprised less than a quarter of the body.[17]

The nationalist faction in Indonesia, broadly speaking, aimed for a unitary state that separates state and religious affairs and that is neutral toward all religions.[18] This faction comprised members from both Muslim and non-Muslim backgrounds, and they were far from homogenous in terms of religious and political outlooks. For instance, the nationalists comprised both the

---

[15] De Silva, *A History of Sri Lanka*, p. 428.

[16] I adopt the original terms used throughout the constitution-making documents. Anshari uses the terms 'Islamic nationalist' and 'secular nationalist'. See Endang S. Anshari, *Piagam Jakarta 22 Juni 1945 dan Sejarah Konsensus Nasional Antara Nasionalis Islamis dan Nasionalis Sekuler Tentang Dasar Negara Republik Indonesia, 1945–1959 (The Jakarta Charter of 22 June 1945 and the History of National Consensus between Islamist Nationalists and Secular Nationalists on the Foundation of the Republic of Indonesia)* (Bandung: Pustaka Perpustakaan Salman ITB, 1981). According to Assyaukanie, Deliar Noer's classification of 'religiously neutral nationalists' and 'Muslim nationalists' is widely accepted. See Luthfi Assyaukanie, *Islam and the Secular State in Indonesia* (Singapore: Institute of Southeast Asian Studies, 2009), p. 5.

[17] R. E. Elson, 'Another Look at the Jakarta Charter Controversy of 1945' (2009) 88 *Indonesia* 105, 109.

[18] RM A. B. Kusuma, *Lahirnya Undang-undang Dasar 1945 (Memuat Salinan Dokumen Otentik Badan Oentoek Menyelidiki Oesaha-oesaha Persiapan Kemerdekaan) (The Birth of the 1945 Constitution (Containing Copies of Authentic Documents of the Investigating Committee for Preparatory Work for Indonesian Independence))*, rev. ed. (Jakarta: University of Indonesia Law Faculty Publishers, 2009), p. 19.

abangan and the *santri* (these terms were used to distinguish Javanese Muslims based on their piety and religious observance). Yet, it was not necessarily the case that *abangans* unequivocally supported a fully secular state or that the more pious Muslims supported an Islamic state. Indeed, various individuals within the nationalist camp held different views on state-religion relations. For example, Mohammad Hatta, a devout Muslim, was committed to secular-socialist political doctrines.[19] His dedication to the separation of church and state was shared by several members of the BPUPKI, including Soepomo (the chief architect of the constitution) and Latuharhary (a Christian from Maluku). Soekarno, despite his *abangan* upbringings, was more open to accommodating religion in the state (although this did not mean that he was amenable to the establishment of an Islamic state or an explicit recognition for Islam in the constitution).[20] For Soekarno, who would later become the first president of Indonesia, Indonesian unity was the primary goal, and achieving this necessitated the rejection of explicit Islamic references in the constitution.

The religionists, on the other hand, sought to establish an Islamic state. This faction was supported by those who emphasized the historical significance of Islam in the polity, focusing on the fact that Islam is the religion of the majority and that it was one of the potent unifying forces behind Indonesian nationalist and anti-colonial consciousness. Hadikoesomo, a prominent modernist Islamic scholar in the BPUPKI, highlighted the importance of a state based on Islamic teachings and principles, arguing that these would ensure unity, peace and harmony in the country. This arrangement, however, would not affect religious freedom as this, he said, is guaranteed under Islamic principles.[21]

Nevertheless, the dominant tendency within the BPUPKI was to establish a unitary state that separates religious affairs from state affairs. Soepomo's ideas were closely linked to his aspiration for an integralistic state in Indonesia. According to this model, individuals form an organic part of the state and the state does not identify itself with the majority or the dominant group. For Soepomo, an Islamic state would not fit his visions for Indonesia and would pose a problem for the minorities.[22] Indeed, both Soekarno and Soepomo

---

[19] Ricklefs, *History of Modern Indonesia*, p. 226.

[20] Kusuma, *Lahirnya Undang-undang Dasar 1945*, p. 19. Soekarno's position was supported by nationalists such as Muhammad Yamin (a Muslim from Sumatera) and A. A. Maramis (a Christian from Manado, North Sulawesi).

[21] Speech by Hadikoesomo on 31 May 1945 in Kusuma, *Lahirnya Undang-undang Dasar 1945*, p. 143.

[22] Speech by Soepomo on 31 May 1945, in Kusuma, *Lahirnya Undang-undang Dasar 1945*, p. 130.

feared that the establishment of religion in a multicultural, multireligious polity would intensify political disputes and complicate the integration of non-Muslims in an independent Indonesia.[23] As a response, on 1 June 1945, Soekarno introduced the *Pancasila* as the philosophical basis of the state. The *Pancasila* contains five principles: Indonesian nationalism (*kebangsaan Indonesia*), humanitarianism (*peri-kemanusiaan*), representative democracy (*demokrasi mufakat*), social justice (*kesejateraan social*) and the belief in God (*ketuhanan*).

It is worth noting that the nationalist-religionist divide that prevailed among the BPUPKI members persisted throughout at least three subsequent constitution-making periods in Indonesia's post-colonial history. However, over time, there was some evolution in the salience of the division and in the causes for which each faction fought. For example, in the post-Soeharto constitutional reforms, the question on state-religion relations pitted nationalists who sought to preserve the *Pancasila* principle of 'the belief in the one and only God' against Islamic-oriented figures who fought to constitutionalize the implementation of *Shariah* law for Muslims. At this stage, the establishment of an Islamic state – which was initially advocated by the religionists in the 1945 and 1955 constitution-making processes – was not even raised. Nevertheless, what is clear is that in all three constitution-making periods, there were persistent efforts to introduce some form of Islamic recognition in the constitution. None of these efforts has ever been successful; instead, the state ideology remains firmly rooted in the *Pancasila*.

The path advocated by Soekarno and his associates, therefore, was one where the state is seen as 'neutral' toward various religious convictions. Unlike the Malaysian and Sri Lankan constitution-makers, the nationalist faction in Indonesia consistently rejected the privileging of a particular religion and explicitly spelled out the role and place of religion in the country. For the likes of Soepomo and Soekarno, the formula that they adopted did not mean that Indonesia would be an 'areligious' state,[24] or that they were predisposed to excluding religion altogether from Indonesia's socio-political life. In fact,

---

[23] Speech by Soepomo on 31 May 1945 in *Himpunan Risalah Sidang-sidang dari Badan Penyelidik Usaha Persiapan Kemerdekaan Indonesia (BPUPKI) (Tanggal 29 Mei 1945–16 Juli 1945) dan Panitia Persiapan Kemerdekaan Indonesia (PPKI) (Tanggal 18 dan 19 Agustus 1945) Yang Berhubung Dengan Penyusunan Undang-undang Dasar 1945 (A Compilation of the Minutes of Meetings of the Investigating Committee for Preparatory Work for Indonesian Independence (BPUPKI) (29 May 1945–16 July 1945) and the Preparatory Committee for Indonesian Independence (18 and 19 August 1945) Relating to the Drafting of the 1945 Constitution)* (Djakarta: Sekretariat Negara Republik Indonesia, 1954), pp. 32–3.

[24] Speech by Soepomo on 31 May 1945 in *Himpunan Risalah*, pp. 32–3.

when Soekarno introduced the *Pancasila* to the BPUPKI, he stressed that an independent Indonesia would be based on the principle of devotion to God and respect among religious adherents.[25] Through this formulation, he articulated his vision for a country that would celebrate both its religious character and its religious diversity. Soekarno also argued that the third *Pancasila* principle – consensus and representative democracy – would provide the best means to protect religion and address religious affairs.[26]

Ethno-Religious Cleavages and the Protection of Group Interests

If the nationalist-religionist divide was a prominent feature of the Indonesian process, the debates on the position of Islam in Malaya were coloured by competing political interests among various groups involved in the constitution-making process, namely, the constitutional drafting commission, the elected representatives from the Alliance coalition and the traditional Malay rulers. The drafting of the constitution was entrusted to an external body known as the Reid Commission. Headed by Lord Reid, the Commission consisted of five jurists from the Commonwealth.[27] There were no local representatives in the Commission; not even members of the Alliance coalition that had won the 1955 federal legislative elections by a solid 81 per cent of the popular vote. The Alliance is a political coalition consisting of three parties that represented the three main ethnic groups in Malaya. United Malays National Organisation (UMNO), the party representing the Malays (who, at the time, comprised about 50 per cent of the population), was undoubtedly the most dominant partner in the Alliance. The MCA (Malayan Chinese Association) and the MIC (Malayan Indian Congress) represented the Chinese and Indian communities, respectively. Despite the absence of local representatives, the Commission nevertheless considered hundreds of written submissions from organizations and individuals who wished to express their views on the constitution. Neither the Alliance nor the Malay rulers had any *de jure* power to make final decisions. Instead, they were asked to make recommendations based on the Commission's report. The Alliance later played an instrumental

---

[25] See Speech by Soekarno on 1 June 1945 in *Himpunan Risalah*, p. 73. Soekarno emphasized that the Indonesian nation must be a nation that is based on God. Similarly, Soepomo argued that religion would become a strong moral basis for the unitary state of Indonesia. Ibid., p. 34.

[26] Speech by Soekarno in Kusuma, *Lahirnya Undang-undang Dasar 1945*, p. 160.

[27] The other members of the Constitutional Commission were Sir Ivor Jennings (an eminent constitutional scholar), Sir William McKell, Justice B. Malik from India and Justice Abdul Hamid from Pakistan.

role in shaping the substance of the constitution, especially on politically sensitive matters involving ethnicity and religion.

Against this background, forming, negotiating and finalizing the constitution became a complicated and contentious affair. Unlike the Indonesian experience, the groups involved in the Malayan process were not competing on the basis of differing philosophical ideas on the state-religion relationship. Rather, what divided them were their agendas and objectives: the Commission was bound by specific terms of reference provided by the colonial power;[28] the rulers of the Malay states were keen on safeguarding their traditional political position within their respective states on issues pertaining to religion, while the Malays (who were mainly Muslims) and the non-Malays (who were mainly non-Muslims) wanted to secure specific group interests on religious, cultural, educational and citizenship matters. For example, the Malays, through UMNO, sought the establishment of an official religion in the constitution and the preservation of Malay special privileges. The non-Malays rejected these demands, fearing that their rights would be impinged upon and that they would eventually become second-class citizens.

The idea of establishing a state religion in the constitution of Malaya was originally not on the Commission's agenda. In the early drafts of the constitution, there was no provision establishing Islam as the religion of the state, nor was there any mention of a state religion in Justice Hamid's initial list of the main heads of subjects to be included in the draft constitution.[29] In fact, despite the Alliance's suggestion that Islam be made the state religion, his notes reiterated the view that such an establishment would be insignificant. The Report of the Federation of Malaya Constitutional Commission in February 1957 (the Reid Report) did not explicitly recommend the establishment of a state religion. A majority of the Commission thought that Malaya should be a secular state like India.[30] For Sir Ivor Jennings, in particular, Islam did not need state protection.[31] The Malay rulers, rather interestingly, also

---

[28] The terms of reference include parliamentary democracy with a bicameral legislature; a strong central government with a measure of autonomy for the states; the provision of a machinery for central-state consultation on certain financial matters specified in the constitution; safeguarding the special position of the Malays and the legitimate interests of other communities. See Report of the Federation of Malaya Constitutional Commission (21 February 1957), DO35/6282.

[29] Sir William Ivor Jennings, 'Working Drafts' in *Papers of Sir Ivor Jennings*, ICS 125/B/10.2.7 (on file with the Institute of Commonwealth Studies, London).

[30] Note on Pakistan and the Reid Commission Report, Constitutional Talks in London, May 1957 on the Future of Malaya (10 May 1957), DO35/6278.

[31] Sir Ivor Jennings, 'Comments on the Reid Report' in *Papers of Sir Ivor Jennings* ('[I] do not think that the religion of a minority or even of a majority, ought to be formally established.

objected to such an establishment, fearing that it would impinge on their traditional positions as the heads of Islam in their respective states.[32] In anticipation of strong objections from the Malay community, the Report nonetheless stressed that *if* any such provision were included, the civil rights of non-Muslims would be unaffected.[33] Interestingly, accompanying the Report was a separate dissenting note authored by Justice Hamid. The note, among others, contained his disagreement with the Commission's refusal to include a provision establishing a state religion – a clear turnaround from his position in the early days of the constitution-making process. At this point, it became clear that Justice Hamid would support the constitutional establishment of Islam, which, according to him, was innocuous. In the end, the constitution reflected what the Alliance leaders and Justice Hamid sought: an explicit declaration of Islam as the state religion, along with the assurance that it would not affect the religious freedom of non-Muslims.

These competing positions on the role of religion in the constitution mirrored the context of the debates on Buddhism during the 1972 constitutional reforms in Sri Lanka. There, the tripartite contest involved: (1) Sinhalese-Buddhists nationalists who advocated stronger recognition and protection of Buddhism above other religions; (2) those who sought recognition of other religions in addition to Buddhism; and (3) those who favoured a secular state. The third view was expressed by members of the Federal Party, which represented the minority Ceylon Tamils.

The impetus for the establishment of Buddhism in the constitution was triggered by dissatisfaction over colonial policies on Buddhist life. Prior to the arrival of the colonial powers, the traditional bond between Buddhism and the state had existed for over 2,000 years. The British colonial government severed the link in the 1840s due to pressures from missionaries who had actively campaigned for the dissociation of the state from Buddhism.[34] The loss of Buddhist monastic political influence and the colonial government's tacit support for missionary activities became key sources of discontent, especially amongst Buddhist monks and laity.[35] These circumstances spurred the

---

For the same reason I dislike the establishment of the Church of England, but I do not propose to make a song and dance about it. I have great many Muslim friends including Justice Abdul Hamid himself and I do not think that Islam needs the power of the state to support it.')

[32] 'Hearing of Counsel on Behalf of Their Highnesses the Rulers', in *Papers of Sir Ivor Jennings*.

[33] See Reid Report, para. 169. The Commission members anticipated objections from the Malay community with respect to their position on state religion, but justified this 'in deference to views of the Malay Rulers'.

[34] De Silva, *A History of Sri Lanka*, p. 431.

[35] Schonthal, 'Constitutionalizing Religion', p. 473.

Buddhist revivalist movement, which was also intertwined with anti-colonial nationalism and demands for complete independence from the British.

The country's first constitution at independence – the Soulbury Constitution – was enacted through a constitutional reform process that began several years before independence. It soon became clear to the Buddhist nationalists that the constitution lacked any special provisions for Buddhism, which, for them, meant that the religion was being severely disadvantaged. While this served to deepen their discontent against the ruling elite and the existing arrangements, it also amplified their demands to restore the central position of Buddhism in the constitutional order. The absence of any reference to Buddhism in the 1948 Soulbury Constitution reflected the political vision of D. S. Senanayake – the country's first prime minister who was instrumental in negotiating the transfer of power from the British government. Senanayake was deeply committed to a secular state, and he envisioned Sri Lanka as a multiracial democracy where no single ethnic group or religion would be privileged above others.[36] In a letter to Senanayake and in a subsequent report, the All-Ceylon Buddhist Congress (ACBC) – an umbrella organization for lay Buddhists who were committed to the restoration of Buddhism – criticized the Soulbury arrangement for its failure to protect Buddhist interests.[37] It is also interesting to note that Senanayake's chief legal adviser was no other than Sir Ivor Jennings – the same individual who would later play a central role in drafting Malaya's constitution and who strongly rejected any special constitutional recognition for Islam.

The momentum for affirmative protection of Buddhism and Buddhist special privileges had thus been set well before the constitution-making process began in 1970. When the United Front, led by the Sri Lanka Freedom Party (SLFP), returned to dominate the legislature with a landslide victory in the parliamentary elections that year, a constituent assembly was convened in July to draft and adopt a new constitution for Sri Lanka. This was seen as an opportune moment to restore Buddhism to its 'rightful place'. Indeed, S. W. R. D. Bandaranaike founded the SLFP in 1951 as a party that would carry the aspirations of the Sinhalese-Buddhist nationalists.[38] As the historian

---

[36] De Silva, *A History of Sri Lanka*, pp. 554–5.

[37] Benjamin Schonthal, 'Buddhism and the Constitution: The Historiography and Postcolonial Politics of Section 6' in Asanga Welikala (ed.), *The Sri Lankan Republic at 40: Reflections on Constitutional History, Theory and Practice* (Colombo: Centre for Policy Alternatives, 2012), pp. 206–7. See also Stanley Jeyaraja Tambiah, *Buddhism Betrayed? Religion, Politics, and Violence in Sri Lanka* (Chicago: University of Chicago Press, 1992), p. 19.

[38] The SLFP is the successor to the *Sinhala Maha Sabha* (Sinhalese Great Assembly), a Sinhalese-centric political movement established by S. W. R. D. Bandaranaike in the 1930s. See De Silva, *A History of Sri Lanka*, pp. 491–3.

K. M. De Silva succinctly notes, Bandaranaike's populist political program was 'unmistakably Sinhalese and Buddhist in content'.[39] Led by Sirimavo Bandaranaike from the 1960s onwards, the SLFP campaigned on the promise that it would pursue constitutional reforms to strengthen both fundamental rights guarantees and protection of Buddhist privileges.[40] This reflected the two initiatives that her husband, S. W. R. D. Bandaranaike, had convened in the late 1950s: (1) a committee for constitutional revision which was tasked, among others, to generate a fundamental rights chapter that includes religious rights; and (2) a commission to address the ACBC demands for special protection of Buddhism.[41]

CONSTITUTIONALIZING RELIGION: BARGAINS,
COMPROMISES AND OUTCOMES

The parallels in the constitution-making contexts and constraints in the three countries are striking, but what is equally noteworthy was how the drafters sought to resolve the contentious points on religion. Political bargains and compromises became a key feature of the constitution-making process. In some instances, the debates and bargains that followed helped loosen rigid preferences amongst different parties involved in the process. Yet, for reasons we shall see later, these exercises produced three different outcomes – one that maintains religious neutrality, one that establishes a state religion and one that sanctions state patronage of religion – in the three countries.

During the first constitution-making process in Indonesia, the nationalist and religionist factions ultimately reached a compromise to entrench 'the belief in the one and only God' as one of the state's philosophical foundations.

---

[39] K. M. De Silva, *Religion, Nationalism, and the State in Modern Sri Lanka* (Tampa, FL: Dept. of Religious Studies, University of South Florida, 1986), p. 23.

[40] Schonthal, 'Constitutionalizing Religion', p. 476. In the SLFP policy statement in November 1964, Mrs. Bandaranaike stated: 'In addition to steps taken by the late Mr. S. W. R. D. Bandaranaike's Government of 1956, and by the present Government to give Buddhism its proper place in the country as the religion of the majority and at the same time guaranteeing complete freedom of worship to all religions, my Government proposes to place before you legislation which will guarantee this *proper place* to Buddhism.' See De Silva, *Religion, Nationalism, and the State*, p. 9 (citing Government of Ceylon, *Hansard, House of Representatives* (November 20, 1964)).

[41] See De Silva, *Religion, Nationalism, and the State*, p. 8. These two bodies are the Joint Select Committee of the Senate and the House of Representatives Appointed to Consider the Revision of the Constitution and the Buddha Sasana Commission. The Commission recommended, among others, the setting up of a Buddha Sasana Council, Buddhist public schools for laity, regularizing the building of temples and establishing *Sangha* courts. See Schonthal, 'Buddhism and the Constitution', p. 210.

This was a slight modification from what Soekarno originally proposed. In the most recent, four-year long constitutional amendment process, this arrangement was retained. However, much like the 1945 experience, this was not without considerable controversy, which necessitated a *quid pro quo* of sorts between the competing political factions in the MPR. Similarly, political bartering was central to the Malaysian experience. The establishment of Islam was accompanied by the promise that non-Malays would be granted citizenship, the right to vernacular education and the right to religious freedom. In Sri Lanka, the 1972 constitution departed from the Soulbury Constitution's neglect of any special protection for Buddhism. The provision on Buddhism that emerged, however, was seen as a careful compromise between demands for special Buddhist protections and guarantees for religious freedom.

Religion and the Pancasila in Indonesia's 1945 Constitution: Bargaining through the Jakarta Charter

The *Pancasila* solution that Soekarno pursued – where the state would be based on 'the belief in God' – was thought to be a sensible middle path. This, as it turned out, was not enough for the religious faction, who continued to demand for a greater recognition for Islam. In June 1945, the opposing factions reached a compromise in the form of the Jakarta Charter.[42] The religious faction gave up its insistence on an Islamic state and agreed instead that the constitutional preamble would contain *Pancasila* values and the principle that the state will be based on 'the belief in God, with the obligation of carrying out Islamic laws for its adherents'. The words containing the state's obligation to implement *Shariah* came to be known as the 'seven words'. This gentlemen's agreement, which was to be cemented in the preamble and article 29 on religion, ensured that the Islamic faction would not create a theocratic Islamic state and that the nationalists would not turn Indonesia into a secular state along the lines of France and the United States.[43]

---

[42] Before the recess of the first session of its meetings, the BPUPKI had appointed an eight-member subcommittee to consolidate the proposals that emerged from the first session. Soekarno, however, convened his own subcommittee, some of which were members of the committee appointed by the BPUPKI but some were substituted for other individuals. For an account of this, see Elson, 'Another Look at the Jakarta Charter Controversy', p. 112.

[43] Testimony by Professor Dahlan Ranuwihardjo, 7th Meeting of the Ad Hoc Commission I (13 December 1999) in *Risalah Perubahan Undang-undang Dasar Negara Republik Indonesia Tahun 1945: 1999–2012 (Reports of the Amendments of the 1945 Constitution of the Republic of Indonesia: 1999–2012)* (Jakarta: Sekretariat Jenderal Majelis Permusyawaratan Rakyat Republik Indonesia, 2002).

Although the Charter was seen as a win-win solution for the competing factions, it was also strongly criticized. Some saw it as a vague compromise, accepted as it were to expedite the goal of creating a united, independent Indonesia.[44] Others disagreed on the extent and practicality of *Shariah* implementation in the state, while some were concerned that the seven words would spur fanaticism and the use of force in Islamic rituals and practices. Despite these objections, Soekarno was adamant in retaining the Charter, emphasizing the great difficulty in reaching a compromise and the need to avoid further deadlocks. By the time the Charter was formulated, Soekarno had also become pressured by time constraints and the desire to accelerate the process of finalizing a constitution and to achieve independence for Indonesia.

Yet, when the constitution was finalized and adopted on the day after the proclamation of independence, the seven words that would have imposed *Shariah* on Muslims were conspicuously missing. On the evening of Independence Day, Hatta (who would later become the first prime minister) received threats of secession by Christian nationalists from East Indonesia. They strongly opposed the seven words on the grounds that their inclusion signalled that the constitution served the interests of only a section of the Indonesian population.[45] Faced with an imminent disintegration of the unitary state that they fought for, Hatta moved swiftly to remove not just the seven words, but other Islamic-inspired elements in the draft constitution. The stipulation that the president must be a Muslim was removed and 'Mukadimah' (an Arabic term for the preamble) was substituted with the Malay term 'Pembukaan'. He convened a discussion with prominent members of the Islamic faction and in a matter of hours, the compromise in the Charter collapsed.[46] They agreed to the changes, although this was done in return for the entrenchment of the phrase 'the belief in the one and only God'. Some scholars argue that this is significant because it resonated with the monotheistic nature of Islam.[47] But for Hatta, the need for national unity and stability in a newly independent country superseded all other considerations. He did just enough to quell the Islamic faction's misgivings by assuring them that they could pursue their agenda again in the future.[48] Soekarno also argued that the

---

[44] Elson, 'Another Look at the Jakarta Charter Controversy', p. 113.

[45] Ibid., p. 120 (citing Mohammad Hatta, *Sekitar Proklamasi 17 Agustus 1945* (*About the Proclamation of 17 August 1945*) (Jakarta: Tintamas, 1969), p. 57); see also Benjamin Fleming Intan, *'Public Religion' and the Pancasila-Based State of Indonesia: An Ethical and Sociological Analysis* (New York: Peter Lang, 2006), p. 42.

[46] For reasons why the Muslim group eventually acquiesced to Hatta's persuasion, see Elson, 'Another Look at the Jakarta Charter Controversy', pp. 124–5.

[47] Testimony by Professor Dahlan Ranuwihardjo, and Intan, *'Public Religion'*, p. 43.

[48] Elson, 'Another Look at the Jakarta Charter Controversy', p. 126.

temporal nature of the constitution meant that the Muslim leaders could later amend the constitution if they so wished.[49]

A decade after independence, a Constituent Assembly was convened to promulgate a new constitution for Indonesia. The proposal for an Islamic state appeared again, pitting the Islamic political parties against secular nationalist parties. The Islamic faction consisted of several Islamic political parties, including Masyumi, Nahdlatul Ulama (NU) and Partai Sarekat Islam Indonesia (PSII). Two of Indonesia's largest Islamic organizations – the NU and Muhammadiyah – together with other Islamic parties advocated the establishment of an Islamic state.[50] The secular nationalists, which included parties like the Partai Nasional Indonesia (PNI – a party whose support base comprised nominal Muslims as well as Christians in the islands outside Java), Partai Komunis Indonesia (PKI – a party who also gained support from Javanese nominal Muslims) and Partai Kristen Indonesia (Parkindo), defended the existing ideological basis of the state rooted in the *Pancasila*.[51] The Christian representatives, in particular, feared that entrenching Islam in the constitution would trigger secession demands from Christians in Indonesia's eastern islands.[52] A change of the state ideology required a two-thirds majority, but the Muslim faction was defeated by fifty-five votes.[53] The gridlock in the Assembly underlined its failure. After four years, it could not conclude its deliberations[54] and failed to draw a new constitution, thereby prompting Soekarno to decree a return to the 1945 constitution. What was established in article 29 of the 1945 constitution with respect to religion, therefore, remained intact.

Religion in the Post-Soeharto Constitutional Reforms

The most recent attempt to amend article 29 on religion and constitutionalize the *Shariah* arose in the post-Soeharto constitutional reforms. The MPR, acting as a constituent assembly comprising both nationalist and

---

[49] Nadirsyah Hosen, *Shari'a & Constitutional Reform in Indonesia* (Singapore: Institute of Southeast Asian Studies, 2007), p. 63.

[50] Nadirsyah Hosen, 'Religion and the Indonesian Constitution: A Recent Debate' (2005) 26 *Journal of Southeast Asian Studies* 419, 426.

[51] Arskal Salim, *Challenging the Secular State: The Islamization of Law in Modern Indonesia* (Honolulu: University of Hawaii Press, 2008), p. 85.

[52] Intan, 'Public Religion', p. 49.

[53] Hosen, *Shari'a & Constitutional Reform*, p. 67. 201 votes were cast for amending article 29 to include the seven words, while 265 votes were cast against.

[54] Adnan Buyong Nasution, *The Aspiration for Constitutional Government in Indonesia: A Socio-legal Study of the Indonesian Konstituante 1956–1959* (Jakarta: Pustaka Sinar Harapan, 1992), p. 405.

Islamic-oriented factions, agreed at the outset that the preamble would be retained.[55] This is symbolically and substantively significant because it signalled the unwavering allegiance to the *Pancasila* as the sole foundation of the state and as the basis for reforms. For the nationalists, the *Pancasila* is an explicit guarantee against the establishment of an Islamic state.

The agreement did not stop the Islamic-oriented factions from launching proposals to incorporate the seven words into the constitution, which they sought to achieve by amending article 29. The initiative was spearheaded by two Islamic parties – the PPP and the PBB. These parties took advantage of the comparably freer political space to advocate their views, since Soeharto's New Order administration banned any discussion of an Islamic state and obligated political parties to make the *Pancasila* as their sole political ideology. There was, however, a shift in strategy: instead of pursuing the establishment of an Islamic state, the proposal focused on the 'special rights of Muslims and the obligation to implement *Shariah* through article 29'.[56] For PPP and PBB, the proposal was not a manoeuvre to establish an Islamic state; rather, the seven words would provide a strong constitutional guarantee for the implementation of Islamic principles to protect Muslims from moral degradation.[57] This time, PPP and PBB were unwilling to compromise, despite alternative proposals by other Islamic-oriented parties on amendments to article 29. For example, the National Awakening (KB) and *Reformasi* factions proposed 'the obligation upon the followers of each religion to carry out their religious teachings'.[58] Hamdan Zoelva of the PBB rejected this formulation, as he believed that only Islam has special, sacred laws.[59] In any case, the parties

---

[55] The Islamic-oriented parties were: the Partai Persatuan Pembangunan (PPP, or United Development Party), Partai Bulan Bintang (PBB, or Crescent Star Party), Partai Keadilan (PK, or Justice Party), Partai Kebangkitan Bangsa (PKB, or National Awakening Party), Partai Amanat Negara (PAN, or National Mandate Party) and the Partai Daulatul Ummah (PDU).

[56] Hosen, 'Religion and the Indonesian Constitution', p. 420.

[57] *Naskah Komprehensif Perubahan Undang-undang Dasar Negara Republik Indonesia Tahun 1945: Latar Belakang, Proses, dan Hasil Pembahasan 1999–2002, Buku VIII Warga Negara dan Penduduk, Hak Asasi Manusia dan Agama* (*Comprehensive Manuscript of Amendments of the 1945 Constitution of the Republic of Indonesia: Background, Process, and Discussion Results, 1999–2002, Book VIII on Citizens and Residents, Human Rights and Religion*) (Jakarta: Sekretariat Jenderal dan Kepaniteraan Mahkamah Konstitusi, 2010), pp. 529–31.

[58] See Salim, *Challenging the Secular State*, pp. 90–1. The *Reformasi* faction consisted PK and PAN. PK explicitly identified Islam as its party ideology, but PAN is a *Pancasila*-based party. Nevertheless, PAN draws its support mainly from the Muslim communities. The National Awakening faction comprised PKB. Both factions supported this formulation so as to guarantee equality among all religions in Indonesia. Hosen, 'Religion and the Indonesian Constitution', pp. 430–2.

[59] Hosen, 'Religion and the Indonesian Constitution', pp. 432–3.

who proposed the insertion of the seven words wanted to enforce the promise that the deletion of the seven words in 1945 was only temporary – that they would later be able to achieve their goals when the constitution is perfected through the legislature. Hosen argues, however, that the demands were more politically motivated than anything else because, in practice, Muslims are already subjected to special regulations on Islamic law even without the constitutionalization of the seven words.[60]

At the other end of the spectrum, the Indonesia Democratic Party – Struggle (PDI-P) and Indonesian National Army and Police (TNI-Polri) factions, who held about 32 per cent of the MPR seats, were most concerned about the prospect of an Islamic state.[61] Their rejection of any changes to article 29 was supported by other nationalist factions such as Golkar (a nationalist party which was very dominant during the Soeharto era) and PDKB (Partai Demokrasi Kasih Bangsa – a party that drew its support from Christian voters). Together, these parties held about 26 per cent of the MPR seats. The nationalists remained committed to the *Pancasila* and rejected any theocratic elements that would allow the state to control the observance of religious duties. For some members, the inclusion of the obligation to carry out one's religious teachings would also be contrary to human rights values.

Notwithstanding the change in strategy, the proposal failed again. Apart from the strong opposition by the nationalists, the factions that sought to amend article 29 were also very divided and their opinions changed throughout the deliberations. Toward the end of the fourth amendment debates, the KB and *Reformasi* factions agreed to retain the original article 29. In the MPR's final plenary session, even the PPP suggested that it would defer to whatever the MPR decided. This was a strong indication that the PPP would go along with the decision of the majority who were overwhelmingly against any amendment to article 29.

In the end, the MPR never voted on the proposal to amend article 29. In what was perhaps a face-saving measure, the PBB rejected the voting

---

[60] Hosen, *Shari'a and Constitutional Reform*, p. 204. When confronted with this statement, Lukman Hakim Saifuddin (PPP) agreed, although he suggested that the constitutional debate opened an opportunity for his party to deliver the aspirations of their supporters. For Zoelva (PBB), however, a constitutional guarantee was essential because statutes and regulations are replaceable.

[61] Ibid., p. 279. Megawati (who, at the time of the constitution-making was the president and the chair of PDI-P) is perceived to be very averse to political Islam. Interview with a member of the Indonesian House of Representatives in Jakarta, Indonesia (18 January 2014).

process, arguing that 'God's law cannot be subjected to voting'.[62] Hosen adds that the PBB feared that an unsuccessful voting outcome would jeopardize the prospects of reopening future debates on including *Shariah* in the constitution.[63] There was never a firm consensus among all parties on the decision not to amend article 29. PBB abstained from the final decision-making process, which led to the retention of article 29 in its original form. Against a more resolute, united and larger group of parties that opposed any amendment to article 29, the two Islamic parties that fought to amend article 29 knew they could not accomplish their goals. In the civil society sphere, even the NU and Muhammadiyah rejected any attempt to formalize *Shariah* in the constitution.[64] This stood in stark contrast to their position during the 1955 deliberations. Indrayana offers another explanation on why and how the deliberations on article 29 turned out the way they did. He suggests that a compromise was struck between competing groups in a closed meeting to avoid a deadlock. The factions proposing to incorporate *Shariah* agreed to withdraw their demands in exchange for a revision to article 31 on the national education system to include a provision on 'improving religious faith and devoutness'.[65] However, they kept these arrangements secret until the final MPR plenary meeting because they wanted to show their constituents that they had been fighting to include *Shariah* in the amendments.[66]

Constitutionalizing Islam as the State Religion in Malaysia

If in Indonesia, the nationalists succeeded in resisting any attempts for constitutional recognition of and obligation to implement Islamic law, the Malayan experience was quite the opposite. Despite earlier objections by a majority of the Reid Commission members and the Malay rulers, the final draft constitution reflected precisely what the Alliance wanted all along: a special constitutional recognition of Islam as the religion of the state. In its memorandum to the Reid Commission in September 1956, the Alliance proposed the following:

---

[62] Hosen, *Shari'a & Constitutional Reform*, p. 199.   [63] Ibid.

[64] Salim, *Challenging the Secular State*, p. 93. According to the chairman of NU, his organization only expects *Shariah* to be implemented as 'communal directives' for Muslims, not codified as state law. Both NU and Muhammadiyah have a combined membership of about sixty million. See Hosen, *Shari'a and Constitutional Reform*, p. 60.

[65] Denny Indrayana, *Indonesian Constitutional Reform 1999–2002: An Evaluation of Constitution-Making in Transition* (Jakarta: Kompas, 2008), p. 289. The revised article 31 states: 'The national education system should be aimed at improving people's religious faith and devoutness and their character as well as sharpening their minds.'

[66] Ibid.

The religion of Malaysia shall be Islam. The observance of this principle shall not impose any disability on non-Muslim nationals professing and practicing their own religions and shall not imply that the State is not a secular State.[67]

At this juncture, there are three crucial questions: (1) Why did the Commission and the colonial government approve the establishment of Islam, despite their initial objection?[68]; (2) What were the bargains that led to the Alliance's unanimous recommendation for inclusion of the provision in the constitution?; and (3) What were the intended effect and meaning of the provision? The constitution-making documents do not offer any explicit reasons for the Commission's U-turn, but several conclusions may be drawn from the various letters and communication records among the British officials.

The prevailing social and political conditions were undoubtedly instructive factors. The colonial government was cognizant of the growing ethnic hostilities and threats of Communist subversion, which they feared would give rise to widespread intercommunal tensions.[69] Some sections of the Malay community had objected to the proposals that emerged from the constitutional discussions, particularly the Commission's treatment of matters on religion and the special position of the Malays. The memoranda submitted to the Commission by various Malay organizations indicated, for the most part, support for the idea of entrenching Islam as the official religion, although they also emphasized the right of minorities to profess and practice their religion. It was thought – even amongst some 'sincere and moderate Malays' – that under the Reid Report's proposals, the Malays 'would give too much away'.[70] This was complicated by debates on *jus soli* citizenship for the Chinese and Indians and the fear that citizenship could later be made conditional upon conversion to Islam. The Malay misgivings piled the pressure on Tunku Abdul Rahman (who would later become the country's first prime minister), who already faced a monumental task of keeping the Alliance coalition together.

The British government and the local leaders knew that it was only a matter of time before these strains evolved into a serious political crisis within the Alliance. What was initially a marriage-of–convenience (UMNO, it was said,

---

[67] Reid Report, para. 169.

[68] Record of a Meeting held in the Commonwealth Relations Office (10 May 1957), CO1030/436. (stating that the Commission 'had recommended that Islam should *not* be made state religion as this might derogate form the powers of the Rulers as the Heads of Religion').

[69] Outward Telegram from Commonwealth Relations Office (19 June 1957), CO1030/436.

[70] Outward Telegram from Commonwealth Relations Office (24 May 1957), CO1030/436.

needed Chinese financial resources and support to win the first elections, while the MCA and MIC knew that they could not progress politically without a working arrangement with UMNO[71]) proved to be an acceptable arrangement – perhaps even the most desirable arrangement under the circumstances – to the British. The Alliance was seen as a stable and useful partner to achieve mutual objectives, especially since independence was conditional upon the coming together of different communities in the polity.[72] The British were thus keen to avoid a disintegration of the Alliance if communal tensions worsened, fearing the formation of a government that felt it could retain the support of and represent only the Malays.[73] One might surmise, therefore, that the Commission and the colonial government were under considerable pressure to secure the Alliance's cooperation and trust, and this eventually led to the concession on the issue of state religion. There was also the question of legitimacy: the Alliance had secured overwhelming support from all major groups in the 1955 elections, and the religion provision was introduced by the Alliance in response to the dominant (i.e., Malay) local opinion.[74]

These local conditions were further complicated by an external factor. News about the Commission's initial refusal to incorporate the provision on Islam reached Pakistan, and soon rumours about the colonial government's motives began to circulate. Various groups alleged that such refusal was part of 'an Indo-British conspiracy to impose on the Malays a constitution which will place the Malays in a permanent ineffective minority in their own country'.[75] In light of the spread of Communist influence in the region at that time, it was claimed that the constitution would open the doors for the Chinese community to 'seize' Malaya for its sole benefit.[76] By then, it became clear to the British government that finalizing the constitution and ensuring a smooth road to independence hinged upon the need to cater – to some extent – to Malay opinion. In other words, there was a need to demonstrate that the arrangements agreed upon in the constitutional conference were 'fully acceptable to the Malays and their interests'.[77] The crucial conduit for this was cooperation with the moderate personalities in the Alliance, particularly the Tunku as its leading and most prominent figure.

---

[71] Letter from Donald MacGillivray to A. M. MacKintosh (26 April 1957), CO1030/440.
[72] Ibid.   [73] Ibid.
[74] Note on Islam as the Religion of the Federation of Malaya (undated), CO1030/440.
[75] See Pakistan and the Reid Commission Report in note 30, above.
[76] See Inward Telegram to the Commonwealth Relations Office from the United Kingdom High Commissioner in Pakistan (4 May 1957), DO35/6282.
[77] See Pakistan and the Reid Commission Report, in note 30, above.

The notion of establishing a state religion whilst maintaining a secular state might seem like a misnomer. Yet, for the Alliance, this was the best solution to appeal to both the Malays and non-Malays. The political settlement was part of a bigger scheme of bargaining among the representatives of Malaya's ethnic groups: Islam would become the religion of the Federation, and in return, the non-Muslims were assured the right to freedom of religion, and the non-Malays were to obtain citizenship and retain the right of education in their mother tongue.[78] The latter two issues appeared to be the most important for the non-Malays – in fact, as the records indicate, more important than the question of state religion. This settlement might have also been driven by two other factors: (1) the Alliance's emphasis on the symbolic significance and the psychological effect of an official religion on the Malay-Muslims,[79] along with the constant assurance that it would not create a Muslim theocracy; and (2) the predominant opinion in UMNO (the biggest and strongest partner in the Alliance) favoured a special position for Islam in the constitution.

Apart from the need to strike a bargain among ethnic groups, the Alliance also found itself in a difficult position vis-à-vis the Malay rulers, who rejected the idea of an official religion of the Federation. In response to this, the Alliance assured the rulers that the proposed arrangement would not affect the traditional positions of each of the individual rulers as heads of religion in their respective states.[80] The contesting parties also agreed that if a federal-level religious department was established for liaison purposes and for federal-state coordination, it would be part of the establishment of the *Yang di-Pertuan Agong* (the king), not of the elected government. The reaching of this agreement would later become one of the bases upon which the British government approved the inclusion of the state religion provision in the constitution.[81]

---

[78] Andrew Harding, 'Sharia and National Law in Malaysia' in Jan Michiel Otto (ed.), *Sharia Incorporated: A Comparative Overview of the Legal Systems of Twelve Muslim Countries in Past and Present* (Leiden: Leiden University Press, 2010), p. 499.

[79] Joseph M. Fernando, 'The Position of Islam in the Constitution of Malaysia' (2006) 37 *Journal of Southeast Asian Studies* 249, 258.

[80] Minutes of the First Meeting of the Working Party of the Constitution of the Federation (22 February 1957), CO941/25.

[81] In response to a question by a member of the House of Commons (Miss Joan Vickers of Plymouth, Davenport) on the reason for the discrepancy between the rulers' views in the Reid Report and the inclusion of article 3, the under-secretary of state for commonwealth relations (Mr. C. J. M. Alport) explained that the rulers' views had changed, and together with the government of Malaya they proposed that the provision establishing Islam as the state religion should be inserted into the constitution. *Hansard*, HC, Vol. 573, col. 713 (12 July 1957).

What appears to be clear at this stage is that the provision on Islam was meant to assume a political significance, rather than a practical effect.[82] It was the result of a political act and a social compromise, motivated by the desire to minimize resistance from various sections of the community. Although the British government expressed misgivings over the ways in which the Alliance dictated the wordings of the constitutional provisions, they were also persuaded by the fact that the arrangements were products of a 'very long political bargaining process'[83] – a process which the Alliance did not want to revisit to avoid further arguments on the substance of the provisions.

The declaration of Islam as the state religion stopped short of establishing an Islamic state along the lines of Pakistan. Justice Hamid reiterated that the arrangement would be 'innocuous'.[84] For him, there was enough positive evidence from similar constitutional arrangements in other countries such as Ireland, Norway, Denmark and Argentina, in the sense that religious establishment was not necessarily detrimental to the exercise of rights.[85] In addition, the Alliance took pains to clarify the nature and effect of the provision: it assured the Commission and the British government that such an establishment would not affect the rights of non-Muslims to profess and practice their religion and that the secular nature of the state would remain intact.[86] In a subsequent discussion of the Commission's report, the Tunku reaffirmed that the 'whole constitution was framed on the basis that the Federation would be a secular state'.[87] Although there was no explanation by the Alliance on what was meant by a 'secular state', the British government understood that this was to mirror the English arrangement with the establishment of the Church of England. It was thought that the Alliance government would create a similar situation in Malaya, where Islam will be the state religion but with full religious rights accorded, as was the case in England, to religious minorities. In the end, the British government conceded that matters on religion are political questions that should be decided by the local leaders, provided there were satisfactory guarantees for religious worship for all religions.[88]

---

[82] Draft Memorandum by Jackson (undated), CO1030/494 (arguing that the establishment of Islam 'has more political significance than practical effect').

[83] Correspondence from Alan Lennox-Boyd to Lord Reid (26 September 1957), CO1030/486.

[84] Report of the Federation of Malaya Constitutional Commission, Justice Abdul Hamid's Note of Dissent (21 February 1957), DO35/6282.

[85] Ibid.

[86] Alliance Party Memorandum to the Reid Commission (27 September 1956), CO889/6.

[87] Minutes of the 19th Meeting of the Working Party of the Constitution of the Federation (17 April 1957), CO941/25.

[88] Record of a meeting held in the Commonwealth Relations Office on 10 May 1957 (21 May 1957), CO 1030/436.

Constitutionalizing Buddhism in Sri Lanka's 1972 Constitution

In January 1971, the Drafting Committee of the Constituent Assembly – headed by Dr. Colvin R. De Silva, a committed Trotskyite and secularist – proposed the Draft Basic Resolution Three (DBR3), which provides that Buddhism shall be given its 'rightful place' and that the state bears the duty to 'protect and foster' Buddhism while assuring the right to religious freedom to all religions.[89] It is notable, however, that earlier drafts of the basic resolution – as in the Malayan experience – did not contain any reference to Buddhism.[90] Instead, it was introduced after the prime minister's letter to De Silva in December 1970, instructing him to incorporate some reference to Buddhism due to prevailing public opinion.[91] Mrs. Bandaranaike wrote:

> There appears to be a considerable demand in the Country for Buddhism as a State Religion, and for the protection of its institution and traditional places of worship. Some provision will have to be made in the new Constitution regarding these matters without, at the same time, derogating from the freedom of worship that should be guaranteed to all other religions.[92]

The formulation of DBR3, to be sure, was the work of De Silva. In keeping with the details of Mrs. Bandaranaike's letter, he constructed a provision that, in his view, would balance and satisfy both the demands for special rights for Buddhism and the protection of religious freedom. What did the formulation in DBR3 mean? Did it mean that Buddhism and Buddhist interests would supersede the fundamental rights of others? Speaking before the Constituent Assembly, De Silva succinctly explained the intention and meaning behind the provision:

---

[89] DBR3 read: 'In the Republic of Sri Lanka, Buddhism, the religion of the majority of the people, shall be given its rightful place, and accordingly, it shall be the duty of the State to protect and foster Buddhism, while assuring to all religions the rights granted by Basic Resolution 5(4).' Basic Resolution 5(4) read: 'Every citizen shall have the right to freedom of thought, conscience and religion. This right shall include the freedom to have or to adopt a religion or belief of his choice, and the freedom, either individually or in community with others in public or private, to manifest his religion or belief in worship, observance, practice and teaching.' This provision was copied verbatim from the ICCPR. See Schonthal, 'Constitutionalizing Religion', p. 478. It is worth noting that DBR3 closely resembled the policy statements and manifesto of the SLFP. See Schonthal, 'Buddhism and the Constitution', p. 213.

[90] Nihal Jayawickrama, 'Reflections on the Making and Content of the 1972 Constitution: An Insider's Perspective' in Welikala (ed.), *The Sri Lankan Republic at 40*, p. 106.

[91] Ibid.

[92] Letter from Sirimavo Bandaranaike to Dr. Colvin R. De Silva (9 December 1970), reproduced in Jayawickrama, 'Reflections', pp. 72–5.

It is intended, and I think in all fairness it should be so stated, that the religion Buddhism holds in the history and tradition of Ceylon a special place, and the specialness thereof should be recognized in the Resolution. It was at the same time desired that it should be stressed that the historical specialness, the traditional specialness and the contemporary specialness which flows from its position in the country *should not be so incorporated in the Constitution as in any manner to hurt or invade the susceptibilities of those who follow other religions* in Ceylon or the rights that are due to all who follow other religions in Ceylon. It is for that reason that, first of all, into the Resolution stating the place being assigned to Buddhism there was incorporated the reference to fundamental rights, Basic Resolution 5(iv).[93]

Despite De Silva's explanation, DBR3 immediately became a subject of immense debate in the Constituent Assembly. Various parties sought to clarify the precise meanings of the resolution – in particular, the relative priority between the special obligations of the state regarding Buddhism and the general right to religious freedom – but they also had different visions as to what and how the religion clause ought to be constructed in order to safeguard their respective interests.

At one end of the spectrum, there were staunch advocates for stronger protection of Buddhism. The United National Party (UNP), led by J. R. Jayewardene, proposed the addition of the words 'inviolable' and 'its rites, Ministers and places of worship' – drawn from the Kandyan Convention of 1815 – to DBR3.[94] Jayewardene also drew on examples in other constitutions, including Malaysia's arrangement on Islam as the state religion. For the UNP, not only would such formulation afford greater specificity on the role of the state with respect to Buddhism, it would also distinguish and elevate Buddhism above all other religions. The effort to assert stronger protections for Buddhism in the constitutional scheme had in fact been the UNP's election manifesto in the 1960s.[95] Along with Mrs. Bandaranaike's promises to fulfil her late husband's visions, it became clear that the political rhetoric and policies in the country were being framed in response to the prevailing sentiments among the Sinhalese-Buddhist majority.

At the other end were Constituent Assembly members who argued that a secular state would best guarantee the rights and interests of all religious

---

[93] Sri Lanka Constituent Assembly Official Report, Debates vol. 1 (Ceylon Government Press, 1972) (29 March 1971), pp. 643–4 and (14 May 1971), pp. 951–2.

[94] Ibid., p. 650. The UNP proposal would have looked like this: 'In the Republic of Sri Lanka, Buddhism, the religion of the majority of the people, shall be *inviolable* and shall be given its rightful place, and accordingly, it shall be the duty of the State to protect and foster Buddhism, *its rites, Ministers, and its places of worship*, while assuring to all religions the rights granted by basic Resolution 5(4).'

[95] Schonthal, 'Buddhism and the Constitution', p. 211.

groups in Sri Lanka. Similar to Jennings's views in Malaya, it was thought that the majority religion did not need state protection. These views were advocated by members of the Federal Party, who represented the Ceylon Tamil minorities. V. Dharmalingam objected to the fact that DBR3 privileged only Buddhism and that special rights were given to Buddhism alone.[96] For the Federal Party, Buddhism's privileged position meant that it could claim a special legal status that other religions could not.

In the middle of the spectrum, there was a proposal for all religions – not just Buddhism – to be granted explicit protection in the constitution. Mr. Aziz, a Muslim member from the ruling coalition, did not oppose the idea of constitutionalizing Buddhism. In fact, he acknowledged the historical role of Buddhism in the polity and the injustices inflicted upon it during the colonial period.[97] However, it was thought that other religions had their fair share of contribution to the state's history and culture and this should be given due recognition. It is worth noting that in terms of political support and alliances, Muslims were largely seen as supporters of the Sinhalese majority for strategic and pragmatic reasons.[98] Indeed, the Muslims, by and large, had almost no disagreement with the constitutionalization of Buddhism in the 1972 constitution-making process.[99] The political strategy adopted by the Muslims in Sri Lanka thus resembled that of the MCA and the MIC in Malaya. It was thought that they had more to gain by avoiding political confrontation with the majority and that their interests would be best secured through cooperation with and goodwill of the majority group.

Nevertheless, De Silva resisted all proposed amendments. The final outcome followed De Silva's initial draft, with two small modifications: the words 'the religion of the majority of the people' were dropped and 'rightful place' was substituted with 'foremost place'. The latter is significant as far as the constitutional position of Buddhism is concerned and was introduced at the direction of Mrs. Bandaranaike, who chaired a smaller committee within the Constituent Assembly which scrutinized the chapter on Buddhism.[100] The entire provision is also said to be a product of a compromise, in which the moderates in the SLFP played a role.[101]

---

[96] Schonthal, 'Constitutionalizing Religion', p. 480, quoting Constituent Assembly Official Report (14 May 1971), pp. 929–30 (translated from Tamil).

[97] Constituent Assembly Official Report (29 March 1971), pp. 640–2.

[98] Farzana Haniffa, 'Conflicted Solidarities? Muslims and the Constitution-Making Process of 1970–72' in Welikala (ed.), *The Sri Lankan Republic at 40*, p. 220.

[99] Ibid., pp. 227–8. [100] Jayawickrama, 'Reflections', p. 106.

[101] Jayampathy Wickramaratne, 'Fundamental Rights in the 1972 Constitution' in Welikala (ed.), *The Sri Lankan Republic at 40*, p. 768.

The ambiguity on the exact nature of the relationship between the two potentially conflicting guarantees in the religion clause remained, but this was also a deliberate and conscious decision by De Silva. Given his ideological leanings, it probably fell short of what was ideal for him, but under the prevailing circumstances, it probably fulfilled both his desire to guarantee religious freedom as well as the wider political pressure to provide special recognition for Buddhism. To some extent, the element of political expediency also prevailed: the issue required majority approval of the legislators, and De Silva knew that opening further debate on the details of the clause would be counter-productive.[102] De Silva clarified his position on this before the Assembly:

> It is after very careful thought that every single word has been introduced into the Resolution, and, as much as I would like to state that I yield to none in my respect for all religions which all peoples in this country and elsewhere follow, I would earnestly urge that any efforts to change the language or the content of what is a very carefully expressed Basic Resolution may result in, shall I say, some kind of unanticipated unbalancing of *what is a very balanced Resolution.*[103]

It is important to note that De Silva could have opted to concede to the demands of those who demanded a stronger assertion for Buddhism. In addition to Jayewardene's proposal, there were, for example, demands to constitutionalize the requirement for the president and prime minister to be Buddhists.[104] Right-wing elements in the SLFP and several Buddhist organisations like the ACBC also demanded that Buddhism be made the state religion.[105] Instead, he strongly rejected these, arguing that no such protection was needed in a country where 74 per cent of the population are Buddhists. Alternatively, he could have yielded to calls for a secular state (in fact, it was what he would have preferred) along the lines argued by Mr. Dharmalingam and the Federal Party. He also rejected this proposal, owing to on-the-ground support for Buddhist protections and the majority sentiments in the popularly elected Assembly. In a public speech in 1987, De Silva argued that the provision on Buddhism should be seen as a compromise of sorts between secularism and Buddhist majoritarianism. That the provision did

---

[102] Schonthal, 'Constitutionalizing Religion', p. 479.

[103] Constituent Assembly Official Report (29 March 1971), pp. 643–4.

[104] Colvin R. De Silva, *Safeguards for the Minorities in the 1972 Constitution* (Colombo: Young Socialist Publication, 1987), p. 11.

[105] Wickramaratne, 'Fundamental Rights in the 1972 Constitution', p. 768.

not explicitly make Buddhism the state religion, according to De Silva, was in and of itself significant.[106]

Stronger Protections for Buddhism in the 1978 Constitution

In 1978, a revision to the constitution – led by the UNP, which had a five-sixths majority in parliament – made a crucial change to the religion clause. The word 'Buddhism' in section 6 of the 1972 constitution was substituted with 'Buddha Sasana' (in what is now article 9 of the constitution). It is worth noting that the UNP's position in the constitution-making processes of the 1970s was markedly different two decades earlier. When it led the government in 1947–1956, its politicians and ministers patronized Buddhist events, but they also maintained that 'Buddhism required no special protection or any specific constitutional guarantees'.[107]

In any case, the process in which the change was done differed from the 1972 constitution. A bipartisan Select Committee of the National State Assembly (the legislature), which comprised representatives from the UNP, SLFP and the Ceylon Workers' Congress, was appointed to consider revisions to the constitution.[108] The Tamil United Liberation Front did not participate, but the Select Committee called for submissions from sixteen organisations, including those representing racial minorities and militant Buddhist organisations.[109]

The alteration to section 6 is substantively significant. For one, the term 'Buddha Sasana' has a much wider connotation – it does not only cover the Buddhist creed, doctrine or belief but also includes institutional aspects such as monks, temples and their lands, relics and so on.[110] This, in essence, widens the scope of the state's duty to 'protect and foster'. In addition, as Schonthal argues, the change distinguishes Buddhism from other religions and implies Buddhism's pre-eminence in the country, which is bolstered by making the provision an entrenched clause in the constitution.[111] This enhanced the status of the Buddhism chapter, allowing it to only be alterable with a two-thirds majority in parliament plus a public referendum. Although the UNP

---

[106] De Silva, *Safeguards for the Minorities*, pp. 10–12.
[107] Tessa Bartholomeusz, 'First among Equals: Buddhism and the Sri Lankan State' in Ian Harris (ed.), *Buddhism and Politics in Twentieth-Century Asia* (London: Pinter, 1999), p. 183.
[108] Jayampathy Wickramaratne, *Fundamental Rights in Sri Lanka*, 2nd ed. (Colombo: Stamford Lake Publication, 2006), p. 28.
[109] W. A. Wiswa Warnapala, 'Sri Lanka's New Constitution' (1980) 20 *Asian Survey* 914, 915.
[110] Schonthal, 'Constitutionalizing Religion', p. 482.   [111] Ibid.

also asserted that the chapter on Buddhism had now been made 'inviolable' (which was exactly what it sought in the 1972 constitution-making process),[112] De Silva's basic 'balancing' structure (or rhetoric, as some might see it) for the provision remained intact. Furthermore, the same constitutional revision exercise introduced stronger protections on religious freedom and fundamental rights as a whole. The freedom of thought, conscience and religion is rendered absolute and entrenched, but the freedom to manifest one's religion is subject to certain restrictions. This is complemented by article 12, which guarantees the right to equality and non-discrimination on the basis of, *inter alia*, race and religion.

Revisiting the Constitutional Position of Buddhism

At the time of writing, Sri Lanka is undergoing major constitutional reforms, which are set in motion following the unexpected fall of former President Mahinda Rajapaksa in the 2015 presidential elections. In December 2015, the prime minister appointed a twenty-member Constitutional Reform Committee, which was tasked to solicit and consider public representations on the content for the new constitution and to provide recommendations to the Constitutional Assembly. Unsurprisingly, religion was a topic attracting much debate. The deep division in public opinion on the constitutional position of Buddhism is reflected in the outcome of the Committee's report: the Committee was unable to reach a consensus, and instead, it proposed six possible permutations on the shape and content of the religion clause for the new constitution. Aside from recommending that article 9 is retained in its current shape and form, the Committee also recommended, among others, that the religion clause states that: (1) Sri Lanka shall be a secular state; or (2) Sri Lanka shall be a secular state while recognizing the role of religion in the spiritual development of people; or (3) Sri Lanka will give all religions equal status.[113] How the Constitutional Assembly seeks to address this contentious question, what will be the path that it eventually adopts, and which similar constitutional provisions (from other countries) that it will look to for inspiration are all important questions that are worth monitoring as the reforms process progresses.

---

[112] Ibid.
[113] Public Representations Committee on Constitutional Reform, 'Report on Public Representations Committee on Constitutional Reform' (May 2016), pp. 18–19, online: www.yourconstitution.lk/PRCRpt/PRC_english_report-A4.pdf.

INCORPORATING THE RIGHT TO RELIGIOUS FREEDOM IN THE CONSTITUTION

The religion clauses in the three constitutions embody constitutional promises of religious liberty, but they must be considered together with other provisions that safeguard (or limit, as the case might be) the right to religious freedom. The Indonesian, Malaysian and Sri Lankan constitutions at independence incorporated some fundamental rights guarantees, although these were far less comprehensive than what we would ordinarily find in international human rights instruments. With regard to Indonesia and Sri Lanka, the lack of fundamental rights guarantees may not come as a surprise, since both constitutions predated the first international human rights instrument – the Universal Declaration of Human Rights. To the extent that there were rights guarantees in the 1945 Indonesian Constitution, they were largely illusory because the state could regulate those rights as it saw fit.[114] This gave the government a blank check to repress its citizens, as evinced by the decades of authoritarianism that Indonesia endured until the fall of Soeharto. In Sri Lanka, the Soulbury Constitution condensed anti-discrimination and religious freedom guarantees into one provision (section 29(2)). As in Indonesia, the bill of rights in the Malayan constitution at independence was decidedly minimalist – it contains only nine main provisions and allows great flexibility to the legislature in regulating rights.

These outcomes reflect the constitution-makers' general resistance to the incorporation of human rights protections. In Indonesia, the omission of a comprehensive set of rights guarantees was a deliberate decision on the part of the 1945 constitutional framers. Soekarno and Soepomo, in particular, staunchly opposed individual rights. They saw these as Western, liberal democratic ideas that are inherently imperialistic and ill-suited to Indonesia's need for a strong sense of communal bond. Instead, they looked to the East and adopted a Japanese-inspired ideology focusing on kinship and mutual cooperation.[115] The coexistence of individual rights and the sovereign powers of the state, it was argued, will only lead to conflict and instability.[116] As a result, guarantees of civil and political rights in the constitution were thin; instead, citizen subservience to the state and its authorities was made paramount.

---

[114] Tim Lindsey, 'Indonesian Constitutional Reform: Muddling towards Democracy' (2002) 6 *Singapore Journal of International and Comparative Law* 244, 253.

[115] Speech by Soekarno on 15 July 1945 in *Himpunan Risalah*, pp. 221–6.

[116] Ibid., p. 226. Soekarno urged his colleagues in the BPUPKI to dispose of individualistic ideas and not include the French-inspired 'rights of citizens' in the constitution. Ibid., p. 230.

Though resistant to the idea of individual rights, Soepomo nevertheless accepted the importance of religious freedom, particularly the freedom of every person to embrace his own religion and to worship according to his religion and beliefs. For Soepomo, this guarantee was not only part of the initial compromise in the Jakarta Charter, but it would also ensure that adherents of other religions would feel at home in Indonesia.[117]

In Malaya, the incorporation of a bill of rights into the constitution was primarily the Reid Commission's initiative, who drew heavily on the Indian Constitution.[118] The opposition came instead from the local leaders involved in the constitution-making process, especially those from UMNO and MCA. However, this did not seem to be explicitly rooted in any strong ideological objection to individual rights, as was the case in Indonesia. Rather, the concerns were couched in the practicalities of incorporating such guarantees and how that would affect the positions and interests of the different communities in the polity. For one, the leaders were concerned that a poorly drafted bill of rights would eventually hamper government expediency. The Malays were anxious to protect their special privileges and interests, which would contradict the right to equality sought by the non-Malays. At that time, the Malays enjoyed many special rights in the states, such as preferential promotion in the civil service, free education and an inalienable right to the most fertile land in the state.[119] The Chinese communities, on the other hand, had a different vision on how to secure their rights and desire for equality in economic, social and political policies. The MCA did not think that a bill of rights would at all be imperative; instead, they thought that the best means to protect the rights and interests of the Chinese community would be by securing citizenship and maintaining a solid political alliance with UMNO.[120] The Alliance leaders nonetheless eventually agreed to a bill of rights due to pressures from the Indian community represented by the MIC.[121] The Alliance submitted to the Commission a short list of rights guarantees, which included the freedom of worship, the freedom to profess, practice

---

[117] Speech by Soepomo on 15 July 1945 in *Himpunan Risalah*, p. 238.

[118] Charles O. H. Parkinson, *Bills of Rights and Decolonization: The Emergence of Domestic Human Rights Instruments in Britain's Overseas Territories* (Oxford: Oxford University Press, 2007), p. 73.

[119] Ibid., p. 74.

[120] Ibid., p. 90. Parkinson argues that the MCA was 'uninterested in a bill of rights' and was 'willing to endorse proposals that were not advantageous to the Chinese community in order to keep its close relationship with the United Malays National Organisation [UMNO]'.

[121] According to Tunku Abdul Rahman, for UMNO and the MCA, it is immaterial whether the bill of rights is included or not. Meeting of the Alliance Party with the Reid Commission (27 September 1956), CO889/6.

and propagate any religion and the freedom of every religion to establish and maintain religious institutions.

In contrast to the Indonesian and Malayan experiences, the Ceylon political leaders, who were involved in proposing a draft constitution to the British government, were keen to incorporate a bill of rights.[122] This was thought to address the fears of the minorities with respect to their position and interests in the political order.[123] However, on the advice of Sir Ivor Jennings, the final draft constitution prepared by the Ceylon Board of Ministers omitted a bill of rights, but included instead section 29(2), which prohibited legislation discriminating against persons of any community or religion and legislation infringing religious freedom.[124] J. R. Jayewardene continued to press for a bill of rights through a shadow constitution despite the decision of the Board of Ministers,[125] and the Tamils also pressed for better rights guarantees.[126] G. G. Ponnambalam, leader of the Tamil Congress and a prominent member of the Bar, for instance, was sceptical of section 29(2)'s ability to protect the rights and freedoms of non-Sinhala minorities. On the other hand, Jennings, who greatly influenced the draft constitution, harped on Britain's relative success in protecting rights despite the absence of a formal bill of rights,[127] and he believed that a fixed regime of rights guarantees would adversely affect government decision-making.[128] Nevertheless, the safeguards for minorities – in the form of section 29(2) – were a condition precedent for independence[129] and the Board of Ministers' proposal was ultimately approved by the Soulbury Commission.

Religious Values as a Limitation on the Exercise of Rights in Indonesia

The post-Soeharto constitutional reforms ushered in prospects for greater human rights protection. In a special session in 1998, the MPR passed Decree 17/1998 on Human Rights, and in 1999, the legislature (DPR – Dewan Perwakilan Rakyat) approved Law 39/1999 on Human Rights. These, as well as the Universal Declaration of Human Rights (UDHR), were the bases for

---

[122] Joseph A. L. Cooray, *Constitutional Government and Human Rights in a Developing Society* (Colombo: Colombo Apothecaries' Company, 1969), p. 34.

[123] Ibid.

[124] Ibid., p. 35. This came to be article 29(2) of the Soulbury Constitution and was modelled after section 5 of the Government of Ireland Act 1920. Ibid.

[125] K. M. De Silva and William Howard Wriggins, *J. R. Jayewardene of Sri Lanka: A Political Biography*, Volume 1: 1906–1956, 2 vols. (Honolulu: University of Hawaii Press, 1988), p. 169.

[126] Ibid.   [127] Cooray, *Constitutional Government and Human Rights*, p. 35.

[128] Schonthal, 'Buddhism and the Constitution', p. 206.   [129] Jayawickrama, 'Reflections', p. 57.

the human rights reforms in the post-Soeharto period. From the early days of the reforms, there was broad consensus among civil society organizations and political factions in the MPR to expand the existing fundamental rights provisions in the constitution. What finally emerged, after the second amendment phase, was a comprehensive set of human rights guarantees. Scholars have lauded Indonesia's achievements on the human rights amendments as 'lengthy and impressive, granting a full range of protection extending well beyond those guaranteed in most developed states'.[130] With respect to religious freedom, the amendments consolidated the existing guarantees by adding the rights to choose and to practice one's religion and to express one's views and thoughts according to his or her conscience. Article 28I further protects the freedom of thought, conscience and religion as a non-derogable right. However, a closer analysis of the religious freedom provisions reveals a striking anomaly: the provision on 'religious values' as a limitation to the exercise of rights.

Since the first of the four phases of amendments, the MPR had unanimously agreed to retain the preamble of the constitution, which contains the *Pancasila* principles. This is significant because it reflects the commitment to the state's pan-religious ideology, as well as the importance of religion and its values in Indonesia. All this would later affect how the limitation clause was drafted. It is worth noting that the 1998 Decree on Human Rights, which became the basis for reforms on the human rights chapter, also referred to religious principles. The Decree's foundational section states that 'the Indonesian people derive their views and attitudes on human rights from religious teachings, universal moral values and culture, as well as the *Pancasila* and the 1945 constitution'.[131]

During the second amendment debates, the *Reformasi* faction introduced and championed the inclusion of the religious values. The faction asserted that such a limitation is the natural consequence of a *Pancasila* state based on 'the belief in the one and only God'[132] and is consistent with the religious character of the state and its people.[133] However, during the deliberations

---

[130] Tim Lindsey, 'Indonesia: Devaluing Asian Values, Rewriting Rule of Law' in Randall Peerenboom (ed.), *Asian Discourses of Rule of Law: Theories and Implementation of Rule of Law in Twelve Asian Countries, France and the U.S.* (Oxon: Routledge, 2004), p. 301.

[131] *Ketetapan Majelis Permusyarawatan Rakyat Republik Indonesia Nomor WVII/MPR/1998 Tentang Hak Asasi Manusia* (MPR Decree No. WVII/MPR/1998 on Human Rights).

[132] Statement by A. M. Luthfi (F-*Reformasi*), 43rd Meeting of PAH I (13 June 2000), in *Risalah Perubahan*. Recall my explanation earlier that the *Reformasi* faction comprised two parties, PK and PAN.

[133] Interview with former member of the MPR's Ad Hoc Committee I from the *Reformasi* faction, in Jakarta, Indonesia (21 January 2014).

there was no clear articulation of what those values are or how to determine them. A Golkar representative even questioned the feasibility of such provision, arguing that conceptions of religious values can vary.[134]

The religious values limitation was not included in the Ad Hoc Committee's final human rights draft, but the *Reformasi* faction pressed on its inclusion in subsequent deliberations. It proposed the following construction: 'in exercising his/her rights and freedoms, each person is obliged to submit to restrictions established by law *and religious values*'.[135] For the faction, the religious values limitation would prevent any unrestrained exercise of rights[136] and balance the demands between rights on the one hand and public order on the other.[137] What appears to have motivated the faction, therefore, was its particularistic conception of rights and its rejection of liberal exercises of human rights that are deemed contrary to Indonesian norms. The *Reformasi* faction continued to insist on the inclusion of the clause at the eleventh hour, drawing strong objections from those involved in finalizing the draft provisions on human rights. Some objected on procedural grounds, arguing that the provisions were already decided in a meeting the day before and no further changes should be made to what had already been agreed upon. Others – even those from the nationalist factions – were more or less supportive or ambivalent about the issue.

The final draft which was ratified by the MPR as the second amendment contained what the *Reformasi* faction fought for, as all factions in the MPR eventually agreed to it. Accounts by a former Ad Hoc Committee member revealed two reasons behind this decision. First, as tensions began to erupt in the MPR, the chairperson suspended the proceedings and faction leaders convened outside the hall to engineer a compromise. A *Reformasi* faction member warned that if the religious values clause was not included in the draft constitution, he would oppose the outcome of the draft.[138] This threat was significant because any decisions on the constitutional amendment must be reached by consensus. Second, there was a race against time to finalize the

---

[134] Statement by Slamet Effendy Yusuf (Golkar), Lobby Meeting Discussing Chapter X on Citizenship (12 June 2000), in *Risalah Perubahan*.

[135] Statement by Muchtar Adam (*Reformasi* faction), 4th Meeting of Commission A (12 August 2000) and statement by Nurdiati Akma (*Reformasi* faction), 5th Meeting of Commission A (13 August 2000), in *Risalah Perubahan*.

[136] Statement by Muchtar Adam (*Reformasi* faction), 4th Meeting of Commission A (12 August 2000), in *Risalah Perubahan*.

[137] Statement by Muchtar Adam (*Reformasi* faction), 6th Meeting of Commission A (14 August 2005), in *Risalah Perubahan*.

[138] Interview with a former member of the MPR's Ad Hoc Committee I in Jakarta, Indonesia (21 January 2014).

amendments on human rights. The Ad Hoc Committee I (PAH I), formed during the 1999 general session of the MPR to deliberate and propose draft amendments, had prepared twenty-one chapters of revisions and additions to the 1945 constitution. Commission A, another committee formed to discuss PAH I's draft amendments, had only about four days to complete its work. Commission A's discussions on human rights at that time had already gone into the wee hours of the morning. A combination of these factors, in the end, persuaded those who opposed the inclusion of religious values to yield to the *Reformasi* faction's demands.

An interview with a prominent member of the *Reformasi* faction who vociferously fought for the inclusion of 'religious values' revealed several important points on the thinking behind the limitation clause. First, it was not thought that the clause would only incorporate or prioritize the values of any single religion. Rather, depending on the circumstances of the case, any religion can assert its own values to restrict rights and a determination of what those values are will be made by the adherents of the respective religions.[139] Second, using Islam as an example, it was asserted that 'religious values' would be those values that are 'universally agreed within the religion', and they are not necessarily exclusively determined by any religious body such as the Indonesian Ulama Council (MUI).[140]

Within scholarly circles, there are contrasting viewpoints on the intentions behind the clause and its effects. Hosen rejects the notion that Islamic-oriented factions sought to establish *Shariah* principles over and above constitutional rights guarantees through the backdoor.[141] For Hosen, 'religious values' is merely one restriction that needs to be considered along with other grounds such as justice, morality, security, public order and democracy.[142] Salim, however, posits that the initial construction proposed by the *Reformasi* faction is telling. For him, that 'religious values' was included alongside 'law' signalled the intention to place *Shariah* 'on a higher level than the constitution'.[143] It is worth noting that at no point in the debates on the clause was *Shariah* referred to. Nevertheless, the difference between what the Islamic faction initially sought and what transpired in the end may only be a question of form. The inclusion of 'religious values' in article 28J(2) is significant, as it is conceivable that particular religious principles may ultimately determine the parameters of rights in Indonesia. Indeed, Hamdan Zoelva, whose faction

---

[139] Interview with a former member of the MPR's Ad Hoc Committee I from the *Reformasi* faction, in Jakarta, Indonesia (21 January 2014).
[140] Ibid.   [141] Salim, *Challenging the Secular State*, p. 109.   [142] Ibid.   [143] Ibid., p. 110.

supported the inclusion of religious values, later interpreted the clause to mean that human rights cannot contradict religious values.[144]

Restrictions on Propagation of Religion in Malaysia

In Malaysia, despite assurances from the Alliance and constitution-makers that the establishment of Islam shall not impinge on the religious freedom of non-Muslims, there were disagreements on the precise parameters of religious freedom. The limitations on religious freedom on the grounds of public order, health and morality appear to have been influenced by similar provisions in the Indian constitution. Apart from emphasizing the right to practice and profess one's own religion, the Reid Commission also highlighted the protection of minority religious groups. The councils constituted to advise the *Yang di-Pertuan Agong* on Islamic religious affairs 'will not be entitled to interfere in any way with the affairs of people of other religious groups'.[145]

However, the explicit restriction on propagation became an important point of contention. This, to be sure, was not new. When the Treaty of Pangkor paved the way for British imperialism in Malaya in 1874, there were no specific injunctions against churches proselytizing Muslims. However, it was recognized that such practice would offend local sensitivities. It was perhaps for this reason that the colonial period introduced regulations restricting proselytizing of Muslim school children and prohibiting Muslim children from attending religious services of other religions, even with parental consent.[146] The constitutions of individual Malay states also preserved the right of state governments to restrict proselytization of Muslims.

In the 1957 constitution-making exercise, opinions were sharply divided. While the Alliance's proposal to the Commission included guarantees to protect the right to propagate, the rulers had different ideas. They sought to exclude the word 'propagate' due to concerns over the legalization of proselytism against Muslims.[147] At the societal level, there was also considerable anxiety amongst the Malay-Muslims on the activities of Christian missionaries. One memorandum brought before the Reid Commission described the extent

---

[144] Hosen, *Shari'a & Constitutional Reform*, p. 128. Hamdan Zoelva was previously the chief justice of the Indonesian Constitutional Court (2013–2015).

[145] Constitutional Proposals for the Federation of Malaya, Cmnd 210 (Her Majesty's Stationery Office, 1957), para. 59.

[146] Hearing of the Malayan Christians' Council before the Constitutional Commission (23 August 1956), CO889/6.

[147] Minutes of the First Meeting of the Working Party.

of such activities,[148] but a subsequent memo by the Malayan Christian Council strongly refuted those claims. It is unclear, from the constitution-making documents, if one argument or the other eventually persuaded the Commission. Even as the Working Party produced its report in April 1957, the details of the religious freedom provision had not been formally agreed upon. Notwithstanding the initial agreement that religious freedom would include the right to profess, practice *and* propagate any religion, the Alliance leaders heeded the rulers' objections and concerns.[149] It was then proposed that the religious freedom guarantee shall not affect existing state laws that restrict the propagation of other religious doctrines among Muslims.

Strengthening Religious Freedom in Sri Lanka?

Since the inception of the Soulbury Constitution, there were strong sentiments against the adequacy of section 29(2) as a means of guaranteeing rights.[150] This culminated in the initiative to incorporate a bill of rights into the constitution, which began with the establishment of a Joint Select Commission on the Revision of the Constitution during S. W. R. D. Bandaranaike's administration.[151] The Commission produced a comprehensive list of fundamental rights, including the right to religious freedom, modelled after provisions in the Indian constitution.[152]

In the 1972 constitution, fundamental rights guarantees, including religious freedom, were spelled out in section 18. Much like the Indonesian framers in 1945 and the Alliance leaders in Malaya, De Silva was not enthusiastic about the prospect of a bill of rights. He seemed particularly concerned that such rights would ultimately erode legislative sovereignty, especially since the draft constitution had made the legislature the supreme instrument of state power, and that fundamental rights would hinder the operation of the government and national development.[153] Eventually De Silva conceded, given the increasing popular support for fundamental rights guarantees.[154] However, the constitutional scheme in place at the time was such that fundamental rights guarantees and enforcement were limited: the legislature exercised judicial power through courts; it could enact laws contrary to the constitution

---

[148] Memorandum by Dato' Panglima Kinta Haji Mohammed Eusoff to the Reid Commission (14 July 1956), CO889/6.
[149] Minutes of the First Meeting of the Working Party.
[150] Cooray, *Constitutional Government and Human Rights*, p. 36.
[151] The committee comprised of representatives from the SLFP, UNP, Federal Party and the Left Parties. See Schonthal, 'Buddhism and the Constitution', p. 208.
[152] Ibid.   [153] Jayawickrama, 'Reflections', pp. 90–1.   [154] Ibid.

with a two-thirds majority approval; the courts were not vested with the power of judicial review; and the constitutionality of a law could only be challenged at the bill stage.[155] The 1978 constitution, which continues to operate today (though with over ten amendments since it was first passed), expanded the scope of rights guarantees. In addition to giving the Supreme Court original jurisdiction over fundamental rights claims, the revision also gave the freedom of thought, conscience and religion – at least the *forum internum* aspect of that right – an 'entrenched' status and rendered it as an absolute freedom, free from limitations.

CONCLUSION

The paths adopted by the constitution-makers in Indonesia, Malaysia and Sri Lanka to constitutionalize religion were markedly varied, although they faced more or less similar social and political constraints. It is clear that across all three countries, there was a need to address majority-minority tensions couched in differing religious interests. Compounding this problem was the popular sentiment that the majority religion should become the religion of the country and ought to shape its culture and political outlook. With respect to the provisions on religious freedom, the establishment of the religious values limitation (Indonesia) and the restrictions on the propagation of other religions among Muslims (Malaysia) are all different manifestations of how the constitution-makers sought to resolve conflicting religious interests and outlooks in the polity. The three different arrangements nevertheless recognize that the state has some role to play in matters pertaining to religion. In Malaysia, the state is involved in the administration of Islamic affairs, and while the constitution does not *obligate* the state to favour Islam above other religions, it *allows* the government to establish and maintain Islamic institutions, and to allocate government funds for Islamic education.[156]

On the state-religion relationship, the Indonesian founding fathers and constitutional reformers rejected the establishment or privileging of Islam in the constitution. Indonesia's approach stands in stark contrast to the arrangements in Malaysia and Sri Lanka, where Muslims and Buddhists are dominant, respectively. In these countries, the founding fathers and constitution-makers decided to tackle competing demands from the majority and minority groups by privileging Islam as the state religion and by providing

[155] Wickramaratne, *Fundamental Rights in Sri Lanka*, p. 26.
[156] Article 12(2), Federal Constitution of Malaysia.

explicit state patronage of Buddhism, alongside other guarantees of rights and freedoms for the minorities.

To be sure, the degrees to which Islam and Buddhism are constitutionalized in these two countries vary. However, their formal constitutional status is symbolically important, as it is significant in terms of appeasing popular sentiments. In Malaya, the motivation, it seems, was to provide a sense of security for the majority Malay-Muslims. That the Alliance emphasized the psychological importance of establishing Islam for the Malays is particularly telling. The establishment of Islam might not have been intended to supersede the rights guarantees in the constitution. Nonetheless, several provisions were included to reassure the Malays that their interests and historical attachment to the land will not be compromised. These provisions include the sanctioning of restrictions on propagation of other religions among Muslims, the constitutional definition of a 'Malay' as one who professes Islam, and the recognition of the special position of the Malays and reservation of quotas (at the discretion of the *Yang di-Pertuan Agong*) in selected areas such as public service and scholarships. In Sri Lanka, the pressures to officially restore the role of Buddhism in the country's social and political spheres amidst the tide of Sinhalese-Buddhist nationalism and Buddhist revivalist movement was too difficult for De Silva to ignore, although he was personally a committed secularist.[157]

Nevertheless, amidst the anxieties on the status of the majority religion across all three countries, compromise was a key feature in all constitution-making experiences. In Indonesia, the 1945 constitution-makers and the MPR reached a consensus in the form of article 29, although there was some form of concession to the Islamic-oriented faction in the shape of article 31 on education and the inclusion of religious values as a limitation on rights. The establishment of MORA several months after independence is also significant because it was both a guarantee against a secular Indonesia and another gesture of compromise toward Muslims who were aggrieved by the collapse of the Jakarta Charter.[158] In Malaysia, the constitutionalization of Islam came with explicit assurances that religious freedom will be protected, as well as a gentlemen's agreement guaranteeing citizenship and vernacular education for the non-Malays. In Sri Lanka, De Silva's formulation of the religion provision,

---

[157] See De Silva, *Safeguards for the Minorities*, pp. 10–12. De Silva remarked: 'I believe in the secular state. But you know when Constitutions are made by Constituent Assemblies they are not made by the Minister for Constitutional Affairs.'

[158] Assyaukanie, *Islam and the Secular State in Indonesia*, p. 69. It is important to note that the MORA does not only represent Muslim interests. Each of the officially recognized religions in Indonesia is represented by respective departments within the Ministry.

though later modified in 1978, was thought to represent a compromise between demands to provide special rights and protections for Buddhism and the fundamental right to religious freedom.

Hirschl sees the benefit of a formal constitutionalization of religion, arguing that such arrangement can 'limit the potentially radical impact of religion by bringing it under state control'.[159] However, this assumes that the state and its apparatus are willing and able to control and co-opt religious authorities and to assert secular principles over religious dogmas. As we shall see in the following chapters, this is not always the case. In addition, the danger with the Malayan and Sri Lankan arrangements is that they are prone to existential conflicts between the protection of the privileged religion versus the rights of those outside of that religion, especially when, over time, constitutional history and the intended meanings ascribed to those constitutional arrangements are neglected.

In light of these challenges, the Indonesian arrangement, which is neither a complete separation of religion and state nor a full-fledged theocracy,[160] seems apt for a polity where religion forms a key part of the collective identity. Religion and religious values are encouraged to play a role in the life of the nation. Through the cross-religious commitment to the *Pancasila*, the Indonesians celebrate the values that are deemed important to the nation, whilst maintaining its 'unity in diversity' philosophy. The 'belief in the one and only God', as Boland argues, is a religiously neutral, 'multi-interpretable formula'.[161] The commitment to the role of religion was evident not only in the speeches of Yamin, Soekarno and Soepomo in 1945, but also in the post-Soeharto constitutional reform debates. Jakob Tobing, for instance, emphasized that the construction of article 29 is already apt for a nation that places considerable importance on religious beliefs and values. The prominence of religion in the state also found support across religious divides. Frans Magnis-Suseno, a Catholic scholar, rejected the secular state idea as this runs contrary to the 'very strong religious orientation' of Indonesians from different religious backgrounds.[162]

In contrast, the Malayan and Sri Lankan arrangements carry a divisive flavour and convey a message of 'otherness' for adherents of minority religions.

---

[159] Hirschl, *Constitutional Theocracy*, pp. 14–16.

[160] Hosen, 'Religion and the Indonesian Constitution', p. 426. According to Hosen, Indonesia has been designed to 'stand in the middle'.

[161] B. J. Boland, *The Struggle of Islam in Modern Indonesia* (The Hague: Martinus Nijhoff, 1971), p. 39. See also Hosen, *Shari'a & Constitutional Reform*, p. 64 (arguing that the term God or *Tuhan* cuts across Christian, Islamic, Buddhist and Hindu concepts of God).

[162] Intan, *'Public Religion'*, p. 162.

With respect to Sri Lanka, a prominent constitutional scholar goes further to argue that the 1972 constitution – drafted in a pro-Sinhalese political climate – sowed the seeds for majoritarianism.[163] One could commend De Silva's attempts to construct a balanced solution on paper, given the prevailing sentiments among the majority of the legislators and the public. But in light of the paths and outcomes from the Indonesian and Malayan experiences, one could also argue that the precise boundaries of the Sri Lankan solution are incredibly vague by comparison. As such, it would also be more prone to abuse or misinterpretation that could disadvantage other religions and religious adherents. While the Malayan leaders and constitution-makers emphasized that the special position of Islam would not affect the secular nature of the state or the rights and freedoms provided in the constitution, De Silva never explicitly addressed demands to clarify the relationship between special protections for Buddhism and religious freedom. It was only several years after the 1972 constitution-making process that De Silva unequivocally stressed that nothing in the Buddhism provision would infringe the rights of other religions in the country.[164] In any case, without the benefit of De Silva's assurance, how the two prongs of the provision should be balanced in cases of conflict remains an important question. Ultimately, as we shall see in subsequent chapters, one will have to give way to the other.

[163] Wickramaratne, *Fundamental Rights in Sri Lanka*, p. 767.
[164] De Silva, *Safeguards for the Minorities*, p. 10.

3

Religion and Religious Freedom in Public Life

Constitutional rights guarantees are typically seen as the main framework and tool to ensure the protection of rights especially for the minorities and, by extension, as a means of managing intergroup relations in a plural society. Notwithstanding the debates expressing doubts on the value and utility of constitutions, there remains a great degree of faith in the importance of constitutions in protecting freedoms and constraining state power.[1] However, what might be overlooked is the potential for constitutional arrangements to undermine, in practice, the very rights that they *ought* to protect. Consider, for example, the constitutional provision that establishes Islam as the state religion in Malaysia and the provision that gives Buddhism the 'foremost place' in Sri Lanka. Both arrangements also cement the guarantee of religious freedom for all other religious adherents. In addition, the constitutional framers affirmed that the establishment of Islam or Buddhism shall not supersede fundamental rights guarantees. Yet, as I shall illustrate in this chapter and also in subsequent chapters, there have been cases in which these arrangements were invoked to justify restrictions on religious freedom.

The main thrust of this chapter is on the interpretation and application of constitutional arrangements. It uncovers the extent to which state policies and practices on religion and religious freedom reflect the guarantees provided in the constitution and reveals the dominant patterns across the three countries. In this respect, the previous chapter's elaboration on the motivations and understandings behind the provisions adopted are important because they help us understand the ways in which the conception and interpretation of those provisions have evolved over time.

---

[1] Frank B. Cross, *Constitutions and Religious Freedom* (New York: Cambridge University Press, 2015), pp. 105–7.

Before delving into the details of religious freedom issues that have emerged in the three countries, I shall first explain the realities and complexities of enforcing religious freedom protection in countries like Indonesia, Malaysia and Sri Lanka, where different groups – often hostile to one another – advance competing visions and claims on religious freedom. We have seen, in Chapter 2, how these tensions found expression in the constitution-making process. In keeping with the book's wider aim of examining the interaction between constitutional law, religion and politics, I shall also explain the interpretation and conception of constitutional arrangements on religion in the state's political projects and discourse. The third section traces the trends and patterns of state policies and practices by focusing on four issues: (1) the role of religious bureaucracies; (2) regulation of houses of worship; (3) religious minorities; and (4) other laws regulating religion.

The analysis points to two overarching conclusions. An obvious pattern is that many of the problems appear to stem from policies geared to protect (at least from the state's perspective) the majority's sensitivities or what is deemed to be in the interests of the majority. This, to some extent, reflects a shift in the conception of the constitutional arrangements on religion. However, as this chapter demonstrates, the degree to which the conceptions change and the way in which they affect religious freedom varies across the three countries. Second, there are variations in the kinds of religious freedom violations in all three countries that do not correspond with the expected outcomes of the arrangements on religion and religious freedom in their respective constitutions. In general, government restrictions on religion and religious freedom are more prevalent in Indonesia than in Malaysia and Sri Lanka.

COMPETING UNDERSTANDINGS OF RELIGIOUS FREEDOM

Freedom of religion, as Scolnicov argues, is a contradiction in terms.[2] On the one hand, 'freedom' implies the absence of constraint; on the other, religion is a comprehensive system of values that govern every aspect of a person's life, and thus the observance of religion and the exercise of religious freedom can become a self-imposed constraint on freedom.[3] This dilemma characterizes the challenges in shaping the metes and bounds of religious freedom in both international and national spheres. For example, if one chooses to embrace a particular religion and that religion (or the religious authorities of that religion, for that matter) provides a set of rules or a value system to which

---

[2]   Anat Scolnicov, *The Right to Religious Freedom in International Law: Between Group Rights and Individual Rights* (Abingdon, Oxon and New York: Routledge, 2011), p. 1.
[3]   Ibid.

the individual must adhere to, can these rules later limit one's freedom to choose how to practice or express his or her religion? Should they? Should the state play a role in enforcing these rules against the individual?

To put these in more concrete terms, consider the case of the Ahmadiyah minority in Indonesia as an example. One of the core teachings of the Qadiani Ahmadiyah sect is that Mirza Ghulam Ahmad – the founder of the Ahmadiyah movement – is a messianic and prophetic figure. The Ahmadis believe that their doctrines are consistent with Islamic teachings and Quranic interpretations. Hence, they consider themselves Muslims, notwithstanding the fact that their doctrines and interpretations are inconsistent with the mainstream Sunni doctrine. However, the position of the Indonesian Ulama Council (Majelis Ulama Indonesia or MUI) is that the Ahmadiyah is a deviant and heretical group: their interpretations and beliefs are deemed contrary to the mainstream principle that Prophet Muhammad is the last prophet, and therefore, the Ahmadis are not Muslims. This appears to be supported by the Indonesian Constitutional Court through its decision in the *Blasphemy Law* case (which will be discussed extensively in Chapter 5). The court argued that the internal authorities of a particular religion shall be empowered to decide the fundamental teachings of that religion and to determine if any religious practices or interpretations are blasphemous or contrary to those teachings. On this line of reasoning, the Indonesian court appears to have contradicted international standards on religious freedom.

Central to the discussion in this chapter is also the idea of a dual conception of religious freedom: as an expressive activity of belief, criticism and inquiry on the one hand, and as an identity which entails equality between religions, on the other.[4] Both originated from the Enlightenment era of liberal thought, where religious freedom follows from the conception of individuals as autonomous, rational, free-thinking citizens, coupled with the notion that every person has the right to equal liberty.[5] These philosophies are now expressed in several international human rights instruments, including the International Covenant on Civil and Political Rights (ICCPR).

On the ground, however, these principles are translated and interpreted according to different ideals in order to serve different interests. The cases later in this chapter demonstrate the different visions on religious freedom and fundamental rights in plural societies. These have already been reflected in the constitutional arrangements in the three countries. The conspicuous omission of the right to choose or change one's religion in the Malaysian set-up, for example, was not a mere oversight. Consider this, then, in tandem

---

[4]   Ibid., p. 31.   [5]   Ibid., pp. 35–41.

with the provision that allows states to control or restrict propagation of other religions among Muslims. Both of these were part of the central demands of the sultans during the constitution-making process, ostensibly, to protect the interests of the Malay-Muslims. For those who subscribe to this anti-proselytism view, religious freedom means the right to be free from organized and active proselytism and does not encompass the right to leave or change one's religion. As this chapter will show, a similar rhetoric was used by the Sri Lankan government and proponents of anti-conversion bills: religious liberty is interpreted as the right to be free from fraudulent or compelled conversions.

In a similar vein, the freedom of religion and conscience may mean the right to interpret a particular religion or faith as one sees fit, whereas others may interpret religious freedom as the right to be free from practices or interpretations that are deemed an insult to their beliefs and the right to be bound by religious law. In the case of Sri Lanka, the demands for, and the subsequent constitutionalization of, Buddhist prerogatives are seen as a manifestation of religious freedom for the majority Buddhists. According to this logic, the state's responsibilities go beyond refraining from encroaching upon rights; they are obliged to positively protect and enforce those rights so that Buddhism can be rehabilitated and afforded a level playing field with Christianity, which enjoyed considerable prestige and influence during the colonial period.[6] This vision of religious freedom as special rights for a certain religion and its adherents is somewhat similar to the justification put forward by the Islamic-oriented faction in the 2002 constitutional amendment process to demand for the constitutionalization of *Shariah* law in Indonesia – that it was the collective right of Muslims to govern their own affairs and to implement their holy law according to the Quran and *Sunnah*.

RELIGION IN THE STATE AND ITS RELATIONSHIP
WITH RELIGIOUS FREEDOM: POLITICS
AND POLITICAL RHETORIC

The Pancasila State of Indonesia

When Soekarno introduced the *Pancasila* before the constitution-making body, he stressed that the 'belief in God' would not only establish Indonesia

---

[6] Benjamin Schonthal, 'Constitutionalizing Religion: The Pyrrhic Success of Religious Rights in Post-Colonial Sri Lanka' (2014) 29 *Journal of Law and Religion* 470. Schonthal argues that special Buddhist rights are 'an imagined liberation-cum-rehabilitation' of Buddhism from centuries of decay and discrimination under colonial rule.

as a 'nation that believes in God' but also that 'every Indonesian should have a God' and that every citizen should be free to worship according to his or her religion or belief.[7] This philosophy thus provides the basis for which religion would be fostered in the state without singling out any particular religion for special protection and for the respect for religious freedom and pluralism. Decades later, this aspect of the *Pancasila* remains relevant in Indonesian political rhetoric. The predominant view – including that of the former president, Susilo Bambang Yudhoyono (SBY) and members of nationalist parties – is that the consequence of this arrangement is that Indonesia is neither secular nor theocratic;[8] instead, it is a *Pancasila* state with religious underpinnings. These views comport with those of the former and current members of the Indonesian Constitutional Court. Former Chief Justice Mahfud, for example, argued that the founding fathers established a *Pancasila* state imbued with religion – a 'religious nation state'.[9] The political allegiance to the *Pancasila* arrangement is indeed quite remarkable and stands in stark contrast, as I will show, to how article 3 on Islam has been conceived among the Malaysian political elites over time.

[7]   See Speech by Soekarno on 1 June 1945 in *Himpunan Risalah Sidang-sidang dari Badan Penyelidik Usaha Persiapan Kemerdekaan Indonesia (BPUPKI) (Tanggal 29 Mei 1945–16 Juli 1945) dan Panitia Persiapan Kemerdekaan Indonesia (PPKI) (Tanggal 18 dan 19 Agustus 1945) Yang Berhubung Dengan Penyusunan Undang-undang Dasar 1945 (A Compilation of the Minutes of Meetings of the Investigating Committee for Preparatory Work for Indonesian Independence (BPUPKI) (29 May 1945–16 July 1945) and the Preparatory Committee for Indonesian Independence (18 and 19 August 1945) relating to the Drafting of the 1945 Constitution)* (Djakarta: Sekretariat Negara Republik Indonesia, 1954), p. 73.

[8]   Interview with a senior Golkar politician in Jakarta, Indonesia (22 January 2014). See also Bayu Galih and Fadila Fikriani Armadita, 'SBY: Indonesia Bukan Negara Sekuler' ('SBY: Indonesia is not a secular country'), *Vivanews* (1 June 2011), online: http://us.nasional.news.viva.co.id/news/read/224041-sby-96indonesia-bukan-negara-sekuler (SBY argues that Indonesia is a country that is based on the belief in God. While it is not a theocracy, it is '[s]till a religious country, not secular'); and statements by Jakob Tobing (F-PDIP), Lobby Meeting of Commission A (20 June 2000), Hamdan Zoelva (F-PBB), 3rd Meeting of PAH I (6 December 1999), and Harun Kamil (F-PG), Lobby Meeting of Commission A (14 June 2000) in *Risalah Perubahan Undang-undang Dasar Negara Republik Indonesia Tahun 1945: 1999–2012 (Reports of the Amendments of the 1945 Constitution of the Republic of Indonesia: 1999–2012)* (Jakarta: Sekretariat Jenderal Majelis Permusyawaratan Rakyat Republik Indonesia, 2002) (all these representatives held the view that Indonesia is not a secular state, but a religious state based on the *Pancasila*).

[9]   Mahfud MD, chief justice of the Indonesian Constitutional Court, speech at the Orientation of House of Representative Members (DPR) of the Republic of Indonesia from PDI-Perjuangan 2009–2014 (8 September 2009). See also 'Sistem Hukum di Indonesia Itu Religius, Bukan Sekuler' ('The legal system in Indonesia is religious, not secular'), *Suara Pembaruan* (29 November 2013), online: www.suarapembaruan.com/home/sistem-hukum-di-indonesia-itu-religius-bukan-sekuler/45730.

These accounts of what the *Pancasila* entails are also largely consistent with most scholarly interpretations. Butt and Lindsey, for instance, posit that the founding principles of Indonesia compel the state to protect religious freedom, encourage the exercise of faith and provide a role for the state in religious matters.[10] For this reason, they argue that Indonesia is not an 'entirely secular state'.[11] Similar views are expressed by scholars like Intan and Hosen who argue that the prominence of religion in the public sphere means that Indonesia is neither secular nor theocratic.[12] There are, to be sure, opposing views. For scholars like Raillon, that the Indonesian arrangement upholds non-establishment and religious neutrality (in the sense that no single religion is put in a privileged position vis-à-vis others) and omits the seven words which would have constitutionally imposed *Shariah* on Muslims, prove the secular nature of the Indonesian constitution.[13] Similarly, Salim suggests that Indonesia is a secular state – his position hinges on the fact that political processes and law-making in the country are irreligious.[14] These differences in opinion appear to be a question of semantics: in particular, what 'secularism' means for each scholar. Nevertheless, the scholarly and political interpretations explained above establish that the *Pancasila* is a principle for religious freedom and pluralism, provides the basis for an interventionist role for the state in religious matters and, in theory, does not elevate one religion above others.

The essence of the *Pancasila*, however, is challenged and contested when it comes to the implementation of state policies. In this respect, Hefner suggests

---

[10] Simon Butt and Tim Lindsey, *The Constitution of Indonesia: A Contextual Analysis* (Oxford and Portland, OR: Hart Publishing, 2012), p. 13.

[11] Ibid., p. 14.

[12] See Benyamin Fleming Intan, *'Public Religion' and the Pancasila-Based State of Indonesia: An Ethical and Sociological Analysis* (New York: Peter Lang, 2006), p. 18 and Nadirsyah Hosen, *Shari'a & Constitutional Reform in Indonesia* (Singapore: Institute of Southeast Asian Studies, 2007), p. 229. Hosen emphasizes that while the state facilitates and encourages religion in public life, political institutions remain free from the control of religion, as would be the case in a theocratic system.

[13] Francois Raillon, 'The Return of Pancasila: Secular vs. Islamic Norms, Another Look at the Struggle for State Dominance in Indonesia' in Michel Picard and Rémy Madinier (eds.), *Politics of Religion in Indonesia: Syncretism, Orthodoxy, and Religious Contention in Java and Bali* (Abingdon, Oxon and New York: Routledge, 2011), p. 94. Cf Raillon's view that despite the establishment of a secular constitution, the state *identity* is neither theocratic nor overly secular. However, later he appears to suggest that the *Pancasila* provides an implicit secularism by placing different religions on a parallel plane. Ibid., p. 110.

[14] Arskal Salim, *Challenging the Secular State: The Islamization of Law in Modern Indonesia* (Honolulu: University of Hawai'i Press, 2008). Throughout his book Salim appears to suggest that Indonesia is a secular state, although at the end he argues that '[a] full separation of religion and the state, is not entirely present as state functions now often overlap with religious functions'. Ibid., p. 77.

that the problems are rooted in the fact that the *Pancasila* did not clarify which religious doctrines or beliefs would fall under the principle of 'belief in the one and only God' and it did not set out 'how the government was to intervene in the religious field to make such a determination'.[15] This raises two problems which I shall briefly address here and explain in detail in the next section. First, if the *Pancasila* allows the state to play a role in encouraging and facilitating religion, how far can and should it go in doing so? Second, does the *Pancasila*-based state tolerate freedom *from* religion or polytheistic beliefs?

There is nothing in the constitution-making deliberations in 1945 and in the post-Soeharto amendments to suggest that freedom from religion was envisioned by the founding fathers and legislators. Throughout the debates, the constitution-makers emphasized that Indonesia is based on the belief in God, as well as the religious nature of the nation and its inhabitants.[16] They did this whilst constantly assuring that the state would safeguard the freedom of religion and worship according to one's religion and beliefs. Intan, however, posits that one of the Indonesian founding fathers (who, quite interestingly, formed part of the Islamic-oriented faction) had suggested that the state would tolerate the freedom not to be religious as well as polytheism.[17] The former chief justice of the Constitutional Court has refined this view further by stating that although there is no prohibition on a person's right to become an atheist, the state may outlaw the spread of atheism as such beliefs are contrary to the spirit of the *Pancasila*.[18] These views seem to support the value that the constitutional framers placed on the *Pancasila* as a commitment to religiosity, religious freedom and pluralism.

The essence and spirit of the *Pancasila* came under challenge during the Soeharto administration, often with perverse consequences on religious freedom and pluralism. In fact, Hefner suggests that religious freedom was

---

[15] Robert W. Hefner, 'Where Have All the *Abangan* Gone? Religionization and the Decline of Non-Standard Islam in Contemporary Indonesia' in Michel Picard and Rémy Madinier (eds.), *Politics of Religion in Indonesia: Syncretism, Orthodoxy, and Religious Contention in Java and Bali* (Abingdon, Oxon and New York: Routledge, 2011), p. 85.

[16] Cf Bob Hering, *Soekarno: Founding Father of Indonesia, A Biography*, Volume 1, 2 vols. (Indonesia: Hasta Mitra, 2003), p. 355 (arguing that the *Pancasila* emphasizes freedom of worship).

[17] Intan, '*Public Religion*', p. 111 (quoting Djohan Effendi, 'Jaminan Konstitusional Bagi Kebebasan Beragama Di Indonesia' ('Constitutional Guarantees for Religious Freedom in Indonesia') in Komaruddin Hidayat and Ahmad Gaus A. F. (eds.), *Passing Over: Melintasi Batas Agama (Passing Over: Crossing Religious Boundaries)* (Jakarta: Penerbit PT Gramedia Pustaka Utama in cooperation with Yayasan Wakaf Paramadina, 1998)).

[18] Irfan Abdul, 'Mahfud Md. Bantah Legalkan Ateisme dan Komunisme' ('Mahfud Md. rejects the legalization of atheism and Communism'), *Tempo.co* (12 July 2012), online: www.tempo.co/read/news/2012/07/12/173416582/Mahfud-Md-Bantah-Legalkan-Ateisme-dan-Komunisme.

comparably better under Soekarno's administration because, at the time, there was a strong emphasis on religious relativism (that is, all religions or religious beliefs are equally valid) and national unity.[19] To be sure, Soeharto upheld the *Pancasila* and stressed that it should be 'honoured forever'.[20] His approach, however, was far more interventionist especially in religious affairs. He outlawed any advocacy for *Shariah* and an Islamic state and obligated all mass organizations to make the *Pancasila* their sole guiding ideology. At the same time, most scholars agree that Soeharto hijacked the *Pancasila* and used religion to further his political goals.[21] The Soeharto government made it compulsory for every citizen to adopt one of the five officially recognized religions – Islam, Protestantism, Catholicism, Hinduism and Buddhism (with the last being given a monotheistic twist), claiming that this was consistent with the proper interpretation of the *Pancasila*.[22] This was part of Soeharto's program of rooting out Communism (which was identified with atheism), although the consequences on religious freedom are much broader and would later continue beyond his administration, as we shall see. Indeed, the view that atheism is incompatible with the *Pancasila* still pervades the social and political spheres today.[23] This is why Hosen, unlike Intan and Hering, posits that '[I]ndonesia recognizes any religion that believes in one God'.[24] Under the presidency of Abdurrahman Wahid – a celebrated activist for pluralism but widely viewed as a weak leader – the five religions were expanded to six to include Confucianism. However, the position of those who fall outside the six official religions, such as the animists and adherents of traditional belief systems, remains difficult. These groups and individuals face official discrimination in matters such as registration of marriages and births and the issuance of national identity cards.[25]

---

[19] Hefner, 'Where Have All the *Abangan* Gone?', p. 85 (quoting Hyung-Jun Kim, 'The Changing Interpretation of Religious Freedom in Indonesia' (1998) 29(2) *Journal of Southeast Asian Studies* 357).

[20] Butt and Lindsey, *Constitution of Indonesia*, p. 229 (citing Z. Adnan, 'Islamic Religion: Yes, Islamic Ideology: No! Islam and the State in Indonesia' in Arief Budiman (ed.), *State and Civil Society in Indonesia* (Clayton, Vic.: Centre of Southeast Asian Studies, Monash University, 1990)).

[21] See, e.g., Luthfi Assyaukanie, 'Muslim Discourse of Liberal Democracy in Indonesia' in Luthfi Assyaukanie, Robert W. Hefner, and Azyumardi Azra (eds.), *Muslim Politics and Democratisation in Indonesia* (Clayton, Vic.: Monash Asia Institute, 2008); Hefner, 'Where Have All the *Abangan* Gone?'; and M. C. Ricklefs, *A History of Modern Indonesia since c. 1200*, 4th ed. (Basingstoke and New York: Palgrave Macmillan, 2008), chapter VI.

[22] Hefner, 'Where Have All the *Abangan* Gone?', p. 85.

[23] Butt and Lindsey, *Constitution of Indonesia*, p. 230.

[24] Hosen, *Shari'a and Constitutional Reform*, p. 195.   [25] Ibid., p. 196.

The way in which the dominant religion, Islam, has been privileged in state administration is arguably another example of the departure from the kind of *Pancasila* that was envisioned by the founding fathers. This is, perhaps, inevitable in a context where the state has a role in facilitating religion in public life and where more than 80 per cent of the population are Muslim. The establishment of the Ministry of Religious Affairs (MORA) in 1946 – which was a compensation of sorts to the Islamic-oriented faction for the rejection of an Islamic state – opened the doors for Islam's *de facto* preferential treatment. While the Ministry was initially thought to be a neutral institution that caters to the officially recognized religious groups in Indonesia, critics argue that it has practically become a Muslim department.[26] With the centralization of Islamic affairs, accelerated as it were under Soeharto, the Ministry's role in regulating religious matters has been significantly enhanced, thereby raising questions on the extent of religious freedom in Indonesia. All this is not to say that article 29 or the *Pancasila* has been explicitly invoked to elevate the dominant religion (Islam) above all other religions or to justify pro-Muslim policies. In this respect, the Indonesian tale is quite different from the Malaysian story, as we shall see. What I shall show later in this chapter, instead, is that current state practices have the *consequence* (intended or otherwise) of prioritizing Islam or majority sensitivities. It is in this sense that the conception of the *Pancasila* articulated by Soekarno and his colleagues has changed over time.

Malaysia: An Islamic State?

During the constitution-making process, the Alliance leaders made it clear that the establishment of Islam would not alter Malaya's secular character. Although there was no explanation as to what 'secular' means, this represented a guarantee against the creation of an Islamic state as demanded by certain sections of the Malay-Muslim community at that time. In the early years following independence, there were attempts at shaking the foundation of article 3. In 1958, a Muslim member of the Federal Legislative Council proposed to prohibit the serving of alcoholic beverages at official functions

---

[26] Ibid. But cf Ibnu Anshori, 'Mustafa Kemal and Sukarno: A Comparison of Views Regarding Relations between State and Religion', unpublished M.A. thesis, McGill University (1994), p. 84 (arguing that the establishment of MORA was to serve Muslim interests), Clifford Geertz, *The Religion of Java* (Chicago and London: University of Chicago Press, 1976), p. 200 (arguing that the MORA was '[f]or all intents and purposes a *santri* affair from top to bottom'), and Salim, *Challenging the Secular State*, p. 46. (arguing that the '[r]eal task of MORA has been to accelerate the unification of Islamic affairs throughout Indonesia').

of the federal government[27] on the basis that the state has the duty to uphold the teachings of Islam and Islamic laws.[28] But the response of the then prime minister, Tunku Abdul Rahman, was telling. He stated, 'I would like to make it clear that this country is not an Islamic state as it is generally understood, we merely provide that Islam shall be the official religion of the State.'[29]

More than forty years later, however, the fourth Prime Minister of Malaysia – Dr. Mahathir Mohamad – declared Malaysia as an Islamic country.[30] This statement has been echoed by his successors, namely, Abdullah Badawi who – in a written reply to a question posed in Parliament – stated that Malaysia is an Islamic state.[31] A few months earlier, his deputy, Najib Razak, who would later become the sixth prime minister, argued that Malaysia has never been a secular state, but is, instead, an Islamic state.[32] Underlying these assertions was the view that the laws and principles of governance in the country are inspired by the fundamental principles of Islam, even if they do not adopt explicit, Islamic-based laws.[33] Put simply, although laws are enacted and enforced by 'secular' institutions such as the Parliament, what makes Malaysia an Islamic state is the substantive manner in which laws conform to Islamic principles – at least those that are understood as such by the political elites and bureaucrats.[34] Dr. Mahathir, for instance, once argued that *Shariah* laws are applicable only to Muslims in personal matters, but the laws of the country, while not Islamic-based, 'can be used as long as they do not come into conflict with Islamic principles'.[35]

---

[27] Ahmad Ibrahim, 'The Position of Islam in the Constitution of Malaysia' in Tan Sri Mohamed Suffian, H. P. Lee, and F. A. Trindade (eds.), *The Constitution of Malaya: Its Development: 1957–1977* (Oxford: Oxford University Press, 1978), p. 54.

[28] Ibid.

[29] Official Report of the Federal Legislative Council Debates (1 May 1958), cols. 4631 and 4671-2.

[30] Andrew Harding, 'Sharia and National Law in Malaysia' in Jan Michiel Otto (ed.), *Sharia Incorporated: A Comparative Overview of the Legal Systems of Twelve Muslim Countries in Past and Present* (Leiden: Leiden University Press, 2010), pp. 505–6. For a list of criteria that the Malaysian government used to justify the 'Islamic state' status, see Nurjannah Abdullah, 'Legislating Faith in Malaysia' (2007) *Singapore Journal of Legal Studies* 264, 270.

[31] Statement by Lim Kit Siang, Hansard No. 44, Eleventh Parliament of Malaysia, Fourth Session, Third Meeting (3 September 2007), pp. 31–2.

[32] 'Malaysia not secular state, says Najib', *Bernama* (17 July 2007), online: www.bernama.com/bernama/v3/printable.php?id=273699.

[33] Ibid.

[34] For a criticism of the institutionalization of Islamic jurisprudence and practices adopted by the Malaysian government, see Tamir Moustafa, 'Judging in God's Name: State Power, Secularism, and the Politics of Islamic Law in Malaysia' (2014) 3(1) *Oxford Journal of Law and Religion* 152. Moustafa argues that the incorporation of Islamic laws and jurisprudence in Malaysia subverts the Islamic legal tradition.

[35] Osman Bakar, 'Islam and Politics in Malaysia' in Shahram Akbarzaden and Abdullah Saeed (eds.), *Islam and Political Legitimacy* (Abingdon, Oxon and New York: Routledge Curzon, 2003), p. 134.

These statements indicate that in the political sphere, there have been efforts to assert a stronger public role for Islam in ways that are inconsistent with what the founders had envisioned. Malaysian political leaders – especially since the Dr. Mahathir era – have also been extremely cautious, if not reluctant, to affirm the limited role of article 3 as espoused by Tunku Abdul Rahman.

Scholars also disagree on the meaning and role of Islam as the religion of the Federation. For Sheridan and Groves, article 3 merely entails the use of Muslim rites in religious parts of federal ceremonies.[36] Shad Faruqi goes a step further, arguing that the provision allows the state to promote 'Islamic education and way of life' for Muslims, establish Islamic institutions and courts and subject Muslims to *Shariah* laws within the specific areas set by the constitution.[37] While practitioners and scholars like Tommy Thomas and Azmi Sharom have consistently affirmed the secular nature of the state,[38] Faruqi is careful not to draw bright lines along the secular-theocratic dichotomy. He underlines that the Malaysia Federal Constitution exhibits both secular and Islamic features, and it is thus neither a fully secular nor fully theocratic state.[39] Although these scholarly opinions vary with respect to the effect of article 3 on the laws and governance of the state, they all agree that article 3 does not provide a basis to supersede fundamental rights protection, especially religious freedom.[40]

---

[36] See L. A. Sheridan and Harry. E. Groves, *The Constitution of Malaysia*, 4th ed. (Singapore: Malayan Law Journal, 1987), p. 31. See also Tommy Thomas, 'Is Malaysia an Islamic State?' (2006) 4 *Malayan Law Journal* xv, xxix.

[37] Shad Saleem Faruqi, 'Freedom of religion under the constitution', *The Sun* (18 May 2006), online: www.sun2surf.com/article.cfm?id=14147. This resonates with the view of Salleh Abas, the former chief justice of the Supreme Court, who argues that article 3 gives the state the 'liberty, power and privilege to establish or maintain or assist in establishing or maintaining Islamic institution or provide or assist in providing institution in the religion of Islam and to incur necessary expenditure for the purpose'. Mohamed Salleh bin Abas, *Selected Articles & Speeches on Constitution, Law & Judiciary* (Kuala Lumpur: Malaysian Law Publishers, 1984), p. 45.

[38] Mohamad refines this view by arguing that Malaysia's secularism is not like the French *laïcité*; rather, it is reflected in the process of adopting laws and institutions. The adoption and transformation of religious bureaucracies in Malaysia are done through secular means, thus akin to a 'secularized adaptation of Islam rather than to a process of desecularization'. See Maznah Mohamad, 'The Ascendance of Bureaucratic Islam and the Secularization of the Sharia in Malaysia' (2010) 83(3) *Pacific Affairs* 505, 506.

[39] Shad Saleem Faruqi, *Document of Destiny: The Constitution of the Federation of Malaysia* (Petaling Jaya: Star Publications, 2008), p. 149.

[40] Faruqi places considerable importance on the fact that the constitution is the supreme law of the land (article 4(1)) and that the establishment of Islam as the religion of the Federation does not extinguish or abolish any 'right or prohibition … law or institution' as provided by article 3(4). Furthermore, although Parliament (in the case of federal territories) and state legislatures may pass laws pertaining to Islam under schedule 9 of the constitution, this does not give them 'a *carte blanche* to pass laws on Islam irrespective of the constitutional guarantees in Article 5 to 13'. See Faruqi, *Document of Destiny*, pp. 126, 135.

To be sure, there are interpretations of article 3 that diverge from the constitutional framers' spirit and ideas in more radical ways. One view sees Islam as the 'state ideology' and as a religion that is sacrosanct vis-à-vis other religions in the country.[41] Accordingly, Islam's role in shaping legal and public policies is supposedly 'far-reaching'.[42] This, by implication, means that constitutional rights protection is secondary. Some have gone even further by arguing that article 3 – perhaps in a manner similar to the Sri Lankan arrangement – obligates the state to preserve and promote Islam and that the Islamic doctrines and laws are integral to the country.[43] Constitutional provisions which allow restrictions on the propagation of other religions among Muslims,[44] sanction government (federal and state) assistance in establishing or maintaining Islamic institutions and provide that the *Yang di-Pertuan Agong* is under oath to safeguard Islam[45] are cited as evidence of Islam's pre-eminence in the polity.[46]

There is no mistaking that this broader conception of Islam as the state religion has gained considerable traction. In some ways, this has allowed the government and politicians to legitimize their perverse conception of the constitutional role of Islam and justify subsequent policies on religion. The process of adopting state-sponsored Islamic symbolism and institutions intensified under the Mahathir administration. One of the most prominent reforms was the separation of the civil and *Shariah* jurisdictions through a constitutional amendment in 1988.[47] The *Shariah* courts' jurisdiction, however, is

---

[41] Shamrahayu A. Aziz, 'Islam as the Religion of the Malaysian Federation: The Scope and Implications' (2006) 14(1) *International Islamic University Malaysia Law Journal* 33, 37 (quoting Abdul Aziz Bari, *Islam dalam Perlembagaan Malaysia* (*Islam in the Malaysian Constitution*) (Petaling Jaya, Malaysia: Intel Multimedia and Publications, 2005)).

[42] Aziz, 'Scope and Implications', p. 38.

[43] See ibid., pp. 39–40 and Mohamed Imam, 'Freedom of Religion under the Federal Constitution of Malaysia – A Reappraisal' (1994) 2 *Current Law Journal* lvii.

[44] Article 11 (4), Federal Constitution of Malaysia.

[45] Fourth Schedule, Federal Constitution of Malaysia.

[46] Aziz, 'Scope and Implications', p. 43. See also Zuliza Mohd Kusrin et al., 'Legal Provisions and Restrictions on the Propagation of Non-Islamic Religions among Muslims in Malaysia' (2013) 31(2) *Kajian Malaysia* 1, 4 (here, the authors posit that article 11(4) is intended to preserve Islam and protect its adherents).

[47] Article 121(1A), Federal Constitution of Malaysia. I will explain the consequences of this amendment on religious freedom in the concluding section of the chapter. Under the Mahathir administration, the government also initiated a series of modernist and progressive Islamic law reforms both as a response to Islamic revivalism as well as to counter the political competition from the Islamic party, PAS. See Donald L. Horowitz, 'The Qur'an and the Common Law: Islamic Law Reform and the Theory of Legal Change' (1994) 42 *American Journal of Comparative Law* 233.

confined to a specific set of issues such as Muslim personal law and offences against the precepts of Islam (provided that these are not offences that are dealt with by civil law).[48] In practice, *Shariah* court judgments are deemed final and could no longer be appealed at the civil courts. The *Shariah* and Civil Technical Committee was established to upgrade the status of *Shariah* courts and to review the compatibility of the laws of the country to Islamic principles.[49] A division within the Attorney General's Chambers (AGC) is tasked to ensure that laws are *Shariah* compliant. However, the AGC's website provides a more modest description of the role of the division, stating that it handles 'matters relating to the implementation, enforcement and drafting of *Shariah* laws at the Federal level'.[50] These are some of the many consequences of the religious revival movement (and the political responses to it) that swept the country since the late 1970s. In the 2013 UMNO general assembly, the prime minister affirmed the government's commitment to uphold Islamic principles and to defend the sanctity of Islam.[51] This is not only a politically powerful statement; it also clarifies the government's stand on article 3 (and, implicitly, its stand on interreligious contests) and showcases how it has evolved from the attitude of the Tunku administration in 1958.

Protecting and Fostering the Buddha Sasana

When the provision on Buddhism was first presented in 1972, Dr. Colvin R. De Silva conceded that the establishment of a secular state in Sri Lanka was already out of the question, as the state bears the duty to protect and foster Buddhism. At the same time, he stressed that the provision would not infringe the rights of other religions in the country,[52] which suggests that the enforcement of one aspect of the provision (concerning Buddhism) would not be

---

[48] See Schedule 9, List II, Federal Constitution of Malaysia.

[49] Tamir Moustafa, 'Liberal Rights versus Islamic Law? The Construction of a Binary in Malaysian Politics' (2013) 47(4) *Law and Society Review* 771, 777–8.

[50] 'What are the functions and roles of the Syariah section', *Attorney General's Chambers*, online: www.agc.gov.my/index.php?option=com_content&view=article&id=187%3Awhat-are-the-functions-and-roles-of-the-syariah-section-attorney-generals-chambers&catid=73%3Aagc-faqs&Itemid=44&lang=en.

[51] 'Full text of Najib's speech at 2013 UMNO General Assembly', *New Straits Times* (7 December 2013), online: www.nst.com.my/latest/full-text-of-najib-s-speech-at-2013-umno-general-assembly-1.425244.

[52] Colvin R. De Silva, *Safeguards for the Minorities in the 1972 Constitution* (Colombo: Young Socialist Publication, 1987), p. 10.

done at the expense of the other aspect (concerning religious freedom). In the following years, however, the political elites have buttressed the position and role of Buddhism in the polity – as we have seen in Chapter 2 – through the constitutional revision in 1978.

There is almost no clear explanation on the intention or understandings behind the 1978 revision.[53] While the declaration of inviolability by President J. R. Jayewardene might allow one to speculate that there was every intention of subordinating religious freedom to the protection of Buddhism, the same constitutional revision process enhanced the protection of fundamental rights in the constitution. In the earlier years of Jayewardene's political career, he espoused a different political outlook than Mr. Bandaranaike.[54] Both shared the vision for Buddhist principles to guide and shape political life. But while Mr. Bandaranaike explicitly rallied around the Sinhalese identity and conventional Buddhism to buttress his political power, Jayewardene was not attracted to such manoeuvers.[55] Yet, from the sixties onwards, the United National Party (UNP) – perhaps responding to the groundswell of Buddhist demands and the political competition posed by the Sri Lanka Freedom Party (SLFP) – inched closer to the SLFP's ideological acceptance of Buddhist restoration.[56]

Given the lingering vagueness on the precise relationship between Buddhist prerogatives and the right to religious freedom, it is not surprising that opinions vary among scholars and members of the legal fraternity. Some have echoed Dr. De Silva's balancing exercise: that the provision obligates the state to protect and foster Buddhism *while* assuring the religious freedom to all other religions, they argue, emphasizes the equal protection of all religions.[57] Bartholomeusz elucidates this further by suggesting that the 1972 constitution accorded Buddhism a 'first among equals, peerless yet parallel' status in the constitutional order.[58] She then goes even further, arguing that the

53 Email conversation with Benjamin Schonthal (25 February 2012).
54 K. M. De Silva and William Howard Wiggins, *J. R. Jayewardene of Sri Lanka: A Political Biography Volume 1: 1905–1956* (Hawaii: University of Hawaii Press, 1988), p. 78.
55 Ibid.
56 Stanley Jeyaraja Tambiah, *Buddhism Betrayed? Religion, Politics, and Violence in Sri Lanka* (Chicago and London: University of Chicago Press, 1992), pp. 60–1.
57 Interview with Dr. Jayampathy Wickramaratne, constitutional scholar and president's counsel, in Colombo, Sri Lanka (10 June 2013) and an anonymous president's counsel, in Colombo, Sri Lanka (11 June 2013). See also Schonthal, 'Constitutionalizing Religion', p. 472 (arguing that 'neither part is given any distinct legal priority').
58 Tessa Bartholomeusz, 'First among Equals: Buddhism and the Sri Lankan State' in Ian Harris (ed.), *Buddhism and Politics in Twentieth Century Asia* (London and New York: Continuum, 1999), pp. 173–93.

1978 revision consolidated this position by making Buddhism the state religion.[59] The latter argument, however, is no longer tenable especially since the Supreme Court declared unconstitutional a bill which sought to establish Buddhism as the state religion in 2005. Nevertheless, some scholars continue to place considerable importance on the strengthening of state obligations vis-à-vis Buddhism. They argue, for instance, that the provision could justify preferential treatment to the Buddha Sasana in financial aid or restrict other religious organizations from propagating their faith;[60] that the Buddhist *Mahasangha*'s (Buddhist clergy) pronouncements and *diktats* greatly influence the state's policies and behaviour;[61] and that the provision opens the possibility for 'transforming Buddhism for official purposes, short of discriminating against other religionists'.[62]

For the historian K.M. De Silva, the introduction of the Buddhism provision does not make Sri Lanka a theocratic state (as some would have actually liked it to be), but at the same time it cannot be said that the country is a secular state.[63] The strengthening of the Buddhism provision in the constitution-making exercise was only the tip of the iceberg. How the provision has been interpreted and applied in practice increasingly reflect scholarly concerns about the potentially far-reaching effects of the provision.[64] Indeed, the trajectory of Sri Lanka's state-religion relationship since independence has changed radically. The first prime minister, D. S. Senanayake, championed secularism and moderation among competing political forces organized along ethnic lines. He vehemently opposed the involvement of monks in public affairs,[65] much to chagrin of the *bhikkus* who thought that they

---

[59] Ibid., p. 182.
[60] A. J. Wilson, *The Gaullist System in Asia: The Constitution of Sri Lanka* (1978) (London and Basingstoke: Macmillan Press, 1980), p. 103.
[61] Dr. M. N. Buch, 'India, Sri Lanka – The Tamil question', *Vivekananda International Foundation* (29 March 2013), online: www.vifindia.org/article/2013/march/29/india-sri-lanka-the-tamil-question.
[62] Wilson, *Gaullist System*, p. 104.
[63] K. M. De Silva, *A History of Sri Lanka*, 1st ed. (Berkeley: University of California Press, 1981), p. 550. See also Buch, 'The Tamil Question' (arguing that Sri Lanka is not quite a theocracy nor is it a secular state like India). Cf Bartholomeusz, 'First among Equals', pp. 185–8 (highlighting the views of some writers that the establishment of Buddhism did not mean that Sri Lanka ceased to be a secular state).
[64] See Farzana Haniffa, 'Conflicted Solidarities? Muslims and the Constitution-Making Process of 1970–72' in Asanga Welikala (ed.), *The Sri Lankan Republic at 40: Reflections on Constitutional History, Theory and Practice* (Colombo: Centre for Policy Alternatives, 2012), p. 227 (arguing that the 1972 constitution institutionalized Buddhism in a manner that casts considerable doubt on the position of other religions and their adherents in the country).
[65] Tambiah, *Buddhism Betrayed?*, p. 26.

had a role to play in society and government – a role, they argued, that had existed from early times.[66] Yet, almost thirty years later, Buddhism became the established religion and monks have become increasingly involved in politics. The establishment of the Jathika Hela Urumaya (JHU) in 2004, a political party led by monks, signalled that the monks intend to remain in political life. In a parliamentary election that year, the JHU fielded over 200 candidates.[67] During the Rajapaksa administration, the JHU formed one of the parties in the government coalition. Although small in numbers (the JHU held three seats in Parliament), the party is said to have possessed significant political clout.

In the executive, Ranasinghe Premadasa – Jayewardene's successor who was known for his pro-Buddhism outlook[68] – expanded the role of Buddhism in the state. He founded the Ministry of Buddhist Affairs (of which he was the first minister) and established a Supreme Advisory Council which, among others, consisted of sixteen monks and presidents of several Buddhist organizations in Sri Lanka.[69] Pressures to further enhance the Buddhism provision continued well into President Chandrika Kumaratunga's administration, which lasted from November 1994 to November 2005.[70] She responded by proposing a draft constitution which sought to accord constitutional recognition of the Supreme Advisory Council in its role as an advisor on matters pertaining to the Buddha Sasana. It is worth noting that Kumaratunga was widely perceived as a secularist who was indifferent to Buddhism, which made her the subject of criticism by influential monks.[71] Although her proposal was eventually unsuccessful, it highlighted the significance of pro-Buddhist pressures on the way the role of Buddhism is to be interpreted and actualized in the state. The policies of the UNP government before Kumaratunga also underscored the concessions to pro-Sinhalese-Buddhist tendencies and its

---

[66] See ibid., chapters 4 and 5. *Bhikkus* are the Theravada Buddhist monks.

[67] Mahinda Deegalle, 'The Politics of the Jathika Hela Urumaya Monks: Buddhism and Ethnicity in Contemporary Sri Lanka' (2004) 5(2) *Contemporary Buddhism* 83, 84.

[68] Mark Juergensmeyer, *Terror in the Mind of God: The Global Rise of Religious Violence*, 3rd ed. (Berkeley, Los Angeles and London: University of California Press, 2001), p. 244.

[69] Premadasa appointed the presidents of the ACBC, the Maha Bodhi Society and the Young Men's Buddhist Association to the Council, along with a Buddhist nun. See Bartholomeusz, 'First among Equals', p. 188. The Council's objective was to protect Buddhism in Sri Lanka, and it was placed under the Ministry of Buddhist Affairs.

[70] Kumaratunga is S. W. R. D. Bandaranaike and Sirimavo Bandaranaike's daughter. Mahinda Rajapaksa succeeded her.

[71] Bartholomeusz, 'First among Equals', pp. 188–9.

weakened commitment to secularism.[72] What all this indicates is the loss of Senanayake's moderate political vision entrenched in the Soulbury Constitution. Indeed, the flaw with Senanayake's approach, as De Silva argues, was its elitist nature and lack of popular support.[73]

It is also important, however, to acknowledge another narrative in the shifting conceptions on the role of Buddhism in the state. From the monks' and Buddhist revivalists' perspective, the shift that had occurred with regard to the role of Buddhism was, in fact, the other way round. Buddhism once enjoyed considerable prestige on the island and *bhikkus* were actively involved in social and political life, contributing to Sinhalese civilization. But since the arrival of the colonialists, the island has trodden on the opposite path. The colonial government's support for Christianity, its missionary activities and subsequent control of the education system were oft-cited as factors that drove the decline of the role of Buddhism in the country.[74] The revival movement, in this respect, only sought to restore what was already on the island for centuries and to remedy the tragic decay of Buddhism and the position of *bhikkus* in the society.

REGULATING RELIGIOUS PRACTICE AND EXPRESSION

State policies and practices may reflect or be influenced by a variety of factors, including (majoritarian) public opinion, pressure groups and media reporting, as well as political parties and their electoral calculations (at both national and local levels). However, as I suggested earlier, policies and practices may also be legitimized – for better or for worse – by particular constitutional arrangements.

There is an inherent tension in the relationship between religious establishment and the freedom of religion. A clear constitutional establishment may provide the basis upon which the favoured religion is singled out for protection and privileges; the adherents of that religion may be subjected to particular laws regulating their religious practices and views; and the special status may be invoked to justify restrictions on other religions and the rights of

---

[72] A. R. M. Imtiyaz, 'The Politicization of Buddhism and Electoral Politics in Sri Lanka' in Ali Riaz (ed.), *Religion and Politics in South Asia* (Oxon: Routledge, 2010), p. 161. D. S. Senanayake, the first prime minister of Ceylon from the UNP during which the Soulbury Constitution operated, was committed to a secular state and religious neutrality. See K. M. De Silva, *A History of Sri Lanka*, 2nd ed. (Colombo: Vijitha Yapa Publications, 2008), pp. 602–3.
[73] Ibid., p. 609.   [74] Tambiah, *Buddhism Betrayed?*, pp. 33–5.

their religious adherents.[75] By contrast, the constitutional disestablishment of religion is thought to advance state neutrality toward all religious beliefs by preventing the privileging of a particular religion or religious group; it may also prevent state intrusion into religious affairs.[76] However, the constitutional recognition of a particular religion (or religion, in the broader sense of the word) may have different meanings in different countries, as the previous chapter illustrates. It may be the case that an established religion is the product of historical, traditional and/or political considerations, with little (intended) practical impact on policymaking. The United Kingdom is one such example – an example which was intended to have been replicated to some degree in Malaysia.

Despite these premises, in practice, it is difficult to accurately predict the effect and consequences of religion clauses on religious freedom. Consider the Pew Forum's Government Restrictions on Religion Index (GRI) as a starting point for comparison.[77] The scores for each country from 2007 to 2012 are reproduced in the following Table 3.1.

Let us disregard, for a moment, the intentions and meanings behind the constitutional arrangements on religion that I have explained in Chapter 2. A plain comparison of the GRI scores among the three countries seems counter-intuitive. In Sri Lanka, where the constitution explicitly obligates the state to protect and foster the Buddha Sasana, one might expect greater state-enforced restrictions on religion and religious freedom. Yet, the extent of such regulation in Sri Lanka – at least according to the Pew Forum's indices – is lower than that of Malaysia and Indonesia. Going deeper into the indicators measured by the latest Pew Forum report, for instance, tells us why: in Malaysia and Indonesia, government restrictions on public preaching reportedly affects all religious groups, compared to only 'some' religious groups in Sri Lanka; government limitations on proselytizing and conversion exists in Malaysia and Indonesia, but not in Sri Lanka; the government regulates the wearing of religious symbols in Malaysia and Indonesia; and there are explicit government bans on particular religious groups in Malaysia and Indonesia,

---

[75] See José Casanova, *Public Religions in the Modern World* (Chicago and London: University of Chicago Press, 1994), p. 55. Casanova argues that within the liberal political tradition, there is a fear of the politicization of religion and that establishment of religion could 'endanger the individual freedom of conscience'.

[76] Ran Hirschl, *Constitutional Theocracy* (Cambridge, MA, and London: Harvard University Press, 2010), pp. 27–8.

[77] The Pew Research Center's Forum on Religion and Public Life has published a series of studies on the restrictions on religion. A complete set of the reports can be found here: www.pewforum.org/category/publications/restrictions-on-religion/.

TABLE 3.1. *Government Restrictions on Religion Index*

Year / Country	Government Restrictions on Religion		
	Indonesia	Malaysia	Sri Lanka
2008[78]	6.8	6.8	4.1
2009[79]	7.0	8.1	3.7
2010[80]	8.6	6.4	6.0
2011[81]	8.2	7.1	5.4
2012[82]	8.3	7.6	5.9
2013[83]	8.5	7.9	5.3

but not in Sri Lanka.[84] While these findings largely comport with the substantive evidence and data reported by various organizations, as we shall see later in this chapter, it also demonstrates that the role and effect of constitutional arrangements on religious freedom are unpredictable.

The Role of Religious Bureaucracies

The existence of state-supported religious bureaucracies is a major indicator of the salience of religion in public life and that the state (and its constitution) is not 100 per cent secular. From time to time, controversies implicating

[78] Period ending mid-2008, based on data collected over a two-year period from July 2006 to June 2008. See 'Rising restrictions on religion – One-third of the world's population experiences an increase', *Pew Research Center: Religion and Public Life* (9 August 2011), online: www.pewforum.org/2011/08/09/rising-restrictions-on-religion2/.

[79] Period ending mid-2009, based on annual data from July 2008 to June 2009. See 'Rising tide of restrictions on religion', *Pew Research Center: Religion and Public Life* (20 September 2012), online: www.pewforum.org/2012/09/20/rising-tide-of-restrictions-on-religion-findings/.

[80] Period ending mid-2010, based on data collected on an annual basis from July 2009 to June 2010. See ibid.

[81] Period ending December 2011. See 'Arab Spring adds to global restrictions on religion', *Pew Research Center: Religion and Public Life* (20 June 2013), online: www.pewforum.org/2013/06/20/arab-spring-restrictions-on-religion-findings/#linegraph

[82] Period ending December 2012. See 'Religious hostilities reach six-year high', *Pew Research Center: Religious and Public Life* (14 January 2014), online: www.pewforum.org/2014/01/14/religious-hostilities-reach-six-year-high/.

[83] Period ending December 2013. See 'Latest trends in religious restrictions and hostilities', *Pew Research Center: Religious and Public Life* (26 February 2015), online: www.pewforum.org/2015/02/26/religious-hostilities/.

[84] See 'Trends in global restrictions on religion, Appendix E: Results by country', *Pew Research Center: Religious and Public Life* (23 June 2016), online: www.pewforum.org/files/2016/06/Restrictions2016appendixE.pdf.

religious freedom may be traced back to the ways in which religious bureaucracies – as the enforcement arm of the state – exercise their powers. As we shall see, the zeal with which these institutions operate, the extent of state and structural (legal) support that they receive, and their influence on policymaking and public opinion vary among the three countries.

In Indonesia, the MORA was established from the very early days of independence. Its tasks, as formulated by Wahid Hasyim (the first minister) were to ensure that everyone is free to adhere and worship according to his own religion and belief and 'to assist, support, protect and promote all sound religious movements'.[85] Although each of the six officially recognized religions is represented by its own director-general, the minister has always been a Sunni Muslim.[86] However, too much should not be read into the ministerial post. After all, Muslims comprise almost 90 per cent of the population and a significant proportion of them are Sunnis. Since its inception, MORA's reach into Islamic institutions and its influence in the centralization and control of Muslim affairs, have expanded considerably.[87] It has local offices and personnel throughout the country – even at the village level – and it possesses authority in governing issues such as marriage, religious education, religious courts and pilgrimage.[88] It was also one of the three ministries that issued a joint decision ordering the Ahmadiyah to cease its religious activities.

The different directions of post-Soeharto developments in Indonesia have, to some extent, shaped the ways in which MORA regulates religion and responds to religious freedom issues. The freer political space has allowed a variety of organizations, agendas and viewpoints – from the more liberal end of the spectrum to the illiberal end – to mushroom, but it has also facilitated a 'conservative turn' in mainstream Muslim discourse and policymaking.[89] Decentralization triggered a redistribution of power from the central to the local governments. While religion remains a matter under the purview of the central government, religious freedom issues often involve questions of overlapping jurisdictions (i.e., religion under the central government and public

[85] B. J. Boland, *Struggle for Islam in Modern Indonesia*, Reprint of 1st ed. (Leiden, The Netherlands: Springer Science+Business Media Dordrecht, 1982), p. 108.

[86] Salim, *Challenging the Secular State*, p. 71.

[87] Ibid., p. 72 (citing Daniel S. Lev, *Islamic Courts in Indonesia: A Study in the Political Bases of Legal Institutions* (Berkeley, Los Angeles and London: University of California Press, 1972)).

[88] Ibid., pp. 73–4.

[89] Zainal Abidin Bagir, 'Advocacy for Religious Freedom in Democratizing Indonesia' (2014) 12 (4) *Review of Faith and International Affairs* 27, 28. See also Martin van Bruinessen (ed.), *Contemporary Developments in Indonesian Islam: Explaining the Conservative Turn* (Singapore: Institute of Southeast Asian Studies, 2013).

order under the local government). The central government has shown a tendency to leave such issues to the local government by framing them as public order concerns, but a major lacuna exists: local regulations cannot be subjected to constitutional review.

Outside the official state apparatus, there is the MUI. Unlike the Malaysian system where there is a *mufti* in each state, there is no such single, dominant figure in Indonesia. Although the MUI has a chairman, it issues *fatwas* in its institutional name. Its *Fatwa* Commission must come to a consensus on a particular issue before them before a *fatwa* can be issued.[90] The MUI's *fatwas* are not legally binding, but their political role and influence cannot be overlooked. Established during the Soeharto period, its first chairman not only envisioned that the MUI would bridge relations between the government and Muslims, he also encouraged Muslims to cooperate with the Soeharto administration.[91] The MUI did not disappoint, in this regard. It was virtually impossible to find a *fatwa* that contradicted government policy (perhaps, in part, because Soeharto screened and approved MUI members), and on the one occasion where it issued a *fatwa* prohibiting Muslims from attending Christmas celebrations, it stirred up a saga which led to the chairman's resignation.[92] All this reinforces the view that the MUI was set up as part of Soeharto's plan to control the *ulama* and public expressions of Islam.

In line with the shift away from authoritarianism in the post-Soeharto era, MUI began enjoying a greater degree of autonomy in its membership selection.[93] This, according to Assyaukanie, has shaped its present character, structure, personnel and, ultimately, the kinds of *fatwas* it issues.[94] Its new-found independence coincided with what some have called 'purification' initiatives, manifested in a series of *fatwas* against liberalism, pluralism, secularism and non-mainstream Muslim groups.[95] Yet, there is still something to be said about the role of the state in protecting or disregarding religious freedom. *Fatwas* against minority religious groups is not a recent

---

[90] Luthfi Assyaukanie, 'Fatwa and Violence in Indonesia' (2009) 11 *Journal of Religion and Society* 1, 4.

[91] Ibid., p. 5 (quoting Nadirsyah Hosen, 'Behind the Scenes: Fatwas of Majelis Ulama Indonesia (1975–1998)' (2004) 15 *Journal of Islamic Studies* 147, 151).

[92] Ibid., p. 6. Soeharto was reportedly upset with the *fatwa* as it was seen as counter-productive to his plans to foster religious harmony. In addition, celebrating Christmas had been a tradition of the Soeharto government. Ibid.

[93] Ibid., pp. 6–7.   [94] Ibid., p. 7.

[95] Bagir, 'Advocacy', p. 28. See also Moch Nur Ichwan, 'Towards a Puritanical Moderate Islam: The Majelis Ulama Indonesia and the Politics of Religious Orthodoxy' in Martin van Bruinessen (ed.), *Contemporary Developments in Indonesian Islam: Explaining the Conservative Turn* (Singapore: Institute of Southeast Asian Studies, 2013), pp. 60–104.

phenomenon; in fact, they have existed since Soeharto's New Order period. The MUI *fatwa* declaring the Ahmadiyah as a deviant Islamic sect was first issued in 1980; a *fatwa* warning Muslims about Shiism's teachings that were deemed contradictory to the fundamentals of Sunni Islam was issued as far back as 1984.[96] However, many observers have highlighted the differing responses by governments during and after Soeharto's New Order administration. A study on the persecution of Ahmadis in Manis Lor, Kuningan (West Java), found that the Ahmadis had been living peacefully in the area for decades until, in 2002, the MUI began pressuring the local government to ban their activities.[97] The regent heeded the MUI's recommendation. There are other similar examples of MUI's growing influence in local politics and governance. Assyaukanie also argues that the Soeharto regime – though known as brutally authoritarian – was more responsive against incidents of religious violence.[98] By contrast, in the post-Soeharto period – in a comparably freer political environment – persecution cases (be they by the state or society) have increased. Human rights advocates have criticized, in particular, the Yudhoyono government for its lethargic response to religious freedom violations, but more interestingly, it has also been seen as a regime that tried to curry favour with the MUI.

In Malaysia, the Malaysian Department for Islamic Development (Jabatan Kemajuan Islam Malaysia, or JAKIM), which is directly overseen by the Prime Minister's Department, is instrumental in carrying out the government's plans, particularly in centralizing matters pertaining to Islam. There is no Ministry of Religion as there is in Indonesia or Sri Lanka. However, there is a minister in the Prime Minister's Department who is assigned a religious affairs portfolio. The co-optation of religious figures into the state administrative structure through JAKIM (or Pusat Islam, in its pre-1997 form) was particularly striking during the Mahathir administration. Like Soeharto, Mahathir was openly authoritarian and suspicious of the *ulama* and political Islam. However, the co-optation of these figures was seen as a strategically sensible move, both as a means to control the religious figures as well as to boost his Islamic credentials and legitimacy, particularly in light of the growing influence of the Islamic party, PAS. In the early years of his administration, the size of the bureaucracy expanded considerably. Its staff increased from 100 in 1982 to 608 in 1987.[99]

[96] Assyaukanie, 'Fatwa and Violence', pp. 8–13.
[97] Rizal Panggabean and Ihsan Ali-Fauzi, *Pemolisian Konflik Keagamaan di Indonesia* (*Policing of Religious Conflict in Indonesia*) (Jakarta: PUSAD Paramadina, 2014), pp. 30, 36.
[98] Assyaukanie, 'Fatwa and Violence', p. 12.
[99] Joseph Chinyong Liow, *Piety and Politics: Islamism in Contemporary Malaysia* (New York: Oxford University Press, 2009), p. 49.

Today, JAKIM reportedly has 3,500-strong staff and is allocated approximately RM800 million of the country's annual budget.

The establishment of JAKIM allows the state to control the kinds of Islamic doctrine and praxis that are developed within the society, and to guard the zeal of religious preachers, teachers and scholars. JAKIM's role in coordinating interstate Islamic affairs and in overseeing the implementation of Islamic laws and aspirations should not be understated. Among others, it writes and vets Friday sermons to be distributed to state religious departments (and subsequently to local mosques); it issues licenses to preachers; and it monitors the spread of 'deviant' Islamic doctrines and facilitates rehabilitation for followers of deviant groups. Although each state maintains its own Islamic bureaucracy and retains jurisdiction in a specified list of Islamic matters,[100] in practice the role of the federal government through JAKIM is more extensive, as it leads efforts to review and standardize Islamic laws throughout the country. Thus, for better or for worse, JAKIM has significantly influenced and defined the parameters of Islam in Malaysia. While it plays a role in moderating the Islamic discourse from the more extremist influences (this was particularly obvious during the Mahathir administration), it has, in the course of time, developed a life of its own.

The institutional monopoly in defining what 'version' of Islam should be fostered and practiced (coupled with solid financial backing from the state) has increasingly steered JAKIM away from its 'moderating' role. If Mahathir's authoritarian style kept the religious authorities in check, subsequent prime ministers have not – for a variety of reasons – been willing and/or able to do so. Thus, JAKIM's accumulation of power and control over time has made it susceptible to intolerant views. Its eagerness to standardize Islamic doctrines and thought by monitoring 'deviant' Islamic teachings has facilitated the persecution of Muslim minorities who do not conform to the mainstream Sunni (Shafie) Islam that the state approves of. It has sought to curb intellectual discourses on Islam by purportedly 'liberal' or progressive Muslim organizations and individuals and to enforce bans on books that it deems misleading, contrary to Islamic teachings in Malaysia, or potentially confusing for Muslims. Well-known cases include the ban on a Muslim women organization's book, *Muslim Women and the Challenges of Extremism*,[101]

---

[100] See Schedule Nine, List II, Federal Constitution of Malaysia.
[101] This ban was subsequently overturned by the High Court in 2010. See Terence Toh, 'Court of Appeal: Banning of Book "Outrageous, Irrational"', *The Star* (27 July 2012), online: thestar.com.my/news/story.asp?file=/2012/7/27/nation/20120727130848&sec=nation.

Irshad Manji's *Allah, Liberty, and Love* and several fictional books by the local writer Faisal Tehrani.

Maznah Mohamad argues that although the 'Islamic state of Malaysia' is a pervasive political rhetoric among the ruling elite, the religious bureaucracy is the main driving force behind efforts to expand a particular version of Islamic doctrine in many aspects of public and private life. It possesses an 'aura of sanctity' as the sole arbiter of the 'correct' version of Islam.[102] On the ground, the bureaucracy is supported by a growing fraternity of Muslim NGOs who share its dogmatic approach and goals on religion, which are often intertwined with broader political and ethno-nationalist aspirations. In contrast, in Indonesia, although MORA plays a significant role in managing Islamic affairs, the Muslim intellectual culture and practices have been far more active, pluralistic and democratic,[103] and the state, therefore, does not maintain a monopoly on religious interpretation in the degree that the Malaysian authorities do.

Unlike Malaysia, where government institutions for religious matters have only been established for Islam, in Sri Lanka there are parallel ministries overseeing the religious affairs of Buddhism as well as three other main religions in the country – Hinduism, Christianity and Islam. Until 2015, when the new administration led by President Maithripala Sirisena came into power, there was a single ministry with distinct departments overseeing religious affairs for all religious groups – the Ministry of Buddha Sasana and Religious Affairs. This is despite the express constitutional obligation on the state to protect and foster the Buddha Sasana. The objective of the Ministry was to 'create a society filled with virtuous values'.[104] One of its functions, apart from carrying out the constitutional obligation with respect to the Buddha Sasana, was to protect the rights of all religions according to the constitution.[105] Each of the different departments operated with different budget and staff (the Buddhist Affairs Department, understandably, had the most resources), functioning as mediators between the government and the religious communities they represent.[106]

---

[102] Mohamad, 'Ascendance', p. 506. Moustafa also argues that the authorities in Malaysia monopolize religious interpretation. Moustafa, 'Judging in God's Name', pp. 161–2.

[103] Norani Othman, 'Islamization and Democratization in Malaysia' in Ariel Heryanto and Sumit K. Mandal (eds.), *Challenging Authoritarianism in Southeast Asia* (London and New York: RoutledgeCurzon, 2003), p. 122.

[104] 'Main functions', *Ministry of Buddha Sasana and Religious Affairs*, online: mbra.gov.lk/en/about-us/main-functions.

[105] Ibid.

[106] Benjamin Schonthal, 'Environments of Law: Islam, Buddhism, and the State in Contemporary Sri Lanka' (2016) 75(1) *The Journal of Asian Studies* 137, 142.

These religious departments were not all established at the same time. In 1979, the government created the Department of Buddhist Affairs,[107] which later evolved into the Ministry of Buddha Sasana in 1990.[108] As in Malaysia, the Ministry was established to facilitate government control over the *sangha*, but the monks' resistance helped them (and the monasteries) to maintain a degree of independence from the state.[109] Nonetheless, within the Ministry there was a Supreme Advisory Council whose objective was to protect Buddhism by advising the government on matters related to the religion.[110] In 2001, a Presidential Commission was appointed by President Kumaratunga to examine the state of the Buddha Sasana. Its report highlighted, among others, the duty of the government as well as Buddhist organizations and population to 'protect the Buddha Sasana by curbing the powerful forces that are against Buddhism'.[111]

When President Mahinda Rajapaksa was elected in 2005, he abolished the Ministry of Buddha Sasana and set up the Ministry of Religious Affairs instead. While this might be seen as an effort to blur the distinction between Buddhism and other religions, Rajapaksa faced grouses by several Buddhist fraternities over the status of Buddhism in the island, as well as pressures on his government to step up efforts to promote and nurture Buddhism.[112] It was no surprise, then, that after his re-election in 2010, he established the Ministry of Buddha Sasana and Religious Affairs. During the Kumaratunga administration, the Ministry was involved in controversial initiatives, such as the drafting of a bill in 2004 which sought to prohibit unethical conversions and criminalize acts that amount to compelling any person to convert to another religion.[113] Although this bill might have been a response to the anxiety about

---

[107] Ibid.. This was followed by the Department of Hindu Religious Affairs, the Department of Muslim Religious and Cultural Affairs (1982) and finally the Department of Christian Affairs (1999).

[108] Mirjam Weiberg-Salzmann, 'The Radicalisation of Buddhism in the Twentieth and Twenty-First Centuries: The Buddha Sangha in Sri Lanka' (2014) 15(2) *Politics, Religion & Ideology* 288, 292.

[109] Ibid.

[110] Mahinda Deegalle, '"Foremost among Religions": Theravada Buddhism's Affairs with the Modern Sri Lankan State' in John Whalen-Bridge and Pattana Kitiarsa (eds.), *Buddhism, Modernity, and the State in Asia: Forms of Engagement* (New York: Palgrave Macmillan, 2013), p. 52.

[111] Bruce Matthews, 'Christian Evangelical Conversions and the Politics of Sri Lanka' (2007) 80(3) *Pacific Affairs* 455, 467 (quoting the Buddha Sasana Presidential Report of 2002).

[112] Ibid.

[113] For an explanation of the details of the bill and how it restricts religious freedom and expression, see Tracy Hesko, 'Rights Rhetoric as an Instrument of Religious Oppression in Sri Lanka' (2006) 29(1) *Boston College International and Comparative Law Review* 123.

conversion among some Buddhists, it was nevertheless drafted in neutral terms, with no particular religion singled out for protection or restriction. In some measure, these examples indicate that although the religious bureaucracy in Sri Lanka caters – in principle – for all religions on the island, in practice it appears to further the interests of the majority religion, a situation which bears much resemblance to Indonesia and Malaysia.

Houses of Worship

In 2014, a study on the policing of religious conflict in Indonesia revealed that social conflicts involving houses of worship are rising in Indonesia.[114] The government, of course, had realized for some time that the construction of houses of worship is a socially and politically sensitive issue. In 2006, it issued a Joint Ministerial Regulation[115] to guarantee and facilitate the building of houses of worship, having consulted representatives from the six officially recognized religions. The Regulation accords the regent or mayor in a regency or city with the power to issue building permits.[116] Apart from satisfying administrative and technical requirements, there are four main conditions that need to be adhered to: (1) there should be at least ninety signatures from the congregation members;[117] (2) it must be supported by at least sixty local residents of other faiths, authorized by the village chief; (3) there must be a written recommendation from the head of the Religious Department office of the district/city; and (4) there must be a written recommendation from the district/city's Forum for Religious Harmony (Forum Kerukunan Umat Beragama, or FKUB).[118]

While these guidelines have generally served their purpose of setting clear benchmarks for all religious groups in Indonesia,[119] there are cases where they have become counter-productive. In some instances, the Regulation has been used as a basis for prohibiting the construction of new houses of worship and for closing down existing ones. The threshold for neighbourhood approval

---

[114] Panggabean and Ali-Fauzi, *Pemolisian Konflik*, p. 4.

[115] *Peraturan Bersama Menteri Agama dan Menteri Dalam Negeri Nomor 9 dan 8 Tahun 2006* (Joint Regulations of the Ministers of Religion and Home Affairs Number 9 and 8 Year 2006), 21 March 2006 [Joint Ministerial Regulation].

[116] Article 6(1)(e), Joint Ministerial Regulation.

[117] The identity of these members needs to be verified by the local office of the district, region, city or province in question.

[118] Article 14(2), Joint Ministerial Regulation. The written recommendation from the FKUB should result from a decision by consensus in an FKUB meeting. Article 15, Joint Ministerial Regulation.

[119] Bagir, 'Advocacy', p. 30.

might seem low, but even if this were satisfied, other local residents may be provoked and mobilized in larger numbers to protest against the building of a particular house of worship. In some notable cases, authorities have shown a tendency to cave in to public (i.e., majoritarian) pressure. In Cilegon (Banten province), for example, the lack of support from local residents (who are majority Muslim) was cited as a reason to deny building permission for a church.[120] In another case, a mosque in North Tapanuli (Sumatera province) was denied a building permit by the local government, even though local approval was obtained.[121]

Critics also argue that the Regulation is enforced overwhelmingly against those who are effectively minorities in areas dominated by another religious majority. From 2009 to 2012, the SETARA Institute reported that fifty-four cases of restriction, demolition or closure of houses of worship – most of which involved the Christian and Ahmadiyah communities – implicated the state. Although, as statistics suggest, a great majority the cases involve churches and/ or non-mainstream Muslim houses of worship, there have been difficulties in building Hindu temples in West Java, as well as mosques in provinces like East Nusa Tenggara and Bali.[122] Despite these reports, MORA has suggested that the number of houses of worship for religious minorities have grown, particularly Protestant churches.[123]

The HKBP Filadelfia (in the Bekasi regency) and the GKI Yasmin (in the Bogor regency) church cases are among the most significant and publicized examples of the challenges in exercising religious freedom in Indonesia. The Filadelfia church was eventually bulldozed in March 2013 under the orders of the local government because it had no proper permit. The church had been

---

[120] There are over 5,000 Christian congregants in this area. SETARA Institute, *Negara Harus Bersikap: Tiga Tahun Laporan Kondisi Kebebasan Beragama/Berkeyakinan di Indonesia 2007–2009* (*State Should Take Action: Three Years Report on the Freedom of Religion and Belief in Indonesia 2007–2009*) (Jakarta: SETARA Institute, 2009), p. 18.

[121] Djibril Muhammad, 'Pemerintah Persulit Pembangunan Masjid Al-Munawar' ('Authorities complicate building of Al-Munawar Mosque'), *Republika* (15 March 2013), online: www.republika.co.id/berita/dunia-islam/islam-nusantara/13/03/15/mjpg22-pemerintah-persulit-imb-pembangunan-masjid-al-munawar.

[122] See SETARA Institute, *Negara Harus Bersikap*, p. 31, and SETARA Institute, *Negara Menyangkal: Kondisi Kebebasan Beragama/Berkeyakinan di Indonesia 2010* (*Denial by the State: Report on the Freedom of Religion and Belief in Indonesia 2010*) (Jakarta: SETARA Institute, 2010), pp. 28–9. See also U.S. Department of State, 'International religious freedom report for 2007' (2007), online: www.state.gov/j/drl/rls/irf/2007/index.htm and U.S. Department of State, 'International religious freedom report for 2008' (2008), online: www.state.gov/j/drl/rls/irf/2008/index.htm.

[123] Bagir, 'Advocacy', p. 30.

in operation since 2000 and was in the midst of a renovation when it was closed down and subsequently demolished. The GKI Yasmin case reveals multiple problems. The half-finished church had previously been issued a construction permit, but this was revoked twice by the mayor of Bogor due to allegations of forged congregation signatures. The Bogor administration then sealed off the church compound in 2010. The case was brought before the Supreme Court and the Indonesian Ombudsman, and both have upheld the church's construction permission. The mayor, however, refused to enforce the Supreme Court's judgment as well as the recommendation of the Ombudsman.[124] Church representatives have rejected suggestions from the local authority to relocate the church.[125] The Yasmin case thus raises serious questions about the rule of law in Indonesia, and its congregation, until today, remains unable to exercise the right to worship.

Unlike Indonesia, there are different regulations on the construction of houses of worship for Muslims and non-Muslims in Malaysia. Proposals for non-Muslim houses of worship must satisfy two main guidelines on population threshold and distance.[126] In cities, places of worship will only be approved if there are at least 2,300 congregation members in a particular area. In rural areas, the threshold would be met if there are at least 1,000 members. Apart from that, the proposed building must be constructed at least 100 metres from the residences of other majority religious adherents and at least 300 metres from the places of worship of other religions. Until 2003, the construction of non-Muslim houses of worship required the approval of state Islamic councils. These regulations do not apply to Muslim houses of worship, and it appears that a congregation of less than 200 members in a particular area would warrant the approval of at least a *surau*.[127]

---

[124] The mayor stood by his decision on the basis that the Bogor District Court has found an individual, Munir Karta, guilty of falsifying ten signatures that are needed as part of the permit approval process. GKI Yasmin, however, argued that those signatures did not form part of its application for the permit. See Ida Indawati Khouw, '3 years on, GKI Yasmin Church remains victim of absence of the state', *The Jakarta Post* (4 December 2011), online: www.thejakartapost .com/news/2011/12/24/3-years-gki-yasmin-church-remains-victim-absence-state.html, and Letter from Ombudsman of the Republic of Indonesia to the President and Chair of the House of Representatives (12 October 2011).

[125] Church representatives have consistently rejected such offers, arguing that the rule of law and the court ruling should be enforced instead. Interview with GKI Yasmin church official in Jakarta, Indonesia (October 2013).

[126] See generally Department of City and Rural Planning of Peninsula Malaysia, 'Planning Guidelines for Temples, Gurdwaras, and Churches' (March 2011).

[127] A *surau* is a smaller version of a mosque. See generally Department of City and Rural Planning of Peninsula Malaysia, 'Planning Guidelines for Mosques and Suraus' (February 2011).

In practice, planning permissions for non-Muslim houses of worship have become increasingly difficult[128] and are 'carefully controlled' by state authorities.[129] In an interview, a government legal officer stressed that the building of houses of worship must take into account of the fact that Islam is the religion of the Federation[130] – a clear violation of the guarantees entrenched in article 3. Although controversial cases are not as prevalent as they have been in Indonesia, reports suggest that permit approvals are sometimes granted very slowly compared to permissions for mosques.[131] There have also been complaints that local policies and decisions have restricted and delayed the building of non-Muslim houses of worship with constant relocations and revocations of previously approved building plans.[132]

For instance, a fourteen-year delay in the erection of a Roman Catholic church in Shah Alam (where approximately 70 per cent of its residents are Muslims) fuelled allegations that state officials have deliberately delayed the construction of the church.[133] Unlike Indonesia, where a significant number of problems involve building permission, problematic cases in Malaysia actually involve the demolition of dispersed, unregistered Hindu temples and shrines in estates or land that are subsequently sold for development purposes.[134] In 2004, a letter addressed to the prime minister by a local political party claimed that one Hindu temple was being demolished every two to three weeks.[135] In some cases, the state governments have failed to relocate the temples, but there have been instances where they have provided alternative allocations of land and borne the costs of constructing new places of worship.[136] The courts have also successfully stepped in in several cases, preventing a developer in the state of Pahang from demolishing a Hindu

---

[128] Interview with a senior academic in Kuala Lumpur, Malaysia (5 August 2013).

[129] U.S. Department of State, 'International religious freedom report for 2003' (2003), online: www.state.gov/j/drl/rls/irf/2003/index.htm.

[130] Interview with an official at the Prime Minister's Department in Kuala Lumpur, Malaysia (July 2013).

[131] See U.S. Department of State, 'International religious freedom report from years 2003–2012', online: www.state.gov/j/drl/rls/irf/index.htm.

[132] See U.S. Department of State, 'International religious freedom report for 2004' (2004), online: www.state.gov/j/drl/rls/irf/2004/index.htm and Suara Rakyat Malaysia (SUARAM), *Malaysia: Human Rights Report 2005* (2006), p. 105.

[133] U.S. Department of State, 2006 Report; see also U.S. Department of State, 2008 Report (about the case of a church in Johor that was finally granted permission to build after a nineteen-year waiting period).

[134] Interview with a senior Hindu organization leader in Petaling Jaya, Malaysia (July 2013).

[135] Suara Rakyat Malaysia (SUARAM), *Malaysia: Human Rights Report 2004* (2005), p. 109.

[136] Interview with a senior Hindu leader in Petaling Jaya, Malaysia (July 2013). See also U.S. Department of State, 2008 Report.

temple on land bought by the developer and ruling, in another case in Kelantan, that the *Orang Asli* had the right to use their land for church services.[137]

In Sri Lanka, different circumstances were at play. The decades-long civil war affected state action against houses of worship. The consequences on religious freedom, in this respect, are different in nature and magnitude compared to Indonesia and Malaysia. For example, the U.S. State Department reports documented the bombing and shelling of Hindu temples and churches in the north of the country during the war.[138] These actions were not necessarily religiously motivated; instead, the destruction of houses of worship was a consequence of the ethnic conflict and war against Tamil-linked militant organizations.

Disputes on the construction of places of worship only began to surface in various reports within the last nine years.[139] In October 2008, the government issued a circular to neutrally regulate the construction of places of worship. The circular stipulates that the building of any new places of religious worship must obtain prior approval from the Ministry of Buddha Sasana and Religious Affairs. Although all religious groups are bound by the same set of regulations, authorities allegedly possess complete discretion in determining the strictness with which they treat the application process and in deciding whether to approve or reject permission.[140]

The result is arbitrary and indiscriminate enforcement, which has made the construction of houses of worship more difficult. While many Buddhist shrines have been constructed – ostensibly under government sponsorship – in predominantly Tamil areas, Christians (especially those belonging to 'non-traditional' or evangelical groups) are burdened by planning permissions that were not always forthcoming. Local authorities have also required churches to obtain the approval of a majority of residents.[141] A government official in charge of Muslim affairs revealed that the impossibility of building mosques

---

[137] See U.S. Department of State, 2007 Report and U.S. Department of State, 2010 Report.

[138] See U.S. Department of State Report, from years 2002–2005, online: www.state.gov/j/drl/rls/irf/index.htm

[139] U.S. Department of State, 2008 Report. Here, it was reported that authorities revoked the permission to construct a new church building in Kelaniya. This case was subsequently brought to the Appeals Court, which approved the church's appeal to proceed with the construction of the church. See also U.S. Department of State, 2010 Report.

[140] Christian Solidarity Worldwide, 'Universal periodic review – 14th session: CSW – Stakeholder submission – Sri Lanka', *Office of the United Nations High Commissioner for Human Rights* (April 2012), online: lib.ohchr.org/HRBodies/UPR/Documents/Session14/LK/CSW_UPR_LKA_S14_2012_ChristianSolidarityNetwork_E.pdf.

[141] U.S. Department of State, 2010 Report.

in multireligious areas are due to objections from local residents.[142] Although the government circular purportedly covers permission for the building of new houses of worship, in practice, it has also been used to question the legality of existing houses of worship. As a consequence, some churches and mosques have been demolished or closed down, although they have existed for decades.[143] The partial attitude of the state authorities toward Buddhism is further supported by claims that shrines or Hindu temples are displaced by Buddhist statues or demolished on the basis that they are built on Buddhist archaeological sites.[144] One source cites the case of a *kovil* located near Temple Trees (the official residence of the president) which had existed for over fifty years, but was later removed under pressure from the military.[145] In some cases, authorities would justify the forced closure of places of worship to protect public peace. For example, some mosques in Sri Lanka often operate as places to slaughter animals, a practice deemed offensive to Buddhists and thus inimical to public peace.[146]

Religious Minorities

In December 2011, mobs attacked the home and a local religious school belonging to Tajul Muluk, a local Shiite leader in Sampang, Madura. The attacks spread rapidly, eventually forcing the Shiites to evacuate their villages in Sampang. At the time of writing, hundreds of 'Sampang Shiites' continue to be internally displaced, living in temporary shelters in the town of Sidoarjo, East Java. In the wake of the incident, the MUI's branches in Sampang and East Java issued separate (but mutually reinforcing) *fatwas* declaring that the teachings of Tajul Muluk were deviant and blasphemous. Shortly after, Tajul was charged under Indonesia's Blasphemy Law and sentenced to two years

---

[142] Center for Policy Alternatives (CPA), 'Attacks on Places of Religious Worship in Post-War Sri Lanka', *Centre for Policy Alternatives* (March 2013), online: www.cpalanka.org/attacks-on-places-of-religious-worship-in-post-war-sri-lanka/, pp. 59–60.

[143] A recent example involved the Assemblies of God church in Kegalle District. Information provided by an NCEASL representative (24 July 2013). See also U.S. Department of State, 2010 Report (on the demolition of a church in Rajagiriya on the basis that it was 'an unauthorized structure', despite claims by the pastor that the church had been authorized and functioning since 1985).

[144] Interviews with various civil society representatives in Colombo and Trincomalee, Sri Lanka (May 2013). In Kurugala, for example, the government was involved in dismantling Sufi shrines because they sat on Buddhist archaeological sites.

[145] Interview with a lawyer and rights activist in Colombo, Sri Lanka (June 2013).

[146] CPA, 'Attacks on Places of Religious Worship', p. 60 (quoting an interview with a politician from Jathika Hela Urumaya).

in prison. The East Java governor then issued a regulation against deviant religious sects on the basis of maintaining public order.

This story is not unique. In February 2011, a similar incident occurred in Cikeusik (West Java), involving Ahmadiyah villagers. The deadly attack cost the lives of three Ahmadis, while others had to immediately leave the village after the attack. The issue of religiously charged societal conflict and violence will be dealt with in Chapter 4. What I intend to highlight here, however, is that the cases involving the Shiites in Sampang and Ahmadis in Cikeusik are not straightforward incidents of local sectarian conflict and violence. Rather, they often implicate various state actors, and the problems can be traced back to government policies targeting religious minorities, both at the local and national levels.

The Blasphemy Law, enacted through a presidential decree in 1965, prohibits a person from publicly advocating or seeking support for religious interpretation or activities that deviate from the core doctrines of a religion.[147] The decree inspired the promulgation of article 156a of the Indonesian Criminal Code, which criminalizes 'deliberate statements or acts in public that constitute animosity towards, misuse, or insult a religion adhered to in Indonesia, or which are intended to prevent others from adhering to any religion based on God'.[148] In 1984, the government formed the Bakor Pakem[149] to monitor religious or belief streams (*aliran kepercayaan*) organizations. These measures do not only target non-mainstream Muslim groups and individuals like Tajul Muluk; they also affect other minority religious movements. Until 2001, Jehovah's Witnesses were banned from practicing their faith. Similarly, Hare Krishna followers were banned in Bali due to strong opposition from the predominantly Hindu Balinese community. Blasphemy prosecutions, formerly uncommon, have grown rapidly since 1998. From 1998 to 2012, there were at least 100 convictions for insulting Islam and/or Christianity.[150]

Many non-mainstream Muslim groups continue to be targeted, but the most prominent cases involve the Ahmadiyah[151] and the Shiites. In fact, in

---

[147] Article 1, Law No. 1, Year 1965 on the Prevention from Abuse of and/or Desecration of Religion.

[148] Article 4, Law No. 1, Year 1965 on the Prevention from Abuse of and/or Desecration of Religion.

[149] Abbreviation for Badan Koordinasi Pengawasan Aliran Kepercayaan Masyarakat (Coordinating Body for Monitoring Communities' Streams of Belief).

[150] Melissa, *Law and Religion in Indonesia: Conflict and the Courts in West Java* (Abingdon, Oxon and New York: Routledge, 2014), pp. 144–8.

[151] The Ahmadiyah reportedly has approximately 500,000 followers throughout Indonesia. Interview with a spokesperson from Jemaat Ahmadiyah Indonesia (JAI) in Jakarta, Indonesia (June 2012).

2008 SETARA reported that if the persecution cases involving the Ahmadiyah were removed from statistics, Indonesia's religious freedom records would appear much more reasonable.[152] A Joint Ministerial Decision issued in 2008 prohibits the Ahmadis from conducting any activities and disseminating information relating to their beliefs.[153] The decision, however, did not enforce an outright ban on the Ahmadiyah. According to the then vice president, Jusuf Kalla, the Ahmadis are still allowed to conduct their worship and religious activities privately within their own community.[154]

Yet, more than twenty-six district and regional governments continue to impose either complete bans or some form of restriction on the Ahmadiyah. These include prohibitions on religious activities, and in some cases, these policies are followed by the closure of Ahmadiyah mosques.[155] For example, the Bogor and Cianjur regencies have banned the Ahmadiyah following mob attacks on the Ahmadis and their properties. In 2002, the Kuningan regency administrators ordered a ban on Ahmadiyah teachings and activities – a move that was not only endorsed by the Regent (*Bupati*) of Kuningan, but also the District People's Representative Council (Dewan Perwakilan Rakyat Daerah or DPRD), the MUI (Kuningan branch) and a host of local Muslim leaders.[156] To date, the central government has not overturned the localized bans. The rationale is that issues involving religious minorities are public order, as opposed to religious, issues and as such, these are matters solely under the jurisdiction of local governments. The consequences of these measures go beyond the inability to practice religion. Adherents of banned or unrecognized religions also face difficulties in registering marriages and births, as well as enrolling children in schools.

Similar trends have emerged in Malaysia in relation to Muslim minorities. The efforts of the government and state religious institutions to standardize

[152] SETARA Institute, *Berpihak dan Bertindak Intoleran: Laporan Kondisi Kebebasan Beragama/ Berkeyakinan di Indonesia 2008 (Siding and Acting Intolerantly: Report on the Freedom of Religion and Belief in Indonesia 2008)* (Jakarta: SETARA Institute, 2009), p. viii. 193 of the 265 reported cases of violations involved the Ahmadiyah. See ibid., p. 38.

[153] *Keputusan Bersama Menteri Agama, Jaksa Agung, dan Menteri Dalam Negeri Republik Indonesia* (Joint Decision of the Minister of Religion, the Attorney General, and the Home Minister of the Republic of Indonesia), No. 3 Year 2008, KEP-033/A/JA/6/2008, No. 199 Year 2008 (9 June 2008).

[154] 'Ahmadiyah can worship, Kalla says', *The Jakarta Post* (11 June 2008), online: www.thejakarta post.com/news/2008/06/11/ahmadiyah-can-worship-kalla-says.html.

[155] SETARA Institute, *Berpihak dan Bertindak*, p. 52. This happened to several mosques in Cianjur, West Java, in 2008.

[156] See Panggabean and Ali-Fauzi, *Pemolisian Konflik*, p. 31. The first order banning the Ahmadiyah activities was followed by a second order two years later, which added an order of surveillance against the Ahmadis. This was signed by the regent, the state attorney and the head of the Ministry of Religion (Kuningan branch). Ibid., p. 32.

and control Islamic practices and doctrines within the Muslim community are supported by various laws. There are laws that criminalize acts in contempt of lawful (religious) authority.[157] Put simply, Muslims may be prosecuted for contradicting a *fatwa* issued by a *mufti* or state or national *fatwa* councils, even though *fatwas* are merely legal opinions according to Islamic jurisprudence. The propagation of other Islamic doctrines among Muslims is also a criminal offence, as are unauthorized religious lectures.[158] As in Indonesia, there are laws outlawing any insults, ridicule or degradation of Islam. These offences fall within the broad framework of offences against the precepts of Islam, the regulation of which is mandated by article 121(1A) and Schedule 9, List II of the Federal Constitution.[159]

What all this means in practice is that doctrines outside the state-approved Sunni doctrine are virtually prohibited. Yet, the arrest of a former *mufti* in 2009 for giving an 'unauthorized' religious lecture at a private home is a potent reminder that even mainstream Sunnis are tightly controlled.[160] In 1996, the National *Fatwa* Council recommended the prohibition of doctrines other than Sunni Islam and endorsed the proposal to amend the Federal Constitution so that only Sunni Islam is recognized as the state religion. Since then, Shiites, Ahmadis and other 'deviant' groups have become easy targets for harassment by religious authorities. Methods of persecution vary – they include raids on mosques and community centres and prohibition on performing Friday prayers.[161] At least sixteen Shiites were detained between 1997 and 2000 under the draconian preventive detention law, the Internal Security Act 1960.[162] In December 2010, 200 Shiites (including children) were

---

[157] See, e.g., s. 12(c), Syariah Criminal Offences (Selangor) Enactment 1995. There are similar laws (for the most part, identically worded) in other states.

[158] See, e.g., ss. 5 and 11, Syariah Criminal Offences (Federal Territories) Act 1997. *Shariah* criminal laws only apply to Muslims.

[159] Both these provisions, as previously explained in Chapter 2, deal with the jurisdiction of the *Shariah* courts.

[160] This was the case of Dr. Mohd Asri Zainul Abidin, who was arrested and charged with the offence of conducting religious lecture without certification of authority under s. 119(1), Selangor Islamic Religious Administration Enactment 2003. It is noteworthy that Dr. Asri is known in some circles as a 'progressive' scholar, and he has, in the past, expressed different opinions from the National *Fatwa* Council on certain issues. See Suara Rakyat Malaysia (SUARAM), *Malaysia: Human Rights Report 2009* (2010), p. 119. Another noteworthy case is that of Fathul Bari Mat Jahaya, an *ustaz* who was arrested by religious authorities in Negeri Sembilan without *tauliah* (a form of accreditation or licence issued by the State *Tauliah* Committee).

[161] Interview with Ahmadiyah Muslim Congregation of Malaysia in Kuala Lumpur (July 2013)

[162] Mohd Faizal Musa, 'The Malaysian Shi'a: A Preliminary Study of Their History, Oppression, and Denied Rights' (2013) 6(4) *Journal of Shi'a Islamic Studies* 411, 438.

arrested by the Selangor Islamic Religious Department for attending a private religious gathering.[163] Two were subsequently charged for acting in contempt of religious authority, but they were acquitted on technical grounds.[164] In other cases, offenders were subjected to religious counselling and rehabilitation.[165] In all these, the government's responses were volatile at best and schizophrenic at worst. In March 2011, a minister stated that Shiites are free to practice, but not to propagate, their religion to others; two years later, another minister declared that Malaysian Shiites have no rights and that only Sunni Islam is recognized.[166]

For non-Muslim minorities, there are laws prohibiting them from propagating non-Islamic religions among Muslims. Pursuant to the constitutional provision allowing states to regulate propagation, at least ten state legislatures in Malaysia have enacted such laws.[167] An enactment in the state of Terengganu, for example, criminalizes the act of persuading or inciting a Muslim to change his or her faith, the use of words of Islamic origin and the public distribution of non-Islamic publications to Muslims.[168] There are identical provisions in other states such as in Kedah, Selangor and Johor, although the punishment for the offences varies across state lines. Proselytizing of non-Muslims, however, is not subject to any restrictions. On this point, Indonesia diverges from Malaysia. Proselytizing is regulated in Indonesia, but the 1979 Joint Ministerial Decision prohibits members of one religion from trying to convert members of other religions. Whether this is enforced equally among all religious groups is a separate question. The State Department reports have documented cases in which local and foreign individuals were arrested and charged for proselytizing Muslims.[169] However, apart from reports of proselytism charges against adherents of non-mainstream

---

[163] Ibid., p. 435. The next biggest crackdown on Shiites occurred in March 2014, where over 100 people were arrested in Perak at a religious celebration. See Syed Farid Alatas, 'Salafism and the persecution of Shi'ites in Malaysia', *Middle East Institute* (30 July 2014), online: www.mei.edu/content/map/salafism-and-persecution-shi'ites-malaysia.

[164] Musa, 'Malaysian Shi'a', p. 435.   [165] See U.S. Department of State, Reports 2004–2012.

[166] See U.S. Department of State, 2011 Report; and Musa, 'The Malaysian Shi'a', pp. 411–12.

[167] See Roger Tan, 'Religion and the law', *The Star* (12 January 2014), online: www.thestar.com .my/Opinion/Columnists/Legally-Speaking/Profile/Articles/2014/01/12/Religion-and-the-law/.

[168] See, e.g., ss. 4, 8, and 9, Control and Restriction of the Propagation of Non-Islamic Religions (Terengganu) Enactment 1980. See also ss. 5–7 of the Enactment and Schedules I and II for prohibited words and expressions.

[169] In 2005, for example, three women from the Christian Church of Camp David in Indramayu, West Java were jailed for attempting to convert Muslim children to Christianity through Sunday school programs. Similarly, in Madura, a foreign citizen and an Indonesian were sentenced to serve time in prison for engaging in proselytizing. See U.S. Department of State, 2005 Report, and U.S. Department of State, 2006 Report.

Muslim groups, there seems to be no indication that Muslims were charged for converting others into Islam.

In Malaysia, the limitation on non-Muslims' religious practice has resulted in the seizure of publications that purportedly offend Muslim sensitivities, including children's books with caricatures of Moses and Noah and Malay-language Bibles, and raids on premises of non-Muslims organizations, typically, for suspicion of proselytizing Muslims or for possessing prohibited publications.[170] The legal debacle over Christians' right to use the word 'Allah' as a reference to God is, to date, the high-water mark of restrictions against non-Muslims. It involved a government prohibition on the use of the word 'Allah' in the Roman Catholic Church's Malay language newsletter. The case raised important constitutional questions about the boundaries of religious freedom in the country, but it was also significant (and unfortunate) in other respects: it deepened the Muslim-Christian divide, reified the adverse consequences of the politicization of religion and reinforced perverse interpretations of the constitution in matters involving religion.

There are comparable trends in Sri Lanka, except that the issues – for the most part – implicate non-Buddhist minorities. To some extent, this is a product of historical discontents rooted in socio-economic and religious competition with the Christians. In recent years, similar discontents have been expressed against Muslims. This is not to say that only interreligious competition exists, while intrareligious tensions do not. Quite the contrary, the latter is a growing concern due to angsts against preachers of orthodox Buddhist doctrine, as well as foreign influences by Middle Eastern *Wahabbi* groups and American Evangelicals.[171] The Kapuwatta Mosque case, which involved the denial of a loudspeaker permit for a mosque in Weligama, is another significant example of an intrareligious dispute that made its way to the Supreme Court and raised broader questions on religious freedom. In some cases, the state has weighed in on these internal schisms by siding with particular groups but not others. According to an activist, for instance, the bulk of state-led religious persecution implicate Protestants (particularly the Evangelicals who are perceived as zealous proselytizers), whereas the Roman Catholic Church is not directly affected.[172]

To operate in the country, religious groups must be incorporated under the Societies and Trust Ordinance or be registered as companies under the Companies Act. Evangelical or 'non-traditional' churches, in particular,

---

[170] See U.S. Department of State Report, from years 2006–2012.
[171] See CPA, 'Attacks on Places of Religious Worship', pp. 33, 72.
[172] Interview with a Christian activist in Colombo, Sri Lanka (June 2013).

are affected by these regulations in ways that established Roman Catholic and Anglican churches are not. The former are often involved in religious propagation, as well as socio-economic activities such as employment training and drug rehabilitation, and they are treated with more suspicion than the established churches.[173] In fact, even the Catholic Church and other Protestant groups see the Evangelicals as a threat.[174] As such, the incorporation or registration of Evangelical churches has – at times – proven to be difficult. The three 'incorporation cases' discussed in Chapter 5 demonstrate this.

The perception of growing cases of 'unethical' conversions by Evangelical Christians and Muslims prompted the government and politicians to respond.[175] A bill proposed by the Ministry of the Buddha Sasana and Religious Affairs in 2004 attempted to prohibit conversions and criminalize activities to persuade or approach any person to convert to another religion. The JHU, a political party closely linked with and led by Buddhist monks, also proposed a similar bill in 2004.[176] These bills would have mirrored the laws in Malaysia that criminalize the propagation of other religions. However, both bills were framed and worded in a generic manner – they did not single out any particular religion for special protection; they were to be of general application, advanced, as it were, to protect the religious rights of all citizens. The Supreme Court nevertheless ruled the JHU Bill unconstitutional, although it noted that the criminalization of 'improper proselytism' is a permissible restriction under article 15(7) of the constitution.[177]

Although the Ministry's bill was eventually abandoned, it signalled the government's intention to restrict religious propagation and address the 'threats' posed by religious minorities.[178] The rationale was that the government needed to protect public order – an argument which has constitutional basis. This reasoning also explains why the police have interfered to prevent worship and prayer services at the hint of mob threats and public pressure. In the meantime, religious minorities have faced other forms of harassment.

---

[173] CPA, 'Attacks on Places of Religious Worship', p. 44.   [174] Ibid., p. 45.

[175] 'Unethical' conversions are conversions deemed to have been secured through fraud, use of material and socio-economic inducements, as well as inter-marriage.

[176] This was the Prohibition of Forcible Conversion of Religion Bill, introduced in Parliament as a Private Member's Bill. It is widely known as the 'JHU Bill'.

[177] The court held that the requirement to notify the divisional secretary of a person's conversion from one religion to another is inconsistent with the guarantee of freedom of thought, conscience and religion in article 10 of the constitution. See Jayampathy Wickramaratne, *Fundamental Rights in Sri Lanka*, 2nd ed. (Colombo: Stamford Lake Publication, 2006), pp. 204–5.

[178] Wickramaratne argues that the rise in unethical conversions in Sri Lanka is led by new Christian churches supported by foreign funding. Ibid.

A Buddhist who converted to Islam was arrested under the Prevention of Terrorism Act and detained without trial for thirty days for writing books about her conversion, which were deemed offensive to Buddhism.[179] Navy and army personnel have interrogated the staff of the National Christian Evangelical Alliance of Sri Lanka and searched its office.[180] Police officers, government officials and politically connected individuals have also reportedly been involved in incidents of violence against religious minorities.[181] In November 2009, police officers and politicians, including the minister of labour, accompanied a mob which destroyed furniture and fittings at the Church of the Foursquare Gospel in Kelaniya.[182] They also threatened the pastor against conducting services and continuing church construction works, even though the Court of Appeal has authorized the construction permission.[183]

Other Laws Regulating Religion

In Indonesia, the Aceh province is accorded special autonomy. One of the consequences of this is that it is the only province in Indonesia that has the explicit approval to implement Islamic laws, including in the commercial and criminal spheres. These are said to be largely accepted and well-practiced norms by local Acehnese, where Islam was historically instrumental in shaping the Acehnese identity,[184] but others have argued that the locals are divided on the implementation of Islamic laws. The regulation and implementation of Islamic law is supported by the establishment of religious institutions such as the Consultative Assembly of Ulama (Majelis Permusyawaratan Ulama) and the religious police.[185] In late 2013, the Aceh legislative council passed a revision on Islamic criminal law, which subjects all violators of offences under Islamic law (such as alcohol consumption, *khalwat* and failure to wear a headscarf for women) – regardless of their religious background – to *Shariah* jurisdiction.[186] To complicate matters further, many

---

[179] CPA, 'Attacks on Places of Religious Worship', p. 58.
[180] U.S. Department of State, 2009 Report.
[181] CPA, 'Attacks on Places of Religious Worship', p. 48.   [182] Ibid., p. 37.   [183] Ibid.
[184] Butt and Lindsey, *Constitution of Indonesia*, p. 182.
[185] Ibid., p. 183. According to the Indonesian Women's Coalition, there are at least forty-six *Shariah*-based laws in Indonesia which, among others, compel women to wear headscarves in public, prohibit alcohol consumption and gambling and require Muslims seeking marriage licenses to be able to read the Quran in Arabic. However, in some areas, such as in Padang, Sumatera and Bulukumba, South Sulawesi, these laws are not enforced and there are no sanctions for non-compliance. See U.S. Department of State Report, from years 2007–2008
[186] This means that both the Islamic criminal law applies to both Muslims and non-Muslims and that violators would be tried in *Shariah* courts. If a non-Muslim is guilty of an offence under

regional legislatures in Indonesia have passed local-level *Shariah* laws that affect the rights of Muslims in their observance of religious norms and duties.[187] There are also local governments that enforce *Shariah*-inspired ordinances that are not classified as *Shariah* laws.[188] Although the central government possesses sole authority over religious issues and these laws cannot, in theory, breach the guarantees entrenched in the constitution, they raise important human rights questions that have not yet been brought before the Supreme Court.[189] Moreover, the minister for home affairs denied suggestions that *Shariah* by-laws exist; instead, he argued that such laws are public order laws that are enacted to address social ills, and as such, these are rightly within the authority of local governments.[190]

In Malaysia, Islamic laws also apply to Muslims but only in personal and family matters, and in a limited sphere of criminal issues relating to Islamic practices and precepts. For instance, public consumption of alcohol, gambling and failure to perform Friday prayers are all punishable crimes. The effect of all these regulations is that Muslims do not have the freedom from religion, or at least from the practices of the religion as defined by state religious authorities. Like Aceh, some states in Malaysia also enforce guidelines on Muslim women's dress,[191] and state Islamic departments maintain an enforcement division that operates much like a religious police squad. Its powers are broad and often unchecked. It does not only police Muslim transgressions of religious laws and practices. In recent years, it has been involved in harassing non-Muslim organizations and premises to combat alleged proselytization activities and to seize religious publications that contain words that are deemed exclusive to Muslims under laws established to control and restrict propagation among Muslims.[192] The raids on the Damansara Utama Methodist

the Criminal Code, they could choose to be tried in a *Shariah* or a regular court. Hotli Simanjuntak and Ina Parlina, 'Aceh fully enforces Sharia', *The Jakarta Post* (7 February 2014), online: www.thejakartapost.com/news/2014/02/07/aceh-fully-enforces-Sharia.html.

[187] Butt and Lindsey, *Constitution of Indonesia*, p. 183.

[188] The Indonesian Women's Coalition reports that there are at least 100 such ordinances. See U.S. Department of State Report, from years 2009–2010.

[189] Ibid.

[190] See U.S. Department of State, 2008 Report. The State Department's 2011 report suggests that the Ministry of Home Affairs has revoked 351 such regulations.

[191] In 2002, 120 Muslim women in Kelantan were fined for violating the dress code. See U.S. Department of State, 2004 Report.

[192] See the Control and Restriction of the Propagation of Non-Islamic Religions (Terengganu) Enactment 1980 and similar laws in other states: Control and Restriction of the Propagation of Non-Islamic Religions (Kelantan) Enactment 1981; Control and Restriction (Propagation of Non-Islamic Religions among Muslims) (Negeri Sembilan) Enactment 1991; Control and Restriction of the Propagation of Non-Islamic Religions (Johore) Enactment 1991; Control and

Church and the Bible Society of Malaysia mentioned above illustrate the ever-expanding powers of religious authorities.[193] In addition to all this, state encroachment into religious practice is also manifested in the difficulties that non-Muslims have faced in obtaining allocation for cemeteries.[194]

UNDERSTANDING THE DOMINANT PATTERNS

The constitutions of Indonesia, Malaysia and Sri Lanka are very clear on religious freedom. Yet, as we have seen in the preceding section, state policies and practices have rendered the practice of religious freedom increasingly difficult, and state interference with religious life has been ever more common. What do these cases say about the relation of religion to the state? How might we understand these trends and patterns?

In some measure, there appears to be underlying suspicions of the 'other' (that is, the religious minorities) in the society, driven, perhaps, by inter- and intrareligious competition.[195] The fear against minorities has been built around the rhetoric that the spread of minority religious beliefs or influence could eventually displace the majority. In Sri Lanka, for instance, Sinhalese-Buddhist groups have accused Muslims – whose population is seen as rapidly growing – of changing the country's demography and Buddhist character. In Malaysia and Indonesia, claims of a larger 'Christianization' agenda or that the Shiites or Ahmadis are out to distort the fundamentals of (Sunni) Islam are increasingly common. The veracity of these assertions may well be subject to challenge, but more worrying is the fact that the state and/or state officials have, at times, been quick to foment and capitalize on these anxieties. For instance, the Malaysian Prime Minister, in a speech marking the *Eid-ul-Fitr* celebration, warned Malaysian Muslims about doctrines and beliefs that 'deviate' from the 'pure' Sunni school of thought;[196] in Sri Lanka, a

---

Restriction of the Propagation of Non-Islamic Religions (Kedah) Enactment 1988; Control and Restriction of the Propagation of Non-Islamic Religions to Muslims (Malacca) Enactment 1988; Non-Islamic Religions (Control of Propagations among Muslims) (Selangor) Enactment 1988; and Control and Restriction of the Propagation of Non-Islamic Religions (Pahang) Enactment 1989.

[193] In the case of the Bible Society of Malaysia, the raid was conducted by both religious enforcement authorities and the police.

[194] See, e.g., U.S. Department of State Report, from years 2003–2005.

[195] The next chapter provides more elaboration on this point.

[196] Dato' Seri Mohd Najib bin Tun Abdul Razak, 'Perutusan Hari Raya Aidiladha 1434h/2013m YAB Perdana Menteri' ('The prime minister's Aidilfitri message'), *NajibRazak.com* (7 August 2013), online: www.najibrazak.com/bm/official-addresses/perutusan-perdana-menteri-sempena-hari-raya-aidilfitri-2013/.

government minister cautioned against 'Muslim expansionism';[197] and in Indonesia, the West Java governor was scheduled to grace an anti-Syiah event in Bandung, although this was later cancelled and he sent one of his officials instead.

State policies and practices reflect or respond to the demands on the ground. In some of the localized bans enforced in Indonesia, for instance, the MUI and other conservative (and influential) religious organizations and leaders played their part in pressuring governments to adopt anti-minority policies. The broader local political dynamics, which will be explored in Chapter 7, is important in this respect. As a consequence, we see potent indications of state practices and policies that drift – whether deliberately or inadvertently – toward appeasing the religious sensitivities of the majority. Regulations that appear neutral on paper – in the sense that they do not explicitly seek to single out any particular religion for special treatment – are not always applied neutrally. All this is often presented as and laced with the protection of public order. Thus, with respect to restrictions on places of worship, authorities have argued that the existence and operation of minorities' houses of worship in an area dominated by another religious group would disturb peace and order amongst the local population. In Sri Lanka, some mosques often operate as places to slaughter animals, a practice deemed offensive to Buddhists and thus seen as a threat to public order.[198] Similarly, prohibitions on the religious practices or activities of Muslim and/or non-Muslim minorities – as most clearly illustrated by the 'Allah' case in Malaysia and the various regulations against the Ahmadis in Indonesia – were advanced on the pretext of maintaining peace. Even the obligation on Malaysian Muslims to conform only to state-approved interpretations of Islamic doctrine and practices is justified, ostensibly, to promote 'order' within the Muslim community.

The significance of these policies and practices on the collective psyche of the majority should not be underestimated. In Sri Lanka, state-supported construction of Buddhist temples, statues and shrines in areas with little or no Buddhist residents (often with military assistance) is seen by both the majority and minority communities as assertion of Sinhalese-Buddhist nationalism and control.[199] In Malaysia and Indonesia, the state's role in restricting the

---

[197] Secretariat for Muslims, *Violations of Muslim' Civil & Political Rights in Sri Lanka* (Report submitted to the UN Human Rights Committee, 9 September 2014), p. 59.

[198] CPA, 'Attacks on Places of Religious Worship', p. 60 (quoting an interview with a JHU (a party which is led by Buddhist monks and forms part of the government coalition) politician).

[199] Ibid., p. 29.

religious activities of non-Muslim and/or Muslim minorities has generated the belief that majority interests should always trump minority concerns. Over time, as we have seen, the state is expected to actively facilitate majority favouritism, dominance and power.

The story, however, is not always discouraging. In Indonesia, the FKUB – a state-supported initiative set up under the 2006 Regulations and supported by local governments – have played some role in mediating disputes on houses of worship. In Langkat, North Sumatera, and Solo, Central Java, the FKUB facilitated efforts to obtain permission for church constructions.[200] Other rights organizations, however, are more skeptical about the role of the FKUB, arguing that it can often legitimize restrictions on houses of worship.[201] Indeed, in some cases in West Java, the FKUB was seen as an obstacle to obtaining permits.[202] There are other positive indications: local courts in Indonesia and Sri Lanka have, from time to time, upheld the right of various religious groups to construct their places of worship. Apart from the Yasmin decision, the Bandung State Administrative Court has previously ruled in favour of two churches by overturning the local government's decision to revoke building permits.[203]

While anxieties over Evangelical Christian activities exist in Malaysia and might explain the severe delays that churches often face in obtaining construction permissions, these cannot adequately explain the actions against Hindu temples. Demolitions seem to have been driven more by development demands than religious enmity,[204] but relocations have become problematic due to refusals to relocate[205] or protests by residents in the relocation area. In 2009, there were stern objections to relocation of a Hindu temple in a predominantly Muslim neighbourhood in Shah Alam, although the relocation would have satisfied planning guidelines. Bowing to public pressure and protests by a small group of Malay-Muslims allegedly linked to a party from the ruling coalition, the opposition-led state government decided to relocate the temple away from the originally planned location.

In any case, the issues presented throughout this chapter raise questions about the role and effect of constitutional provisions on religion and religious

---

[200] U.S. Department of State, 2008 Report and U.S. Department of State, 2010 Report.
[201] SETARA Institute, *Tunduk Pada Penghakiman Massa: Laporan Kebebasan Beragama dan Berkeyakinan di Indonesia 2007 (Bowing to Public Pressure: Report on the Freedom of Religion and Belief in Indonesia 2007)* (Jakarta: SETARA Institute 2009), p. 24 and SETARA Institute, *Negara Harus Bersikap*, pp. 13–14.
[202] U.S. Department of State, 2008 Report.   [203] U.S. Department of State, 2010 Report.
[204] Interview with a senior leader of a Hindu organization in Petaling Jaya, Malaysia (July 2013).
[205] See, e.g., SUARAM, *Report 2009*, p. 123.

freedom. Constitutions can produce unintended, at times even perverse, consequences on religion and religious freedom. This is particularly obvious in cases where constitutional arrangements were invoked to legitimize restrictions on religious freedom, even though this may well contradict the spirit and intention underlying those arrangements. And, not only do we see varying degrees of religious freedom problems across all three countries, the impact of the arrangements on religion appear to be antithetical to what is conventionally *expected* of establishment or disestablishment models. Indonesia, a country without a constitutionally established religion, appears to regulate religion and to protect the dominant religion more extensively than a country that bears the constitutional obligation to protect and foster Buddhism. More ironically, in the country where the establishment of Islam was intended to have limited practical effect, there is an ever-increasing regulation of religion (sometimes premised on the need to protect the sanctity of Islam), often with adverse effects on the freedom of non-Muslims and Muslims alike. In Malaysia, state policies and practices increasingly seek to conform, whether implicitly or explicitly, to rigid religious doctrines defined by an exclusive group of religious bureaucrats whose opinions carry significant and/or symbolic weight in public life. The crucial takeaway is this: constitutions and their effects are unpredictable. But more importantly, these are all signs of evolving conceptions and interpretations of constitutional arrangements, sometimes, in surprising, even alarming ways.

4

Religious Freedom in Divided Societies
and the Role of the State

As the previous chapter demonstrates, Indonesia, Malaysia and Sri Lanka are conflicted on religious freedom – at least as far as state practices and policies are concerned. Despite the constitutional arrangements that were put in place to safeguard religious freedom, the situation on the ground paints a bleak picture of the standards of the rule of law and rights-protection. What is particularly alarming, as we have seen, is that the very provisions that were designed to protect religious freedom have been utilized in perverse ways to justify restrictions on rights.

The patterns of religious conflict and private (i.e., non-state) abuses of religious freedom present another complicated story. Of the three countries under study, Malaysia stands in a unique position vis-à-vis Indonesia and Sri Lanka. It is unique in the sense that the organized and aggressive mob-led violence that are prevalent in the latter two countries are extremely rare in Malaysia. Religious animosities and provocation, to be sure, are present and ever-increasing in Malaysia. There have also been episodes of religiously motivated attacks against individuals and places of worship, but the scale is unlike what has occurred in Indonesia and Sri Lanka.

This general observation appears to be consistent with the Pew Forum's Social Hostilities Index from 2008 to 2013, which measures acts of religious hostility by private individuals and organizations, including cases of mob violence, harassment and intimidation. In general, the Pew Forum reported 'very high' levels of social hostilities in Indonesia and Sri Lanka, as opposed to 'low' levels of social hostilities in Malaysia.[1] Much of this is evident through cases on houses of worship disputes and on other issues involving the freedom

---

[1] The Pew Research Center's Forum on Religion and Public Life has published a series of studies on the restrictions on religion. These studies measure both government restrictions on religion (Government Restrictions Index, GRI) and social hostilities on religion (Social

to practice and express one's religion. In Indonesia and Sri Lanka, objections against the building of churches, for example, have sometimes resulted in violent conflict and arson attacks. Such incidents are relatively uncommon by comparison in Malaysia. Another striking example is the persecution of non-mainstream Muslims. In Malaysia, there is hostile propaganda against the Shiites and Ahmadis, but intolerance has yet to grow into violence. By contrast, there are widely reported cases of violent (and deadly) attacks against Ahmadis and Shiites in several Indonesian provinces.

This raises two questions. First, why the variation across the three countries? Second, what do these cases tell us about the protection and enforcement of constitutional guarantees of religious freedom? It is beyond the scope of this book to provide a comprehensive explanation of the history, roots, causes and consequences of religious conflict and intolerance in the three countries. These issues warrant a comprehensive study in their own right. My aim in this chapter is more modest: it is to shed some light on the complexities in protecting religious freedom in the three countries and to reinforce our understanding on how perverse conceptions of law and constitutional arrangements may drive societal intolerance. This can be evaluated by examining the role of hard-line or intolerant organizations, executive action (or inaction, as the case might be) against manifestations of religious intolerance and local political dynamics. In doing so, I shall highlight what Horowitz calls – in his study of Indonesia – the 'rule of law deficit'.[2]

THE ROLE AND INFLUENCE OF HARD-LINE ORGANIZATIONS

The existence of religious conflict and its adverse effects on the freedom of religious practice and expression is not a new phenomenon in Indonesia. During the transition to democracy in the late 1990s and early 2000s, Indonesia experienced some of the deadliest religious conflicts in its modern history. The animosities were laid raw and bare: in conflicts that plagued the Maluku and Sulawesi islands, for example, rival Muslim and Christian extremist groups openly encouraged their followers to attack persons of other faiths.[3] In 1998, a provocative speech, allegedly made by a Christian politician

---

Hostilities Index, SHI). A complete set of the reports can be found here: www.pewforum.org/category/publications/restrictions-on-religion/.

[2] Donald Horowitz, *Constitutional Change and Democracy in Indonesia* (Cambridge: Cambridge University Press, 2013), pp. 233–46.

[3] See U.S. Department of State, 'International religious freedom report for 2001' (December 2001), online: www.state.gov/documents/organization/9001.pdf. The speech was attributed to Theo Syafei, who confessed to making the speech (which was recorded and distributed)

from the PDI-P (Partai Demokrasi Indonesia-Perjuangan), was said to have sparked an anti-Muslim riot in Kupang, East Nusa Tenggara. Although the violence and death toll eventually subsided, killings and attacks on houses of worship continued to occur for several years.[4]

The role of private actors was significant in these conflicts as well as much of the recent religiously motivated violence. There are several organized movements involved in coordinating attacks against minorities, 'policing' vice and immoral activities especially during the month of *Ramadhan* (this is colloquially known as 'sweeping') and enforcing their ideas of vigilante justice. Some of them actually began to mushroom during the post-Soeharto era. These groups include Front Pembela Islam (Islamic Defenders' Front, or FPI), Laskar Jihad (which has been disbanded since October 2002), Gerakan Reformis Islam (Islamic Reformist Movement, or GARIS) and Forum Umat Islam (FUI). They were formed for a variety of objectives and reasons, including to combat 'immoral' activities; to counter 'Christianization' and apostasy; to mobilize against communist-influenced movements; and to defend the sanctity of Islam.[5] The FPI is perhaps the most notorious of these hard-line organizations. Established in 1998, the FPI has its roots in the civilian security unit (*Pamswakarsa*) established by state security forces to help control public disorder and combat pro-democracy protests in the aftermath of Soeharto's fall.[6] They were endorsed and supported by influential military and police elites such as General Wiranto and the former Jakarta police chief.

To be sure, these hardliners comprise a miniscule percentage of Indonesian Muslims. However, their public presence is increasingly visible (especially through their massive public rallies in the streets of towns and cities in

---

but denied that he made the speech in Kupang in 1998. See Jan Sihar Aritonang and Karel Steenbrink, *A History of Christianity in Indonesia* (Leiden: Brill, 2008), p. 222.

4 See U.S. Department of State Report, from years 2003–2006, online: www.state.gov/j/drl/rls/irf/index.htm.

5 See Ismail Hasani and Bonar Tigor Naipospos, *The Faces of Islam 'Defenders'* (Jakarta: Pustaka Masyarakat Setara, 2010). In an interview, a representative of the Association of Indonesian Churches (Persekutuan Gereja Indonesia, or PGI) admitted that there are foreign-funded Evangelical organizations that engage in aggressive proselytizing. However, the PGI does not condone such activities due to its potential for disrupting interreligious harmony in the country. Interview with a senior leader of the PGI in Jakarta, Indonesia (October 2012).

6 Robert W. Hefner, 'Muslim Democrats and Islamist Violence in Post-Soeharto Indonesia' in Robert W. Hefner (ed.), *Remaking Muslim Politics: Pluralism, Contestation, and Democratization* (Princeton: Princeton University Press, 2004), pp. 273, 285. Hefner's article provides a concise but insightful account of the history of the three largest Islamist paramilitaries in Indonesia – the FPI, Laskar Jihad and Laskar Mujahidin. For a detailed study of hard-line Muslim organizations in Indonesia, see Hasani and Naipospos, *The Faces of Islam 'Defenders'*.

Indonesia); their ability to rally the masses is unmistakable; and they are vociferous in exploiting religious tensions. They are emboldened, in some cases, by support from local religious leaders (*ulama*) as well as the lack of decisive police action in cases of violence. What is equally interesting is that in many of the cases of mob violence, the individuals and perpetrators of violence were not from the localities themselves; rather, reports suggest that they were mobilized from other districts. In a deadly anti-Ahmadiyah incident in 2011, an influential local *ulama* reportedly sought the support of FPI members from a neighbouring district to facilitate the dissolution of the Ahmadiyah in Cikeusik.[7]

As in Indonesia, Sri Lanka has been plagued by its own history of communal violence. The civil war that lasted for over three decades was largely ethnic-oriented, pitting the Sinhalese against the Tamils, but the acts of violence nevertheless impaired the ability of people to practice their religion. The Tamil Tigers – considered a terrorist organization by the Sri Lankan government – were implicated in many deadly attacks on places of worship, most notably the Temple of the Tooth in Kandy,[8] which is considered the holiest Buddhist shrine in the country. There were also many cases of religious violence perpetrated by Buddhist mobs and monks, most of which were aimed at Christian organizations and churches.[9] A great majority of these cases appear to be motivated by discontents over proselytism and conversions, along with the perception that Muslims and Christians pose an existential threat to the Sinhalese-Buddhists in their own homeland. As I have explained in preceding chapters, these grievances were not new; rather, they had existed even before independence and remained in the background until the end of the war.[10]

The Sri Lankan equivalents to the hard-line groups in Indonesia are the Bodu Bala Sena (Buddhist Power Force, or BBS), Sinhala Ravaya and Ravana

---

[7] Rizal Panggabean and Ihsan Ali-Fauzi, *Pemolisian Konflik Keagamaan di Indonesia* (*Policing Religious Conflict in Indonesia*) (Jakarta: PUSAD Paramadina, 2014), p. 69.

[8] See U.S. Department of State, 'International religious freedom report for 2003' (2003), online: www.state.gov/j/drl/rls/irf/2003/index.htm.

[9] Although many cases implicate the Buddhist majority, there was one case in 2003 in which Hindu mobs attacked a church in Kaluvenkerni and set Christian homes ablaze. See U.S. Department of State Report, from years 2003–2008, online: www.state.gov/j/drl/rls/irf/index.htm.

[10] The Sinhala-Muslim riots in 1915 perhaps remain the deadliest conflict with minority Muslims in Sri Lankan history. These were largely driven by economic interests and considerations of the Sinhalese but, as Dewasiri noted, they became important in framing subsequent Sinhalese-Buddhist versus Muslim grievances. See Nirmal Ranjith Dewasiri, *New Buddhist Extremism and the Challenges to Ethno-Religious Coexistence in Sri Lanka* (Colombo: International Centre for Ethnic Studies, November 2016), pp. 7–8.

Balaya. These groups present themselves as the defenders of Sinhalese-Buddhist interests. These are new organizations that have only emerged in post-war Sri Lanka, but they have been widely implicated in recent religious conflicts in the country. Among the three, the BBS was first to be established in 2012. Its *raison d'etre* is to protect the Sinhalese-Buddhists, who it sees as a small (and vulnerable) global minority. Whereas similar groups in Indonesia are not necessarily led by the clergy, hard-line organizations like the BBS are predominantly led by and composed of Buddhist monks, some of whom are active political party members.[11]

Organizations like the BBS have a unique ability to rally the masses and pit Sinhalese-Buddhists against other ethnic and religious groups by turning seemingly normal societal disputes into religious conflict. In the Aluthgama incident in 2014, what was initially a traffic altercation involving Muslim youths and a Buddhist monk later morphed into a deadly anti-Muslim riot (with victims from both the Sinhalese and Muslim communities) after a provocative speech by a BBS leader.[12] In the context of Sri Lankan society, confronting and countering violence by the BBS monks triggers conflicting emotions and responses. This is because monks are, in general, venerated figures in the society. Yet, the lack of clear state disapproval of their violent acts bolsters these hard-line organizations, as is the case in Indonesia. Their modus operandi and activities also bear much resemblance to their Indonesian counterparts – they engage in attacks against practices and establishments perceived to be insulting to Buddhism (such as hotels with 'Buddha Bars') and mobilize the masses against 'Christianization' and 'Islamization' in the country.

In Malaysia, groups like Perkasa and ISMA (Malaysian Muslim Solidarity) are advocates of Malay-Muslim supremacy and self-styled defenders of Islam and the Malays. These are also relatively new organizations. In a story similar to that of Indonesia, these movements have become increasingly vocal and visible as the democratic space opened up in the years following

---

[11] This is not to say that all Buddhist monks in the country are part of or support these groups. In fact, the mainstream Buddhist clergy has distanced itself from the BBS. The CEO of the BBS, however, is a layperson who had previously served in the government. See Eric Ellis, 'The monks' army', *The Global Mail* (undated), online: tgm-archive.github.io/sri-lanka/monks-army .html. Sources also suggested that the monks who are involved in these organizations are often from the younger cohort of radicalized monks, some of whom possess criminal records for offences such as drunk driving. Interview with various civil society and political actors in Colombo, Sri Lanka (June 2013). See Dewasiri, *New Buddhist Extremism*, p. 24.

[12] Tim Hume, '"Fascists" in saffron robes? The rise of Sri Lanka's Buddhist ultra-nationalists', *CNN* (18 July 2014), online: edition.cnn.com/2014/07/17/world/asia/sri-lanka-bodu-bala-sena-profile/.

Mahathir's resignation. The rhetoric and objectives of these groups are comparable to those of the ethno-nationalist organizations in Sri Lanka. Take ISMA as an example. It began as a student movement in 1997 and was later consolidated in its current form in 2005. ISMA declares itself as a Malay nationalist organization guided by the principles of Islam. What drives its existence and function is the emotional, historical attachment to Islam's 'glorious' past in the Malay homeland and the desire to revive and relive that past. As a result, its outlook is decidedly anti-Western, and it adopts an antagonistic attitude toward those outside the Malay-Muslim fold (or those it identifies as 'liberal' Malay-Muslims). Among other socio-economic and welfare-oriented objectives, ISMA aims to protect Islam as the country's constitutional identity and sees itself as a unifying force for the Malay-Muslims, particularly against challenges posed by the 'chauvinist Chinese' and 'evangelical Christians'.[13] To promote its cause, it relies – as do like-minded organizations in Sri Lanka and Indonesia – on a kind of discourse that paints minorities as opportunists who are out to confuse, weaken and displace the majority.[14] At the same time, ISMA also identifies itself as a dynamic, moderate and progressive organization.

Despite their hostility and provocative rhetoric against minorities – which are by and large disseminated through social media and public discussions – these groups have not been reported to engage in the kind of violence that similar groups in Indonesia and Sri Lanka perpetrate. In fact, the May 1969 riots remains the deadliest occasion of ethnic violence in post-independence Malaysia – since then, religiously or ethnically motivated communal violence has been almost non-existent.[15] It is also important to emphasize that the organized, hard-line groups in Indonesia and Sri Lanka are not the sole instigators of mob violence. In some cases, local residents have also been involved in leading attacks against minorities and places of worship. In any case, although the minorities in these three countries are and will always be

[13] Ikatan Muslimin Malaysia (ISMA), *Buku Pengenalan Ikatan Muslimin Malaysia* (*Introductory Book of the Malaysian Muslim Solidarity*), online: isma.org.my/v2/buku-pengenalan/
[14] Groups like the BBS, in their rallies, have spread allegations that food at Muslim-owned restaurants were spat into before being served to Buddhist customers; that undergarments sold at Muslim-owned stores have been infused with chemicals to make Buddhist women infertile; and that Muslim doctors are secretly sterilizing Buddhist women. Some of these allegations, unfortunately, do gain currency on the ground. Interview with a civil society organization representative in Colombo, Sri Lanka (June 2013).
[15] Another notable case is the Kampung Medan riots in 2001, which claimed six lives. The incident was triggered by a dispute between Malay and Indian residents relating to concurrent events in the village – a Malay (Muslim) family held a wedding event, and at the same time, a wake was being held by the Indian (Hindu) family.

the prime targets, those within the majority group (Muslim or Buddhist, as the case may be) who do not share their views or struggles are also regarded as 'traitors' and thus susceptible to intimidation and harassment.[16]

MANIFESTATIONS OF INTOLERANCE AND VIGILANTE JUSTICE

As we have seen, majority-minority disputes over building of houses of worship are a recurring problem. Building plans proposed by the minorities are sometimes treated with great suspicion amongst the majority community. In a case in Ende (East Nusa Tenggara), for instance, the apprehensiveness of local residents about the existence of a mosque necessitated a series of compromises between minority Muslims and majority Catholics. Among other things, Muslims agreed to refrain from building a dome and using loudspeakers.[17] Although the Ende case did not result in violence (Catholic residents in the area responded, instead, by putting on loud music during the call for prayers), it illustrates deep societal tensions in what some might regard as routine exercises of religious freedom. Competing visions of religious freedom are thus obvious in cases like these. For adherents of the majority religion in a particular area, the presence and activities of other religions (especially those known as evangelizing religions like Islam or Christianity) may sometimes be perceived as a threat to their freedom *from* the influence of other religious beliefs. For the minorities, however, the establishment of a place of worship is simply viewed as a fundamental right to practice and manifest their religion. These tensions, however, should not be taken lightly. Indeed, disputes over the legality of houses of worship or religious gatherings have been one of the main triggers for serious conflict in both Indonesia and Sri Lanka.

Hard-line groups like the FPI have led protests against allegedly illegal churches, arguing that they are simply enforcing the 2006 Ministerial Regulation that regulates the construction and expansion of houses of worship. In a similar vein, local Catholic leaders in Ende objected to the mosque on the basis that the Muslims have not strictly complied with the requirements

---

[16] For example, in Indonesia, there was an attempted mail-bomb attack on a prominent Muslim activist, Ulil Abshar Abdalla, who is widely known for the support for liberalism and pluralism. In Malaysia, a civil society activist associated with Sisters in Islam was at the centre of ISMA's smear campaign. She was listed as one of the masterminds behind the Coalition of Malaysian NGOs' report to the UN in the recent Universal Periodic Review, which was deemed an insult to Islam.

[17] Panggabean and Ali-Fauzi, *Pemolisian Konflik*, pp. 276–7.

of the Regulation.[18] Nonetheless, when hard-line organizations are implicated, there is greater propensity for protests and harassment to turn violent.
In some cases, attacks were driven by objections against Christians' use of
private homes, shop houses or public spaces for worship services. The attacks
sometimes go beyond harassment, intimidation and destruction of property. In
2010, for example, an FPI-led attack led to the violent assault on a pastor and a
congregation member from the Pondok Timur Batak Protestant Church.[19]

Similar trends exist in Sri Lanka. For many years, harassment, death threats
and physical assaults by mobs have affected the ability of churches to hold
worship services, but in extreme cases, the attacks have led to deaths.[20] From
2009 to 2012, there were at least 138 recorded attacks against Christians and
churches around the country,[21] while in 2013 and 2014 alone there were a total
of 157 anti-Christian attacks.[22] In the past four years, however, animosities
against Muslims have increased considerably, prompting the UN High Commissioner for Human Rights to highlight the 'significant surge in attacks
against religious minorities' by extreme Sinhalese-Buddhist nationalists and
Buddhist monks.[23] There were in fact very few violent incidents between
Buddhists and Muslims from 2003 to 2011.[24] Some observers posit that the
Dambulla incident in 2012 – where Buddhist monks attacked a mosque on the

[18] Recall – from the explanation in Chapter 3 – that the decree stipulates, among others, the
requirement that a building proposal must be endorsed by local residents. Panggabean and
Ali-Fauzi suggest that the decree has not facilitated the building of house of worship. Instead,
its rigid requirements have actually worked to amplify animosities between different religious
groups, when previously construction approvals could be achieved by informal negotiations
and consensus among local leaders. Ibid., p. 280.

[19] U.S. Department of State, 'July-December, 2010 International Religious Freedom Report'
(2011), online: www.state.gov/j/drl/rls/irf/2010_5/. The attackers were later sentenced to prison
terms ranging from five to seven months for their roles in the assault.

[20] Ibid. (The case of Jeevana Diya Church in Kurunegala District.)

[21] Data obtained from the National Christian Evangelical Alliance of Sri Lanka (NCEASL), via
email conversation (July 2013).

[22] Gehan Gunatilleke, *The Chronic and the Acute: Post-War Religious Violence in Sri Lanka*
(Colombo: ICES and Equitas, 2015), p. 25. The author utilizes data obtained from the
NCEASL.

[23] Oral Update of the High Commissioner for Human Rights on Promoting Reconciliation and
Accountability in Sri Lanka; A/HRC/24/CRP.3/Rev.1 (25 September 2013).

[24] See U.S. Department of State Reports, from years 2003 to 2011, online: www.state.gov/j/drl/rls/
irf/index.htm. Cf a report from the Center for Policy Alternatives in Sri Lanka on an attack on
a 300-year-old Muslim shrine in Anuradhapura in September 2011. The attack was perpetrated
by a mob led by Buddhist monks on the basis that Muslims were planning to turn the
shrine into a mosque and that the shrine sat on a land bestowed on the Sinhalese-Buddhists
centuries ago. The police claimed that they did not receive any complaints about the incident
and were not at the scene, despite photographic evidence to the contrary. See Center for Policy
Alternatives, 'Attacks on Places of Religious Worship in Post-War Sri Lanka', *Centre for Policy*

basis that it was an illegal building on sacred Buddhist land[25] – was the starting point for the post-war anti-Muslim movement. Since then, there has been a spate of attacks against mosques and hate campaigns targeting Muslim businesses and socio-religious practices.[26] The hate campaigns have focused, among others, on banning Muslim dietary practices (the anti-*Halal* movement) and religious garb (the *hijab*). In 2013, the BBS attacked the Sri Lanka Law College, alleging that exam results were manipulated in favour of Muslim students.[27] Some of the attacks were also motivated by allegations that churches and mosques were operating illegally without prior registration with the government, although there is no legal requirement to register new or existing houses of worship.[28]

The sense by hard-line groups that they were merely 'enforcing' law and order is also visible in hate campaigns and sectarian violence against non-mainstream Muslims in Indonesia. The Indonesian case is distinctive in this respect: various studies have established a connection between sectarian violence and the issuance of *fatwas* declaring certain minority Muslims as 'deviant'.[29] The persecution of the Ahmadis in Manis Lor, Kuningan is an instructive case. Not only did the local MUI declare the Ahmadiyah as 'deviant', it also recommended the local government to seize assets belonging to the Ahmadis.[30] All this, along with several years of state and society-led harassment, culminated in the 2007 anti-Ahmadiyah violence. Various organizations, rallying under a single movement called the Gabungan Umat Islam Indonesia (Coalition of Indonesian Muslims, or GUII), mobilized hundreds of individuals to attack an Ahmadiyah mosque and houses belonging to the Ahmadis.[31] As in a similar episode of violence in Tasikmalaya just months earlier, the mobs carried out the attacks undeterred by police presence.[32]

Alternatives (March 2013), pp. 59–60, online: www.cpalanka.org/attacks-on-places-of-religious-worship-in-post-war-sri-lanka/.

[25] U.S. Department of State, 2012 Report.

[26] See CPA, 'Attacks on Places of Religious Worship', pp. 51–2. See Gunatilleke, *The Chronic and the Acute*, pp. 21–4.

[27] Farzana Haniffa et al., *Where Have All the Neighbours Gone? Aluthgama Riots and Its Aftermath: A Fact Finding Mission to Aluthgama, Dharga Town, Valipanna and Beruwela* (Colombo: Law and Society Trust, 2014), p. 10.

[28] CPA, 'Attacks on Places of Religious Worship', p. 59.

[29] See Luthfi Assyaukanie, 'Fatwa and Violence in Indonesia' (2009) 11 *Journal of Religion and Society* 1 and Panggabean and Ali-Fauzi, *Pemolisian Konflik*.

[30] Panggabean and Ali-Fauzi, *Pemolisian Konflik*, p. 51.   [31] Ibid., p. 34.

[32] Not all cases of violence implicate the organized hard-line movements. In some cases, individuals or local residents were responsible for attacks against Ahmadiyah mosques. For example, in August 2008, members of the Ciputat Muslim Community Forum sealed a mosque on the grounds that the Ahmadis have breached the decree prohibiting them from

The Monas incident in June 2008 was also, perhaps, one of the most significant cases of violence led by hard-line organizations. Various Muslim and
non-Muslim intellectuals, activists and DPR members who had grouped
themselves as the National Alliance for the Freedom of Faith and Religion
(Aliansi Kebangsaan untuk Kebebasan Beragama dan Berkeyakinan, or
AKKBB), organized a protest rally against the 2008 Joint Ministerial
Decision against the Ahmadiyah.[33] They were swiftly met by the hardliners
even before the rally began, who then proceeded to attack rally-goers indis-
criminately, including women and children.[34]

Intrareligious tensions are not alien to Sri Lanka, although there may well
be a difference in the scale and nature of such conflicts as compared to
Indonesia and Malaysia. For one, there are no overt state-sponsored restrictions against non-mainstream religious groups. There are several reported
cases of violent intra-Buddhist conflicts, but these were largely acts of harassment and intimidation; none of these cases resulted in deaths or large-scale
property destruction.[35] In 2007, Sunnis and Ahmadis in Negombo clashed
over the latter's right to hold prayers at a local mosque and over allegations that
an Ahmadi was killed by a local Sunni group. In these incidents, the police
provided protection to the Ahmadis but did not take action on the murder
allegations.[36] There are also intrareligious tensions among the Christians,
that is, between the traditional and evangelical churches. In November 2011,
Cardinal Malcolm Ranjith, who heads the Catholic Church, called on the
government to control the spread of 'American fundamentalist churches'
who have allegedly converted Buddhists and Catholics through material
inducements.[37]

In Malaysia, interreligious relationships were generally regarded as 'amic-
able' for many years.[38] However, Malay-Muslims who renounce their faith
and convert to other religions face difficulties in practicing and expressing
their new religion openly. There is a great degree of social stigma against
them. Some have faced death threats,[39] but there has been no report of violent
conduct toward them. Muslim organizations, motivated by a strong sense of
exclusivity, also do not generally participate in interfaith bodies formed among

---

proselytizing activities and in Sukabumi (West Java) local residents vandalized two Ahmadiyah
mosques. See U.S. Department of State, 2009 Report.

[33] See Chapter 3.   [34] Hasani and Naipospos, *The Faces of Islam 'Defenders'*, pp. 141–2.

[35] Dewasiri, *New Buddhist Extremism*, pp. 18–19.

[36] U.S. Department of State, 2007 Report.   [37] U.S. Department of State, 2011 Report.

[38] U.S. Department of State, Report from years 2003–2006.

[39] Jane Perlez, 'Once Muslim, now Christian and caught in the courts', *The New York Times*
(24 August 2006), online: www.nytimes.com/2006/08/24/world/asia/24malaysia.html?_r=0.

other non-Muslim organizations and they have strongly rejected proposals for a national interreligious council in 2004. The establishment of the council was seen as a move that would put Islam on par with other religions – this situation, for them, betrays the special position of Islam as the religion of the Federation. Moreover, the view that Islamic matters should remain exclusively within the purview of Muslims and should not be discussed with other faiths is pervasive. As a result, there is little tolerance within certain sections of the society for religious expression or opinion that does not conform to their views. Perkasa and several Muslim NGOs, for example, have filed police reports against newspapers or individuals who espouse views that they deemed an insult to Islam.[40]

In 2010, religious violence began to rear its head. This was triggered, in part, by a High Court ruling allowing a Catholic publication to use the word 'Allah' in its Malay-language newspaper. In just over a week following the decision, several places of worship, including churches, a Sikh temple and mosques were attacked and desecrated.[41] A church in a suburb of Kuala Lumpur sustained the worst damage from an arson attack.[42] None of these incidents were mob-led but that such attacks are rare in Malaysia prompted immediate condemnation from government, political parties, religious leaders and civil society organizations. In another prominent case, fifty Muslim residents in Shah Alam placed a cow's head at the gates of the state government's office and stepped on it as a mark of protest against the decision to relocate a Hindu temple to their neighbourhood.[43] Although this case is more aptly classified as an insult to a religious belief than a violation of religious freedom, it highlights intolerant undercurrents within the society which can, over time, evolve into more serious conflicts.

What these cases demonstrate is that religious tensions tend to take a physical form when majority sensitivities are offended. The presence of non-Muslim houses of worship in a predominantly Malay-Muslim area is not always objected to because of fears of proselytism and conversion. The Hindu

---

[40] U.S. Department of State, 2010 Report. In 2010, Muslim NGOs filed a complaint against a former mufti for an article entitled 'The Challenge of the Reformist Movement', which allegedly insulted Islam.

[41] Ibid.

[42] Seth Mydans, 'Churches attacked in Malaysian "Allah" dispute', *The New York Times* (8 January 2010), online: www.nytimes.com/2010/01/09/world/asia/09malaysia.html.

[43] U.S. Department of State, 2010 Report. There was also a case where a group of Muslim demonstrators demanded a church to remove a cross outside its building. See '50 stage protest against cross on new church', *The Star* (20 April 2015), online: www.thestar.com.my/news/nation/2015/04/20/50-stage-protest-against-cross-on-new-church/.

temple case, for instance, was triggered because the very existence of temples in a particular area (where Muslims are the majority) is deemed offensive to Muslim sensitivities.[44] In the wake of the attacks on the Metro Tabernacle Church, a representative of the Muslim Lawyers Association also seized the opportunity to remind the public that the attack proved that the use of the word 'Allah' among non-Muslims was a sensitive issue for the Muslim community.[45] What he failed to mention, however, is that the rejection of the use of 'Allah' by non-Muslims is not a view that is shared by all Muslims in the country.

VIOLENCE, OMISSION AND IMPUNITY

How have states responded to the various manifestations of religious intolerance and incidents of religious violence? If the previous chapters documented the ways in which the state persecutes religious groups and restricts religious freedom through its policies and practices, here I shall highlight the problem of state *inaction* and complicity with intolerant forces, and how, in turn, these affect the extent to which constitutional rights (to religious freedom) can be enforced and practiced. There are several issues that must be considered at the outset to contextualize the situation in all three countries.

The first concerns the nuances in state responses against religious persecution and religious violence. There are three striking patterns. On one end of the spectrum, the state actively facilitates societal persecution and violence, particularly through its officials and security apparatus. On the other end, it displays willingness and/or ability to anticipate conflict and intervene against it, followed by a full course of investigation and prosecution of the perpetrators. In between these two extremes is a 'hands-off' approach, in the sense that it takes the position of a 'bystander': it does nothing to prevent or halt acts of harassment and violence.

---

[44] See Andrew Willford, 'The Letter of the Law and the Reckoning of Justice among Tamils in Malaysia' in Yew-Foong Hui (ed.), *Encountering Islam: The Politics of Religious Identities in Southeast Asia* (Singapore: Institute of Southeast Asian Studies, 2012), pp. 133, 137.

[45] 'Leaders of Metro Tabernacle Church forgive attackers', *The Star* (9 January 2010), online: www.thestar.com.my/story.aspx/?file=%2f2010%2f1%2f9%2fnation%2f5441174. A similar issue surfaced in Sri Lanka in 2013, where a group of Buddhist monks associated with the BBS stormed a hotel in Beruwala for organizing a Nirvana-themed dinner event for tourists. The BBS CEO objected to the event for the inappropriate use of words associated with Buddhism to describe a dinner party. Two of the hotel's managers were subsequently arrested and charged for 'hurting religious feelings'. See 'Hotel managers arrested over "Nirvana style" dinner event', *The Sunday Times* (27 January 2013), online: www.sundaytimes.lk/130127/news/hotel-managers-arrested-over-nirvana-style-dinner-event-30406.html.

The second issue involves local religious personalities, whose role and influence add another dimension to religious conflict and contestation. In countries like Indonesia, Malaysia and Sri Lanka, religious figures are generally revered. In some provinces, districts or localities, they are the point of reference for local religious, social and political matters. The authority of these figures often goes unquestioned; in fact, to challenge such authority would be considered an affront to the society's values and order. The role of such personalities is so significant that in some cases they may make or break religious tensions and conflict. Consider the province of East Java, home to one of the most serious sectarian conflict involving minority Shiites (the Sampang Shiites). The prominence of religious leaders is unmistakable – not only do they weigh in on religious doctrines (chiefly, by warning against the 'threat' and deviance of non-mainstream groups) and advise the local government on how to deal with such groups, they also determine who locals should vote for in elections. These determinations are, by and large, heeded by the local population.[46]

Lackadaisical Executive?

A state's omission in dealing with societal harassment or violence against religious groups can both worsen intolerance and breed a culture of impunity. Complicating matters further is the potential for particular governmental policies and practices to trigger violence by vigilante groups. In Sri Lanka, for example, the debate on anti-conversion legislation became a source of societal tension and led to an increase in extremist Buddhists-led attacks on evangelical Christian churches.[47] Likewise, in Indonesia, government decrees against minority religious sects and their activities are seen as triggers for vigilantism and have spurred incidents of rights violations.[48]

The lack of effective government response against religious violence has been consistently highlighted as a pressing problem in Indonesia.[49] According

---

[46] Various interviews in Surabaya, East Java (24 May 2016).

[47] U.S. Department of State, 2005 Report.

[48] See SETARA Institute, *Berpihak dan Bertindak Intoleran: Laporan Kondisi Kebebasan Beragama/Berkeyakinan di Indonesia 2008* (*Siding and Acting Intolerantly: Report on the Freedom of Religion and Belief in Indonesia 2008*) (Jakarta: SETARA Institute, 2009), p. 38. SETARA reported that before the ministerial decree was issued in June 2008, there were 48 cases of violations, compared to 145 cases after the decree was issued. Based on these data, SETARA concluded that the decree had serious implications on the Ahmadiyah as it became a legitimizing tool for hard-line groups and individuals to pursue the Ahmadis.

[49] See U.S. Department of State, Report from years 2003–2012.

to statistics from 2007 to 2012, there were 283 cases of state omission, which encompass instances where the state failed to prevent or halt societal violence and where it failed to prosecute and punish the culprits.[50] A closer study of specific cases nevertheless reveals a degree of variation in the extent of government or police involvement in preventing violence and protecting victims thereof. In some cases, the police, although present, were merely spectators to mob violence. A prominent example is the deadly attack against Ahmadis in Cikeusik in 2010, where the police were outnumbered by mobs consisting of over a thousand people.[51] In some cases, arrests of the perpetrators of violence were not followed by criminal prosecution; in others, the punishment passed by court was minimal. This was clear in the Cikeusik case: not only did the court sentence the individuals charged for killing several Ahmadis to between three to six months' imprisonment,[52] an Ahmadi who attacked the mob leader was sentenced to a longer jail time. A study by SETARA also revealed that no FPI member was ever penalized from 1998 to 2001 for their violent activities.[53] However, there were occasions where the government was more pro-active in preventing violence and protecting minorities: heightened security measures have been taken to guard churches during Christmas celebrations and terror threats have also been swiftly dealt with. In Central Sulawesi, which has a history of deadly Muslim-Christian

[50] See SETARA Institute, *Tunduk Pada Penghakiman Massa* (*Bowing to Public Pressure*) (Jakarta: SETARA Institute, 2009), p. 2; SETARA Institute, *Berpihak dan Bertindak Intoleran*, p. 45; SETARA Institute, *Negara Harus Bersikap: Tiga Tahun Laporan Kondisi Kebebasan Beragama/Berkeyakinan di Indonesia 2007–2009* (*The State Should Take Action: Three Years Report on the Freedom of Religion and Belief in Indonesia 2007–2009*) (Jakarta: SETARA Institute, 2009), p. 39; SETARA Institute, *Negara Menyangkal: Kondisi Kebebasan Beragama/Berkeyakinan di Indonesia 2010* (*Denial by the State: Report on the Freedom of Religion and Belief in Indonesia 2010*) (Jakarta: SETARA Institute, 2010) p. 89; SETARA Institute, *Politik Diskriminasi Rezim SBY: Laporan Kondisi Kebebasan Beragama/Berkeyakinan di Indonesia 2011* (*Political Discrimination by the SBY Regime: Report on the Freedom of Religion and Belief in Indonesia 2011*) (Jakarta: SETARA Institute, 2012), p. 23, and SETARA Institute, *Kepimpinan Tanpa Prakarsa: Laporan Kondisi Kebebasan Beragama/Berkeyakinan di Indonesia 2012* (*Leadership Without Initiative: Report on the Freedom of Religion and Belief in Indonesia 2012*) (Jakarta: SETARA Institute 2013), p. 41.

[51] Julian Millie, 'One year after the Cikeusik tragedy', *Inside Indonesia*, Edition 107, (January–March 2012), online: www.insideindonesia.org/weekly-articles/one-year-after-the-cikeusik-tragedy. The police had anticipated an attack against the Ahmadis and tried to persuade them to leave their village. However, the Ahmadis refused and before long, the mobs arrived and began attacking the victims.

[52] 'Light Cikeusik sentencing highlights legal discrimination: Rights group', *The Jakarta Post* (29 July 2011), online: www.thejakartapost.com/news/2011/07/29/light-cikeusik-sentencing-highlight-legal-discrimination-rights-group.html.

[53] Hasani and Naipospos, *The Faces of Islam 'Defenders'*, p. 85.

conflict, local police protected houses of worship during religious services. Reports in 2009 and 2010 also indicated that the police have made progress in preventing incidents of religious violence.[54] The leaders of the FPI involved in the infamous violence against religious freedom activists at the National Monument in June 2008 were arrested, charged and sentenced to eighteen months in prison.

In Sri Lanka, police responses to religiously-motivated attacks against persons and properties have also been varied. An analysis of various reports and accounts by civil society members also reveals several trends. First, no actions have been taken against perpetrators of violence. One source also revealed how police stood as passive spectators when monk-led mobs attacked Muslim-owned premises and other places of worship.[55] In some cases, the police have even accompanied the aggressors to demand churches to stop holding services.[56] There have also been instances in which the police have attempted to investigate incidents of violence against persons and property, but no further actions were taken to arrest and prosecute the perpetrators. In fact, it is suggested that authorities were, in general, reluctant to detain and charge those involved in attacks on minorities, especially if they were Buddhist monks.[57] A more positive pattern involves cases where the police have been willing and able to provide protection by dissolving mob threats and attacks.[58] Government officials were quick to condemn violence against places of worship, especially when these incidents heightened during 2003 to 2004.[59] The police then followed suit by conducting investigations and arresting the attackers.[60] Such instances, however, are far and few between. During President Rajapaksa's administration, in particular, there was a strong sense of lawlessness due to the authorities' reluctance and inability to ensure that

---

[54] U.S. Department of State, 2009 Report and U.S. Department of State, 2010 Report.

[55] Interview with civil society activist and legal researcher in Colombo, Sri Lanka (June 2013).

[56] See U.S. Department of State, Report from years 2003 to 2005 and 2008 to 2009. See a case involving the Assembly of God Church in Kaluthara in 2008 and another case in Trincomalee, where the pastor was advised to yield to protests against church meetings as the police could not guarantee his safety. No actions were taken by the police in the attacks against churches and Christians in Thanamalwila and Ratnapura in 2003, as well as the 2004 attacks against a Christian NGO and Catholic shrine.

[57] Ibid. This source also suggested that not a single Buddhist monk has been called into account for instigating violence against minorities. See U.S. Department of State, 2012 Report.

[58] See U.S. Department of State, 2007 Report. For instance, when the Assembly of God church in Yakkala were harassed and threatened by mobs which prevented churchgoers from attending services, the police mobilized to disperse the aggressors.

[59] See U.S. Department of State, 2005 Report. President Kumaratunga declared that these incidents will not be tolerated and ordered a full investigation into them.

[60] Ibid.

instigators of violence feel the full force of the law. A fact-finding mission on the Aluthgama riots led by a team of Sri Lankan academics, for instance, found that the state turned a blind eye to the BBS's 'orchestrated' violence.[61] Efforts to lobby the authorities to prevent the BBS from staging a rally in Aluthgama proved futile, as it was thought that such prevention would only worsen the problem.[62]

In contrast to the situation in Indonesia and Sri Lanka, the Malaysian police and authorities have been quick to react to any signs of disorder or tensions. In 2006, they reacted 'quickly and forcefully' to protect Catholics at a church in Ipoh who were harassed by more than 1,000 Muslims due to allegations of child conversion.[63] The government was also quick to denounce the spread of the false rumour, and the police mobilized to detain those responsible for spreading it.[64] Following threats of a large protest at a church in Klang due to the dispute over the Christians' use of 'Allah', the police mobilized to guard the church and members of public from various religious backgrounds who had gathered to support the church.[65]

Although – as I have explained previously – the police have been involved in raids and arrests against non-mainstream religious groups, there are also suggestions that they have been willing to respond to societal threats against these groups. The Ahmadiyah community, in particular, claims to have been relatively well-protected by the police in the face of harassment and intimidation by local residents.[66] In addition to all this, the government tightly controls public discussions of racially and religiously sensitive issues, and it has prosecuted the perpetrators of the Metro Tabernacle Church arson in 2009.[67] However, in the past few years, government interventions have been increasingly selective, appearing to be more protective of the sensitivities of the majority. While the government has reacted quickly against inflammatory statements and conduct capable of offending Muslims and provoking interethnic unrest, it remained tight-lipped in the face of death threats against a prominent Muslim lawyer who criticized the encroachment of the *Shariah* courts upon the civil courts' jurisdiction. Calls by Perkasa to burn Malay-language Bibles containing the word 'Allah' have also not been seriously dealt with.

---

[61] Farzana Haniffa et al., *Where Have All the Neighbours Gone?*, p. 2. [62] Ibid., pp. 16–17.
[63] See U.S. Department of State, 2007 Report. [64] Ibid.
[65] Account by an eyewitness who was present at the church gathering (January 2014).
[66] Interview with Ahmadiyah Muslim Congregation of Malaysia in Kuala Lumpur, Malaysia (July 2013).
[67] See U.S. Department of State, 2010 Report. In the Metro Tabernacle Church case, the government also allocated funds to repair the damaged church.

Contextualizing Police Responses

My interviews with civil society members, lawyers and victims of religious violence in Jakarta and Colombo revealed that the influence of hard-line groups sometimes pervades the police force. In Indonesia, the problem of corruption makes quid pro quo pecuniary agreements the norm between these entities (especially at the district level). Some local police members are even fearful of these groups. An FPI member admitted that the police is a reliable partner in its efforts on moral policing (gambling and vice).[68] The police, on their part, are sometimes forced to take a practical stand for personnel safety and public order. In fact, in Panggabean and Ali-Fauzi's study, a member of police intelligence in the Kuningan Regency revealed that cooperation with organizations like the FPI would actually further public peace and order – to prevent conflicts from turning deadly.[69] The motivation here appears very modest: a strategy for damage limitation rather than conflict prevention or law enforcement. The drawback, however, is that the police are sometimes forced to yield to pressures by the intolerant groups to restrict the movement and activities of persecuted minorities.[70] The role of religious personalities is also vital because the police at local levels are said to be reluctant or unable to act in the absence of explicit backing by the local *ulama*.

Similarly, in Sri Lanka, the police force is dominated by the Sinhalese-Buddhists, who may have reservations about confronting monks. In the Aluthgama incident, the BBS leader's fiery speech against the Muslims – threatening them that the BBS was ready to protect the Sinhalese at all costs – was also said to appeal to the sentiments of the police and army present at the scene.[71] Even though it was clear that violence was imminent, the police nevertheless permitted the BBS rally to continue.[72] Eyewitness accounts suggest that the Special Task Force did little to contain the violence; in fact, pleas for help as houses were looted and burned were largely ignored.[73]

It would of course be misleading to suggest that the police and the perpetrators of violence have consistently enjoyed a harmonious, reciprocal relationship. Throughout late 2000 to 2001, there were indications that the police were actively pursuing the FPI, often resulting in violent confrontations

---

[68] Panggabean and Ali-Fauzi, *Pemolisian Konflik*, p. 55.   [69] Ibid.

[70] This was apparent with regard to the Ahmadis in Manis Lor. Although the police were largely successful in preventing large-scale violence in 2007 and 2010, in subsequent years they began advising Ahmadis to restrict their activities or conduct them inconspicuously. Ibid., p. 56.

[71] Hume, '"Fascists" in Saffron Robes?'.

[72] Haniffa et al., *Where Have All the Neighbours Gone?*, pp. 16–17.   [73] Ibid., pp. 22–3, 42–4.

between them.[74] In the Aluthgama riots, although the police failed to contain the violence, 135 people were reportedly arrested. However, a deal was struck between the BBS and the inspector general of police: seven arrested people were released in exchange for the BBS's cancellation of a meeting in Mawanella.[75] The BBS leader who provoked what has been deemed one of the worst sectarian violence in post-war Sri Lanka was neither charged nor prosecuted. These nuances may well explain why there is a tendency for religiously motivated violence to spin out of control in Indonesia and Sri Lanka. In Malaysia, despite the shortcomings of the executive, there is some confidence that the government will spring into action and mobilize the police at any sign of violence or disorder.[76] The police, to be sure, has also been beset by allegations of corruption, but there has been no indication of an 'association' of sorts with hard-line groups, and it has proven to be responsive in curtailing violence.

The Lack of Accountability and Power Dynamics

How the executive branch reacts to religious conflict may tell us a lot about a country's political leadership, as well as the strength of the rule of law and legal institutions. These, by extension, help us understand why the nature and scale of such conflicts are more severe in some countries than in others. One important point here concerns the ability of courts to make their decisions stick vis-à-vis the other government branches. The inability to do so shakes the core ingredient of the rule of law: that the government and the governed are constrained by laws that must be enforceable.[77] What might then follow, as we shall see, is the problem of accountability amongst political actors and a culture of impunity amongst the perpetrators of violence.

The Indonesian experience with several religious freedom cases, in particular, showcases the inability of the judiciary to either bind or secure cooperation from other political branches through its decisions. Much like the ghosts of corruption that continue to linger around the judiciary (as well as most of Indonesia's social, economic and political spheres), the courts are up against a long history in which government officials, politicians and lawmakers were

---

[74] Hefner, 'Muslim Democrats and Islamist Violence', p. 286.

[75] Haniffa et al., *Where Have All the Neighbours Gone?*, p. 49.

[76] Recall the example explained previously on how the government and police responded toward an arson attack against a church in the aftermath of the High Court's ruling on the 'Allah' case.

[77] Brian Z. Tamanaha, 'The History and Elements of the Rule of Law' (2012) *Singapore Journal of Legal Studies* 232, 233.

unaccountable and whose decisions were rarely invalidated.[78] The failure of
the DPR to remedy problems of the Blasphemy Law six years on is one striking
example, but the Constitutional Court is not alone in not being able to make
its judgments stick. In the Yasmin church case, the former mayor of Bogor was
able to defy the Supreme Court's decision with virtually no repercussions. The
current mayor, Bima Arya Sugianto, has pledged to resolve the dispute, but
with no indication that he will uphold the Supreme Court's decision. Various
accounts suggested, however, that there has been some (albeit slow) progress
in discussions between disputing parties.[79] While the Yasmin church representatives have pushed for a legal solution (that is, through an enforcement of
the Supreme Court's decision and the ombudsmen's recommendations), the
mayor's approach appears to be a cautious and pragmatic one, seemingly
preferring a political as opposed to a legal solution.

While this may be understandable, given the complexities and sensitivities
surrounding the case, it also raises a broader conceptual question: how do we
balance political and legal solutions and can this balance be achieved – if at
all – without undermining the rule of law? Similar issues in resolving criminal
actions and/or rights disputes with religious undertones outside the courts exist
in Sri Lanka, but here, there is an added element of governmental pressure.
Insiders suggest, for instance, that in the aftermath of the attacks against a
Muslim-owned clothing chain in Colombo, the owners were strongly advised
by government sources not to pursue charges against the Buddhist monks who
perpetrated the attacks.[80]

A closely related point to all this concerns the prevailing political and power
dynamics surrounding the executive branch.[81] How these play out in all three
countries under study, to be sure, are different. In Indonesia, for instance,
local government officials that are popularly elected – be they the governor,
the regent or the mayor – may wish to take accountability to their voters
seriously. In other words, they may feel empowered to use their mandate as a
justification to ignore or sidestep judicial decisions and constitutional rights
guarantees. Sources posit that this sense of popular legitimacy explains why
the previous mayor of Bogor, Diani Budiarto, took the very bold step of
ignoring the Supreme Court's decision in favour of the church.[82] It is worth

---

[78]   Simon Butt, 'Indonesia's Constitutional Court: Conservative Activist or Strategic Operator?' in
       Bjorn Dressel (ed.), *The Judicialization of Politics in Asia* (Oxon: Routledge, 2012), p. 107.
[79]   Various interviews in Jakarta and Bogor (March 2016).
[80]   Interview with a human rights lawyer in Colombo, Sri Lanka (June 2013).
[81]   In Chapter 7, I shall explain, in greater detail, how electoral politics shape the government's
       policies and practices on religion and religious freedom.
[82]   Interviews with various civil society activists and politicians in Jakarta, Indonesia (June and
       October 2012).

noting that in the Yasmin church case, there are important political realities that the mayor must face: there are strong objections to the presence of the church among influential sections of the local community[83] – sections that form the core voter base of the mayorship. From a practical standpoint, to scrupulously uphold the law and further the values of pluralism, is not a natural, first-choice solution. However, more often than not this legitimizes intolerant forces within the society and drives majority tyranny – the latter being one of the problems that should be minimized with a functioning rule of law.

Compounding these issues is leadership weakness at the national level. The Susilo Bambang Yudhoyono (SBY) administration enjoyed great popular support, but its policymaking capabilities were often crippled by political infighting and horse-trading amongst his coalition members.[84] In some circles, SBY was viewed as a weak and indecisive leader who was very sensitive about his reputation and thus unwilling to take risks and make firm decisions. For some observers, including those from his own party (Partai Demokrat), these issues affected the way in which the SBY government responded to religious freedom issues on the ground, although privately, SBY was concerned about the plight of religious minorities.[85] Such ambivalent attitudes can trickle down to the national police and the *Satpol*,[86] affecting their readiness to act against societal harassment and violence. On the other hand, some observers have defended SBY's hands-off approach: they argue that issues of violence and conflict are public order (as opposed to religious) issues within the purview of elected local governments, and thus there is little that the president could do to resolve such local-level conflicts.[87]

---

[83] Interview with a deputy minister in Jakarta, Indonesia (June 2012) and conversation with a member of one of the biggest political parties in Indonesia, in Jakarta, Indonesia (January 2014).

[84] In the 2009 presidential elections, SBY garnered over 60% of the popular votes. His candidacy was supported by four other main political parties – Partai Amanat Negara (PAN), Partai Keadilan Sejahtera (PKS), Partai Kebangkitan Bangsa (PKB) and Partai Persatuan Pembangunan (PPP). These are all, incidentally, Islamic-oriented political parties. I will discuss this in greater detail in Chapter 7.

[85] Interviews with various members of various civil society organizations and members of political parties in Jakarta, Indonesia (June 2012). See a series of interviews by Tempo with Jalaludin Rakhmat – an elected member of the DPR and a leader of the Shia community in Indonesia. In the interview, Rakhmat suggests that the Shiites generally maintain good relations with SBY and his administration. 'Kisah Kang Jalal Soal Syiah Indonesia' ('Kang Jalal's Story on Indonesian Shiites'), *Tempo* (3 September 2012), online: www.tempo.co/read/news/2012/09/03/173427066/Kisah-Kang-Jalal-Soal-Syiah-di-IndonesiaBagian-2.

[86] *Satpol* is the Indonesian acronym for the Civil Service Police Unit. It is established under the auspices of the Ministry of Home Affairs and is therefore distinct from the national police force. The *Satpol* operates locally to maintain public order and enforces only laws and regulations issued by the mayor.

[87] Interview with a deputy minister in Jakarta, Indonesia (June 2012).

Similar problems of weak political leadership in dealing with religious intolerance exist in Malaysia, especially in the post-Mahathir era. Much like the criticisms levelled against SBY in Indonesia, the current Malaysian prime minister, Najib Razak, though privately a progressive individual, is unwilling to risk his already fragile support both within his own party and the wider electorate. The consequence is the adoption of seemingly contradictory positions on matters involving religious tolerance and conflict. On one end of the spectrum, the prime minister has spearheaded initiatives such as the Global Movement for Moderates Foundation (GMMF)[88] – an organization that advocates moderation in international relations and foreign policy through, inter alia, the commitment to upholding human rights, democracy and good governance. Of late, however, the prime minister has increasingly pandered to the sensitivities of right-wing conservatives in the country by asserting, for instance, that 'human rightism', liberalism and pluralism are new forms of threats to Muslims.[89] The government thus foments some level of conservatism (even intolerance) in the society by allowing groups like Perkasa and ISMA to operate, hoping that this would bolster its public image as the defender of majoritarian (Malay-Muslim) interests. But at the same time, it keeps these discourses on a leash, not allowing them to escalate into serious violence. In some measure, the latter reflects the government's circumspection with the country's experience with the 1969 ethnic riots, and it has thus been relatively quick at countering any signs of public disorder.

Yet, this weakened political leadership, along with the realization that the government needs to play to the majority gallery, has emboldened particular religious demagogues to assert their power and influence. The problem is magnified when the executive and bureaucracy have managed to escape scrutiny over their policies and practices due to systemic governance problems. That the parliament acts as a rubber-stamping authority of executive policies breeds a culture of non-accountability, and the tradition of strict enforcement of party discipline means that legislative and executive members from the ruling party are forced to toe government lines or risk being driven out of office. Politicians are reluctant to question religious edicts and authority, lest they be accused of disobeying the *ulamas* and being un-Islamic.[90]

---

[88] The prime minister first mooted this idea in his speech at the United Nations General Assembly in 2010.

[89] 'Speech by the prime minister at the 57th National Quran Recitation Ceremony', *Prime Minister's Office* (13 May 2014), online: www.pmo.gov.my/?menu=speech&page=1676&news_id=716&speech_cat=2.

[90] The political leadership allows muftis to have free reign in order to buttress its political support. Interview with a former politician and minister in the Prime Minister's Department (August 2013).

Taken together, these conditions have facilitated the emergence of figures who enjoy significant clout in executive decision-making and who use the state as a proxy to monopolize religious discourse. This is the upshot of decades-long of state control over religion, which has its roots in the premiership of Dr. Mahathir Mohamad. The difference, however, was that Dr. Mahathir's authoritarian character allowed him to control any discourses that might provoke religious intolerance and kept religious authorities and clerics at bay.[91]

In Sri Lanka, the powerful executive presidency that defined the Rajapaksa presidency became a significant source of discontent. For many observers, the abuse of power and extensive control over other political branches created a degree of lawlessness in the society: those within or close to the president's circles were reportedly able to act with a degree of impunity; corruption became widespread; and law enforcement was, as a government lawyer admitted, 'lethargic'.[92] Power was virtually concentrated in the hands of President Rajapaksa, whose immediate family and loyalists became the centre of gravity for Sri Lankan social, political and economic life.[93] Three of the president's brothers held prominent positions in the government: his younger brothers, Gotabaya and Basil, held the secretary of defence and minister of economic development portfolios, respectively; his older brother, Chamal, was the Speaker of the Parliament.

Under these circumstances, coupled with the majority-centric political program that the regime adopted for strategic purposes, we may begin to piece the puzzles regarding its approaches to religious conflict and religious freedom. Although some believed Rajapaksa to be personally committed to pluralistic values,[94] he also recognized the fact that since the end of the war in 2009, his government drew its strength and legitimacy from the wave of Sinhalese nationalist support. Ethno-religious nationalism was deemed a factor worth harnessing to ensure his continued electoral success and power.[95] As a result, the government was cautious about being seen to side with the minorities in religious disputes. They were also reluctant to pursue the monks who led religious provocation and attacks. While some have pinned this on

---

[91] An insider suggested that Dr. Mahathir kept a tight lid over the influence and activities of the religious bureaucracy and clerics, much to the resentment of the latter. Interview in Kuala Lumpur, Malaysia (December 2013).

[92] Interview with a prominent government lawyer in Colombo, Sri Lanka (June 2013).

[93] Neil DeVotta, 'Sri Lanka's Ongoing Shift to Authoritarianism', *East West Center Asia Pacific Bulletin*, No. 201 (22 February 2013).

[94] Jehan Perera, 'Inter-Religious Empathy That Waits to Be Harnessed', *National Peace Council of Sri Lanka Newsletter* (2014) (on file with author).

[95] Ibid. Various interviews in Colombo, Sri Lanka (October 2016).

the desire to prevent further monk-led violence, there are also claims that Rajapaksa was held back by personalities within his own cabinet.[96] One also has to remember that monks are revered figures in Sri Lanka, which makes prosecuting them a politically difficult decision – especially for the monks who champion the Sinhalese-Buddhist cause. The question of legality, therefore, did not seem to arise with respect to any actions that further the prominence of Sinhalese-Buddhist interests and nationalistic sentiments.

The consequences of a powerful executive that lacks accountability and weak rule of law are also reflected in the practice of patronage politics that empower intolerant groups engaged in spreading religious hate speech or anti-minority rhetoric. In Sri Lanka, the BBS and other like-minded organizations were thought to have enjoyed tacit support from influential government officials.[97] Many saw the defence secretary's participation in officiating the BBS's cultural and training centre as a significant indication of the state's patronage over the organization. In the 2014 Aluthgama incident, the fact that the BBS leader who provoked the anti-Muslim riots walked free fuelled further speculation about the BBS's impunity and protection from the government. This is, of course, not unique to Sri Lanka. In Malaysia, Perkasa has also allegedly received funding from government agencies[98] and it maintains a support base within the UMNO party.[99] A controversial preacher from India – who is known to have made religiously provocative statements – delivered lectures in the country, sometimes, with explicit support from government ministers.[100]

In Indonesia, hard-line organizations like the FPI, though small in numbers, are influential lobbyists in local politics, often striking bargains and agreements with local elites contesting in gubernatorial, mayoral or other district-level elections. In return for a pledge of electoral support, politicians provide implicit legitimation for the FPI's demands and activities by passing

---

[96] See Hume, '"Fascists" in Saffron Robes?'. These suggestions were also revealed in an interview with an influential SLFP politician in Colombo, Sri Lanka (October 2016).

[97] In several interviews conducted in Colombo in 2013 and 2016, various civil society members, academics, lawyers and politicians alleged that the former president's brother, Gotabaya Rajapaksa, was a key figure in providing political patronage to the BBS.

[98] 'Perkasa admits getting aid from Putrajaya', *The Malaysian Insider* (25 December 2013), online: www.themalaysianinsider.com/malaysia/article/perkasa-admits-getting-aid-from-putrajaya.

[99] Interview with an UMNO politician in Kuala Lumpur, Malaysia (July 2013).

[100] 'Deputy minister: Zakir Naik "voice of moderation" needed to fix tarnished Islam', *The Malaymail Online* (19 April 2016), online: www.themalaymailonline.com/malaysia/article/deputy-minister-zakir-naik-voice-of-moderation-needed-to-fix-tarnished-isla.

local regulations which, among others, ban deviant religious groups.[101] When General Wiranto ran for the presidency in 2004, the FPI mobilized in support of Wiranto and campaigned to discredit SBY[102] (a highly popular candidate who eventually became president for two consecutive terms). FUI Cirebon (Forum Ukhuwah Islamiyah Cirebon) reportedly maintains strong links with local political leaders in the city of Cirebon, through which it has been able to strengthen its presence and 'enforcement' actions in the locality.[103] Some of the more influential personalities in these organizations are members of political parties and even elected members of parliament.[104] To add to this, some MUI figures and Islamic-oriented political parties such as the PKS and PPP have repeatedly called for the Ahmadiyah to be banned.[105] These trends signal to the public and other state apparatus of where governmental prejudices lay. To some extent, they have also shielded agent provocateurs from the full force of the law and weakened public confidence in the capability of the government to protect citizens impartially.

UPHOLDING LAW AND POLITICAL COMPROMISE

There is enough evidence to illustrate that decisiveness and police action can prevent or, at the very least contain, violence. In Indonesia, this was evident in cases of sectarian conflict in Manis Lor and Bangil. In Manis Lor, the local police – in anticipation of violence – coordinated with the district police for personnel reinforcement. Both the heads of the district police and country police sent a stern warning that violence would not be tolerated and that should it occur, the perpetrators of violence will be swiftly arrested.[106] Although the regent's 2004 Joint Decision Letter (*Surat Keputusan Bersama*, or SKB) which outlaws Ahmadiyah activities and teaching was still in force, the police was determined to avoid the kind of violence that engulfed the village in 2007.

A more recent case concerns the persecution of Ahmadis in Bangka Belitung, who were forced to leave their homes and were relocated by the local government.[107] In that case, direct intervention from the Jokowi

---

[101] There were allegations that such agreement was struck between the FPI and a candidate in the West Java gubernatorial election in 2013.

[102] Panggabean and Ali-Fauzi, *Pemolisian Konflik*, p. 138.   [103] Ibid., p. 161.   [104] Ibid., p. 166.

[105] See SETARA Institute, *Berpihak dan Bertindak Intoleran*, pp. 74–5.

[106] Panggabean and Ali-Fauzi, *Pemolisian Konflik*, pp. 40, 54–5.

[107] This was done in response to public order concerns. Propaganda against the Ahmadis were spread through social media, focusing, among others on the allegation that the Ahmadis beginning to 'dominate' Bangka and would outnumber Sunni Muslims.

administration – the president sent his staff to personally oversee the situation and instructed that under no circumstances should the Ahmadis be forced to leave their village – helped allay the conflict.[108] In Malaysia, although the government allows intolerant attitudes and discourse to simmer – and indeed at times it has also actively facilitated such discourses – it has shown greater willingness and ability to put a lid over any sign of unrest, due to its general aversion toward open ethnic violence and conflict. The police have also generally acted quickly, as we have seen, to any signs of ethnic and/or religious conflict.

That aside, the cases and issues expounded here raise several points for reflection. The first concerns the approach to resolving religious conflict in the society – an issue which was most apparent in the Yasmin church case in Indonesia, but is equally relevant in Malaysia and Sri Lanka. The mayor of Bogor is not necessarily alone in his choice of approach to deal with the Yasmin church case. The rule of law requires formal legality to ensure a degree of legal certainty and predictability, but even some have admitted that adherence to formal legality might not always be 'appropriate or socially beneficial'.[109] There are complexities in the Yasmin case that might well be relevant in the mayor's calculations: the contesting accounts of the validity of the signatures obtained from residents; the refusal of the church to relocate to a different location; the strong objections from sections of the local residents; and the anxieties amongst locals (even those who do not categorically reject the church) about the wisdom of constructing the church, knowing that it would only attract vigilante groups to the area. In situations where violence is imminent or at least foreseeable, an exercise of discretion and political compromise could well provide a win-win situation between hostile parties and avoid a potentially fractious, zero-sum game. Indeed, in the Bangka case, the president – whilst affirming protection for the Ahmadis – also stressed that any disputes must be resolved through dialogue.[110]

Yet, political solutions and compromise are largely dependent on political will, as we shall see in Chapter 7. There is a danger that if political survival becomes largely dependent on the mobilization of majoritarian religious sentiments, then there may be less willingness or incentive to resolve the conflict amicably between contesting religious groups. To the extent that the rule of law may offer some protection from majoritarian passions, prejudice and arbitrary decision-making, an over-reliance on political solutions alone

---

[108] Interview with a member of the presidential staff in Jakarta, Indonesia (March 2016).
[109] See Tamanaha, 'The History and Elements of the Rule of Law', p. 242.
[110] Interview with a member of the presidential staff in Jakarta, Indonesia (March 2016).

may worsen conflict, especially in a context where the view that 'democracy as majority rule' is prevalent across the three countries. These are the dilemmas that Indonesia, Malaysia and Sri Lanka are continuing to grapple with.

A second point that is worth pondering on is the potential for laws (be they constitutional or ordinary laws) to be used as a weapon for oppression or to trigger intolerance. We have seen some evidence and tendencies for this in Chapter 3, but they can also exist at the societal level. In Malaysia and Sri Lanka, groups like ISMA and the BBS invoke the constitutional provisions on Islam and Buddhism to push authorities to adopt pro-active policies in favour of the majority religion (or ethno-religious group) and to justify discrimination of religious minorities. In the Manis Lor case in Indonesia, violence escalated after the issuance of the regent's Joint Decision Letter (first in 2002 and again in 2004). The Joint Ministerial Regulation that was intended to facilitate the building of houses of worship by providing clear standards and rules is thought to have amplified disagreements between contesting religious groups and bred intolerance. It provides a justification for particular groups to object to the building of houses of worship (be they mosques or churches) on the grounds that procedures have not been complied with.[111] Ironically, prior to the regulation, residents in Ende and Kupang, regardless of their religious background, worked together to construct houses of worship in the area.[112] These examples show that societal conflict and/or private abuses of religious freedom do not occur in a vacuum.

---

[111] See Panggabean and Ali-Fauzi, *Pemolisian Konflik*; and Melissa Crouch, 'Implementing the Regulation on Places of Worship in Indonesia: New Problems, Local Politics and Court Action' (2010) 34 *Asian Studies Review* 403.
[112] Panggabean and Ali-Fauzi, *Pemolisian Konflik*, p. 311.

5

Constitutional Adjudication on Religion
and Religious Freedom

If we were to go by normative international standards, the fact that a religion is established as a state religion or that the followers of a particular religion comprise the majority of the population should not affect fundamental rights or justify any discrimination against other religious minorities.[1] Similarly, the fact that a set of principles is enshrined as the official state ideology in constitutions should not impair the exercise of religious freedom.[2]

The European Court of Human Rights (ECtHR) has adjudicated many notable cases involving this intersection between state ideology, religion and fundamental rights. The European human rights regime maintains a record of according states with the autonomy (through the margin of appreciation doctrine) to determine the parameters of religious freedom vis-à-vis the principle of secularism or an underlying national ideology, in general. It has been argued, however, that such broad autonomy has on occasion militated against minority protection.[3] For example, when the ECtHR heard the Turkish case concerning a ban on headscarves in public universities, it emphasized the importance of secularism within Turkey's constitutional, political and democratic

---

[1] Office of the High Commissioner for Human Rights, *General Comment No. 22: Article 18 (Freedom of Thought, Conscience, and Religion)*, para. 9, CCPR/C/21/Rev.1/Add.4 (30 July 1993), online: www.unhchr.ch/tbs/doc.nsf/(Symbol)/9a30112c27d1167cc12563ed004d8f15? Opendocument.

[2] Ibid., para. 10.

[3] Martin Wählisch, 'ECHR Chamber Judgment Case of *S.A.S. v. France*: Banning of Burqas and Niqabs Legal?' *Cambridge Journal of International and Comparative Law Online* (July 2014), online: cijl.co.uk/2014/07/21/echr-chamber-judgment-case-s-s-v-france-banning-burqas-niqabs-legal/. For a critique of the application of the principle of secularism to restrict religious freedom in the ECtHR jurisprudence, see M. Todd Parker, 'The Freedom to Manifest Religious Belief: An Analysis of the Necessity Clauses of the ICCPR and the ECHR' (2006) 17 *Duke Journal of International & Comparative Law* 91.

order.[4] The wearing of a headscarf in a higher education setting was deemed problematic, especially in light of the growing political significance of religious symbols in the country in recent years.[5] Likewise, in a string of ECtHR decisions involving school bans on religious attire,[6] the court dismissed the applicants' complaints as the ban was deemed legitimate to protect the constitutional principle of secularism in France, the rights of others and public order.

The courts in Indonesia, Malaysia and Sri Lanka have not been spared the task of adjudicating similar controversies. In this chapter, I focus on three cases: the *Blasphemy Law* case in Indonesia, the 'Allah' case in Malaysia and the incorporation cases in Sri Lanka. They will illuminate our understanding of three important issues: (1) the competing visions and claims of religious freedom that were advanced by parties involved in the constitutional challenges; (2) the courts' reasoning in upholding or rejecting the constitutional challenge; and (3) how constitutional law and constitutional provisions may be invoked in perverse ways to restrict religious practice and expression. Taken together, the analysis will illustrate how legal and political demands for the protection of religion (or the dominant religion), on the one hand, and religious freedom, on the other, have played out in the courts and how conceptions of the constitutional arrangements on religion have evolved in the three countries.

DEFINING THE CONSTITUTIONALIZATION OF RELIGION AND THE PARAMETERS OF RELIGIOUS FREEDOM: THREE CASE STUDIES

Regulating Religious Interpretation and Practices: The Blasphemy Law in Indonesia

The *Blasphemy Law* case was not the first time the Indonesian Constitutional Court was called upon to determine the boundaries of article 29

---

4   *Leyla Şahin v. Turkey*, Application No. 44774/98, Grand Chamber, European Court of Human Rights (10 November 2005). The court did not rely on the principle of secularism alone to justify the restrictions on religious freedom. Rather, it considered this in tandem with the pursuit of public order and the protection of the rights and freedoms of others. See *Leyla Şahin v. Turkey*, paras. 115–116, and Anat Scolnicov, *The Right to Religious Freedom in International Law* (Oxon: Routledge, 2010), p. 178.

5   *Leyla Sahin v. Turkey*, para. 115.

6   See *Ranjit Singh v. France*, Application No. 27561/08, Court (Fifth Section), European Court of Human Rights (30 June 2009); *Jasvir Singh v. France*, Application No. 25463/08, Court (Fifth Section), European Court of Human Rights (30 June 2009); *Aktas v. France*, Application No. 14308/08, Court (Fifth Section), European Court of Human Rights (30 June 2009); and *Bayrak v. France*, Application No. 43563/08, Court (Fifth Section), European Court of Human Rights (30 June 2009).

or, more specifically, cases juxtaposing 'the belief in one and only God' vis-à-vis religious freedom.

In 2008, the court delivered an instructive decision in a case that raised questions concerning the reach of article 29, the place of Islamic law in the constitutional order and the jurisdiction of religious (*Shariah*) courts.[7] The petitioner challenged the constitutionality of the Religious Courts Law on the basis that the limited jurisdiction of such courts infringed his right to religious freedom.[8] Islam, he argued, requires Muslims to adhere to the full panoply of Islamic law (including criminal law), and the fact that the state restricts the application of Islamic law to mainly personal law matters was inconsistent with article 29 of the constitution.[9] Implicit in his argument was the belief that the religion clause requires the state to enforce religious laws and religious orthodoxy.

The court, in a short but unanimous judgment, rejected the constitutional challenge.[10] With regard to article 29, the court emphasized the 'middle path' conception – that Indonesia is neither a theocratic nor a secular state – and stressed that the *Pancasila* requires national laws to conform to the nation's ideology and to develop religious tolerance.[11] The Constitutional Court also added that the state, in treating its citizens, must not draw any distinctions between the majority and minority.[12]

This decision affirmed the broad powers of the state in regulating religious practices, but it also limited the reach of religious laws in a country that pays special constitutional recognition to religion.[13] More importantly, it illustrates that the national ideology or the basis of the state (*dasar negara*) can be invoked to restrict the exercise of religious freedom. There were similar

---

[7]   Constitutional Court of Indonesia, Decision No. 19/PUU-VI/2008, Examination of Law No. 7, Year 1989 on the Religious Courts as amended by Law No. 3, Year 2006 (12 August 2008) [*Religious Courts* case]. The religious courts in Indonesia are the *Shariah* courts that deal with a limited scope of Islamic law (marriage, succession, gifts, bequeaths, payment of alms, charitable gifts, gifts to the needy and *Shariah* economic matters).

[8]   Ibid., pp. 4–5.   [9]   Ibid., p. 7.

[10] The petitioner's specific challenge based on article 29(1) (which provides that the Indonesian state is based on the belief in the one and only God) was rejected. The court reasoned that that articles 24(2) and 24A(5) provide that religious courts are one of the four branches of the Indonesian judiciary and the bounds of their jurisdiction are determined by legislation. Ibid., p. 23.

[11] Ibid., p. 24. The court also added that the petitioner failed to understand the nature of the state-religion relationship in Indonesia.

[12] Ibid.

[13] Simon Butt and Tim Lindsey, *The Constitution of Indonesia: A Contextual Analysis* (Oxford and Portland, OR: Hart Publishing, 2012), p. 226.

considerations in the *Blasphemy Law* decision, which the court delivered less than a year after the *Religious Courts* case.

The Blasphemy Law had its roots in the state's desire to safeguard public order and national unity. In this respect, the state identified the growth of spiritual or belief groups that promote teachings or doctrines that are contrary to established religious principles as a threat to national unity and to existing religious groups in the country.[14] A law that prevents the abuse or desecration of religion, it was believed, would further religious harmony and ensure that Indonesians are free to worship according to their own religion.[15] Under this law, there are only six officially recognized religions in Indonesia (Islam, Protestantism, Catholicism, Buddhism, Confucianism and Hinduism), but the practice of other religions such as Judaism, Zoroastrianism, Shintoism and Taoism are not prohibited – they are allowed to exist so long as they do not contravene the Blasphemy Law and other laws in the country.

Articles 2 to 4 set out the sanctions against blasphemy or religious deviance: those who offend the law will be ordered to cease their activities; the president, on the advice of the minister for religious affairs, the attorney general and the home affairs minister may also declare an offending organization illegal and subsequently seek to disband it; and failing the ministerial or presidential actions, the offending organizations and their members may face criminal charges with a maximum sentence of five years imprisonment.[16] Pursuant to this law, in 2008, the government issued a Joint Ministerial Decision against the Ahmadiyah[17] – a minority Muslim sect whose religious doctrines and interpretations are deemed to have deviated from the teachings of Islam. As the previous chapter explains, the law has also been routinely used – especially in the post-Soeharto period – to persecute and prosecute members of non-mainstream religious groups and deviant 'sects'.[18]

[14] See Elucidation on Law No. 1 of 1965 on the Prevention on Abuse and/or Desecration of Religion, online: www.kemenag.go.id/file/dokumen/UU1PNPS65.pdf (translated from Indonesian).

[15] Ibid.

[16] Article 4 of the Blasphemy Law inserts a provision from the Criminal Code that deals with the punishment for blasphemy. Article 156a criminalizes deliberate statements or acts in public which constitutes animosity toward, misuse or insult against a religion adhered to in Indonesia, or which is intended to prevent others from adhering to any religion based on God.

[17] Joint Decision of the Minister of Religion, the Attorney General, and the Minister of Home Affairs of the Republic of Indonesia, No. 3 Year 2008, KEP-033/A/JA/6/2008, No. 1999 Year 2008 (9 June 2008), arts. 2 and 3. The decree calls for the Ahmadiyah to disband and cease all religious activities that deviate from the principal teachings of Islam. It also prohibits any support for religious interpretations that deviate from the fundamental teachings of a religion and bans any unilateral action from the general public against Ahmadiyah members.

[18] Simon Butt and Tim Lindsey, *The Constitution of Indonesia*, p. 236.

In 2009, several Muslim and Christian NGOs and human rights organizations challenged the law's constitutionality before the Constitutional Court, claiming that it violated constitutional guarantees of religious freedom and equal treatment.[19] They argued that the law undermined religious freedom by allowing the state to determine the 'correct' religious interpretation and to punish those who do not conform to state-approved interpretations.[20] The government, by contrast, argued that the law furthers, rather than restricts, religious freedom by protecting religious adherents from the desecration of their religion.[21] Its defence of the law's constitutionality was couched in pragmatic terms: outlawing blasphemy would ensure religious harmony, tolerance and public order in the context of Indonesia's plural society; the restrictions are perceived as limited, as they only prohibit deliberate acts or statements promoting deviant religious interpretations that are made in *public*; and according to the then minister for religious affairs, the law does not enforce a blanket prohibition on religious interpretation or religious activities resembling a particular religion.[22]

The court agreed with the government and upheld the constitutionality of the law. The decision was built around three important points. The first was pitched at a conceptual level. For the court, as a nation that upholds the principle of the 'belief in one and only God' and is based on religious values, the Indonesian Constitution does not protect the freedom *from* religion, nor does it endorse anti-religious ideas or the defamation or desecration of any religious teachings and doctrines.[23] The second and third points evinced more practical considerations. The court held that the law did not completely restrict religious freedom; rather, it only prohibits public acts or statements that 'advocate or seek public support for' religious interpretations that deviate from the 'fundamental doctrines' of that religion.[24] Here, the court distinguished between the freedom of religion as an internal belief (*forum internum*) and the freedom to express one's religion or beliefs (*forum externum*). The

---

[19] Interestingly, several other religious organizations such as the Indonesian High Council of Confucianism, the Indonesian Hindu Society and Indonesian Federation of Buddhist Organizations joined the proceedings as related parties. In their statements before the court, they rejected the petition challenging the constitutionality of the law. Two other related parties – Nahdlatul Ulama and Muhammadiyah (the two biggest Muslim organizations in Indonesia) – also provided statements before the court rejecting the petition.

[20] Constitutional Court of Indonesia, Decision No. 140/PUU-VII/2009, Examination of Law No. 1, Year 1965 on the Prevention from Abuse of and/or Desecration of Religion (Arts. 1, 2(1), 2(2), 3 and 4(a)) (19 April 2010) [*Blasphemy Decision I*], p. 270.

[21] Ibid., p. 241.   [22] Ibid.   [23] Ibid., p. 275.

[24] Ibid., p 287. Here, the court suggested that the law did not prohibit interpretations or acts (that resemble a religion adhered to in Indonesia) which are done in private.

latter, according to the court, implicates the religious freedom of others, social relations and the public interest, and hence it can be restricted based on public order and religious values considerations.[25] Finally, the court's motive was, in part, preventive – it took pains to stress the threat of societal conflicts if religious interpretations are left unregulated and if religious sensitivities are not protected.[26] The law, in this respect, would operate to prevent public disorder.

In 2013, the Constitutional Court revisited the Blasphemy Law on petition by a group of Shiites. This time, the review focused on article 4's criminalization of blasphemy.[27] In essence, the applicants' arguments revolved around the uncertainties and vagueness of the law. They argued that it was unclear what constitutes 'publicly' for the purposes of article 4.[28] Justice Harjono had in fact raised this point in his concurring opinion to the 2010 decision. If a person commits the purportedly 'blasphemous' act, but only does so before a limited group of followers or religious congregation, is the person criminally liable under the law? Although Justice Harjono acknowledged the flaw, he thought that the issue would be best addressed by the legislature.[29] The second claim centred on the uncertainty as to what constitutes 'animosity, abuse, or insult towards a particular religion' and who possesses the competence or authority to determine whether a statement or act is deviant or insulting.[30] The petitioners pointed out an example in which a local Indonesian Ulama Council (MUI) branch had declared the teachings of one Oben Sarbeni as deviant, but there were no other religious organizations that have made similar declarations.[31]

---

[25] Ibid., pp. 292–3. [26] Ibid., p. 287.

[27] Article 60(1) and (2) of Law No. 8 of 2011 amended Law No. 24 of 2003 on the Constitutional Court so that the court could review laws which had previously been brought before it, provided that a different basis of argument is introduced to the court. Article 4 of the Blasphemy Law provides criminal sanctions based on article 156a of the Indonesian Criminal Code, which provides maximum sentence of five years imprisonment for a person who deliberately and publicly expresses or performs an act which: '(a) in essence constitutes animosity towards, misuse of, or defamation of a religion adhered to in Indonesia; or (b) is intended [to cause] people not to adhere to any religion based on the one and only God.' The Elucidation on article 4 states that the criminal act referred to in sub-clause (a) is one 'which is solely (in its essence) intended to be hostile or offensive. Therefore, any description, whether in writing or verbal, that are made objectively, *zakelijk*, and academically, about a particular religion and accompanied by efforts to avoid words or a set of words that are hostile or offensive in nature, are not criminal according to this clause'.

[28] Constitutional Court of Indonesia, Decision No. 84/PUU-X/2012, Examination of Law No. 1, Year 1965 on the Prevention from Abuse of and/or Desecration of Religion (Arts. 1, 2(1), 2(2), 3 and 4(a)) (9 April 2013) [*Blasphemy Decision II*], p. 9.

[29] *Blasphemy Decision I*, p. 311. [30] *Blasphemy Decision II*, p. 14. [31] Ibid., p. 12.

As expected, the government focused its arguments on the necessity of retaining the Blasphemy Law to protect public order and inter- and intra-religious harmony. In this regard, the government claimed that the public dissemination of religious interpretations that 'lacks sound methodological basis' can provoke public disorder.[32] These arguments echoed the government's position in the 2010 case that the law furthers, rather than restricts, religious freedom by protecting religious harmony.[33]

The court again dismissed the constitutional challenge in a judgment that mirrored its 2010 decision, emphasizing the need to maintain public order. The court rejected the argument that the meaning of 'publicly' was vague; instead, it agreed with the government's assertion that such meaning can be sufficiently determined from the Indonesian Criminal Code and its commentaries.[34] This reasoning, however, failed to specifically address the questions raised by Justice Harjono on the interpretive issues surrounding the word 'publicly'. The court also rejected the second claim raised by the petitioners on the basis that these are implementation as opposed to constitutional problems.[35] Instead, the court argued that the general courts may exercise their discretion in deciding whether or not a particular act constitutes blasphemy and – quoting its 2010 decision – that the basic doctrines and teachings of a particular religion are decided internally by the authorities of that religion.[36] Who these 'internal authorities' are and what would happen if a particular religion lacks a 'central authority' remain unanswered questions. There is also a crucial inconsistency in the court's argument. While on the one hand it accepted that one's interpretation of a religion is part of his or her freedom of conscience (*forum internum*),[37] it also endorsed an important qualification to religious freedom – that any religious interpretation must be consistent with the fundamental religious teachings, by using 'appropriate methodologies' based on recognized religious sources.[38]

Battling over God's Name and Defending the Sanctity of Islam: The 'Allah' Case in Malaysia

Questions about the precise role of Islam as the religion of the Federation are not new or uncommon. I have previously alluded to the 1988 case of

---

[32] Ibid., p. 117.

[33] *Blasphemy Decision I*, pp. 34–5 (statements provided by the minister of religious affairs and the minister of law and human rights).

[34] *Blasphemy Decision II*, p. 144. According to the commentaries, 'publicly' or 'in public' means: (1) 'a place that is visited by the public or where the public can listen . . .'; (2) a public place where there is a lot of people; and (3) a place for public viewing.

[35] Ibid., pp. 145–7.   [36] Ibid., pp. 145–6.   [37] *Blasphemy Decision I*, pp. 288–9.

[38] Ibid., p. 289.

Che Omar, which dealt with the meaning and consequences of 'Islam' in article 3 of the constitution. The case, to be sure, was not one about religious freedom. Instead, the Supreme Court had to determine whether a mandatory death sentence for drug trafficking offences was unconstitutional on the basis that it was against Islamic injunctions.[39] In a short judgment, the Supreme Court reiterated the limited role of Islam in the constitutional order. The framers of the constitution, the court argued, understood that the operation of Islamic law would be confined to personal law matters for Muslims only.[40] More importantly, the court affirmed that the law of the country remains secular (as opposed to theocratic) and emphasized that if the constitutional framers intended for Islam to have a significant role in the constitutional order, they would have included an explicit constitutional provision to invalidate any laws contrary to Islamic injunctions.[41]

Twenty-five years later, the views in *Che Omar* were dismantled by the Court of Appeal in the infamous 'Allah' case. In January 2009, the Ministry of Home Affairs granted the Catholic Church a publication permit for its weekly publication (*The Herald*). The permission was subject to two conditions: (1) a prohibition on the use of the word 'Allah' in the Malay language edition of the publication; and (2) the front page of the publication must be stamped with the word '*terhad*' ('limited'). The latter meant that distribution is restricted to churches and Christians only. The prohibition followed a Ministry directive in 1986 which lists sixteen prohibited words (including 'Allah') that are exclusive to Islam and cannot be used by other religions in their publications. However, the government had been allowing the use of Malay-language Bibles (known as '*Al-Kitab*') bearing the word 'Allah', provided that they are used only in churches by Christians and that they are endorsed with the words 'not for Muslims'.[42]

At first glance, this might be seen as a routine, straightforward case of judicial review of restrictions on the right to religious practice. Indeed, from the Catholic Church's perspective, the prohibition on the use of 'Allah' simply violated the constitution's articles 3 and 11 on religious freedom and article 10 on freedom of speech and expression.[43] However, it became clear that this was not just any religious freedom issue; instead, it was one that was politically

---

[39] *Che Omar bin Che Soh v. Public Prosecutor* [1988] 2 Malayan Law Journal 55. The appellant in that case argued that according to Islamic law, drug offences do not constitute offences that are punishable by death. He sought a declaration that the law (the Firearms (Increased Penalties) Act 1971) was unconstitutional as it was contrary to Islamic law.

[40] Ibid.   [41] Ibid.

[42] *Titular Roman Catholic Archbishop of Kuala Lumpur v. Menteri Dalam Negeri & Another* [2009] 2 Malayan Law Journal 78, 106–7 [*The Herald Decision I*].

[43] Ibid., p. 91.

loaded and entangled with considerations about ethno-religious insecurities and suspicions. The government's defence of the Ministry's decision revealed its conceptions of how religious freedom should be defined and practiced. It suggested that religious freedom can and should be restricted to avoid religious 'confusion' and public disorder, as well as to avoid aggravating majority religious sensitivities. For the government, *The Herald* could have used an alternative word to refer to 'God' in its Malay language publications.[44] The right to practice one's religion, in its view, only extended to practices or activities that are 'integral' to the religion – in this case, the Christian faith. This attempt to define and limit the scope of permissible religious practices is comparable to the Indonesian experience with the *Blasphemy Law* case. In any event, the government contended that the prohibition on using 'Allah' was only limited to *The Herald* and that such use contravened existing state enactments to control the propagation of religions other than Islam among Muslims.[45]

In October 2013, the Court of Appeal reversed a High Court decision in 2010 which had declared that the prohibition on the use of 'Allah' was unconstitutional. For the High Court, the claim that the use of 'Allah' would endanger public order and national security was baseless and far-fetched.[46] It also relied on 'uncontroverted historical evidence' submitted by the Church that 'Allah' has long been used by Christians and Muslims in Arabic-speaking countries, Malay-speaking Christian natives in Malaysia, and some of the earliest Malay Bibles in Malaya.[47] Based on this evidence, the court argued that the use of 'Allah' was integral to the practice and propagation of Catholicism to Malay-speaking Catholics.

For the Court of Appeal, however, the High Court did not fully appreciate the public order threat posed by the unrestricted use of 'Allah'. Just as its counterparts in Indonesia, the court's arguments appear to be dictated by

---

[44] Ibid. The alternative word referred to here is the Malay translation for God, which is *'Tuhan'*. See Chapter 3 for a brief overview of the enactments. The enactments in all states are almost identical. The prohibited words include 'Allah', *'ulama'*, *'hadith'*, *'haj'*, *'mufti'* and *'fatwa'*. There are also certain expressions that are considered exclusive to Muslims such as *'Insya Allah'* and *'Alhamdulillah'*. See Non-Islamic Religions (Control of Propagation amongst Muslims) (Selangor) Enactment 1988, Schedule, Part I.

[45] Ibid., p. 102.

[46] Ibid., pp. 103–16. The Catholic Church's affidavit states that '[i]n the fourteen years of the said publication there has never been any untoward incident arising from the Applicant's use of the word "Allah" in the said publication.' Ibid., p. 97.

[47] Ibid., pp. 96–103. The word 'Allah' as a reference to God in Malay Bibles has been used since the early seventeenth century. It was used in the first edition of Matthew's Gospel in Malay, published in 1629, and in the first complete Malay Bible published in 1733. See Daud Soesilo, 'Translating the Names of God: Recent Experience from Indonesian and Malaysia' (2001) 52(4) *The Bible Translator* 414, 416.

pragmatic concerns – it referred to a series of violent protests and attacks on several houses of worship that unfolded after the High Court decision in favour of the Catholic Church, all of which were deemed enough to justify the government's prohibition.[48] While the High Court considered that the position of Islam as the religion of the Federation was irrelevant to the constitutionality of the restrictions imposed on the Catholics, the Court of Appeal gave more credence to article 3.[49] It argued that the use of 'Allah' by *The Herald* could adversely affect the 'sanctity of Islam' envisaged under article 3(1) and the right for other religions to be practiced in peace and harmony.[50] Finally, the court assessed whether a particular religious practice was in fact essential and integral to the religion. It concluded – relying upon its own research of Bible history and the Christian tradition – that the use of 'Allah' was never an integral part of Christian religious practice.[51] This fortified its assumption that allowing *The Herald* to use 'Allah' will only lead to confusion among the Muslims.

The consequences of the Court of Appeal's decision on both the position of Islam and the protection of the religious rights of minorities in Malaysia are potentially far-reaching. Although the court was careful to limit the application of the prohibition (so that it applies only to *The Herald*), the decision expanded the role and effect of the provision on Islam in unprecedented ways. In other words, in matters pertaining to religious freedom and policymaking, in general, the state is obligated – the court argued – to defend the sanctity of Islam and to have regard to the position of Islam as the religion of the Federation.[52] What is also striking was the court's unquestioning acceptance of the government's suspicions about the faith, beliefs and activities of different religious communities in the country. The fear, in this respect, was that the 'confusion' among Muslims could facilitate proselytization and subsequent conversions of the Malay-Muslims to Christianity. As we have seen, these concerns also permeate sections of the Malay-Muslim community on the ground.

Protecting Buddhism and Restricting Propagation of Religion: The Incorporation Cases in Sri Lanka

Constitutional contests on the scope and meaning of the state's obligations toward Buddhism are also not a recent phenomenon. In fact, there were

---

[48] *Menteri Dalam Negeri & Others v. Titular Roman Catholic Archbishop of Kuala Lumpur* [2013] 6 Malayan Law Journal 468, 493 [*The Herald Decision II*].
[49] Ibid., p. 511.   [50] Ibid., p. 493.   [51] Ibid., pp. 495–6.   [52] Ibid., pp. 493, 509.

judicial review cases concerning the Buddhism clause in the early and mid-1970s – even before the clause was revised to its current form.[53] However, discussions have largely centred on the 'incorporation cases', which raised important questions regarding the relative priority of Buddhist protection vis-à-vis religious rights (of minorities) under article 9. More specifically, these cases showcase the tensions between the right to convert, the right to religious practice and expression, as well as the preservation of Buddhism in Sri Lanka.

Before delving into the details of these cases, there is an important comparative point on Sri Lanka vis-à-vis the other two countries: while the cases in Indonesia and Malaysia demonstrate the courts' tacit approval of state control over the 'correct' or 'essential' religious interpretation or practices, the Sri Lankan Supreme Court has explicitly rejected such approaches. In 1985, the court examined a claim that a compulsory monthly salary contribution to the National Security Fund violated the freedom of thought, conscience and religion. The petitioner argued that the use of the Fund to purchase arms and weapons resulting in violence and the destruction of human life was against the tenets of his Buddhist faith.[54] The court held that religious beliefs – illogical or incomprehensible though they might be – are constitutionally protected and it was not the function of the court to question the correctness with which a person has perceived or interpreted his faith.[55] This position was affirmed in the *Nineteenth Amendment Bill* case, as we shall see in the next section.[56]

The 'incorporation cases' were three separate constitutional challenges to Private Members' Bills which sought to legally incorporate Christian organizations in Sri Lanka. These organizations had specific, stated aims which included religious propagation activities as well as the provision of socio-economic assistance to those in need. One of those organizations was an order of Catholic nuns, Menzingen.[57] The organization established itself as a vehicle for the propagation of Catholicism and sought to carry out activities

---

[53] See Benjamin Schonthal, 'Securing the Sasana through Law: Buddhist Constitutionalism and Buddhist-Interest Litigation in Sri Lanka' (2016) 50(6) *Modern Asian Studies* 1996, 2012.

[54] Jayampathy Wickramaratne, *Fundamental Rights in Sri Lanka* (Colombo: Stamford Lake Publications, 2006), p. 178 (quoting *Premalal Perera v. Weerasuriya* (1985) 2 Sri Lanka Law Report 177).

[55] Ibid., p. 177.

[56] See ibid., pp. 932–4. The court in this case stressed that the conception and enforcement of religious obligations for every person were beyond the reach of the state and that to restrict the right of worship on the basis of offending morals was problematic as what constitutes 'morals' differs across all religious beliefs.

[57] The organization is called the 'Provincial of the Teaching of the Holy Cross of the Third Order of Saint Francis in Menzingen of Sri Lanka' [Menzingen].

relating to religion, education, vocational training and maintaining orphan-ages.[58] Petitioners against the bill argued before the Supreme Court that the incorporation of Menzingen would not only allow the propagation of Cath-olicism, but it would also facilitate the conversion of particularly vulnerable individuals (such as children, the sick and the destitute) through the allure of material and economic benefits. They held a particular conception of the Buddhism clause and the right to religious freedom which shaped their belief that Menzingen's incorporation would be unconstitutional. First, they argued that Menzingen's 'economic' activities would go beyond the observance and practice of religion, and these would not be protected by the right to manifest one's religious belief in article 14(1).[59] Second, freedom of thought, con-science and religion was construed as encompassing freedom *from* other religious influences. It was thought that the prospective conversions that would result from Menzingen's activities would infringe the freedom of thought, conscience and religion protected by article 10. Finally, they con-tended that the objectives and activities of Menzingen would threaten the existence of Buddhism, thereby infringing article 9. This case, as in the two incorporation cases before it,[60] demonstrates the continuing anxiety among Buddhists of a perceived 'Christianization' threat to the position of Buddhism in the polity and Buddhist religious life.

The Supreme Court, as it did in the previous two cases, held in favour of the petitioners. Its decision was revealing of its mindset and orientations toward religious propagation and the role of Buddhism. For the court, that Menzingen's proposed activities combined religious observance and practice with the provision of material benefits to defenceless and vulnerable people were suspect. This, it held, violated article 10, because such practices would

---

[58] See *A Bill Titled 'Provincial of the Teaching of the Holy Cross of the Third Order of Saint Francis in Menzingen of Sri Lanka (Incorporation)'*, Supreme Court of Sri Lanka Special Determination, S.C.S.D. No. 19/2003 (25 July 2003) [*Menzingen* case].

[59] Ibid., pp. 2–3. The petitioner highlighted three activities that were '[e]conomic or financial in nature', listed in the clause 3 of the bill: (1) teaching in schools; colleges or other educational institutions; (2) serving in nursing homes, clinics and hospitals; and (3) maintaining day care centres, orphanages, elderly care centres and nursing homes for the sick, destitutes, aged, orphans and infants.

[60] The two previous cases are: (1) *The Christian Sahanaye Doratuwa Prayer Centre (Incorporation) Bill*, Supreme Court of Sri Lanka Special Determination, S.C.S.D No. 2/2001 (24 May 2001) [*Prayer Centre* case] and (2) *The New Wine Harvest Ministries (Incorporation) Bill*, Supreme Court of Sri Lanka Special Determination, S.C.S.D No. 2 /2003 (16 January 2003) [*New Wine Harvest* case]. In both decisions, the Supreme Court held that the incorporation of the Christian organizations was unconstitutional. The former case did not raise any questions on the violation of article 9.

necessarily result in improper pressure or influence over a person's right to freely choose or adopt his religion or belief.[61] The court also distinguished the right to propagate a religion and the right to practice and manifest one's religion; it held that the former was not protected because there was no express right to that effect in the Constitution.[62]

By adopting this strict textualist approach, the court carved an additional restriction on the right to religious freedom and denied what many Christians consider to be part of the manifestation of their religious belief. However, in the remaining parts of its judgment, the court hinted at a more restrictive reading of the limitation imposed on propagation – it argued that even if propagation was a guaranteed right under the constitution, the protection of such right did not extend to a right to convert another person to one's own religion, as this would violate the freedom of conscience.[63] This reflects the concern, which was obvious throughout the judgment, over conversions attained through 'improper' means, compulsion or material inducements.

The right to propagate a religion is, of course, not an absolute right. The International Covenant on Civil and Political Rights (ICCPR) and the Sri Lankan Constitution both recognize that such right may be legitimately restricted to further goals such as public order, health and morality. Previous reports by the UN Special Rapporteurs to the Sub-Commission on Prevention of Discrimination and Protection of Minorities have also highlighted the need to prohibit coercion or improper inducements in securing religious conversions.[64] Yet, as in the cases in Malaysia and Indonesia, what was revealing about the *Menzingen* decision was not just the court's curious rationale on religious freedom questions, but also its assumptions about the nature and

---

[61] *Menzingen* case, p. 6.

[62] Ibid., p. 7. In drawing such distinction, the court followed its decision in the *Prayer Centre* case, which held that although the constitution guarantees the right to manifest one's religion, it does not protect the right to propagate and spread another religion. Here, the court referred to an Indian case (*Rev. Stanislas v. State of Madhya Pradesh* (1977) All Indian Rep. S.C. 908 which held that there is no fundamental right to convert another person to one's own religion because that would contravene the freedom of conscience. It also argued that unlike the Indian Constitution, the Sri Lankan Constitution contains no express fundamental right to propagate one's religion. *Prayer Centre* case, p. 23.

[63] Ibid.

[64] See Special Rapporteur of the Sub-Commission on Prevention of Discrimination and Protection of Minorities, *Study of Discrimination in the Matter of Religious Rights and Practices*, UN Doc. E/CN.4/Sub.2/200/Rev.1 (1960) (by Arcot Krishnaswami) and Special Rapporteur of the Sub-Commission on Prevention of Discrimination and Protection of Minorities, *Elimination of All Forms of Intolerance and Discrimination Based on Religion or Belief*, UN Doc. E/CN.4/Sub.2/1984/28 (3 August 1984).

effect of religious propagation.[65] The court did not offer any explicit basis for its assumptions. The other important point was the court's declaration that the propagation of Christianity would 'impair the existence of Buddhism',[66] thus rendering the bill inconsistent with article 9. This reasoning also lacked any explanation, but more significantly, this line of argument went beyond its two previous decisions on the constitutionality of the incorporation bills. Its decisions in those cases – the *Prayer Centre* case and the *New Wine Harvest* case – did not address the question of whether the proposed activities of the organizations would threaten the position of Buddhism.

PROVISIONS ON STATE-RELIGION RELATIONSHIP: CHANGING CONCEPTIONS?

The preceding case studies are only part of a bigger set of constitutional contests showcasing the salience of the constitutional provisions on religion, both in the claims of litigants as well as judicial reasoning. The diverse ways in which litigants have invoked and interpreted the religion clauses are striking, particularly when we compare them against the underlying motivation and spirit behind the adoption of those clauses.

For one, there is a belief that the religion clause requires the state to enforce religious laws and principles or even to elevate divine laws and principles above the country's 'secular' laws. This peculiar conception of what the religion clause entails was especially evident in the Indonesian *Religious Courts* case and the Malaysian case of *Che Omar*, but it has also gained ground outside the courts. In Malaysia, for instance, there is growing acceptance amongst Muslim interest groups, the state Islamic bureaucracies and Muslim civil society movements that article 3 requires the state to ensure that 'Islamic' laws and principles are elevated and entrenched in law-making and governance. The series of public rallies in Jakarta in late 2016 – precipitated by accusations that the Jakarta governor had insulted the Quran and Islam – have opened opportunities for several Muslim movements to advocate a '*Shariah*-based Indonesian state'.

In another variation, some have invoked the provisions on religion to enforce religious orthodoxy or mainstream religious doctrines and practices.

---

[65] Wickramaratne argues that the court failed to appreciate the distinction between propagation as an act of evangelism versus improper proselytism. See Wickramaratne, *Fundamental Rights in Sri Lanka*, p. 201.

[66] *Menzingen* case, p. 7.

As we have seen, the defence of the Indonesian Blasphemy Law was grounded in the belief that a *Pancasila* state could not endorse 'deviant' religious practices and teachings. In Malaysia, a government prohibition against the use of 'Allah' in a Christian publication, the wearing of a *serban* (Muslim headgear) to schools and the wearing of a *purdah* in civil service were justified on the basis that these were practices that were not essential or non-mandatory to a particular religion. In other words, they are not part of the accepted, mainstream religious practices. In Sri Lanka, a Buddhist monk's application to be enrolled and admitted to the Bar in 1977 triggered a very controversial constitutional challenge by several lay Buddhist organizations (including the Young Men's Buddhist Association and the All Ceylon Buddhist Congress) to frustrate the application.[67] For the petitioners, the state's duty to protect Buddhism included reinforcing the orthodox notion that Buddhist monastic life must be separated from worldly concerns.[68]

In other instances, the religion clauses have been invoked in a less radical, but nevertheless significant, fashion: they sought to compel the state to protect and defend the sanctity of religion (or the majority religion, as the case might be) from various external threats, real or imagined. By extension, the state is required to entrench and enhance the superiority of the dominant religion vis-à-vis other religions in the constitutional order. In Malaysia, for example, this has translated into claims that the position of Islam as the state religion meant that in cases of civil-*Shariah* jurisdictional conflict, the *Shariah* court should always prevail.[69]

The highest courts in these three countries have responded to these claims and pressures in varying ways. In fact, there is no perfect consistency in the direction that these courts have taken. In the case of Sri Lanka, as we shall see, the courts have not always endorsed the idea that actions or practices that threaten the status of Buddhism would violate article 9. What I want to emphasize here, however, is indications of changing conceptions on the religion provisions emerging from the courts. One such indication rests in the ways in which courts have invoked such provisions (i.e., the belief in one and only God in Indonesia, the establishment of Islam as the religion of the Federation in Malaysia and the provision that obligates the Sri Lankan state to give Buddhism the foremost place and to protect and foster the Buddha Sasana) to define the boundaries of religious freedom in these countries.

---

[67] Schonthal, 'Securing the Sasana', p. 22.   [68] Ibid., pp. 23–4.

[69] See *Subashini A/P Rajasingham v. Saravanan Thangathoray & Other Appeals* [2008] 2 Malayan Law Journal 147.

Can Pancasila Restrict Religious Freedom?

Since its inception in August 2003, only a handful of cases involving questions on the constitutional role of religion in the state and religious freedom have come before the Indonesian Constitutional Court. I have explained two such cases – the *Religious Courts* case and the *Blasphemy Law* case – where the court interpreted religious freedom in the context of the *Pancasila's* first principle, 'belief in the one and only God'.

The two cases demonstrate that the use of the 'belief in the one and only God' in article 29 to restrict religious freedom may yield different consequences. Recall that the *Religious Courts* case involved the claim that the exercise of one's religious freedom hinged on one's ability to adopt and be subjected to the full panoply of *Shariah* law. The outcome in this case illustrates how the state-religion arrangement can thwart any attempts to widen the scope and reach of Islamic laws among Muslims. This comports with the constitutional framers' understanding of the *Pancasila* in limiting the role of Islam in the state and affirms their explicit rejection of constitutionally sanctioned *Shariah* obligations for Muslims. Yet, in stressing that religious activities cannot 'diverge from the *Pancasila*',[70] the *Blasphemy Law* decision demonstrates that article 29 can also be used in a way that is counterproductive to religious tolerance and the protection of the religious rights of minorities (especially those who do not conform to mainstream religious doctrines and views). This is a far cry from Soekarno's pluralistic understanding of the *Pancasila* as a principle that encourages religiosity but which nevertheless embraces a broad conception of 'God'.[71]

The *Blasphemy Law* case also cemented another important principle for human rights jurisprudence in Indonesia: since the *Pancasila* is the state's philosophical foundation and the state encourages religion and religiosity,[72] 'religious values' becomes a legitimate – even natural – constraint on rights.

---

[70] *Blasphemy Decision I*, p. 273. The court also stressed that aside from the *Pancasila*, the Indonesian Constitution is imbued references to religious values and religiosity. Consequently, 'the Indonesian nation is a nation that believes in God'. Ibid.

[71] It is significant that article 29(2) protects the freedom to worship according to one's religion *and beliefs*. The latter accommodates the traditional, spiritual and mystical groups, as well as belief streams (*aliran kepercayaan*) that exist all over Indonesia and do not necessarily subscribe to the main religions' idea of 'God'. In the post-Soeharto constitutional amendment process, there were attempts by several political parties, such as Golkar, PAN and PK (who formed the *Reformasi* faction) to remove the word 'beliefs' from article 29(2), but they were unsuccessful. Article 29(2) in the constitution today is in the same form as it was from the original 1945 constitution.

[72] *Blasphemy Decision I*, p. 275.

Chapter 2 has shown how this provision was inserted at the eleventh hour in the constitution-making process, leaving little room for legislators to determine its precise meanings and limitations. For the court, 'religious values' was a 'key consideration' in determining the constitutionality of laws.[73] In other words, what appears to follow from article 29 is that the state is compelled to uphold religious values against exercises of rights that are deemed incompatible with such values.

The exceptionalist undertones in the court's reasoning were clear. Despite its repeated acknowledgment of the ICCPR standards on religious freedom in its judgment, the court distinguished Indonesian constitutional norms from 'Western' norms to justify the use of 'religious values' as a basis for upholding the law – even if this meant violating Indonesia's obligations under the ICCPR.[74]

The inherent subjectivity and vagueness of the term 'religious values' are fraught with difficulties. If the exercise of religious freedom must conform to 'religious values', one is pressed to ask: what are such values and who determines them? The court did not explicitly address these questions, but the judgment – particularly on the point that religious interpretations must follow the correct methodology and that a religion's 'internal authorities' would determine the fundamental doctrines of that religion[75] – indicates that the court would defer to mainstream religious standards. In the case of Islam, the court added, the *ulama* would possess the authority in interpreting Islamic teachings. The state's role, then, is confined to enforcement: it would merely enforce what has been agreed upon by the religious authorities.[76] What the court seemed to ignore, in this regard, is the fact that religious views and interpretations are profoundly diverse, even amongst Indonesian religious scholars and the MUI. Opinions and *fatwas* against groups like the Ahmadiyah and Shia, for instance, vary across regions and localities in the country. In practice, in the case of Islam, 'authority' is almost always dominated by orthodox Sunni religious leaders. By going down the path that it did, the court provided an avenue through which religion and religious practices can be controlled within the state's narrow official framework.[77]

---

[73] Ibid.

[74] 'Indonesia's respect for international law and conventions, including those concerning human rights,' said the court, 'must be based on the philosophy and constitution of the Republic of Indonesia'. Ibid. To date, Indonesia has not entered any reservations to its ratification of the ICCPR. The constitutional amendment which cemented the religious values limitation was passed in 2000, but Indonesia only ratified the ICCPR on 23 February 2006.

[75] *Blasphemy Decision I*, p. 289.   [76] Ibid.

[77] Butt and Lindsey, *The Constitution of Indonesia*, p. 240.

Radical Shifts in the Conception of Article 3 on Islam

The seeds for the transformation of the meaning of article 3 had been sown before the 'Allah' case, but the ways in which the decision dealt with article 3 are unprecedented. A careful reading of the judgment not only suggests that the court had its mind fixed on a peculiar understanding of article 3, but it also reveals the court's underlying tendencies in matters implicating Islam.

The court, to begin with, went further than declaring that article 3 on Islam can restrict the exercise of religious freedom. Having identified the propagation of other religions to Muslims as the 'most possible and probable threat to Islam',[78] it suggested that article 3, when considered with the provision allowing states to regulate propagation (article 11(4)), meant that Islam should be *immune* from any threats to weaken its special position.[79] To cement these views, the court stated that a minister was obliged to defend the sanctity of Islam and to consider Islam's special constitutional position in his decision-making. The provision that other religions – despite the establishment of Islam as the state religion – may be practiced 'in peace and harmony', was construed not as a safeguard for religious freedom as the framers had intended, but as protection for Islam.[80] As if to annihilate the limited role of article 3 envisioned by the constitutional framers, the court also completely ignored article 3(4), which provides that Islam does not and cannot operate as an automatic trump card against other constitutional provisions (including fundamental liberties).[81]

A similarly broad interpretation of article 3 has been especially obvious in cases on Muslim apostasy or conversion, as well as in those implicating the role of the state in controlling religious doctrines and praxis. Some judgments have relied excessively on the idea that Islamic laws and principles override other 'secular' considerations. In a conversion case in 2007, the Federal Court implied that a Muslim's ability to exercise his or her freedom to change a religion is subject to Islamic norms, principles and procedures.[82] This means that the establishment of Islam and the principles of the religion were made to precede fundamental rights guarantees in the constitution.[83] When the case

---

[78] *The Herald Decision II*, p. 490.   [79] Ibid., p. 469.

[80] The court stated that the phrase 'in peace and harmony' was intended to protect and insulate Islam from any possible threats to it. Ibid., p. 490.

[81] See Shad Saleem Faruqi, *Document of Destiny: The Constitution of the Federation of Malaysia* (Petaling Jaya: Star Publications, 2008), p. 346.

[82] *Lina Joy v. Majlis Agama Islam Wilayah Persekutuan & Another* [2007] 4 Malayan Law Journal 585, 593.

[83] See Andrew Harding, 'Sharia and National Law in Malaysia' in Jan Michiel Otto (ed.), *Sharia Incorporated: A Comparative Overview of the Legal Systems of Twelve Muslim Countries*

was tried at the High Court, the trial judge declared that subjecting religious freedom to the constitutional establishment of Islam reflected the intentions of the constitutional framers.[84] In an earlier case concerning the constitutionality of a ban on the wearing of *serbans* for Muslim students, the High Court rejected the notion that the role of Islam under article 3 was confined to official rituals and ceremonies.[85] Instead, the court argued, article 3 envisioned Islam as a complete way of life and, consequently, regulations contrary to Islam can be invalidated.[86] Still more questionable was the presiding judge's assertion that the Malay rulers had demanded the establishment of Islam as the religion of the Federation so as to recognize the supremacy of Islam.[87] These arguments, as Chapter 2 has illustrated, have no historical basis.[88]

The attempt to buttress the superiority of Islam in the constitutional set-up was also evident in the court's assessment of the importance of the use of 'Allah' in Christian doctrines and traditions. In some measure, the analysis saw the court affirming the need to consider the impact of Christian religious practices on Islam and the Muslim community. Recall that in the *Blasphemy Law* decision, the Indonesian Constitutional Court avoided making any explicit judgments on the 'correct' principles and doctrines in a particular religion. Instead, it left these issues to be determined by the religion's 'internal authorities'. Even then, the court avoided naming an authoritative religious body to make such determinations. I have also briefly noted that the Sri

---

in *Past and Present* (Leiden: Leiden University Press, 2010), p. 564. See also *Kamariah bte Ali & Others v. Governments of the State of Kelantan, Malaysia & Another* [2002] 3 Malayan Law Journal 657. This is also another case on apostasy, but is nevertheless pertinent in demonstrating how courts have transformed the meaning of Islam as the religion of the Federation vis-à-vis fundamental rights protection. There, the court held that '[a]rticle 11 cannot be interpreted so widely as to revoke all legislation requiring a person to perform a requirement under Islam or prohibit them from committing an act forbidden by Islam ... this was because the standing of Islam in the Federal Constitution was different from that of other religions'. Ibid., pp. 658–9.

[84] *Lina Joy v. Majlis Agama Islam Wilayah Persekutuan* [2004] 2 Malayan Law Journal 119, 129.

[85] *Meor Atiqulrahman Ishak and Others v. Fatimah Sihi and Others* [2000] 5 Malayan Law Journal 375, 383.

[86] Ibid., pp. 384–5.

[87] Ibid., p. 384. In the judgment, the court asserted that the provision on Islam was included as part of a bargain which led to the grant of citizenship to the non-Malays. It argued that it was unfathomable that the Malay rulers who fought to include Islam as the religion of the Federation would limit the role of Islam to mere rituals and ceremonies. This interpretation was incorrect, and it certainly did not reflect the position taken by the Malay rulers during the constitution-making process. As we have seen in Chapter 2, the provision was inserted at the insistence of the Alliance leaders.

[88] As Faruqi observes, the constitutional framers had explicitly rejected the idea that Islam would operate as a comprehensive value system that governs the life of the nation. Faruqi, *Document of Destiny*, p. 348.

Lankan Supreme Court rejected the task of ascertaining whether a particular religious belief or interpretation is correct or sensible.

By contrast, a two-judge majority in the 'Allah' case saw it fit to determine whether a Christian organization *should* use the word 'Allah' in its Malay-language publications. In a rather debatable series of reasoning and conclusion, a judge argued that the use of 'Allah' was not integral to the Christian faith, based on a 'quick research on the history of the language of the Bible'.[89] Another judge examined the appropriateness of the Christians' insistence to use 'Allah' in their religious publications by referring to selective Internet sources disputing such use in the Christian tradition.[90] For the court, this lack of consensus on how and when to use 'Allah' weakened claims about the importance of such use within the Christian community.[91] Yet it is worth noting that in the course of its analysis, the court disregarded the historical evidence previously submitted by the Catholic Church in the High Court to show that Christians in Malaysia (especially the Malay-speaking natives in Sabah and Sarawak) had been using the word 'Allah' as a reference to God for many years. It also ignored a previous (and a more nuanced) Federal Court decision that laid down a five-step test to determine the constitutionality of laws affecting religious practices.[92] In that case, the importance of the disputed practice to a religion was only one of the five factors that a court must consider in its decision-making. Eventually, in the 'Allah' case, the court found itself injudiciously expanding the grounds on which religious freedom can be restricted and validating the claims that protecting Islam and saving Muslims from confusion outweighed the religious rights of minorities.

De Silva's 'Balanced Solution' in Practice: A Mixed Response

Whereas the highest courts in Malaysia, through a number of decisions, appear to incrementally assert the superiority of Islam as the state religion over fundamental rights, the Sri Lankan Supreme Court has delivered mixed signals on what 'protecting Buddhism' entails. In fact, Sri Lanka's highest courts have not always validated claims that the Buddhism chapter required the state to protect Buddhism in ways that could override other 'secular' considerations, including the government's nationalization policies and fundamental rights.[93] This appears counter-intuitive, because a plain comparison of the religion provisions in both constitutions suggests that the

---

[89] *The Herald Decision II*, pp. 495–6.
[90] Ibid., pp. 513–21 (opinion by Justice Mohamad Zawawi Salleh).   [91] Ibid., p. 522.
[92] *Meor Atiqulrahman bin Ishak v. Fatimah bte Sihi* [2006] 4 Malayan Law Journal 605.
[93] Schonthal, 'Securing the Sasana', pp. 1981–2002.

Sri Lankan arrangement would provide more leeway for courts to prioritize Buddhist prerogatives.

The three incorporation cases were all examined against the backdrop of intense public concern about evangelism, proselytism and the status of Buddhism in Sri Lanka.[94] Only the *New Wine Harvest* and *Menzingen* petitions explicitly raised questions about the balance between Buddhist prerogatives versus the protection of religious rights.[95] However, it was in *Menzingen* that the court cemented an expansive interpretation of the state's duties under article 9: the right to exercise one's religion exists so long as it does not adversely affect the Buddha Sasana.[96] In this regard, the propagation of Christianity and proselytism were seen as the kinds of religious practices that would threaten the Buddha Sasana.

Almost a year later, the court considered a petition challenging the constitutionality of a bill that sought to criminalize forcible and unethical conversions from one religion to another (known as the 'JHU Bill').[97] The bill was to have implications for the freedom to practice and express one's religion as it targeted propagation and proselytism activities. Like the cases preceding it, the *JHU Bill* case illustrates the competing claims on religious rights and on two seemingly incompatible halves of article 9 – the state's duties to protect and foster the Buddha Sasana, on the one hand, and the guarantee of religious freedom, on the other. For the proponents of the bill, criminalizing forced conversions was consistent with the state's duty to protect and foster the Buddha Sasana; the freedom of thought, conscience, and religion in article 10; and the right to practice and manifest one's religious beliefs under article

---

[94] Benjamin Schonthal, 'The Legal Regulation of Buddhism in Contemporary Sri Lanka' in Rebecca Redwood French & Mark A. Nathan (eds.), *Buddhism and Law: An Introduction* (Cambridge: Cambridge University Press, 2014), p. 150.

[95] In the *New Wine Harvest* case, the petitioner (who was the secretary of the All Ceylon Buddhist Congress) argued that the bill would open the door for the organization to engage in the propagation of Christianity and for the fraudulent conversions into Christianity. See *New Wine Harvest* case, pp. 9–11, and Priyalal Sirisena, 'Bill to establish Christian institution challenged in SC', *The Island* (18 January 2003), online: www.island.lk/2003/01/18/news10.html.

[96] *Menzingen* case, pp. 6–7.

[97] Clause 2 of the Prohibition of Forcible Conversion of Religion Bill '[p]rohibits acts to convert or attempts to convert any persons from one religion to another by the use of force, allurement, or any fraudulent means'. The supporters of the bill said that it did not seek to enforce a blanket prohibition on conversions, but only on those that were deemed unethical. See Manohara de Silva, 'Proposed Legislation on Unethical Conversions' in A. R. B. Amerasinghe and S. S. Wijeratne (eds.), *Human Rights: Theory to Practice: Essays in Honour of Deshamaya R. K. W. Goonasekere* (Colombo: Legal Aid Commission and Human Rights Commission of Sri Lanka, 2005), p. 187.

14(1)(e).[98] Conversely, its opponents (the petitioners in this case) argued that the bill was framed in explicit terms to prioritize Buddhist prerogatives and target Christian practices.[99] For them, this violated article 9 because state patronage of Buddhism cannot be exercised at the expense of the religious rights of others.[100]

The Supreme Court, however, did not fully resolve the question about the relative priority of Buddhist protections vis-à-vis fundamental rights under article 9.[101] In what was a mixed response, it ruled, without much elaboration, that the bill's prohibition on acts or attempts to convert a person from one religion to another through force, allurement or any fraudulent means (clause 2) did not contravene article 9 as the petitioners had claimed.[102] The court also ruled, again without any further explanation, that the clause was a permissible restriction on the right to practice and manifest one's religion, as provided by article 15(7).[103] In the end, the bill was never presented to parliament for adoption.

That the court made no effort to illuminate an understanding of article 9 was, perhaps, a calculated decision in order to avoid making a clear decision

---

[98] See submission by president's counsel A. A. de Silva in Wasantha Ramanayake, 'SC to communicate determination of anti conversion bill to president and speaker', *Daily News* (11 August 2004), online: archives.dailynews.lk/2004/08/11/new12.html.

[99] Written Submissions by the Solidarity for Religious Freedom to the Supreme Court of Sri Lanka, 4, August 2004 (on file with author). The preamble of the bill referred to the predominance of Buddhism in article 9, stating that the 'Buddhist and non-Buddhist are now under serious threat of forcible conversion and proselytizing by coercion or by allurement or by fraudulent means'.

[100] See also Wickramaratne, *Fundamental Rights in Sri Lanka*, p. 202 (arguing that the obligation to protect and foster the Buddha Sasana is without prejudice to other religions. Buddhism is only the first among equals; other religions are not subordinated to it.).

[101] Benjamin Schonthal, 'Constitutionalizing Religion: The Pyrrhic Success of Religious Rights in Post-Colonial Sri Lanka' (2014) 29 *Journal of Law and Religion* 470, 487. For a detailed description of the decision, see Schonthal, 'Constitutionalizing Religion' and Wickramaratne, *Fundamental Rights in Sri Lanka*, pp. 203–5. Wickramaratne describes this decision as a 'very balanced' one, in light of the court's effort to distinguish true evangelism on the one hand, and improper proselytism on the other.

[102] *Prohibition of Forcible Conversion of Religion Bill*, Supreme Court Special Determination, S.C. Nos 02–22/2004 (12 August 2004), pp. 12–13. However, the court recommended particular amendments to clauses in the bill which dealt with the meaning of 'force', 'fraudulent' and 'allurement'. There were other clauses in the bill that the court held were in conflict with article 10. Ibid., pp. 13–14.

[103] Ibid. In article 15(7), the exercise of the freedom to manifest one's religion in the Sri Lankan constitution is subject to restrictions in the interests of national security, public order and the protection of public health or morality, or for the purpose of securing due recognition and respect for the rights and freedoms of others, or of meeting the just requirements of the general welfare of a democratic society.

in favour of one group over the other.[104] To some, this might seem unsatis-
factory, and indeed one could argue that the court was sidestepping its
responsibility to decide an important constitutional question. But the *JHU
Bill* case could also be viewed in a more positive light. The path that the court
took was in fact the one that it crucially missed in *Menzingen*. It could have
struck down the *Menzingen* bill without invoking article 9 and, subsequently,
without sending a less than favourable message to the minorities about their
fundamental rights in the country's constitutional order. Invoking the restrictions in article 15(7) to address concerns over improper proselytism and
conversion – along the lines that it did in the *JHU Bill* case – would have
been a less jarring approach to minority interests and sensitivities. Unfortunately, the decision in *Menzingen* only served to legitimize and amplify
exclusivist claims to religion and religious rights by the majority.

Just months after the *JHU Bill* case, the Supreme Court took another
different turn. This time, the case concerned a bill to amend article 9 of the
constitution, which was also introduced by the Jathika Hela Urumaya (JHU)
party.[105] The bill not only sought to impose stronger restrictions on the
freedom of religion for both Buddhists and non-Buddhists,[106] it also proposed
to make Buddhism the official religion of the state.[107] Interestingly, the
proposal adopted a language similar to the Malaysian provision on Islam:
aside from elevating the status of Buddhism as the official religion, it stated
that other religions 'may be practiced in peace and harmony with the Buddha
Sasana'. The consequence, therefore, is more far-reaching than the Malaysian
arrangement because the practice of religious freedom would only be protected so long as it does not affect the Buddha Sasana.

The court declared the bill unconstitutional for violating the freedoms of
religion and to manifest one's religion, and the right to equality and non-
discrimination. The more crucial point concerns the court's conception of the

---

[104] Schonthal argues that the court made a politically strategic move. It did not want to assert
    Buddhist superiority over fundamental rights, as that would disenfranchise the groups
    (the non-Buddhists, the secularists and the liberals) who were strong government supporters at
    the time. At the same time, it did not want to appear to subordinate Buddhist protection to
    fundamental rights due to the risk of alienating Buddhist nationalists who were growing in
    numbers. Schonthal, 'Constitutionalizing Religion,' pp. 487–8.
[105] See Nineteenth Amendment to the Constitution (Private Member's Bill), Gazette of the
    Democratic Socialist Republic of Sri Lanka (29 October 2004), Supplement, p. 2 [Nineteenth
    Amendment Bill].
[106] For example, Buddhists are required to bring up their children as Buddhists (article 9.4,
    Nineteenth Amendment Bill) and the conversion of Buddhists into other religion and the
    propagation of other religion among Buddhists are prohibited (article 9.5).
[107] Article 9.1, Nineteenth Amendment Bill.

meaning and parameters of article 9. It emphasized that the Sri Lankan Constitution is secular and that the special position of Buddhism is balanced by the assurance that the rights of other religions are equally protected from any interference.[108] The court also added that Parliament cannot enact legislation which enforces the preference for one religion at the expense of other religions.[109] This decision appeared to restore the meaning behind the provision on Buddhism as was intended by De Silva. Three years later, however, the court's reasoning in a case concerning a loudspeaker permit for a mosque to broadcast their call to prayers[110] seemed to suggest that the parameters of acceptable religious practices would also be determined from a distinctively Buddhist worldview. Although the court reiterated that Sri Lanka is a secular state and that the restrictions on religious practices that amount to noise pollution were compatible with secularism,[111] it also noted a Buddhist scholar's writings on the metes and bounds of religious worship according to the Buddha, which emphasized the importance and benefit of quieter prayers as opposed to loud prayers that 'disturbs' the environment.[112] The implication of this reference and decision, as Abeyratne notes, is that the practices of minority religions are now assessed in relation to what is mandated as appropriate and proper according to Buddhist principles.[113]

THE PUBLIC ORDER RESTRICTION

The contestations involving religion and religious freedom reflect broader social and political concerns amongst different religious groups in the society. The growing apprehension about the spread of minority religions and deep insecurities about the survival of the majority community of believers, for instance, have elevated the belief that the state must intervene to protect majority interests. The histories and experiences in all three countries have shown that these anxieties can trigger violence and religious vigilantism. Malaysia has, by and large, been spared the kinds of societal violence we see in Indonesia and Sri Lanka, but poorly managed tensions may evolve into deadly outcomes. There is thus some reason to take the Indonesian court

---

[108] Wickramaratne, *Fundamental Rights in Sri Lanka*, p. 933.   [109] Ibid., p. 934.

[110] *Kapuwatta Mohideen Jumma Mosque v. OIC Weligama*, S.C. Application No. 38/2005 (FR); S.C. Minute of 9/11/2007.

[111] Rehan Abeyratne, 'Rethinking Judicial Independence in India and Sri Lanka' (2015) 10 *Asian Journal of Comparative Law* 99, 125.

[112] Ibid. (quoting *Church of God (Full Gospel) v. K.K. R.M.C Welfare Association*, AIR 2000 SC 2773).

[113] Ibid.

seriously when it expressed concerns that striking down the Blasphemy Law would spur religious vigilantism. These situations require courts to balance the protection of rights and freedoms against the need to secure public order and national security. However, the court's peculiar rationale deserves greater scrutiny, especially since the case involves constitutional rights issues.[114]

The Indonesian court's public order argument focused on concerns that 'deviant' religious interpretation or activities will agitate adherents of the blasphemed religion and that minorities could become targets of violence by extremists who reject religious pluralism.[115] In a similar vein, the Malaysian Court of Appeal endorsed the government's view that *The Herald's* use of 'Allah' would provoke religious antagonisms between Christian and Muslim communities. It also stressed two points: (1) the threat to the sanctity of Islam as the religion of the Federation is a public order concern;[116] and (2) for the government to exercise its discretion to protect public order, it need not wait for actual violence to occur.[117] In any case, what is clear from both decisions was that the courts were more anxious about a majority-led backlash and its potential to trigger interreligious conflict. The courts' idea of 'order' also appears to hinge on the protection and preservation of the majority community of believers in the respective countries.

What both the Malaysian and Indonesian courts failed to scrutinize in detail was that the threats to public order are posed not by those whose religious practices the courts sought to circumscribe. Rather, they were instigated by those who object to those practices (or to the existence of the minorities, as the case might be). The courts did not attempt to balance these competing considerations. Given the courts' reasoning, it is conceivable that individuals or groups may stoke violence and disorder to justify restrictions against the minorities. Pursuing or protecting 'public order', therefore, may easily disguise religious intolerance and the persecution of minorities and, by extension, legitimize tyranny of the majority.

Another obvious shortcoming of the two decisions is the assessment of whether the restrictions imposed on religious freedom were in fact proportional to the public order aim the governments sought to achieve. In the 'Allah' decision, the court accorded great deference to executive decision-making in a situation that it perceived as a grave threat to public order and national security. The judgment evinced the majority judges' suspicions about Christian proselytism and its effects on the Muslim community. Yet, its rationale was curious, particularly in light of the fact that Malay-language

---

[114] The incorporation cases did not address the question of 'public order'.
[115] *Blasphemy Decision I*, pp. 292–3, 304.   [116] *The Herald Decision II*, p. 493.
[117] Ibid., pp. 506–7.

Bibles have been allowed to use 'Allah' as a reference to God and that the Sikhs have also been using 'Allah' in their religious literature and practices. There was no evidence to suggest Christians had taken advantage of the use of the word 'Allah' to seek Malay-Muslim converts. In fact, from the very beginning, the Catholic Church emphasized that the use of 'Allah' in its Malay-language publication would only serve the interests of its Malay-speaking congregation, especially those from the states of Sabah and Sarawak.

In Indonesia, the court believed that the Blasphemy Law was a solution to avoid widespread violence, but its preventive effect now seems obsolete in light of the growing cases of intolerance and violence against religious minorities in the country. In just ten months after the 2010 decision, for instance, Ahmadis in Cikeusik, West Java, faced brutal and deadly mob attacks in which three Ahmadis were murdered.[118] The police stood by as the attacks were carried out, and the perpetrators received lighter prison sentences than the victims who fought in self-defense. In January 2012, SETARA Institute reported that there were 114 cases of religious freedom violations against the Ahmadiyah in 2011.[119] This is more than a two-fold increase in the number of violations against them in 2010 (fifty cases). Violence against the Shiites also peaked in 2011 and 2013, with the infamous case involving Shiites from Sampang whose properties were burned and destroyed by mobs and who were subsequently forced to flee their village.[120]

When public peace is at stake, especially in a religiously divided society, it is understandable that the protection of public order becomes one of the prime considerations of the government. However, the over-reliance on the idea that the religious rights of minorities should be restricted because the majority might instigate widespread violence to protest the exercise of such rights, as we have seen, is profoundly problematic. What seems to be an issue, in this respect, is the notion of 'public order' that the courts have adopted. The conceptions of the Malaysian and Indonesian courts appear to be limited to the realms of preserving public peace, tranquility and the 'harmonious co-existence'[121] between different religious groups. This narrow view of public order is not necessarily wrong, but it can – in the manner invoked by the

---

[118] 'Court Hands Two Muslim Killers Light Sentences', *South China Morning Post* (29 July 2011), A10.

[119] SETARA Institute, *Politik Diskriminasi Rezim SBY: Laporan Kondisi Kebebasan Beragama/ Berkeyakinan di Indonesia 2011* (*Political Discrimination by the SBY Regime: Report on the Freedom of Religion and Belief in Indonesia 2011*) (Jakarta: SETARA Institute, 2012), p. 28.

[120] *Blasphemy Decision II*, p. 74 (evidence given by Samsu Rizal Panggabean, researcher at the Center for Security and Peace Studies, Gadjah Mada University, Jogjakarta, Indonesia).

[121] See *The Herald Decision II*, p. 493. The Malaysian court also conceived the disruption to public order as a disruption to the 'even tempo of life in the community'.

courts in the two countries – thwart the essence of fundamental rights protection. There is thus a case to be made, in light of the two decisions, for a broader and richer definition of public order – one that sees 'public order' as part of a set of rules or values to ensure a well-functioning society, which includes the respect for human rights and religious diversity.[122] This could facilitate stronger protection for religious freedom, particularly in the face of majoritarian demands.

THE (PERVERSE) CONSEQUENCES OF CONSTITUTIONAL ARRANGEMENTS

So far, I have demonstrated how competing interests and the majority-minority divide manifest themselves in issues implicating religion and religious freedom. Minorities often assert the religious freedom protection enshrined in the constitution, while there are sections of the majority who seek greater visibility and influence of the dominant religion and greater protection of the interests of that religion. For example, in Malaysia and Sri Lanka, Malay-Muslims and Sinhalese-Buddhists have argued for the right to be free from any indoctrination or influence from the Christian faith, not only as a matter of the protection of an individual right to religious freedom, but also as a matter of preserving the dominant community identity. It is very unlikely that these divisions will disappear, at least in the near future. However, improvements in the rule of law – which would include ensuring law is enforced equally across the board, as well as ensuring acts of religious violence and vigilantism do not go unpunished – could strengthen the protection and enforcement of constitutional rights for all.

That aside, the cases elaborated in this chapter, as well as the issues and controversies described in Chapter 3, tell us that constitutional arrangements could have perverse consequences. I focus on two main observations, both of which could be broadly construed as signs of an emerging 'constitutional perversion' in the three countries.

The first concerns the great paradox that constitutional safeguards for religious rights do not necessarily secure religious freedom after all. In fact,

---

[122] See UN Commission on Human Rights, *Siracusa Principles on the Limitation and Derogation Provisions in the International Covenant on Civil and Political Rights*, UN Doc. E/CN.4/1985/4 (September 28, 1984); Roel De Lange, 'The European Public Order, Constitutional Principles and Fundamental Rights' (2007) 1 *Erasmus Law Review* 3, 23; and Parker, 'The Freedom to Manifest Religious Belief'. The *Siracusa Principles* provides that public order should be interpreted in the context of the purpose of the human rights that the state seeks to restrict.

violations and restrictions of religious rights have been facilitated by particular arrangements in the constitution – the clauses that permit restrictions on fundamental rights (such as restrictions in the interests of public order) and specific provisions on religion (the 'belief in the one and only God' in Indonesia; the restriction against propagation among Muslims in Malaysia; and the provisions on Islam and Buddhism in Malaysia and Sri Lanka, respectively). Article 29 of the Indonesian Constitution was rooted in the founding fathers' pluralistic conception of religious life in Indonesia.[123] In the Malaysian Constitution, the framers entrenched article 3, but with explicit assurances that the position of Islam was merely symbolic and that it would have limited practical effect on the laws and practices of the country. In a similar vein, article 9 of the Sri Lankan Constitution was thought to be the best formula to balance demands for state patronage of Buddhism and the protection of religious rights. Yet these arrangements, no matter how innocently intended by the constitution-makers, have produced unintended and troubling consequences for the state of religious freedom in the three countries. Instead of guaranteeing religious freedom, they have been utilized to expand the symbolic and substantive importance of the dominant religion in the legal, social and political spheres.

By some (generous) accounts at least, all this simply indicates the inevitable shifting conceptions of constitutional arrangements over time. A more nuanced examination of these patterns, however, indicates an underlying motivation to pander to the interests and sensitivities of the dominant religion or religious group in the country. This underlies my second point: constitutional provisions have been invoked and interpreted to advance a defensive posture over the majority's religious fervour. Or, at the minimum, the arrangements have indirectly forced the state to consider how their policies affect the interests and demands of the majority religious group. Indeed, implicit in the arguments presented before the courts was the sense that the dominant community was entitled to some form of special protection from the state in cases where majority-minority interests came into conflict, and constitutional provisions were the means to achieve that end.

Constitutional jurisprudence indicate that courts have increasingly (though admittedly not exclusively) sided with hegemonic demands and majoritarian

---

[123] According to an Islamic scholar, Professor Dawam Rahardjo, the essence of the *Pancasila* was 'not to allow the majority to impose its views on minorities'. Francois Raillon, 'The Return of Pancasila: Secular vs. Islamic Norms, Another Look at the Struggle for State Dominance in Indonesia' in Michel Picard and Rémy Madinier (eds.), *Politics of Religion in Indonesia: Syncretism, Orthodoxy, and Religious Convention in Java and Bali* (Oxon: Routledge, 2011), p. 104.

sentiments. Some of these decisions were rife with latent suspicions and distrust of minorities, while others emphasized the need to prevent further conflict. For example, the court in *Menzingen* declared that the organization's propagation objectives contravened the freedom of thought, conscience and religion based on its assumption that its religious and socio-economic activities would *necessarily* result in conversions by allurement. Similar inclinations to protect majority sensitivities were obvious in the 'Allah' decision in Malaysia, where the court thought it was apt to restrict the rights of Catholics to protect Muslims from 'confusion' over who 'Allah' is.[124] This reinforces the majoritarian undertones of a decision which held that article 11(4)'s prohibition on religious propagation to Muslims allowed states to pass laws to protect Islam from other Islamic schools of thought or doctrines of Islam that did not conform to the Sunni doctrine.[125] All this indicates that majority interests, when in conflict with minority rights, supersede the latter.

In the Indonesian case, the Constitutional Court was determined to restrict religious interpretation and expression so as to ensure that mainstream sensitivities are not offended. One manifestation of its majoritarian-centric approach rests in its approval of the role of 'internal authorities' of a particular religion to decide the range of 'correct' or acceptable interpretation and practices. For Islam, the Ministry of Religious Affairs (MORA) acts based on the information and consensus it receives from Islamic organizations.[126] These institutions, however, are dominated by mainstream Sunni Muslims. In this respect, the decision has had the effect of streamlining the doctrines and practices associated with Islam. All this, taken together, reinforces the deviation from Soekarno and Soepomo's vision of the *Pancasila* as a common national ideology that 'does not unite itself with the dominant group in the country'.[127] By contrast, just over a year before the *Blasphemy Law* decision, the court in the *Religious Courts* case declared – in reference to the *Pancasila* – that 'the state's service to its citizens does not depend on whether adherents to a particular religion, ethnic group, or race are in the majority or the minority.'[128]

---

[124] *The Herald Decision II*, p. 507.
[125] *Mamat bin Daud & Others v. Government of Malaysia* [1988] 1 Malayan Law Journal 119.
[126] *The Blasphemy Decision I*, p. 289.
[127] RM A. B. Kusuma, *Lahirnya Undang-undang Dasar 1945 (Memuat Salinan Dokumen Otentik Badan Oentoek Menyelidiki Oesaha-oesaha Persiapan Kemerdekaan) (The Birth of the 1945 Constitution (Containing Copies of Authentic Documents of the Investigating Committee for Preparatory Work for Indonesian Independence))*, rev. ed. (Jakarta: University of Indonesia Law Faculty Publishers, 2009), p. 127.
[128] *Religious Courts* case, p. 24.

How might we understand the discrepancies between the two decisions? One possible answer is that it might have been easier for the court to reject claims for a stronger and wider application of Islamic law in Indonesia, especially since this was very clearly rejected by the constitution-makers both in 1945 and in the post-Soeharto era. As Chapter 2 has shown, the rejection of an explicit constitutionalization of *Shariah* for Muslims was also supported by the two largest Islamic organizations in Indonesia – the Nahdlatul Ulama (NU) and Muhammadiyah. There might also have been wider practical and democratic considerations at play. As Butt notes, most Indonesians are 'unlikely to favour a classic or rigid version of Islamic law, nor an expansion of the fields of Islamic law enforced by the state',[129] because while they retain a strong sense of Islamic identity and observance to Islamic rituals, they also hold to local cultural practices that are not necessarily underpinned by Islamic doctrines.[130] To incorporate a wider spectrum of Islamic law in Indonesia, he argues, would 'misrepresent the wishes of most Indonesian Muslims'.[131]

If anything, these cases demonstrate that courts are faced with a difficult task in adjudicating constitutional claims from different (and often hostile) groups. Because religious identity is a significant social marker in Indonesia, Malaysia and Sri Lanka, legal battles on constitutional rights, both in process and outcomes, may turn into bitter, winner-takes-all contestations. The *Menzingen* case, for instance, illustrates how the explicit declaration of the relative superiority of Buddhism to minorities' religious rights by the Buddhist petitioners and, subsequently, by the Supreme Court, could raise anxieties among the minorities about their socio-political position in the country. For the Buddhists, such favourable results represent a symbolic assertion of their political power and dominance. In Malaysia, the 'Allah' decision was a significant legal and moral victory for right-wing Malay-Muslim groups in their quest to ensure

---

[129] Simon Butt, 'Islam, the State and the Constitutional Court in Indonesia', *Sydney Law School Legal Studies Research Paper No. 10/70* (July 2010), p. 17. Raillon cites a survey by the Center for the Study of Islam and Society in May 2007 which found that only 22% of Indonesians support *Shariah* as the basis of the state. Raillon, 'The Return of Pancasila', p. 110. A survey in 2007 found that only a third of the respondents supported particular principles or values that are associated with the more restrictive varieties of *Shariah*. See Indonesian Survey Institute, 'Trend Dukungan Nilai Islamis versus Nilai Sekular di Indonesia' ('Trends of support for Islamist values versus secular values in Indonesia'), *Lembaga Survei Indonesia* (October 2007), online: www.lsi.or.id/riset/310/trend-dukungan-nilai-islamis-versus-nilai-sekular.

[130] Butt, ibid., p. 17.

[131] Ibid., p. 18. Note that despite the central government's careful rejection of more comprehensive implementation of Islamic law, some regional governments have passed legislation that are inspired by *Shariah*. Some of them do so in more explicit terms than others. These laws have not been challenged before the Supreme Court, and the central government has been very slow in striking down such laws.

the political survival of the Malay-Muslims in their homeland. That survival is seen as dependent on the preservation of Islamic supremacy in the country. For the non-Malay Christians, this was yet another setback to religious and non-discrimination rights that have become increasingly eroded over the years.[132] A more challenging situation arises when some of these contests are perceived as lose-lose outcomes. For instance, in the case of a Christian in Indonesia who was accused of insulting Islam, hard-line organizations dissatisfied with the perceived light sentence he received proceeded to attack churches.[133]

In the next chapter, I will explore how judicial decision-making might also be shaped by the institutional design of the judiciary and driven by strategic and ideological factors. However, it is important to acknowledge the public pressure that courts face in dealing with cases like these. The judgments in the *Blasphemy Law* and 'Allah' controversies, as well as in the incorporation cases, were all delivered in a climate of heightened tensions between different religious groups implicated in these cases. In the Indonesian and Malaysian cases, hundreds of members of right-wing organizations staged demonstrations outside the courtroom as the decisions were delivered. In the wake of the High Court ruling that the restriction on the use of 'Allah' was unconstitutional, several houses of worship were attacked and vandalized. During *Blasphemy Law* hearings, expert witnesses and lawyers were openly threatened – both inside and outside the courtroom – with physical violence and assault. The context in which the courts operate is thus important in understanding how and why religious freedom protections are on the wane. At the same time, these judicial approaches have also deepened religious schisms in societies that are already deeply divided and whittled away the protection of legal rights for minorities. The obvious danger here is that the constitution does not serve its conventional purpose as a restraint on the will of the majority, but rather one which is used as a guise for a majority-empowering agenda.

---

[132] In Chapter 7, I will provide a detailed examination of the relationship between electoral and identity politics on the one hand and rights enforcement on the other.

[133] See Melissa Crouch, 'Preface' to Ihsan Ali Fauzi et al., *Disputed Churches in Jakarta*, Tim Lindsey and Melissa Crouch (eds.), Rebecca Lunnon (trans.) (Asian Law Centre and the Centre for Islamic Law and Society at the University of Melbourne, The Paramadina Foundation (Jakarta) and the Center for Religious and Cross-Cultural Studies (CRCS), Postgraduate School, Gadjah Mada University (Yogyakarta), 2011).

6

Judicial Institutions and the Rule of Law Deficit

We have seen that state practices and policies implicating religion and religious freedom are increasingly geared toward appeasing majoritarian sensitivities or what the state deems to be in the interests of the majority community. The cases and examples elaborated in the previous chapters also demonstrate the ways in which the state's peculiar conception, interpretation and application of particular constitutional arrangements on religion and religious freedom may serve to undermine religious freedom. I argue that this is indicative of a larger phenomenon, which could be understood as a 'constitutional perversion'.

Could the courts be counted on to enforce constitutional commitments and protect religious freedom? Our examination of judicial decisions indicate that the courts themselves have – to some extent – facilitated the perversion of constitutional arrangements on religion and religious freedom, especially in cases implicating the minorities. Not only do these decisions fail to protect and uphold religious freedom, but more often than not, they also appear to reflect and validate the preferences of the government of the day and/or the majority's sentiments. This tendency is troubling because it raises questions about the court's ability and willingness to fulfil its role as an impartial constitutional adjudicator and protector of minority rights.

The primary aim of this chapter is to account for these patterns by focusing on the role of the judiciary as a key rule-of-law institution. What explains the judicial approaches to questions implicating religion and religious freedom? Do particular features of institutional design promote particular judicial attitudes in resolving such questions? To what extent do judges' ideological or political preferences, or their concerns about public reaction, affect their choices and responses? To what extent are judges constrained by the prevailing political dynamics and the preferences of politicians? In answering these questions, this chapter addresses a broader set of issues that is central to this study as a whole, namely, the significance of constitutionalism and the rule of law and the role of politics in defining the protection of rights in the three countries. All this, by extension, shall illuminate an understanding of the conditions that may facilitate or undermine constitutional guarantees as well as the changing conceptions of those provisions over time.

There are two preliminary points. First, the analysis focuses primarily on the highest judicial institutions empowered to conduct constitutional review. In Malaysia, the superior courts (the High Court, Court of Appeal and Federal Court) have jurisdiction over the constitutionality of legislative and executive acts, but the Federal Court holds the proverbial last word. In Indonesia and Sri Lanka, only the Constitutional Court and Supreme Court, respectively, possess constitutional review powers. The second point concerns the peculiarity and limitations of the Indonesian system. The Constitutional Court may only review the constitutionality of statutes passed by the legislature only. Other laws and regulations that are in Indonesia's hierarchy of laws[1] are technically not subject to constitutional review. Although the Supreme Court may examine laws that are hierarchically below statutes, they have no powers to do so against the constitution.[2]

My goal here is not to articulate a definitive theory or explanation that applies to all three countries under study. In fact, as we shall see, there are different considerations, factors and conditions at play in each country that might explain why courts and judges have adopted the paths they did in constitutional contests on religion. However, the evidence and analysis that I present in this chapter point to several conclusions.

First, to some extent, institutional design matters in determining judicial independence and, consequently, the willingness of judges to enforce constitutional commitments on religion and to protect religious freedom from state encroachment. *Ex post* control mechanisms may influence judges' willingness and ability to insulate themselves from political interference, but appointment processes may also shape the types of judges that comprise the bench. Indeed, the lesson to be drawn from the Malaysian and Sri Lankan experiences is that retaliation against judicial activism can be quick and conspicuous, with damning consequences for the judiciary. Second, design is,

---

[1] Under article 7(1) of the Law No. 10 of 2004 on Rules on Establishing Legislation (amended in 2011), the hierarchy is as follows: (1) the 1945 constitution; (2) People's Consultative Assembly (MPR) decrees; (3) statutes or interim emergency laws; (4) government regulations; (5) presidential regulations; (6) provincial regulations; and (7) county/city regulations.

[2] Simon Butt and Tim Lindsey, *The Constitution of Indonesia: A Contextual Analysis* (Oxford and Portland, OR: Hart Publishing, 2012), p. 88.

in and of itself, inconclusive in explaining the rigor with which judges enforce religious freedom guarantees. Institutional design features cannot fully explain, for example, why courts have been willing to uphold rights in other cases but not in cases implicating religion. As the case studies examined in this book also attest, anticipated public reaction, as well as judges' ideologies and interpretive methods may also be important in shaping judicial responses on sensitive religious issues.

The point here is that institutional design and judicial behaviour cannot be seen as mutually exclusive factors in explaining why judges and courts adopt the approaches they did in constitutional contestations involving religion. It will also become obvious throughout this chapter that the problems with the practices and policies on religion and religious freedom (and the breakdown of the rule of law) in individual cases can be attributed, directly or indirectly, to the wider governance issues stemming from the existence of a powerful executive and the lack of check and balances.

THE SIGNIFICANCE OF INSTITUTIONAL DESIGN

Scholarship on courts and judicial review has highlighted the significance of institutional design in ensuring judicial independence. Ginsburg, for example, posits that mechanisms for appointment and accountability, term length, court size, access to the court and the effect of judicial decisions are the five principal design features that constitute judicial power.[3] Keith's large-scale empirical study confirmed the nexus between the adoption of constitutional provisions providing guaranteed terms for judges and separation of powers, on the one hand, and improvements in states' human rights behaviour on the other.[4] Other scholars emphasize the significance of specific institutional design features: Rios-Figueroa, for instance, argues that appointment, tenure and removal mechanisms are the most important institutional design features for judicial autonomy, and the combination of these three

---

[3] Tom Ginsburg, *Judicial Review in New Democracies* (Cambridge: Cambridge University Press, 2003), pp. 34–5. Some of these features, such as terms of office, the finality of decisions and the exclusivity of judicial authority, are identified by Keith as the measures for judicial independence. See Linda Camp Keith, 'Judicial Independence and Human Rights Protection around the World' (2000) 85 *Judicature* 195, 196–7. Madison argued that the members of each political branch should have 'as little agency as possible in the appointment of the members of the others' and viewed permanent tenure as crucial to securing judicial independence. See James Madison, 'The Federalist No. 51' in *The Federalist Papers*, online: www.congress.gov/resources/display/content/The+Federalist+Papers#TheFederalistPapers-51.

[4] Keith, 'Judicial Independence', pp. 199–200.

design features may incentivize judges to decide according to their sincere preferences.[5] In a bid to underscore the relevance of politics vis-à-vis the judiciary, my focus for this chapter is on this narrower set of indicators – modes of appointment and removal mechanisms.

Countries around the world have adopted various mechanisms in order to ensure some degree of independence among members of the highest judicial office and to protect them from political interference. In robust, established democracies such as the United States, the president nominates candidates to the Supreme Court, but they go through a rigorous screening process (which includes confirmation proceedings before the Senate) and they are then appointed for life. In the United Kingdom, Supreme Court candidates are selected and recommended by an independent Judicial Appointments Commission, although the Lord Chancellor retains the final say in appointments. In relatively younger democracies, similar multibody appointments systems have been established. In Taiwan, for example, the president appoints members of the Council of Grand Justices – who are initially nominated by a committee – with the approval of the legislature.[6]

There are thus many ways to configure judicial appointment systems. In general, scholars distinguish three principal types of appointments mechanisms, which Ginsburg describes as professional, cooperative and representative.[7] In theory, if one considers the separation of powers and checks and balances theses vis-à-vis judicial independence, the concentration of appointment power in a single actor or institution is more likely to compromise judicial independence. Unchecked powers might allow politicians to appoint judges who would rubber-stamp and advance the government's agenda. This, in turn, may dilute the effectiveness of constitutional constraints on governmental exercises of power and compromise the protection of rights. This premise is based on the idea that the dispersal of judicial appointment powers is more conducive to judicial independence because

[5] Julio Rios-Figueroa, 'Institutions for Constitutional Justice in Latin America' in Gretchen Helmke and Julio Rios-Figueroa (eds.), *Courts in Latin America* (Cambridge: Cambridge University Press, 2011), pp. 27, 51.

[6] Ginsburg argues, however, that this system is a *de facto* single-body appointments mechanism because the nomination committee is formed by the president and the legislature is dominated by the largest political party, whom the president typically belongs to. See Ginsburg, *Judicial Review*, p. 43.

[7] Ibid., p. 43. See also Rios-Figueroa, 'Institutions', p. 29 (drawing the distinction between appointments done: (1) by judges; (2) by at least two different state or non-state institutions; and (3) by a single, non-judicial organ. The first and second method would guarantee a measure of independence, while the third would not.).

no single authority or institution is able to determine the composition of the bench and impose its preferences on it.[8]

Two further points are worth noting. First, there are instances in which appointments mechanisms appear similar in principle – in the sense that multiple actors are involved to ensure a degree of accountability – but the implications on judicial independence may work out very differently in practice. Second, there is an ever-present possibility that judges who are appointed through a *de jure* or *de facto* single-institution method may nevertheless decide, once they are on the bench, to assert their own preferences and views over those of their appointing institution.[9] As such, removal mechanisms and the length of tenure are equally important design features to consider. As in mechanisms of appointment, there are reasons to stress the importance of checks and balances in removal mechanisms and to avoid the concentration of removal powers in a single entity. It has also been argued that security of tenure would increase the ability of judges to insulate themselves from the dominant political fervour or political interference.[10] Yet, for some, security of tenure does not always produce predictable judicial responses, in that judges may nevertheless choose defer to the preferences of the government of the day.[11]

In Indonesia, the selection of constitutional court judges follows Ginsburg's representative appointment model. Here, the powers of appointment are dispersed across three different institutions representing the three branches of government – the Supreme Court, the People's Representatives Council (DPR) and the president. Each institution may appoint three judges. According to the Constitutional Court Law, the nomination and election of the justices must be transparent and participatory.[12] Each of the three appointing institutions shall set their own procedures for selecting and electing judges,

---

[8] Daniel M. Brinks, '"Faithful Servants of the Regime": The Brazilian Constitutional Court's Role under the 1988 Constitution' in Gretchen Helmke and Julio Rios-Figueroa (eds.), *Courts in Latin America* (Cambridge: Cambridge University Press, 2011), pp. 128, 134. Brinks posits that the degree of judicial autonomy increases with the rise in the number of veto players in both *ex ante* and *ex post* modes of control.

[9] Ibid., p. 131 (arguing that 'ex ante control is less precise because one can never fully predict how a particular judge will act . . .').

[10] Ginsburg, *Judicial Review*, p. 46. Madison argues for permanent tenure, as this could insulate judges from being dependent on their appointers. See Madison, 'Federalist No. 51'.

[11] Gretchen Helmke and Jeffrey K. Staton, 'The Puzzling Judicial Politics of Latin America: A Theory of Litigation, Judicial Decisions, and Interbranch Conflict' in Gretchen Helmke and Julio Rios-Figueroa (eds.), *Courts in Latin America* (Cambridge: Cambridge University Press, 2011).

[12] Article 19, Law No. 24 of 2003 on the Constitutional Court.

but these must be conducted in an objective and accountable manner.[13] Practices, however, vary. The DPR is known to have carried out open fit-and-proper tests to appoint three judges during the 2008 to 2013 selection period.[14] Similarly, the president convened a commission to conduct such tests for his nominees during the same period. However, the president's appointments to the court in late 2013 have been greatly scrutinized and criticized for the lack of transparency.[15]

Unlike Indonesia, the Malaysian and Sri Lankan systems place the power of appointment in the hands of the executive. In Malaysia, multiples stages are involved. The power of appointment rests with the constitutional monarch – the *Yang di-Pertuan Agong* (YDPA) – who acts on the advice of the prime minister. Before making the appointment, the YDPA is required to consult with the Conference of Rulers – a body comprised of the sultans of the nine Malay states and the heads of state of the other four states in the Federation. There are no comparable fit-and-proper proceedings in Malaysia, although the Conference is said to provide a checks and balance mechanism for appointments.[16] Nevertheless, this appears to be a matter of formality, since the Conference cannot veto the prime minister's proposal. The prime minister, on the other hand, considers the views of the Conference (as well as the chief justice, in the case of appointments of judges other than the chief justice), but he is not bound by them. The unspoken rule (and indeed, the net result) is that the prime minister wields a lot of power in appointing judges to the highest courts in the country so that the system becomes a *de facto* single-body appointment mechanism.

This bears much resemblance to the mechanism in Sri Lanka before the Nineteenth Amendment to the constitution in May 2015. The Sri Lankan Constitution expressly concentrated the power of appointment in the presidential office. The Eighteenth Amendment, introduced by the government in

---

[13] Article 20, Law No. 24 of 2003 on the Constitutional Court.

[14] 'Transparency in selecting constitutional judges', *Tempo.co* (15 August 2013), online: en.tempo.co/read/news/2013/08/15/080504615/Transparency-in-Selecting-Constitutional-Judges.

[15] This concerns the appointment of Justice Patrialis Akbar (a former legislative member from PAN and former minister of law and human rights under President Susilo Bambang Yudhoyono's administration). A constitutional law expert alleged that the appointment was a political bargain between the Partai Demokrat (President Yudhoyono's political party) and PAN, although PAN officials were quick to deny this. See 'Refly: Ada Barter Politik Terkait Penunjukan Patrialis' ('Refly: There is a political barter in Patrialis' appointment'), *Kompas* (30 December 2013), online: nasional.kompas.com/read/2013/12/30/1815358/Refly.Ada.Barter.Politik.Terkait.Penunjukan.Patrialis.

[16] Shad Saleem Faruqi, *Document of Destiny: The Constitution of the Federation of Malaysia* (Petaling Jaya: Star Publications, 2008), p. 640.

	Indonesia	Malaysia	Sri Lanka
Constitutional Provision on Judicial Independence	**Art. 24 (1):** The judicial power shall be independent and shall possess the power to organise the judicature in order to enforce law and justice.	No comparable provision on judicial independence.	No comparable provision on judicial independence.
Modes of Appointment	**Art. 18 (1) of Constitutional Court Law 2003:** Three institutions – the Supreme Court, the president and the legislature – are involved in appointing judges. Each institution may appoint three candidates.	**Art. 122B:** The YDPA makes the appointment of all superior court judges based on the advice of the prime minister and after consulting the Conference of Rulers. For judicial appointments other than the heads of the superior courts (the chief justice of the Federal Court, the president of the Court of Appeal and the Chief Judge of the High Court) the prime minister shall consult such heads before appointing judges to their respective institutions.	**Art. 107 (1):** Power of appointment is solely in the hands of the president. *After the Nineteenth Amendment, which was passed in May 2015, the appointment of the chief justice, the president of the Court of Appeal and other judges of the Supreme Court and Court of Appeal must be approved by the Constitutional Council. The ten-member council includes the prime minister, the leader of the opposition, the speaker of Parliament and seven other persons appointed by the president. Five of the presidential appointees will be made through the nomination from both the prime minister and the leader of the opposition. One appointee must be nominated by a majority of members of Parliament who are not affiliated with the political parties of either the prime minister or the leader of the opposition.

(continued)

TABLE 6.1. (*continued*)

	Indonesia	Malaysia	Sri Lanka
Removal Mechanism	**Art. 23 (4):** The president holds the power to dismiss judges, on the recommendation of the chief justice of the Constitutional Court.	**Art. 125:** The king may dismiss judges, but the prime minister or the chief justice (after consulting with the prime minister) must first make a representation for removal to the king. The king may then convene a special tribunal to investigate the allegations and may remove judges based on the tribunal's recommendations.	**Art. 107(2):** Judges shall hold office during good behaviour. The president may order the removal of a judge, after a majority of members of Parliament presents a resolution for removal on grounds of misbehaviour or incapacity. The Speaker is also involved in the process. The resolution for removal shall only be entertained by the Speaker or placed on the Order Paper of Parliament if the notice of the resolution is is signed by at least one-third of the total number of members of Parliament and sets out full particulars of the alleged misbehaviour or incapacity.
Term Length	**Art. 22:** Five years, with the possibility of re-election for a second five-year term. Mandatory retirement age is 70 years.	**Art. 125:** Permanent tenure – judges hold office until they reach the mandatory retirement age of 65 years.	**Art. 107 (5):** Permanent tenure – judges hold office until they reach the mandatory retirement age of 65 years.

2010, established a bipartisan Parliamentary Council to provide its observations on judicial appointees, but the president is not bound by them. To provide some context for subsequent discussions on the judiciary and the rule of law in Sri Lanka, it is worth noting that there had previously been a Constitutional Council empowered to approve recommendations on judicial appointees made by the president.[17] The Eighteenth Amendment eliminated the Constitutional Council, along with its veto powers in appointment matters, as well as presidential term limits. As a result, the executive presidency became the most powerful institution in the country, with little checking mechanism on its exercises of power. The arrangements in Malaysia and Sri Lanka, therefore, lack any concrete safeguards to protect the independence and integrity of the judiciary. The Nineteenth Amendment, which was part of the new President-elect Maithripala Sirisena's 100-day reform program, restored the Constitutional Council and its crucial role in judicial appointment.

The Perils of Unchecked Powers

The diffusion of appointing power has – to some extent – allowed the Indonesian Constitutional Court to insulate judges from short-term political pressures and to operate within a wider policy space. No single institution monopolizes the appointments process, nor can any single political branch directly dictate judicial decision-making. These problems were so endemic during Soeharto's New Order administration that judicial intimidation and corruption were regarded as standard features of the regime. That three separate institutions are now involved in determining the composition of the court also allows a degree of diversity – in terms of both background and ideological preferences – within the bench. This mechanism allows a mix of career and non-career judges to serve the court.[18] Indeed, since its inception, there have been justices who were distinguished academics as well as those who previously served as members of the MPR (a few of them were, incidentally, among those involved in the post-Soeharto constitutional amendment process). The career judges nominated by the Supreme Court are viewed as more moderate and legalistic than their non-career counterparts, who tend to

[17] Jayampathy Wickramaratne, *Fundamental Rights in Sri Lanka*, 2nd ed. (Colombo: Stamford Lake Publication, 2006), p. 80.

[18] Marcus Mietzner, 'Political Conflict Resolution and Democratic Consolidation in Indonesia: The Role of the Constitutional Court' (2010) 10 *Journal of East Asian Studies* 397, 404.

be more academic and activist.[19] The Indonesian design, therefore, has helped the Constitutional Court to free itself (albeit not completely, as the rest of the chapter shall demonstrate) from the judiciary's troubled history.

By contrast, experiences from Malaysia and Sri Lanka show just how vulnerable executive-dominated appointment systems are and how they can cripple the effectiveness of judicial institutions. In Sri Lanka, for example, the judiciary was tested by the impeachment of Chief Justice Shirani Bandaranayake in 2013. I shall explain her removal in detail shortly, but first I wish to emphasize the dangers of the president's virtually absolute power of appointment. Shortly after Bandaranayake was impeached, the president appointed Mohan Peiris to the highest judicial office in the country. Peiris was not a career judge, and it was no coincidence that he was formerly an attorney general and a trusted legal advisor to the president and his cabinet. Peiris was widely known as a strong government loyalist, who often blocked efforts to hold the government accountable for human rights violations.[20] In short, the concentration of power in the hands of the executive not only risks political interference with the court's day-to-day business; it also allows the placement of ideologically biased judges who share (or are at least sympathetic to) the government's interests and political agendas.

There were similar instances of overt political interference with the judiciary in Malaysia. In 2007, an explosive appointment-fixing scandal emerged, exposing the grim state of the country's judiciary. Colloquially known as the 'Lingam Tape Scandal',[21] the case centred on the role of a senior lawyer in fixing the appointment and promotion of the then Chief Judge of the High Court of Malaya, as well as several other senior members of the judiciary. Also implicated in the case was the then prime minister, a former deputy minister in the Prime Minister's Department who was in charge of legal affairs and a close associate of the prime minister, who is a well-known businessman in Malaysia. A Royal Commission of Inquiry set up to investigate the case found, among others, evidence of a concerted effort to undermine the then chief

---

[19] See Bjorn Dressel and Marcus Mietzner, 'A Tale of Two Courts: The Judicialization of Electoral Politics in Asia' (2012) 25 *Governance: An International Journal of Policy, Administration, and Institutions* 391, 405 and Mietzner, 'Political Conflict', p. 417.

[20] See 'Sri Lanka: Appointment of new chief justice undermines rule of law', *International Commission of Jurists Press Release* (15 January 2013), online: www.icj.org/sri-lanka-newly-appointed-chief-justices-long-record-of-blocking-justice/.

[21] V. K. Lingam was the senior lawyer implicated in the scandal. He was taped being in a phone conversation with the then Chief Judge of the High Court of Malaya (who later went on to become the president of the Court of Appeal and the chief justice of the Federal Court) and was allegedly delving into details of fixing the appointment and promotion of that Chief Judge, along with several other senior justices.

justice's (Dzaiddin Abdullah) recommendation to the prime minister for the post of the Chief Judge of the High Court of Malaya, because the recommended individual did not see eye to eye with the prime minister.[22] The Commission also exposed details about judicial corruption and bribery implicating a former chief justice[23] and determined that there were elements of political patronage in the appointment and promotion of the justices implicated in the scandal.[24] Two important lessons may be drawn from the Lingam Tape Scandal. First, as in Sri Lanka, a powerful prime minister can ensure that only judges who share similar ideological preferences (or at least those who would be willing to further the government's agenda) are appointed. Second, this case shows that judicial appointments are not only open to manipulation by the executive, but also by politically connected private parties who might have stakes in a judiciary that is subservient to the executive.

With respect to removal and/or reappointment mechanisms, Indonesia has also adopted a multistage process involving several actors. The Constitutional Court Law explicitly lists conditions that would warrant a dismissal, but the recalcitrant judge may first defend him/herself before the Honorary Council of the Constitutional Court.[25] A presidential decree is required to complete the dismissal process, but only upon request by the chief justice.[26] Further strengthening the mechanisms to ensure judicial independence are the procedures for reappointment. Judges at the court serve for one five-year term, but they may seek reappointment for a second five-year term. The prevailing consensus among scholars is that a longer term of appointment correlates with greater independence as judges can insulate themselves from the predominant political sentiments.[27] The possibility of reappointment, Ginsburg argues, may be averse to judicial independence because judges seeking to remain in office might pander to the interests of the institutions that

---

[22] Commission of Enquiry on the Video Clip Recording of Images of a Person Purported to be an Advocate and Solicitor Speaking on the Telephone on Matters Regarding the Appointment of Judges: The Report, Vol. 1 (Putrajaya: BHEUU, May 2008), p. 66.

[23] Ibid., pp. 71–3.

[24] F. S. Shuaib, 'Malaysian Judicial Appointment Process: An Overview of the Reform' (2011) 7 *Journal of Applied Sciences Research* 2273, 2274.

[25] Articles 23(2) and (3), Law No. 24 of 2003 on the Constitutional Court. The conditions for a 'dishonorable dismissal' include the commission of acts of misconduct, the violation of the oath of office, the failure to attend five successive hearings without valid reasons and being sanctioned with imprisonment for committing a criminal act punishable by a term of imprisonment.

[26] Article 23(4), Law No. 24 of 2003 on the Constitutional Court.

[27] Ginsburg, *Judicial Review*, p. 46. Hamilton also argues that permanent tenure would be the best defence against encroachments upon judicial independence. See Alexander Hamilton, 'The Federalist No. 78' in *The Federalist Papers*, online: www.congress.gov/resources/display/content/The+Federalist+Papers#TheFederalistPapers-78.

appoint them.[28] The Indonesian system, however, found a way around this: judges do not necessarily have to seek reappointment from the institution that initially appointed them to the court. There is, therefore, no dependence for survival on the first appointing institution, nor is there any need to pander – at least in theory – to the preferences of that institution.[29]

Compare this to the removal mechanisms in Malaysia and Sri Lanka, which, much like their systems of appointment, accord significant powers to the executive. Abuse of power is an obvious threat to judicial integrity and independence, as the experiences from these countries illustrate. The Malaysian judiciary was taught a haunting lesson in 1988, and it is one that it has yet to recover from. A case on political infighting within the United Malays National Organisation (UMNO) – the dominant party in the ruling coalition – was brought to the courts for resolution. It involved a suit challenging the legality of UMNO's internal elections brought by a narrowly defeated faction within the party against the incumbents led by Dr. Mahathir.[30] The details of the decision and the political battles that resulted therefrom are complicated. But suffice it to say that the High Court's ruling played into the hands of Dr. Mahathir's faction, which then prompted the defeated faction to launch an appeal to the Supreme Court.[31] Against this, Harding notes, the UMNO-dominated government had to ensure that nothing should disturb the status quo.[32] The upshot of this controversy saw the suspension (and eventual dismissal, following a tribunal recommendation to that effect) of the president of the Supreme Court and the removal of two other judges[33] – an outcome which many saw as being far from accidental. It was also unsurprising that the reconstituted Supreme Court bench that heard the appeal held in favour of Dr. Mahathir's faction. As many observers have noted, this saga delivered a critical blow to the independence of the Malaysian judiciary,[34] which was once widely regarded as an autonomous institution with high integrity.

[28] Ginsburg, *Judicial Review*, p. 47.

[29] For a concise but insightful account on the politics of the reappointment of judges, see Mietzner, 'Political Conflict', p. 415.

[30] *Mohd Noor Bin Othman v. Mohd Yusof Jaafar* [1988] 2 Malayan Law Journal 129.

[31] The Supreme Court, which was the highest court in the country, became the Federal Court in 1994.

[32] Andrew Harding, *Law, Government and the Constitution in Malaysia* (The Hague and London: Kluwer Law International, 1993), p. 146.

[33] The tribunal set up to investigate the President of the Supreme Court (Salleh Abas) was fraught with suspicions: it was chaired by a judge who would succeed Salleh Abas should he be dismissed; it applied a civil standard of proof; and it employed a broad test of judicial misbehaviour. See Harding, *Law, Government, and the Constitution*, pp. 146–7.

[34] See Ibid., p. 147; Chandra Kanagasabai, 'Malaysia: Limited and Intermittent Judicialization of Politics', in Bjorn Dressel (ed.), *The Judicialization of Politics in Asia* (Oxon: Routledge, 2013), pp. 202, 206; Donald L. Horowitz, *Constitutional Change and Democracy in Indonesia*

The Sri Lankan situation is not short of controversy either. Executive interference with the judiciary is not a recent phenomenon, but the most controversial and significant incident yet came with the impeachment of Chief Justice Bandaranayake in January 2013. Like most of her predecessors, Bandaranayake often toed government lines, delivering, in particular, judgments that bolstered the executive presidency.[35] Her attitude began to change after the infamous 'Mannar incident'. What began only as a local fishing dispute between Muslim and Tamil fishermen in the district of Mannar soon turned controversial when a cabinet minister allegedly threatened a District Court judge to overturn his decision in favour of the Tamil fishermen. This was followed by violent mob attacks against the Mannar Court Complex, which then prompted the Bar Association of Sri Lanka, lawyers and judges to boycott judicial proceedings nation-wide. Since then, the writings were on the wall for Bandaranayake's impeachment due to the strong tension between the judiciary and the executive. Compounding this was the sense that Bandaranayake was beginning to pose a threat to President Rajapaksa's regime due to her opposition to several government-sponsored bills and her pro-devolution position.[36]

The final straw came when the Supreme Court ruled unconstitutional a bill that would have sanctioned the consolidation of three development authorities under the Ministry of Economic Development (headed by Basil Rajapaksa). It would have expanded control over the developmental budget with virtually no oversight.[37] In November, almost immediately after the Supreme Court delivered its judgment, parliamentarians from the ruling coalition initiated impeachment proceedings against Bandaranayake on the

---

(Cambridge: Cambridge University Press, 2013), p. 236; Datuk George Seah, 'Crisis in the Judiciary: The hidden story', *The Malaysian Bar* (1 May 2004), online: www.malaysianbar.org.my/administration_of_justice/crisis_in_the_judiciary.html.

[35] Neil DeVotta, 'Sri Lanka's Ongoing Shift to Authoritarianism', *East West Center Asia Pacific Bulletin*, No. 201 (22 February 2013).

[36] Interview with a prominent legal researcher and civil society activist in Colombo, Sri Lanka (June 2013). Devolution is a politically and ethnically sensitive issue. The Thirteenth Amendment to the constitution, passed in 1987, devolved powers to provincial councils as a political solution for the ethnic conflict in the country. However, the Rajapaksa regime was said to be reluctant to implement devolution as mandated by the Thirteenth Amendment, despite promising during and after the civil war that he would do so.

[37] The bill is called the *Divineguma* Bill, introduced into Parliament in August 2012. For a brief but insightful explanation on the bill and why the Supreme Court declared it unconstitutional, see DeVotta, 'Sri Lanka's Ongoing Shift', p. 37, and International Crisis Group, 'Sri Lanka's authoritarian turn: The need for international action', *Asia Report*, No. 243 (20 February 2013), p. 5, online: www.crisisgroup.org/~/media/Files/asia/south-asia/sri-lanka/243-sri-lankas-authoritarian-turn-the-need-for-international-action.pdf.

ground of misconduct. The impeachment process went by very quickly by Sri Lankan standards – in December, a parliamentary select committee (comprised mainly of government elites) found Bandaranayake guilty of financial and official misconduct, without affording her basic due process guarantees; by mid-January, two-thirds of the Parliament voted to impeach Bandaranayake, a decision which the president ratified; and a few days later, Mohan Peiris was appointed as the new chief justice. The impeachment process, according to many observers, was flawed and lacked basic due process guarantees.

Structural Independence and Judicial Exercises of Power

In light of the foregoing analysis and illustrations, one might conclude that the Malaysian and Sri Lankan systems risk producing judges who lack independence, while the Indonesian mechanism produces judges that are likely to be more independent. Indeed, until recently, the Indonesian Constitutional Court has been widely hailed as one of best success stories of the Indonesian constitutional reform and democratic transition. The court, particularly under the leadership of Jimly Asshiddiqie (the first chief justice), earned considerable public trust and respect against the background of a notoriously corrupt judiciary that lacked accountability and was regarded as the 'worst in Asia',[38] and a country that suffered from serious rule of law deficits that continues to linger in the post-Soeharto period.[39] Indeed, the very aim of creating a new judicial institution imbued with constitutional review powers was to sever any links with the severely tarnished reputation of the Supreme Court.[40]

Emboldened by its independence, the Constitutional Court has not been shy – sometimes even overly bold, according to some commentators – to assert its autonomy in politically sensitive issues, such as electoral disputes.[41] The court's activism has not struck a chord with everyone. Former President

---

[38] Lilian Budianto, 'Indonesia's judicial system rated worst in Asia: Survey', *The Jakarta Post* (15 September 2008), online: www.thejakartapost.com/news/2008/09/15/indonesia039s-judicial-system-rated-worst-asia-survey.html.

[39] Horowitz, *Constitutional Change*, p. 233. Horowitz argues that there was a delayed development in the rule of law, even as democracy began to consolidate.

[40] Ibid., p. 241.

[41] See Dressel and Mietzner, 'Tale of Two Courts', pp. 401–2. For an explanation of some of the key electoral affairs decisions by the court, see ibid., pp. 402–4. For an account of the expansion of judicial function by the Constitutional Court, see Horowitz, *Constitutional Change*, pp. 242–3. See also Simon Butt, 'Indonesia's Constitutional Court: Conservative Activist or Strategic Operator?' in Bjorn Dressel (ed.), *The Judicialization of Politics in Asia* (Oxon: Routledge, 2013), pp. 98, 101–2 (explaining the role of the court's first chief justice, Professor Jimly Asshiddiqie, in building the court's reputation and competence).

Yudhoyono and his vice president, Jusuf Kalla, for instance, openly expressed their discontent with the court's verdicts. However, those who are unhappy, particularly from the government, have not been able to directly attack the court and undermine its independence along the lines that have occurred in Malaysia and Sri Lanka.[42] These observations largely apply to electoral or political disputes, but there were also cases in which the court's activism saw the expansion of civil liberties and individual freedoms, especially those relating to the rights to free speech, expression and association.[43] Of particular significance was its affirmation of the rights of former members of the Indonesian Communist Party to run for elections.[44] The court has also demonstrated its readiness to uphold rights that are not expressly mentioned in the constitution, and for that it has earned praise from scholars like Lindsey and Butt who laud the court's achievements in developing a body of rights jurisprudence that has previously been absent in Indonesia.[45] A lot of this, perhaps, can be credited to the way in which the Constitutional Court is structured and designed, particularly in terms of its appointment and removal mechanisms.

Contrast this with the situation in Malaysia and Sri Lanka. Whereas the Indonesian Constitutional Court has been able to fend off direct government interference, the Malaysian court has faced conspicuous interference by the executive. While the investigations against Chief Justice Salleh Abas during the 1988 judicial crisis were ongoing, the executive engineered a constitutional amendment to place judicial power under the purview of the legislature.[46] The bill was quickly passed and it came into effect in June 1988, thus officially subordinating the judiciary to the executive-dominated legislature. Two months later, Abas was dismissed. Prior to the UMNO case, courts at various levels had delivered several controversial decisions challenging executive authority in matters implicating fundamental rights.[47] All this annoyed the

---

[42] Dressel and Mietzner, 'Tale of Two Courts', p. 406 (quoting an interview with former Chief Justice Jimly Asshiddiqie in Jakarta in September 2009). See also Mietzner, 'Political Conflict', p. 413 (arguing that Vice President Jusuf Kalla 'frequently phoned judges and released his anger over their decisions, giving lengthy lectures on why they obstructed the government's work').

[43] See generally Mietzner, 'Political Conflict'.   [44] Ibid., p. 409.

[45] See Butt and Lindsey, *Constitution of Indonesia*, p. 222.

[46] Before the amendment, article 121(1) states: '[t]he judicial power of the Federation shall be vested into High Courts of coordinate jurisdiction and status'. The amended provision now states: '[T]here shall be two High Courts of coordinate jurisdiction and status ... and the High Courts and inferior courts shall have such jurisdiction and *powers as may be conferred by or under federal law*' (emphasis added).

[47] These decisions include a Supreme Court decision that upheld the quashing of an order to revoke the employment pass of a foreign journalist because he was deemed a threat to national security (*J.P. Berthelsen v. Director General of Immigration* [1987] 1 Malayan Law Journal 134) and a High Court decision rejecting the home minister's reasons for refusing to grant a

prime minister, who thought that judges had gone overboard by circumscribing decisions made by Parliament and the policymaking powers of the executive – acts which he considered undemocratic.[48] He also made his criticisms clear in an interview with *Time Magazine*, hinting that the government would work to overrule courts' decisions that interfered with the government's policies and decisions.[49]

Taken together, these events have led to declining standards of judicial independence and integrity over time. The judiciary's (especially the Federal Court's) willingness to challenge executive authority in politically sensitive matters and in fundamental rights issues has generally been on the wane.[50] Judicial enforcement of the rights to personal liberty and freedom of speech, for instance, has been ineffective, but this is also partly attributable to legislation that heavily circumscribes judicial review of executive powers in security matters.[51] On matters implicating religion and religious freedom, the Federal Court has avoided serious scrutiny of the constitutionality of government interventions implicating religion and religious freedom. Aside from rejecting the Catholic Church's leave to appeal in the 'Allah' case, it has also issued decisions unfavourable to religious freedom and the minorities by refusing to adjudicate matters involving conversion (deciding instead that conversions should be decided upon by the *Shariah* courts).[52] The Court of Appeal, on

publication license to *Aliran*, an NGO (*Persatuan Aliran v. Minister for Home Affairs* [1988] 1 Malayan Law Journal 440). For an overview of other decisions, see Kanagasabai, 'Judicialization of Politics', pp. 206–7. See also Harding, *Law, Government and the Constitution*, pp. 142–4.

[48] See Ratna Rueben Balasubramaniam, 'Has Rule by Law Killed the Rule of Law in Malaysia?' (2008) 8 *Oxford University Commonwealth Law Journal* 211, 213.

[49] In the interview, Dr. Mahathir remarked: '[T]he judiciary says (to us), "Although you passed a law with a certain thing in mind, we think that your mind is wrong, and we want to give our own interpretation." If we disagree, the Courts will say, "We will interpret your disagreement". If we go along, we are going to lose our power of legislation. We know exactly what we want to do, but once we do it, it is interpreted in a different way, and we have no means to reinterpret it our way. If we find out that a Court always throws us out on its own interpretation, if it interprets contrary to why we made the law, then we will have to find a way of producing a law that will have to be interpreted according to our wish.' Quoted in Kanagasabai, 'Judicialization of Politics', pp. 206–7.

[50] See ibid., p. 210. As Kanagasabai correctly notes, however, that there have been sporadic exercises of judicial activism, but these were largely dependent on the individual judges hearing the cases. See also Faruqi, *Document of Destiny*, pp. 398–401 (arguing that responses to human rights issues have been mixed).

[51] Faruqi, *Document of Destiny*, p. 398.

[52] See *Haji Raimi bin Abdullah v. Siti Hasnah Vangarama binti Abdullah and Another* [2014] 4 Current Law Journal 253 and *Lina Joy v. Majlis Agama Islam Wilayah Persekutuan & Another* [2007] 4 Malayan Law Journal 585.

occasion, has displayed more willingness to push the envelope. However, as a senior judge revealed, judges have had to pay their price for their bouts of activism, including the prospect of non-promotion.[53]

As in Malaysia, Sri Lanka's judicial integrity and independence has been tested and compromised. Survivability is a very important consideration for Sri Lankan judges, and this could be dictated by judges' willingness to support the government's agenda and majoritarian sentiments.[54] There were, to be sure, spells of bravery amongst the Supreme Court judges who occasionally stood up against the government and the political elites. However, as scholars argue, corruption is not only widespread at the Supreme Court; it is also endemic at the lower-level courts. DeVotta posits that 'telephone justice' – a practice where the attorney general or president calls judges and instructs them to deliver specific rulings – is thought to be a common practice.[55] Patronage politics is also another significant problem. There were cases in which retired judges were appointed to positions in the government post-retirement[56] and judges' family members were rewarded for judicial obedience.[57] All in all, the core message is clear: compliant judges will be rewarded with various perks and incentives; recalcitrant or even activist judges will be severely punished, and sometimes, even subjected to death threats and intimidation.[58]

The executive has not been shy to openly criticize the court. President Kumaratunga – Rajapaksa's predecessor – publicly admonished a Supreme Court judge for obstructing government progress and accused another judge of accepting financial bribes.[59] Both these cases illustrate efforts by the executive to undermine the authority and integrity of the Supreme Court. In the Bandaranayake case, an overt, government-led campaign against the former chief justice took place in the media and on the streets.[60] A senior judge was reportedly physically attacked by armed men following his

---

[53] Interview with a senior judge in Kuala Lumpur (August 2016).

[54] Interview with a senior lawyer and activist in Colombo, Sri Lanka (June 2013).

[55] DeVotta, 'Sri Lanka's Ongoing Shift'.

[56] Interview with a legal academic in Colombo, Sri Lanka (June 2013).

[57] DeVotta, 'Sri Lanka's Ongoing Shift'. DeVotta states, for example, that Chief Justice Bandaranayake's husband was installed as the chairman of the National Savings Bank – an appointment which was widely viewed as being related to her position at the court.

[58] Ibid. See also International Crisis Group, 'Sri Lanka's Judiciary: Politicised Courts, Compromised Rights', *Asia Report*, No. 172 (30 June 2009).

[59] International Bar Association (IBA), 'Sri Lanka: Failing to Protect the Rule of Law and Independence of the Judiciary', *IBA Human Rights Institute Report* (London: IBA, November 2001), p. 31.

[60] International Crisis Group Report No. 172, p. 5.

criticisms of the government's conduct as an attack against judicial independence.[61]

The psychological effect of such bullying should not be underestimated, as these may produce timid judges who are cautious of their actions, especially where such actions are contrary to the policies and interests of the government of the day. In Sri Lanka's case, the role and influence of the chief justice is also an important consideration. There is an unspoken culture of deference toward the chief justice, who wields significant influence over the judiciary and approves the composition of the judicial bench for a particular case.[62] As chief justices are typically close to the executive, all these factors have worked in ways that adversely affect the judiciary's robustness in protecting fundamental rights and its reluctance to get entangled in politically sensitive cases.[63] Still, some have argued that in cases involving religion and rights, the court has been seen as relatively impartial.[64]

The foregoing accounts underscore the importance of institutional design in facilitating judicial independence. The executive branches in Malaysia and Sri Lanka have shown their ability to retaliate against judges who deliver unfavourable decisions against the ruling elite. Although those decisions did not implicate questions on religion, the attacks against the judiciary forewarn judges about the costs of going against government policies. Thus, one might deduce that a weak judiciary – comprising persons favourable to the ruling government, or operating in an environment of fear about possible attacks on it – would be inimical to religious freedom protection. However, the Indonesian experience (and the Sri Lankan case, if one accepts the view that the court has been impartial in its treatment of religion cases) offers a cautionary tale to this view.

As we have seen previously, the Indonesian Constitutional Court has been particularly bold in resolving electoral disputes and in expanding its rights jurisprudence. But when we consider certain decisions implicating religion

---

[61] Ibid., pp. 5–6.

[62] International Bar Association (IBA), 'Justice in Retreat: A Report on the Independence of the Legal Profession and the Rule of Law in Sri Lanka', *IBA Human Rights Institute Report* (London: IBA, 2009), pp. 31–2. According to the report, Sarath Silva, who sat as chief justice from September 1999 to June 2009, would choose to sit in politically sensitive cases, while the more independently minded judges would routinely be excluded from such cases. Ibid., p. 32.

[63] Kishali Pinto-Jayawardena, 'Protecting the Independence of the Judiciary: A Critical Analysis of the Sri Lankan Law' in *Sri Lanka: State of Human Rights 1999* (Colombo: Law & Society Trust, 1999), pp. 170, 179–80.

[64] Benjamin Schonthal, 'Constitutionalizing Religion: The Pyrrhic Success of Religious Rights in Post-Colonial Sri Lanka' (2014) 29 *Journal of Law and Religion* 470, 471.

or religious freedom, the Indonesian story paints a mixed picture. The two decisions on the Blasphemy Law are prime examples of both judicial reluctance to protect minorities and its willingness to defer to majoritarian sensitivities. Similarly, the court upheld the constitutionality of the controversial Anti-Pornography Law (which, for some, was an attempt at enforcing the more conservative varieties of Islam), which has raised considerable concern among Muslims and non-Muslims alike.[65] Although the constitutional challenge against the law was not advanced on the basis that it was contrary to religious freedom guarantees, some of the petitioners nevertheless suggested that the breadth of what constitutes 'pornography' under the law could eventually affect the observance of particular religious rituals and the existence of religious structures.[66] The law neither explicitly authorizes exceptions for artistic and cultural expressions nor traditional rituals; instead, it gives the government the discretion to make exceptions through laws and regulations.[67] However, the court, in a move that crossed into the borders of judicial law-making, held that there are five exceptions from the law: arts, literature, customs, science and sports.[68] A detailed assessment of this decision is beyond the scope of this chapter, but it is important to note that the Blasphemy Law and Anti-Pornography Law decisions represent important symbolic and moral victories for their proponents. These decision and laws, and the intolerance and religious rights violations nurtured by them, are yet another setback for minorities in Indonesia.

JUDICIAL BEHAVIOUR AND APPROACHES TO RELIGIOUS FREEDOM

If institutional design alone affects the independence of the courts to the point that constitutional guarantees are disregarded, how do we explain shifts in judicial approaches over time? As Helmke and Rosenbluth note, and as the

---

[65] See Pam Allen, 'Challenging Diversity?: Indonesia's Anti-Pornography Bill' (2007) 31 *Asian Studies Review* 101.

[66] An example that the petitioners pointed out was the ancient Buddhist temples which houses sketches or paintings that may be deemed pornographic under the law. See Constitutional Court of Indonesia, Decision No. 10–17-23/PUU-VII/2009, Concerning the Examination of Law No. 44, Year 2008 on Pornography (30 December 2009), p. 19 [*Anti-Pornography Law Decision*].

[67] See Article 13(1), Law No. 44 of 2008 on Pornography [Anti-Pornography Law]. Article 14, however, mentions a possible exception for education and health purposes. The government has the discretion to determine and regulate the use of pornographic material for such purposes.

[68] *Anti-Pornography Law Decision*, p. 383.

Indonesian examples show, the creation of judicial independence on paper –
through various aspects of institutional design – is not always enough.[69] Many
scholars have also argued that notwithstanding the ways in which courts are
designed, judges may *behave* in varying ways, expected or otherwise, once
established. How, then, might we explain the problems of religious freedom
enforcement from the perspective of judicial behaviour? What might explain
the decisions and choices that judges make?

Judges as Strategic Actors or Legal Formalists?

At the heart of the strategic theory of judicial behaviour is the idea that judges
make decisions by taking into account the policy preferences of other government branches and how those branches would react to their decisions.[70]
In other words, judges would take an intermediate path that they believe is
palatable to both branches. This theory, therefore, is linked to institutional
design and the concentration or dispersal of political powers, which we discussed previously. Of course, this is not to say that courts cannot exercise their
discretion at all. Rather, they do so by carefully navigating the political constraints that they find themselves in.[71] Acting strategically, by accommodating
such constraints, allows courts to avoid direct conflict with other branches of
government, especially if they anticipate that such confrontation may ultimately prompt political actors to attack the court and its independence.[72]

In countries like Malaysia and Sri Lanka, where *ex post* controls over the
judiciary are virtually concentrated in the hands of the executive, and where
there is a history of executive attacks against the judiciary, it is tempting to
conclude that unfavourable judicial decisions involving religious issues are
driven by judges' strategic considerations of government preferences. This
point becomes even more persuasive when we consider the extent to which
politicians utilize and manipulate religious issues and sentiments to maintain
or bolster their political power.

Before the onslaught against the Malaysian judiciary in 1988, judges had,
by and large, adhered to the path of strict legalism.[73] Indeed, as Chief Justice

[69] Gretchen Helmke and Frances Rosenbluth, 'Regimes and the Rule of Law: Judicial
Independence in Comparative Perspective' (2009) 12 *Annual Review of Political Science*
345, 359.

[70] Ginsburg, *Judicial Review*, p. 67.   [71] Ibid., p. 68.

[72] Keith E. Whittington, 'Legislative Sanctions and the Strategic Environment of Judicial
Review' (2003) 1 *International Journal of Constitutional Law* 446, 447.

[73] Khoo Boo Teik, 'Between Law and Politics: The Malaysian Judiciary since Independence'
in Kanishka Jayasuriya (ed.), *Law, Capitalism and Power in Asia* (London: Routledge, 1999),
pp. 174, 188.

Abas once noted, 'the court's role is not to dispense social justice, but only to apply the law as it is written'.[74] This presents judges as unconstrained actors who deliver judgments according to good faith interpretations of the law and precedent. Remarkably, it was this formalistic approach that allowed the court to safeguard the intent and spirit behind article 3 on Islam. As we have seen in Chapter 5, the 1988 case of *Che Omar* – which was decided by the Abas court – clarified the parameters for the role of Islam in the constitutional order, stating that it was merely restricted to rituals and ceremonies and rejecting any assertions that Malaysia was an Islamic state.[75] Post-1988, however, judges have increasingly veered from the formalistic path. The 'Allah' judgment is a good example. The court's explicit declaration that the exercise of religious freedom must take into account the position of Islam as the religion of the Federation, can neither be justified from the express language of article 3, nor supported by the precedent in *Che Omar*. When the Federal Court considered and later dismissed the Church's application for leave to appeal in 2014, it did not address the fundamental questions regarding article 3 that were presented to it.[76] In a more recent case concerning the constitutionality of a *Shariah* state law that restricts freedom of expression, the Federal Court argued, in part, that the constitutional right to free speech must be read together with position of Islam as the religion of the Federation.[77] A few years earlier, in the religious conversion case of *Lina Joy*, the Federal Court implied that the ability of a Muslim to exercise one's freedom to change one's religion was subject to Islamic norms and principles. The dissenting judgment in *Lina Joy*, however, displayed greater fidelity to constitutional history and *Che Omar*, arguing that article 3 was never intended to supersede other constitutionally protected rights and privileges.[78]

---

[74] Gordon P. Means, *Malaysian Politics: The Second Generation* (Singapore: Oxford University Press, 1991), p. 143.

[75] The court suggested that if Islam in article 3 were to have a wider role, the constitution-makers would have inserted a provision stating that any law contradicting Islamic injunctions would be void. See *Che Omar Che Soh v. Public Prosecutor* [1988] 2 Malayan Law Journal 55.

[76] *Titular Roman Catholic Archbishop of Kuala Lumpur v. Menteri Dalam Negeri & Others* [2014] 6 Current Law Journal 541. See also Jaclyn Neo, 'What's in a Name? Malaysia's Allah Controversy and the Judicial Intertwining of Islam and Ethnic Identity' (2014) 12 *International Journal of Constitutional Law* 751. In the religious headgear case (Meor Atiqulrahman), the High Court's warped conception of article 3 – though made in *obiter* – was never addressed by the Court of Appeal and Federal Court. The appellate courts also did not deliver any authoritative interpretation of article 3 in the context of religious freedom. See Neo, 'What's in a Name?', p. 761.

[77] *ZI Publications Sdn Bhd & Another v. Kerajaan Negeri Selangor* [2016] 1 Malayan Law Journal 153, 160.

[78] *Lina Joy v. Majlis Agama Islam Wilayah Persekutuan & Another* [2007] 4 Malayan Law Journal 585, 631.

These decisions may be indicative of the court's recognition of the strategic constraints surrounding it. It is difficult to find any sound constitutional basis – whether based on a textual application of article 3, precedent or the historical understanding of the provision – for the way in which the court interpreted article 3 to justify the restriction on rights. Instead, as the 'Allah' decision shows, the court appeared to have taken into account factors such as the anticipated reaction of the majority Malay-Muslims to perceived threats against their religion, the need to protect them from religious 'confusion', as well as the importance of particular practices within a religious faith or community. With the growth of Malay-Muslim organizations whose causes are centred on the belief that Islam and the Malay identity are under threat in 'their' homeland, judges might also see the need to be protective of majoritarian sentiments or risk public backlash. This concurs with scholarly views that strategic decision-making may not solely depend on how other political branches react; judges might also consider the likelihood of compliance with their decisions[79] and the views of their colleagues, the wider legal community and/or the public.[80] In the 'Allah' case, the hostile environment in which the court delivered its decision was also visible: as pressure groups and activists descended on court grounds, they recited prayers and reminded the court of its duty to protect Islam. While it is conceivable that these pressures and movements could influence judicial decision-making, it is of course difficult to precisely gauge the breadth of public support for such pressure groups. However, what is clear is that they have increasingly become vocal and their influence amongst the Malays should not be underestimated. Some of these organizations are also thought to receive state patronage through UMNO, the dominant political party in the ruling coalition.

With respect to its strategic interactions with other political branches, there is not a lot of wriggle room for the court. The typical model of the strategic interaction theory posits that judges' decisions will fall in between the ideal policy preferences of the other two political branches – the legislature and the executive.[81] A diffused political environment would allow courts more

---

[79] Brinks, 'Faithful Servants', p. 132.
[80] Javier Couso and Lisa Hillbink, 'From Quietism to Incipient Activism: The Institutional and Ideological Roots of Rights Adjudication in Chile' in Gretchen Helmke and Julio Rios-Figueroa (eds.), *Courts in Latin America* (Cambridge: Cambridge University Press, 2011), pp. 99, 101.
[81] Gretchen Helmke and Julio Rios-Figueroa, 'Introduction: Courts in Latin America' in Gretchen Helmke and Julio Rios-Figueroa (eds.), *Courts in Latin America* (Cambridge: Cambridge University Press, 2011), pp. 14–15.

space to exercise its judicial power.[82] In Malaysia, however, the legislature is executive-dominated and the ruling coalition has always held a two-thirds majority in parliament, at least since the 1970s until the 2008 general elections. The legislature has thus merely acted as a rubber-stamp on government policies. In this situation, judges' calculations are dictated by a single political branch, leaving them with much less flexibility than what the standard strategic interaction model envisions. Indeed, the Federal Court has exercised considerable restraint in checking legislative and executive exercises of authority, and it maintains a habit of interpreting the bill of rights narrowly.[83]

All this must be considered in the context of Malaysia's social and political development since the 1980s, where the country has experienced a wave of religious resurgence inspired by the Iranian revolution. The ruling party has been very conscious about projecting an 'Islamic' image, in part to counter the growing support for an opposition Islamic political party. What followed was a series of policies designed to assure the Malay-Muslim electorate that the government was committed to championing Islam alongside its modernization initiatives: it expanded the religious bureaucracy; it co-opted religious authorities in governing public and private life; and it separated the civil and *Shariah* jurisdictions in 1988. The result, as a constitutional scholar notes, is that civil courts have been very careful in meddling with anything that implicates (or is perceived to implicate) Islam, even where important constitutional rights questions arise.[84]

As in Malaysia, the institutional set-up and political circumstances in Sri Lanka restrict judges' range of strategic choices. The 1978 constitutional reforms created a powerful executive office, and the president wielded strong powers in appointing and sanctioning judges.[85] In practice, the same ruling coalition has, by and large, controlled both the executive and the legislative majority.[86] Consequently, strategic judicial behaviour requires pandering to the preferences and interests of the government of the day. In fact, a report by the International Commission of Jurists in 2009 highlights the court's inaction in issues implicating 'core presidential authority or policy'.[87]

---

[82] Ginsburg, *Judicial Review*, p. 18.   [83] Balasubramaniam, 'Rule of Law', p. 216.

[84] Interview with a constitutional scholar in Kuala Lumpur, Malaysia (August 2013).

[85] As I stated in Chapter 1, given the cases studied in this book, my analysis and arguments do not take into account the latest constitutional amendments in 2015.

[86] There is one exception to this. In December 2001, during the presidency of Chandrika Kumaratunga (Sri Lanka Freedom Party), Ranil Wickremesinghe's United National Party won the legislative elections. Wickremesinghe became the prime minister until Kumaratunga dismissed his government and called for fresh elections in August 2004.

[87] International Crisis Group Report No. 172.

To what extent can all this explain judicial attitudes in cases involving religion and religious freedom? One crucial difference between Malaysia and Sri Lanka is that while the Malaysian court has gradually deviated from the original understandings and spirit behind article 3, the Supreme Court has not been as consistent in its responses on the relative priority between the protection of Buddhism vis-à-vis the protection of religious freedom, despite operating in a fervent Sinhalese-Buddhist political environment. As we have seen, the court in *Menzingen* suggested that religious freedom cannot be exercised in ways that would adversely affect the Buddha Sasana. Yet, in the *Nineteenth Amendment* case, it held that the protection of the Buddha Sasana must not come at the expense of religious freedom and that the special position of Buddhism was balanced by the assurance that the rights of other religions were equally protected from any interference.[88] Then, in the *Kapuwatta* case, the court reaffirmed Sri Lanka's secular nature (without at all addressing article 9 on Buddhism), but it also went on to draw the boundaries of permissible religious expression according to Buddhist principles.

These inconsistent treatments of the relative priority between the protection of Buddhism vis-à-vis religious freedom complicates the task of concluding what precisely motivates decisions in one way than another. If judges were indeed acting strategically by deferring to presidential or executive preferences, one would expect that their decisions on the meaning of article 9 would not change so drastically within a year. In fact, the three incorporation cases (*Prayer Centre*, *New Wine Harvest* and *Menzingen*), the *JHU Bill* case and the *Nineteenth Amendment* case all arose during the same regime – that is, during President Chandrika Kumaratunga's administration. However, one point to bear in mind here is that all the cases elaborated were heard by different benches, and in Sri Lanka, the chief justice could 'pre-decide' the outcomes of a particular case by controlling the allocation of cases amongst judges.[89]

Leaving aside – for a moment – these difficulties, there is more consistency in the Supreme Court's approaches to issues on the religious freedom of minorities. The three incorporation cases discussed in the previous chapter demonstrate that the court was not willing to uphold the right to propagate one's religion due to its suspicion that the exercise of such right might result in conversions secured through fraudulent means.[90] The court's reaction to the

---

[88] Wickramaratne, *Fundamental Rights*, p. 933.   [89] IBA, 'Justice in Retreat', pp. 31–2.

[90] In the three incorporation cases discussed previously, the court denied the incorporation of Christian organizations on the basis that their proposed objectives and activities (especially with respect to the propagation of the Christian faith) would be contrary to the freedom of thought, conscience and religion.

JHU's anti-conversion bill was mixed: while other clauses in the bill were deemed unconstitutional, the provision criminalizing conversions by force, allurement, or fraudulent means was judged to be conditionally constitutional and consistent with the requirements of article 15(7) of the constitution. It was also significant that the court recommended the removal or modification of the problematic clauses, after which the bill as a whole could be easily passed in parliament by a simple majority.[91]

There are several ways of explaining the court's approaches on religious freedom. The first rests in the court's strict textualist approach in interpreting what the right to religious freedom entails. In the *Menzingen* and *Prayer Centre* decisions, for instance, the court refused to uphold the right to propagate one's religion on the basis that such a right is not explicitly protected in the constitution. The court was not willing to construe the right to propagate as part of the right to manifest and practice one's religion.

Second, the political context in which these decisions were delivered is an important consideration, which suggests that the court's decisions reflected the strategic constraints it operated under. The court was adjudicating these cases against the background of strong public anxiety over the spread of Christianity through missionary activities. Therefore, much like the Malaysian situation where strategic decision-making takes into account public opinion, the judgments reflect the court's implicit refusal to validate activities that are perceived as unfriendly to the dominant religious fervour. In other words, the court might have considered the need to protect majoritarian interests or risk public backlash. The latter is a real and proven danger, as the Mannar incident and other reported cases of judicial intimidation have shown.[92]

Moreover, since the late 1950s, national politics, as we have seen in Chapter 2, have centred around the promotion and protection of Sinhalese-Buddhist interests. President Kumaratunga – initially indifferent to Sinhalese-Buddhist causes – eventually caved in to right-wing pressures.[93] She began making concessions to fierce proponents of Sinhalese-Buddhist rights, one of which was evident in the constitutional recognition of the Supreme Advisory Council consisting of Buddhist monks and representatives of Buddhist

---

[91] Roshini Wickremesinghe, 'The Role of Government and Judicial Action in Defining Religious Freedom: A Sri Lankan Perspective' (2009) 2 *International Journal of Religious Freedom* 29, 38.

[92] Pinto-Jayawardena, 'Protecting the Independence', p. 178. Pinto-Jayawardena argued that judges who delivered unpopular decisions would face intimidation by thugs.

[93] According to a source, Kumaratunga sought to maintain a good balance the competing demands between protecting and fostering Buddhism on the one hand, and upholding religious freedom on the other. Interview with a former government official and diplomat in Colombo, Sri Lanka (June 2013).

organizations. It was also under the Kumaratunga administration that the government promulgated the anti-conversion bill through a committee of multireligious individuals appointed by Prime Minister Ranil Wickremesinghe and then approved by President Kumaratunga.[94] Under such circumstances, one may begin to understand why the court delivered a careful, mixed response to the constitutionality of the bill. The criminalization of conversions would be constitutional if particular terms were redefined, and the court suggested that provisions (or parts of some provisions) which were unconstitutional could simply be removed so that the bill would pass the constitutional hurdle.[95] The court also strategically avoided opening the Pandora's Box by leaving questions about the relative priority between the protections of Buddhism vis-à-vis religious freedom unaddressed. In addition, Sarath Silva, the then chief justice appointed by President Kumaratunga, had a widely known inclination for populist decisions that appeal to Sinhalese-Buddhist sensitivities.[96] Kumaratunga was also infamous for publicly reprimanding the judiciary in cases where decisions have gone against the government.[97]

Compared to Malaysia and Sri Lanka, the Indonesian Constitutional Court judges need not worry about being arbitrarily removed for unpopular decisions against the government's interests, because no single political actor holds such a prerogative. As noted previously, although the legislature is not involved in the dismissal process for constitutional court judges, the president exercises removal powers at the advice of the chief justice and there are well-defined grounds for removal. In addition, judges do not have to seek reappointment from their initial appointing institution. As Butt argues, the court has demonstrated considerable activism, even in resolving politically charged cases. It has, for example, been fearless in reviewing electoral disputes and laws; some of its decisions have also proved to be quite controversial, including those where it has enforced rights that are implicit in the constitution.[98]

---

[94] A. R. M. Imtiyaz, 'The Politicization of Buddhism and Electoral Politics in Sri Lanka' in Ali Riaz (ed.), *Religion and Politics in South Asia* (Oxon: Routledge, 2010), pp. 146, 172 note 34. The bill was introduced as a Private Member's Bill by an MP from the JHU, who was at that time a member of the government coalition.

[95] *Prohibition of Forcible Conversion of Religion Bill*, Supreme Court Special Determination, S.C. Nos 02–22/2004 (12 August 12 2004), p. 15.

[96] International Crisis Group Report No. 172.

[97] Jayawardena argues that Kumaratunga was especially quick to engage in 'unrestrained criticism' against the judiciary when the courts decided cases against her government. The president also reportedly issued a statement that '[t]he judiciary would pose difficulties for the executive if they are wholly outside anyone's control'. See Pinto-Jayawardena, 'Protecting the Independence', pp. 178–84.

[98] For an overview of the court's jurisprudence in politically charged cases, see Horowitz, *Constitutional Change*, pp. 242–3 and Simon Butt, 'Indonesia's Constitutional Court:

Yet, as we have seen in Malaysia and Sri Lanka, strategic decision-making may entail considerations of the public's views, not just those of other political actors. Judges may also want to ensure that their decisions stick, in order to preserve the integrity and authority of the court in the long run. For these reasons, Butt highlights the mixed approaches that the Constitutional Court has exhibited in exercising its powers. While some cases demonstrate the court's boldness in challenging the government, in other cases it has exercised some restraint, for instance, by carefully avoiding striking down statutes after declaring them unconstitutional. These instances, according to Butt, are hallmarks of a politicized rather than an activist institution.[99] By adopting a forward-looking, 'strategic pragmatism' approach, the court would allow itself – in the long run – to maintain or expand its activism.[100]

Recall the *Blasphemy Law* case, where the Constitutional Court raised concerns over the problems with the parameters of word 'publicly'. While the court upheld the constitutionality of the law, it also held that only the legislature could remedy the law's vagueness and loopholes. In effect, the court cautiously signalled to the legislature that something needed to be done, but without compelling the legislature to do so. In the *Religious Courts* case, where the petitioner insisted on the application of the full corpus of Islamic law (which, to him, was central to his freedom of religion), the court pointed out that it was merely empowered to act as a 'negative legislature' and it could only invalidate – as opposed to amend – statutes that were inconsistent with the constitution.[101] In this case, the court opted to maintain the status quo with regard to demands for a greater place for Islam in the polity, bearing in mind, perhaps, that the constitutionalization of *Shariah* was explicitly rejected throughout Indonesia's constitution-making history.

Both cases are important in so far as they define the constitutional position of religion vis-à-vis religious rights and endorse the powers of the state in regulating religious freedom, but the outcomes are different. The *Religious Courts* case reflects the settled understanding – one that is shared by every government since independence – of the predominance of the *Pancasila* principles and the restricted role of Islamic law in the constitutional order.[102] The *Blasphemy Law* case, on the other hand, affirmed the prominence of the

---

Conservative Activist or Strategic Operator?' in Bjorn Dressel (ed.), *The Judicialization of Politics in Asia* (Oxon: Routledge, 2013), pp. 102–7.

[99] See Butt, 'Indonesia's Constitutional Court', p. 99   [100] Ibid.

[101] Simon Butt, 'Islam, the State and the Constitutional Court in Indonesia', *Sydney Law School Legal Studies Research Paper* No. 10/70 (July 2010), p. 15 (citing R. Michael Feener, *Muslim Legal Thought in Modern Indonesia* (Cambridge: Cambridge University Press, 2007)).

[102] Butt and Lindsey, *Constitution of Indonesia*, p. 226.

Pancasila, but in doing so it throws into doubt the promise of respect for religious pluralism that the founding fathers had envisioned.

These two examples comport with Butt's strategic pragmatism thesis. The court recognized the need to avoid offending the political branches, because retaliation may come in forms other than an outright removal of judges: politicians may seek to weaken the court by appointing subpar judges; they may pass laws that undermine or circumvent the court's decisions; they may completely ignore those decisions; or in extreme cases, they might move to dissolve the court.[103] In other words, although institutional design may insulate the court from the kinds of interference that we have seen in Malaysia and Sri Lanka, the court may nevertheless be mindful of other forms of political backlash, some of which have affected several other institutions during the post-Soeharto reform period.[104]

An amendment to the Constitutional Court Law in 2011 served as a timely reminder for the court to tread more carefully in its decision-making exercises. The amendment (which was introduced by the then minister for law and human rights who became one of the sitting justices of the court but was removed in January 2017) requires the court to choose between invalidating a statute (or provisions thereof) that it finds to be unconstitutional or leaving the law in force.[105] In other words, the court could no longer adopt the tactics that it did – for example, dictating the application of laws or directing the legislature to enact new laws within a specific time frame. This sent a signal from the legislature that it was aware of the court's manoeuvres and that it was jealously guarding its law-making powers. Time will tell if the court will circumvent or

---

[103] See Butt, 'Indonesia's Constitutional Court', p. 107. Butt suggests that the Constitutional Court's rulings can be categorized into four types: (1) it declares that a law is unconstitutional, but only from the date of the court's decision; (2) it declares that a statute is unconstitutional but because the costs of striking down the statute would be too high, the court asks the government to take steps toward compliance; (3) it finds that a law breaches the constitution but instead of immediately invalidating the law, the court sets a deadline for the legislature to pass a new law; and (4) it decides that the law is 'conditionally constitutional', that is, the law is valid so long as it is applied within the bounds that the court sees as constitutional. See ibid., pp. 108–10.

[104] See ibid., p. 107. One such example is the Judicial Commission. See Simon Butt, *Corruption and the Law in Indonesia* (Oxon: Routledge, 2011). Butt also highlights a case concerning a law on electricity, which was struck down by the court. The decision prompted heavy criticisms against the court and it certainly did not sit well with the executive and the legislature. The government responded. It did not directly attack the court, but proceeded to enact regulations similar to the invalidated law. The regulations, however, were out of the court's reach as it has no jurisdiction to review government regulations. Butt, 'Indonesia's Constitutional Court', p. 108.

[105] Ibid., p. 112.

abide by this,[106] but it is clear that the court has reasons to make its decisions palatable to other political actors in order to safeguard its authority and integrity in the future.

Alternative Explanation: Ideological Biases

Strategic considerations may not necessarily be the sole or dominant explanation for judicial attitudes across these countries. Indeed, we must be cautious in concluding that judges were strategically pandering to the preferences of the government simply because they failed to deliver rights-enforcing decisions. In the Sri Lankan cases, the written judgments evince the court's formalistic approach in interpreting the right to religious freedom. But what do we make of the court's contradictory approaches – illustrated in the *Menzingen* and *Nineteenth Amendment* cases – in deciding whether the provision on Buddhism trumps fundamental rights of minorities?

Couso and Hillbink's findings on judicial behaviour in Chile's Constitutional Tribunal provide a useful comparative example on the significance of the attitudinal theory of judicial behaviour. In Chile, judges were historically reluctant to defend rights and to assert their judicial powers across different regimes, but they then drastically began to show signs of increased activism in rights adjudication.[107] In light of these changing attitudes, Couso and Hillbink argue that strategic considerations *alone* cannot explain the Chilean judges' approaches toward rights. Rather, their ideological predispositions, moulded by their professional training, socialization and changes in the constitutional discourse within the legal academy, are also important in explaining why they adopted the paths that they did.[108]

We could extrapolate these arguments to the Malaysian and Sri Lankan experiences. If the Sri Lankan judges are merely strategic actors who act based on the anticipation of how the government would respond to their decisions, we would expect the second decision on article 9 (*Nineteenth Amendment*) to follow the first decision (*Menzingen*), because the political context and regime remained unchanged. In addition, both cases were heard by different

---

[106] The then chief justice, Mohammad Mahfud MD, announced that the court accepted the amendment. See 'MK Legowo Sambut UU Baru' ('Constitutional Court accepts the new law'), *Hukumonline* (22 June 2011), online: www.hukumonline.com/berita/baca/lt4e 017327806e1/mk-legowo-sambut-uu-baru.

[107] Couso and Hillbink, 'From Quietism to Incipient Activism', p. 123.

[108] Ibid. The authors also assert that institutional changes, which saw the appointment of judges coming from the academic and political spheres, have also helped spur judicial activism in rights adjudication. Ibid., p. 110.

benches,[109] raising the possibility that different ideological predispositions were at play in the two cases. The *Menzingen* decision also appear to indicate clearer prejudices, particularly on the question regarding Christian propagation activities – the court held that the combination of propagation practices with activities advancing social welfare would *necessarily* impose improper pressures on vulnerable, prospective converts. This bias seems more marked when we consider the fact that there are other incorporated religious bodies in Sri Lanka whose objectives include the propagation of religion and the provision of social welfare. Likewise, in Malaysia, the limited role ascribed to Islam in *Che Omar* has not been followed by the Federal Court in subsequent decisions (as well as in several High Court and Court of Appeal decisions). These decisions, to be sure, arose under the same government regime – by 'regime' I mean the political coalition that forms the government of the day. (The Barisan Nasional coalition has dominated the federal government since independence.) Thus, as in Sri Lanka, it is possible that the changing conceptions on the role of Islam in article 3 have been facilitated by (changing) judicial ideologies.

There are, of course, challenges in discerning the precise ideological leanings of judges. In countries like Malaysia and Sri Lanka, access to judges for personal interviews is difficult. Written judicial decisions sometimes do not offer much insight into judicial ideologies: in Sri Lanka and Indonesia, for example, judges at the Supreme Court and Constitutional Court do not write individual judgments like their counterparts in Malaysia. Further, Sri Lankan Supreme Court determinations typically lack the sort of lengthy analysis that we see in the Malaysian and Indonesian judgments. My subsequent arguments, therefore, are derived from analysing particular circumstances that might shape judicial ideologies. What I will demonstrate is that particular ideological biases that are prevalent among judges in the three countries may be shaped and conditioned by three main exogenous and endogenous factors: the mechanisms of judicial appointment, the allegiance to a fundamental national philosophy and the judges' private religious or political convictions.

Consider, first, the cases of Malaysia and Sri Lanka, where the power to appoint judges to the Federal Court and Supreme Court, respectively, is virtually the sole prerogative of the executive. A cursory view of history provides some evidence in which the executive appointed judges who share their ideological preferences and would advance their political agenda. The

---

[109] The *Menzingen* case was heard by Justice Bandaranayake, Justice Yapa and Justice Jayasinghe. The *Nineteenth Amendment* case was heard by Justice Weerasuriya, Justice Tilakawardene and Justice Raja Fernando.

appointments of Chief Justice Sarath Silva (who, as I noted previously, was known for his pro-government and pro-Sinhalese-Buddhist tendencies) and Chief Justice Mohan Peiris (who has had a long association with the Rajapaksa regime) are two of the most important examples in Sri Lanka. Sarath Silva's case is particularly revealing because he had been appointed ahead of Justice Mark Fernando, the most senior judge who was widely tipped to become the next Chief Justice. Fernando's disadvantage, however, was that he had a reputation for delivering decisions that circumscribed executive and legislative excesses of power.[110]

In Malaysia, changes in the composition of the then Supreme Court after the 1988 judicial crisis, combined with the revelations in the Lingam Tape inquiry, are important illustrations of how the prime minister can dictate the composition of the courts and reject the nomination of judges who do not share his views and political interests. During Dr. Mahathir's administration, the government was very keen to ensure that its policies and decisions went unchallenged. This position was remarkably different from that of his predecessors – all of whom were trained lawyers who understood the importance of the rule of law and judicial independence.[111] Analysts see 1988 as the turning point – since then, the executive has facilitated the appointment of ideologically pro-establishment judges to the highest court, and many of these appointments are highly questionable.[112] Against this background, it is perhaps unsurprising that the changes and expansion in the role of Islam in the constitutional order vis-à-vis religious freedom have occurred after the *Che Omar* decision in 1988. All this, in turn, bolstered the government's control over religious matters, be they for Muslims or non-Muslims.[113] This is not to say that the Indonesian system is not vulnerable to ideological biases dictated by judges' appointing institutions, especially if one considers Ginsburg's

---

[110] Kishali Pinto-Jayawardena and J. C. Weliamuna, 'Corruption in Sri Lanka's Judiciary' in Transparency International, *Global Corruption Report 2007: Corruption in Judicial Systems* (Cambridge: Cambridge University Press, 2007), pp. 275–6. Fernando's punishment continued under the Sarath Silva leadership. He was 'excluded from almost all important constitutional cases' from 1999 to 2003, forcing him to retire prematurely in 2004. Ibid., p. 277.

[111] Kanagasabai, 'Judicialization of Politics', p. 214.

[112] Interview with a constitutional law scholar in Kuala Lumpur, Malaysia (August 2013).

[113] See the line of cases explained in Chapter 5: *Meor Atiqulrahman bin Ishak v. Fatimah bte. Sihi* [2006] 4 Malayan Law Journal 605 (on the constitutionality of a ban on Muslim religious headgear); *Sulaiman bin Takrib v. Kerajaan Negeri Terengganu (Kerajaan Malaysia, intervener) & other applications* [2009] 6 Malayan Law Journal 354 (concerning religious practices or activities that disobey *fatwas* against deviant religious teachings); *Lina Joy v. Majlis Agama Islam Wilayah Persekutuan & Another* [2007] 4 Malayan Law Journal 585 (on the conversion of a Muslim to Christianity); and *Menteri Dalam Negeri & Others v. Titular Roman Catholic Archbishop of Kuala Lumpur* [2013] 6 Malayan Law Journal 468.

argument that representative appointment mechanisms may also produce appointees who are 'pure agents of the appointers'.[114] However, even if this were the case, there is some degree of ideological diversity within the Indonesian Constitutional Court bench.[115]

Due to the politically charged nature of religious issues, how they can be manipulated to mobilize political support, and how, in turn, they may determine the survival of politicians and regimes in Indonesia, Malaysia and Sri Lanka, governments may want to ensure that they can exercise control over religion (in whichever direction that is politically beneficial to them). When defective judicial appointment systems are thrown into the picture, all this can result in an ethnically unbalanced court composition at all levels, which is an obvious problem in Malaysia.[116] At present, an overwhelming number of judges are Malay-Muslims. It would of course be unfair to insinuate that a judge's ethnic and religious identities can, *per se*, influence his or her decisions. However, given the climate of Muslim religious fervour and the propaganda of the threat – real or imagined – to Islam and the Malay race, combined with the state's politicization of Islam, we cannot completely discount the possibility these wider elements may shape a judge's personal preferences and decisions.

According to a legal practitioner and a senior judge, many Malay-Muslim judges in Malaysia are increasingly inclined to prioritizing their religious predispositions over the constitutional guarantee of fundamental rights.[117] Some judges have also publicly declared that they are 'Muslims first, judges second'. Some are concerned about threats to Malay-Muslim political dominance, while others are motivated by a deep sense of personal duty to protect Islam. A retired Federal Court judge, for instance, suggested that in issues implicating Islam and the state, one of the prime concerns amongst most judges on the bench is the need to preserve the sanctity of Islam, the Malay identity and the prominence of Malay political power.[118] This mirrors the remarks made by a retired chief justice in a public forum, in which he suggested that there are efforts to take advantage of the 'weaknesses and disunity' of the Malay community to seize political power from the Malays.[119]

[114] Ginsburg, *Judicial Review*, p. 44.   [115] Ibid.

[116] Interview with a constitutional law scholar in Kuala Lumpur, Malaysia (August 2013).

[117] Interview with a civil liberties lawyer in Kuala Lumpur, Malaysia (August 2013) and conversation with a retired judge (June 2016).

[118] Interview with a retired Federal Court judge in Putrajaya, Malaysia (January 2014).

[119] Speech by Tun Abdul Hamid Mohamad, 'Human Rights from the Perspective of Islamic Traditions and the Malaysian Constitution', National Forum on Human Rights (24 January 2014) (translated from Malay; all translations are my own).

With respect to the 'Allah' dispute, the former judge argued that there was an underlying motivation to lure the Malays to Christianity by convincing the Malays of the parallels between Islam and Christianity.[120] These ideological preferences to enhance the protection of Malay-Muslim interests (as opposed to upholding fundamental rights) may drive the perversion of constitutional provisions. If all this holds water in Malaysia, it may well do the same in Sri Lanka because of the interrelatedness of the Sinhalese and Buddhist identities. Moreover, similar propaganda has proliferated amongst the Sinhalese-Buddhist majority: that the position of Buddhism (and as a result, the Sinhalese identity) is under threat due to a Christianization agenda and the spread of Western influence in the country since the British colonial period.

Unlike the Malaysian and Sri Lankan cases, one distinctive factor that drives Constitutional Court judges in Indonesia is the allegiance to the *Pancasila*. The *Pancasila* is the *grundnorm* of the Indonesian state and a core feature of the Indonesian identity. It is a set of principles that bind the polity under the nation's *Bhinneka Tunggal Ika* motto and must be fully accepted by all citizens.[121] As a result, although the mechanism of appointment allows the selection of Constitutional Court judges from diverse professional backgrounds (some were prominent academics, while others were career judges and politicians), they are nevertheless largely mainstream judges whose legal training and thinking are shaped by the *Pancasila*. The *Blasphemy Law* case best illustrates how judges committed to the *Pancasila* strove to uphold a law that would otherwise be inimical to fundamental rights under international standards. To uphold the *Pancasila* values and the religious underpinnings of the state in defining the parameters of religious freedom in Indonesia was, for the court, important as a matter of principle, despite the shortcomings of the law.

There are two further possibilities with regard to this *Pancasila*-driven approach. The first is that the paths taken by a majority of the judges in the *Blasphemy Law* case may have been based on their sincere belief that the *Pancasila* and the protection of the state's 'unity in diversity' character necessitated the restriction on religious expression and practices that may offend the religious sensitivities of others. The notion that a *Pancasila*-based state necessarily warrants restrictions on the exercise of rights on the basis of religious values appears widely accepted among judges, although this, as some have suggested, did not mean that the values of any particular religion

---

[120] Ibid.   [121] Butt and Lindsey, *Constitution of Indonesia*, p. 237.

are elevated above others.[122] A former chief justice, writing extra-judicially, affirms that a *Pancasila*-based state does not sanction atheistic beliefs, the freedom to promote anti-religious ideas and acts that constitute an insult to or desecration of religious teachings.[123] The second possibility is that the direction in which the *Pancasila* is applied or interpreted in relation to religious freedom may be conditioned by a judge's personal convictions (including those of a religious character). The notions that blasphemy should be criminalized and that 'deviant' religious groups should be restricted reflect the more mainstream, if not dominant, views in Indonesia. A former chief justice, for example, suggests that the fact that religion is an important element in Indonesia means that 'the protection of religious freedom must be integrated with the protection towards the purity of religious teachings', and the state must therefore take steps to realize such protection.[124] This interpretation may have been done in good faith, but it nevertheless departs from the respect for pluralism that Soekarno and the founding fathers envisioned.

Beyond ideologies on ethnicity, religion and executive-judiciary relations, how judges understand their role in the constitutional order is also important. Deference to executive power may not always be the result of strategic considerations; rather, it may be a reflection of the judges' understanding of their functions. Sri Lanka is a case in point. There is not only a lack of jurisprudential understanding of the role of courts in fundamental rights cases,[125] but as I indicated earlier, there is a reported practice of deference toward the chief justice (who is, more often than not, friendly to the regime in power). Some practitioners and academics in Sri Lanka suggest that some judges tend to view themselves as mediators in human rights cases,

---

[122] Interview with three sitting judges of the Indonesian Constitutional Court in Jakarta, Indonesia (October 2012 and January 2014). See also Moh. Mahfud M.D., 'Kebebasan Agama dalam Perspektif Konstitusi' ('Religious freedom in constitutional perspective'), presentation at the Conference of Religious Leaders of the ICRP: Strengthening Religious Freedom in Indonesia, Demanding Commitment from Elected President and Vice President (5 October 2009), online: www.mahfudmd.com/index.php?page=web.MakalahWeb&id=3&aw=1&ak=8.

[123] Hamdan Zoelva, 'Negara Hukum dalam Perspektif *Pancasila*' ('Law state in the perspective of *Pancasila*') (30 May 2009), online: hamdanzoelva.wordpress.com/2009/05/30/negara-hukum-dalam-perspektif-pancasila/. The former chief justice also opined that the concept of religious freedom envisioned by the founding fathers did not accommodate atheistic beliefs or anti-religious propaganda. See also Moh. Mahfud MD, 'Kebebasan Agama' and Nadirsyah Hosen, 'The Constitutional Court and 'Islamic' Judges in Indonesia (2016) 16(2) *Australian Journal of Asian Law*, Article 4.

[124] Moh. Mahfud MD, 'Kebebasan Agama'. Former Chief Justice Mahfud also argues that although religious freedom is guaranteed, the '[f]reedom to deviate from religion' is not allowed.

[125] Interview with a legal academic and practitioner in Colombo, Sri Lanka (June 2013).

not as active defenders of constitutional rights through judicial review. There have been instances where courts have asked victims of rights violations to withdraw their cases when the government had made an offer to compensate them.[126] The result is that the government is able to act with some degree of impunity, as courts are reluctant to reprimand them for acting *ultra vires* the constitution.

SITUATING WEAK JUDICIAL INSTITUTIONS AND RULE OF LAW

Strong rule of law, fashioned by an independent judiciary committed to upholding fundamental rights without fear or favour, is necessary to ensure the enforcement of constitutional guarantees. An analysis of the Indonesian, Malaysian and Sri Lankan cases reveals that not only does defective institutional design of the judiciary leave very little scope for judicial independence, but the existence of an all-powerful executive also contributes to the fragility of the rule of law. To exacerbate all this, a culture of corruption permeates through political and law enforcement institutions, and political elites and civil society groups have often exploited religious divides in the society for their own ends. An International Commission of Jurists report on Sri Lanka, for example, aptly summarized the state of fundamental rights in the country, highlighting that its problems were symptomatic of 'both a breakdown in institutions and a failure of political will'.[127]

The Indonesian judiciary has long carried the reputational burden as a corrupt institution that merely rubber-stamps governmental exercises of power. The three decades of authoritarian rule under Soeharto consolidated the breakdown in the separation of powers that began in Soekarno's 'guided democracy' era. The idea of an integralistic state pursued by the nation's founding fathers denied the need for human rights protection but focused on a strong, authoritative executive. Many view the post-Soeharto democratic reforms as an impressive – though far from perfect – overhaul of Indonesian constitutionalism. A Constitutional Court, which emerged with more integrity and independence than ever before, is frequently mentioned as one of the positive outcomes of the reform.[128]

Nonetheless, as the local saying goes, nothing is predictable in Indonesia. In October 2013, a corruption scandal returned to haunt the judiciary: Chief

---

[126] Ibid.   [127] International Crisis Group Report No. 172.
[128] See Horowitz, *Constitutional Change*, p. 244, and Butt, 'Indonesia's Constitutional Court', p. 102.

Justice Akil Mochtar was caught red-handed at his residence as several million dollars changed hands, allegedly for favourable decisions in two electoral disputes that the Constitutional Court had previously adjudicated. A court that had been basking in its prestige – perhaps even complacently – began to lose public confidence and respect.[129] Just over a month after the chief justice's arrest, a violent protest erupted in the courtroom as the court delivered its verdict in a Maluku election dispute.[130] Sources posit that corruption had in fact existed in the court for several years, but the lack of evidence made it difficult to pursue such cases.[131] This episode severely damaged the integrity of the court and prompted some to raise questions over the transparency of its appointment system.[132] The latter was made worse by an administrative court decision invalidating the presidential decree that appointed Justice Patrialis Akbar (who was formerly the minister of law and human rights and a DPR member from PAN) to the court.[133] In February 2017, Justice Patrialis Akbar was dishonourably dismissed after being implicated in a corruption case.

By contrast, the Malaysian and Sri Lankan judiciaries have not seen the kind of long-standing, institutionalized corruption that their Indonesian counterpart experienced throughout its post-independence history. In fact, the Malaysian judiciary enjoyed considerable prestige as an independent and competent institution until the events that unfolded in 1988. Similarly, the Sri Lankan judiciary was widely viewed as competent and independent since the country gained independence in 1948.[134] However, it gradually transformed into a cautious institution, then deferential, and now largely irrelevant.[135] The upshot of this is that corruption has become a serious

---

[129] See 'Ujian Penjaga Konstitusi' ('Test for guardians of the constitution'), *Kompas* (10 January 2014), online: nasional.kompas.com/read/2014/01/10/0837457/Ujian.Penjaga.Konstitusi.

[130] See 'Kisruh di Sidang MK, Akumulasi Kekecewaan Publik' ('Chaos in Constitutional Court, accumulation of public frustration'), *Kompas* (16 November 2013), online: nasional.kompas .com/read/2013/11/16/1441030/Kisruh.di.Sidang.MK.Akumulasi.Kekecewaan.Publik.

[131] Butt suggests that there had been two allegations of bribery during 2010–2011, but investigations failed to lead to any evidence. See Butt, 'Indonesia's Constitutional Court', p. 102.

[132] Indonesian Center for Law and Policies Studies, *The Re-Election of Constitutional Judges as a Momentum in Reorganizing the Public Officials Elections*, Indonesia Law Reform Weekly Digest, 35th ed. (October 2013).

[133] 'PTUN Batalkan Keppres Pengangkatan Patrialis Akbar' ('Administrative Court invalidates presidential decree appointing Patrialis Akbar'), *Kompas* (23 December 2013), online: nasional .kompas.com/read/2013/12/23/1818029/PTUN.Batalkan.Keppres.Pengangkatan.Patrialis.Akbar. Justice Patrialis Akbar refused to vacate his post, and the president then appealed against the decision, which was subsequently overturned by the State Administrative High Court.

[134] International Crisis Group Report No. 172.

[135] Jayantha de Almeida Guneratne, Kishali Pinto-Jayawardena, and Gehan Gunatilleke, *The Judicial Mind in Sri Lanka: Responding to the Protection of Minority Rights* (Colombo: Law and Society Trust, 2014).

disease – the Judicial Services Commission that is supposed to prevent corruption is largely defunct; corrupt judges who toe government lines would be shielded from disciplinary action; and bribes for the issuance of summons and favourable trial dates are common.[136] It is also interesting to note the common mantra embraced by the governments of all three countries in times where judicial independence and integrity were eroded (especially in the Soeharto, Dr. Mahathir and President Rajapaksa's administrations): economic development and political stability take precedence over the protection of human rights and the rule of law. By espousing this outlook, anything that can potentially challenge the state's agenda to consolidate its power and development will be quickly silenced and, as a result, weak rule of law institutions emerged.

Leaving aside the threats of corruption, the Indonesian Constitutional Court has otherwise been able to progressively build and maintain its independence in the post-Soeharto reform period. Competitive politics between and within political branches is pertinent in this respect, because it generates political diffusion. As we have seen at the beginning of this chapter, scholars emphasize the importance of political fragmentation in securing judicial independence – an assertion which rests on the assumption that fragmented power would make it harder to sanction judges for their decisions.[137] Writing in reference to Indonesia, Horowitz suggests that judicial independence in newly independent countries is conditional upon the existence of strong political competition.[138] Since the fall of the New Order regime (in which Soeharto's party, Golkar, dominated national politics), robust competition meant that no single party has dominated the legislature or the executive. In Malaysia, however, political competition has historically been very weak. The ruling coalition, Barisan Nasional (BN), has, with very few exceptions, consistently garnered a supermajority in Parliament.[139] However, since 1998, the political landscape is changing as the BN faced a formidable opponent in the form of the Pakatan Rakyat. Much healthier competition exists in Sri Lanka between the dominant UPFA and the United National Party (UNP), but since 2000, the UPFA has dominated both the legislative and executive elections,[140] with the UNP being largely viewed as weak, indecisive and unable to expand its electoral influence beyond Colombo.[141]

---

[136] Pinto-Jayawardena and Weliamuna, 'Corruption', p. 277.
[137] See Helmke and Rios-Figueroa, 'Introduction', p. 6.
[138] Horowitz, *Constitutional Change*, p. 235.
[139] Except 1969, 2008 and 2013. See Balasubramaniam, 'Rule of Law', p. 56.
[140] Between 2000 and 2010, there were four legislative elections. Three of these – in 2000, 2004 and 2010 – were won by the UPFA.
[141] Interview with a political economy scholar in Colombo, Sri Lanka (June 2013).

CONCLUSION

The three case studies have challenged some important assumptions underlying institutional design of the judiciary and judicial behaviour in protecting
and enforcing constitutional guarantees. The Malaysian and Sri Lankan
experiences demonstrate that the security of tenure on paper is inconclusive:
the power of the executive to remove and discipline judges with virtually
no checks and balances can produce compliant judges who are fearful of
reprisal and are cowed in the face of arbitrary exercises of government
power. Ironically, in Indonesia, where Constitutional Court judges may seek
reappointment for a second term, the independence and integrity of the
court have been widely celebrated, at least until the corruption scandals
implicating the former chief justice and another justice. The crucial factor
in the Indonesian set-up, in this respect, is that judges do not have to seek
reappointment from the institutions that appointed them in the first term.
Yet, despite the more balanced power of appointment in the Indonesian case
(as compared to the Malaysian and Sri Lankan systems), the *Blasphemy Law*
case demonstrates the Constitutional Court's reluctance to uphold the religious freedom for minorities.

All this brings us to the point about judicial behaviour: there are indications
that judges in all three countries act strategically in adjudicating politically
charged cases on religion and religious freedom, but strategic behaviour may
not necessarily be the sole explanation for judicial attitudes across these
countries. Constitutional contestations on religion in the three countries are
often framed as majority-minority battles, set against the background of societies that are not only religiously divided, but where competing groups are
deeply suspicious of one another. Unfortunately, as our discussion shows,
judges themselves may not be immune from sectarian propaganda centred
on the alleged threat posed by the minorities to the survival of the dominant
ethnic and religious groups in these countries.

Where strategic behaviour is present, it is not solely determined by the
expected responses of other political branches. Anticipated public reactions
also matter. Just as championing the religious interests and sensitivities of the
majority is important for politicians to garner popular votes and maintain
political power (as we shall see in the next chapter), a majoritarian approach
may also be important for the courts. In Malaysia and Sri Lanka, for example,
anxiety over Christian missionary activities has always been prevalent among
the majority Malay-Muslims and Sinhalese-Buddhists, but in recent years the
rhetoric has become increasingly hostile amidst claims that Christianization
efforts are threatening the dominant positions of the Malay-Muslims and

Sinhalese-Buddhists. An opinion poll conducted by the Merdeka Centre, for instance, found that 83 per cent of the Malays in Peninsular Malaysia agreed that the use of 'Allah' is exclusively for Muslims.[142] Against this, there may be genuine concerns of a public backlash that might trigger serious disorder. Courts – as the Indonesian case most prominently illustrates – may also be concerned about their ability to ensure that their decisions are respected and implemented on the ground. This can be a complex affair, especially since politicians in Indonesia are accustomed to acting without restraint and regard for constitutional principles. Taken together, all these factors may explain why a court that has achieved a great degree of institutional independence is nevertheless reluctant to be bolder in politically charged religious issues.

---

[142] 'Poll: Eight in 10 Malays say Allah solely for Muslims', *The Star* (26 February 2013), online: www.thestar.com.my/News/Nation/2013/02/26/Poll-Eight-in-10-Malays-say-Allah-solely-for-Muslims/.

7

Religion, Electoral Politics and Religious Freedom

One striking point that has come across previous chapters is the way in which religion and religious issues are inextricably linked to local political dynamics. The analysis in Chapter 2 on constitution-making processes and outcomes is particularly instructive, but the chapters on state practices and constitutional contestations involving religion also reveal the underlying tendencies to use religion to further particular political goals – be they the preservation of the hegemony of the religious majority or the ruling elite's interests. In this chapter, I will delve deeper into the relationship between religion and politics by evaluating the role of electoral competition in shaping state policies on religion and the protection of religious freedom.

In a study of Hindu-Muslim violence in India, political scientist Steven Wilkinson makes three important and interrelated observations.[1] First, electoral incentives determine whether the state will work to prevent anti-minority violence. More specifically, when minority votes matter for electoral support, governments will prevent violence and provide security to the Muslim minority in India. The second point centres on the existence of political competition. Wilkinson posits that higher levels of political competition or party fractionalization (that is, where there are three or more parties competing in an election) correspond to lower levels of Hindu-Muslim violence. This is because, Wilkinson argues, politicians will have more incentives to appeal to minorities who are key swing voters (either directly or through coalition with minority parties) to win elections. There are, however, instances where two-party competition can push governments to prevent violence or even provoke it. When a party in power relies on minority support, politicians have incentives to prevent violence against one of its support bases. By contrast, when a

---

[1]   Steven I. Wilkinson, *Votes and Violence: Electoral Competition and Ethnic Riots in India* (Cambridge: Cambridge University Press, 2006), pp. 138–40.

ruling party lacks minority support, Wilkinson contends that it can both provoke and/or allow violence to take place.

Wilkinson's study sheds light on the political or electoral conditions in which governments are more likely to safeguard minority interests. However, as this chapter will show, while Wilkinson's overarching theory on the relationship between electoral incentives and government action or inaction in communal violence can be extrapolated to this study on religion and religious freedom in Indonesia, Malaysia and Sri Lanka, there are important divergences in circumstances and outcomes across the three countries. In Malaysia and Sri Lanka, the desire to maximize Malay-Muslim and Sinhalese-Buddhist votes, respectively, has led ruling coalitions – at various points in time – to appease the majority in how they handle religious issues. This strategy has also seen ruling parties co-opt or support right-wing movements in the society. The rest of the chapter will demonstrate how and why all this has occurred and why religious minorities have failed to gain leverage in policy decisions that affect their interests and rights.

The Indonesian story is more complex. There is a high level of party fractionalization, and multiple cleavages exist within the majority community. In 2014, for instance, twelve parties competed in the national legislative elections. Although Muslims in Indonesia nowadays subscribe to the mainstream Sunni school of thought, their religious practices and observance, their views on interreligious relations and their political affiliations are very diverse. According to Wilkinson's study, these are some of the conditions that should increase the government's willingness to protect minorities.[2] However, there are potent indications that the government as well as political parties in Indonesia are increasingly seeking to appease a broader base of the Muslim electorate. In some cases, as we shall see, political elites themselves have resorted to inflaming sectarian passions and mobilized supporters along religious lines in order to discredit their opponents.

The point that this chapter makes, in short, is that in all three countries, government responses and policies implicating religion reflect the ruling coalition's political calculations vis-à-vis the majority and minority electorates. Where politicians have turned toward appeasing the majority, there is potent evidence that minority interests take a back seat. It is not necessarily the case that minority votes and voices are unimportant. However, for reasons that we

---

[2] Ibid., p. 160. In his study of India, Wilkinson also identified another condition – the importance of Muslim votes in national politics. Muslims comprise 12% of the Indian population and Wilkinson deems that this is enough to constitute a significant voting bloc. See ibid., pp. 41–4.

shall see later in this chapter, the incentives to appeal to them have significantly diminished. To arrive at these conclusions, I organize this chapter in two main parts. In the next section, I provide an overview of the history and interaction between religion and politics in the society. This provides a useful background for understanding how and why local politics are mobilized along religious lines and the extent to which religion can be manipulated for political ends and reify divisions within the society. I then assess the circumstances and conditions that shape politicians' electoral incentives for or against the protection of religious freedom (especially for minorities) across the three countries. The analysis will also help us understand why conceptions of state-religion relations have changed over time in a direction that favours the dominant religious group and why constitutional guarantees on religious freedom have proven to be malleable in practice.

RELIGION IN POLITICS AND SOCIETY: AN OVERVIEW

Indonesia

I have previously explained that although Muslims comprise almost 90 per cent of the Indonesian population, their professed doctrines and practices are not homogenous. Unlike Malaysia, Indonesia has historically been more accommodating to diverse forms of Islamic thought and political movements, with different perspectives on critical issues such as the Islamic state and the way Islam is translated into public life.[3] Much has been written on the Muslim society in Indonesia and its political attitudes and tendencies. The most common typologies that have been used or referred to by Indonesianists are those that were developed by Clifford Geertz and Deliar Noer. Geertz, based on his study on a small community in an East Java village, distinguished three groups of Javanese Muslims – the *santri*, the *abangan* and the *priyayi*.[4] The *santri* are identified as observant Muslims, while the *abangan* are nominal Muslims who are less tied to formal Islamic rituals and who subscribe to what Hefner calls 'non-standard' Islamic practices that incorporate mystical and spiritual elements.[5] Deliar Noer, on the other hand, classifies Indonesian

---

[3]   Norani Othman, 'Islamization and Democratization in Malaysia' in Ariel Heryanto and Sumit K. Mandal (eds.), *Challenging Authoritarianism in Southeast Asia* (Oxon: RoutledgeCurzon, 2003), p. 122. Othman also argues that Islam in Indonesia thus differs remarkably from that in Malaysia and that the Muslim intellectual culture has been far more active and democratic in Indonesia. Ibid.

[4]   Clifford Geertz, *The Religion of Java* (Chicago: Chicago University Press, 1960).

[5]   Robert W. Hefner, 'Where Have All the Abangan Gone? Religionization and the Decline of Non-Standard Islam in Contemporary Indonesia' in Michel Picard and Rémy Madinier (eds.),

Muslims into two groups: 'traditionalists' and 'modernists'.[6] The former assimilates Islam with local traditions; the latter combines a scripturalist approach to Islam based on the Quran and *Sunnah*, free from innovations and superstitions, with an open attitude toward modern scientific advances.[7]

In terms of political affiliations, historically, the *santris* tended to align themselves with Islamic political parties such as the Masyumi and the Nahdlatul Ulama (NU) – both of which were prominent parties that fought for the establishment of an Islamic state until the 1960s. Masyumi was dissolved in 1960, while NU ceased to become a political party in the 1980s. NU, however, maintains an affiliation with the Partai Kebangkitan Bangsa (PKB), which was set up in 1999. The *abangans* supported some of the early secular parties such as the Partai Nasionalis Indonesia (PNI) or the Partai Komunis Indonesia (PKI).[8] During Soeharto's New Order period, they tended to affiliate with Golkar and in more recent years, they are said to be largely aligned with the PDI-P.[9] As Assyaukanie correctly argues, however, the *abangan-santri* dichotomy is contentious and their respective political affiliations have also changed considerably over time.[10] Others argue that the *abangan-santri* distinction is losing contemporary relevance.[11] The same can also be said of the traditionalist-modernist dichotomy and their perceived political affiliations. The traditionalists mostly belong to the NU and they have traditionally been politically aligned to the PKB, while the modernists are largely

---

Politics of Religion in Indonesia: Syncretism, Orthodoxy, and Religious Convention in Java and Bali (Oxon: Routledge, 2011), pp. 71, 73–5. Hefner stresses that although some have popularized the idea that *abangans* were non-observant Muslims, *abangans* nevertheless view themselves as Muslims – they acknowledge the authority of the Quran and *Sunnah*, but practice an 'ethnicized variety' of Islam. For criticisms of Geertz's classification, see Luthfi Assyaukanie, *Islam and the Secular State in Indonesia* (Singapore: Institute of Southeast Asia Studies, 2009) and M. C. Ricklefs, *A History of Modern Indonesia since C. 1200*, 4th ed. (Stanford: Stanford University Press, 2008), p. 197.

6   Deliar Noer, *The Modernist Muslim Movement in Indonesia, 1900–1942* (Singapore: Oxford University Press, 1973).

7   Ricklefs, *History of Modern Indonesia*, p. 203.

8   Assyaukanie, *Islam and the Secular State*, p. 4 and Ricklefs, *History of Modern Indonesia*, p. 277.

9   Assyaukanie, *Islam and the Secular State*, p. 6 (quoting Mark R. Woodward, 'Indonesia, Islam, and the Prospect for Democracy' (2001) 21(2) *SAIS Review* 29). See also R. William Liddle, 'New Patterns of Islamic Politics in Democratic Indonesia', *Asia Program Special Report*, No. 110 (Washington, DC: Woodrow Wilson Center, 2003), p. 7.

10   Assyaukanie, *Islam and the Secular State*, p. 4. Assyaukanie also stresses that *santris* are not a homogenous group. Ibid., p. 226.

11   Azyumardi Azra, 'Bali and Southeast Asian Islam: Debunking the Myths' in Kumar Ramakrishna and See Seng Tan (eds.), *After Bali: The Threat of Terrorism in Southeast Asia* (Singapore: World Scientific, 2003), pp. 39–40. See also Ricklefs, *History of Modern Indonesia*, p. 356 and Hefner, 'Where Have All the Abangan Gone?', pp. 80–4. Hefner's article provides a good explanation of the factors that led to the decline of the *abangans*.

Muhammadiyah members. The Muhammadiyah was once closely identified with Partai Amanat Negara (PAN). However, all these affiliations are not static. Muhammadiyah is no longer formally or exclusively connected to PAN, and there is great diversity in political support and affiliation amongst Muhammadiyah members.[12] A senior Muhammadiyah figure, for example, was a member of Golkar's central leadership. There are also Partai Persatuan Pembangunan (PPP) and Partai Keadilan Sejahtera (PKS) cadres who are Muhammadiyah members. Likewise, there are active politicians in the PDI-P, the Partai Demokrat and Golkar who are prominent NU members.

What seems obvious at this point is that there is great diversity and fluidity in religious thought, ideological views and political affiliations in Indonesia. Personal religiosity does not always reflect one's political allegiances and, as we shall see, pragmatically driven politics has led to changing attitudes among political parties in matters involving religion. Abdurrahman Wahid, a religious scholar with a *santri* background who founded the NU-based political party, PKB, was a strong advocate of liberal democratic values and religious pluralism, and he was deeply committed to the *Pancasila*.[13] Similarly, although a large section of Indonesian Muslims are conservative in their beliefs and practices, they do not always vote for an Islamic party or a Muslim politician.[14] According to a senior Golkar politician, while religious observance has increased throughout Indonesia, supporters of nationalist parties have, by and large, remained supporters of those parties instead of shifting their support to parties with an explicitly Islamic ideology, such as the PKS.[15]

Against this background, it is worth recollecting and emphasizing the Soeharto factor in relation to the attitudes of Indonesian Muslims toward Islamic political parties. To some extent, the repression of political Islam during the Soeharto presidency is said to have adversely affected views against such parties.[16] Soeharto ensured that the *Pancasila* was the sole ideological basis (*asas tunggal*) of the state, including political parties and civil society organizations. There was no negotiation on this, as Soeharto envisioned

---

[12] Conversation with a prominent Muhammadiyah leader in Jakarta, Indonesia (October 2012).

[13] Assyaukanie, *Islam and the Secular State*, p. 18. Although the PKB's members largely comprise NU members and traditionalist Muslims, the party's ideological basis is the *Pancasila* and its membership is open to non-Muslims.

[14] Nithin Coca, 'Is political Islam rising in Indonesia?', *Al Jazeera* (12 May 2014), online: www.aljazeera.com/indepth/features/2014/04/political-islam-rising-indonesia-2014429132534 17235.html. See also Azra, 'Debunking the Myths', p. 42.

[15] Interview with a senior Golkar politician and DPR member in Jakarta, Indonesia (January 2014). See also Azra, 'Debunking the Myths', p. 40 and Saiful Mujani and R. William Liddle, 'Personalities, Parties, and Voters' (2010) 21 *Journal of Democracy* 35, 38.

[16] Assyaukanie, *Islam and the Secular State*, p. 3. Soeharto's presidency lasted over three decades, from 1967 to 1998.

the *Pancasila* as a means of binding and controlling the polity. Muslim organizations like the NU and Muhammadiyah were torn on entrenching the *Pancasila* as their ideological foundation, but they eventually accepted it. Despite Soeharto's hostility to political Islam, he eventually became friendly to the development of Islam at the societal level in the second half of the New Order period. Skilled at manipulating religion to consolidate his power, he began – especially in the 1990s – to adopt more conciliatory policies toward Islam and Muslim organizations. He reached out to ultraconservative Muslims in the Indonesian Islamic Propagation Council, provided patronage to a Muslim intellectual organization and co-opted Muslim figures into the armed forces and the cabinet.[17] At the same time, Soeharto was also committed to a program for religious tolerance.[18]

The fall of Soeharto led to the proliferation of new political parties, including Islamic parties such as the PAN (from the moderate varieties) and the Partai Bulan Bintang (PBB) and PKS (from the more puritanical varieties). The PPP, which survived the collapse of the New Order, immediately switched its political ideology from the *Pancasila* to Islam. Some of these parties, as we saw in Chapter 2, immediately seized the freer political space to demand the inclusion of the 'seven words' (which would have obligated the state to enforce *Shariah* law for Muslims) in the constitution. At the same time, many Islamic movements that were previously suppressed by Soeharto mushroomed. Some of them – such as Hizbut Tahrir Indonesia (HTI) – exploited the newfound freedom to expound extremist views and activities, often acting as self-styled law enforcers in the name of religion. Unlike the Islamic political parties that have accepted and participated in the democratic process, some of these organizations are more hostile to democracy.

In spite of these developments, support for Islamic parties in Indonesia has declined since independence. In the 1955 general elections, for instance, Masyumi and NU received almost 40 per cent of the total votes nationally.[19] The former's support base was largely drawn from outside Java, while the latter's support was concentrated in East and Central Java.[20] The religio-political

---

[17] See Azra, 'Debunking the Myths', p. 41; Hefner, 'Where Have All the Abangan Gone?', p. 86; and Donald L. Horowitz, *Constitutional Change and Democracy in Indonesia* (Cambridge: Cambridge University Press, 2013), pp. 35–6.

[18] R. William Liddle, 'The Islamic Turn in Indonesia: A Political Explanation' (1996) 55 *Journal of Asian Studies* 613, 624.

[19] Marcus Mietzner, 'Comparing Indonesia's Party Systems of the 1950s and the Post-Suharto Era: From Centrifugal to Centripetal Inter-Party Competition' (2008) 39 *Journal of Southeast Asian Studies* 431, 434.

[20] Ibid.

polarization in electoral competition was clear, as nationalist and Islamic parties mobilized for support according to the narrow interests of their constituencies.[21] As we shall see later in this chapter, this has changed significantly. In the four elections since Soeharto's departure, the electoral gains of Islamic parties have waned: they secured 13 per cent, 18.1 per cent, 15 per cent and 14.8 per cent of the total votes in the 1999, 2004, 2009 and 2014 legislative elections, respectively.[22] As Chapter 2 also demonstrates, the support for the establishment of an Islamic state or the constitutionalization of *Shariah* has also declined over time. After the collapse of such efforts in the 1955 constitution-making process, even *santris* have largely taken a critical tone toward calls for an Islamic state.[23] The two largest Muslim organizations in Indonesia – the NU and Muhammadiyah – explicitly rejected efforts to reintroduce the 'seven words' into the constitution during the post-Soeharto constitutional reforms.

Nevertheless, the use of religious symbolism in elections remains one of the strategies for political mobilization, especially in conservative constituencies. Politicians seeking electoral victory need to portray support for and observance of religious activities. In some districts, gentlemen's agreements are struck with local religious leaders for electoral support.[24] In the 2014 presidential election campaign, Prabowo Subianto – a candidate from Gerindra (Great Indonesia Movement – a nationalist party) – embraced the endorsements and pledge of support by the Front Pembela Islam (FPI). On the other hand, the PDI-P candidate, Joko Widodo (Jokowi), was subject to a smear campaign questioning his religious orientations and religiosity. Jokowi's campaign team had to respond by proving that he has performed the mandatory Muslim pilgrimage and that he is able to recite the Quran and lead mass prayers. In his tenure as the Governor of Jakarta, Widodo drew protests from locals and hard-line organizations when he appointed a Christian woman as the head of an urban village (*Ketua Lurah*) where the majority population is Muslim.

Malaysia

In 2004, Bridget Welsh wrote that religion has become the 'defining domestic ethnic marker' in Malaysia.[25] In retrospect, there are many indications that the

---

[21] Ibid., p. 435.
[22] By 'Islamic parties' I mean the parties whose formal ideological base is Islam, i.e., PPP, PKS and PBB. As for PAN and PKB, although their support bases are largely Muslims, the *Pancasila* is their formal ideological foundation.
[23] Assyaukanie, *Islam and the Secular State*, p. 2.
[24] Conversation with a Partai Demokrat politician in Jakarta, Indonesia (January 2014).
[25] Bridget Welsh, 'Shifting Terrain: Elections in the Mahathir Era' in Bridget Welsh (ed.), *Reflections – The Mahathir Years* (Washington: John Hopkins-SAIS, 2004), pp. 119, 121.

foundations for Welsh's claim had been set well before 2004. We have seen throughout the previous chapters how the interrelatedness of Islam and the Malay identity led to demands for recognition of Islam in the constitution and how inseparability of these ethnic and religious affiliations has become embedded in the Malay psyche. The religious overtones of social and political movements in Malaysia began to intensify in the late 1970s and 1980s, inspired as they were by the Iranian revolution. *Dakwah* (religious preaching) movements – some of which had been established before the revival – proliferated throughout the country, calling for stronger adherence to Islamic ideals and principles.[26] These organizations espoused various interpretations of Islam, including the propagation of a 'pure' Islamic way of life. Some sought to achieve their objectives through more radical and militant means, while others maintained active participation in politics and the civil society sphere.[27]

These developments are significant for several reasons. First, from the perspective of law and governance, they presented a challenge to the government's control and authority in interpreting and defining the parameters of Islam in the polity. I have alluded to the issue of state monopoly over religious interpretations in Chapter 3, but here I want to emphasize its political significance. For example, there are laws stipulating that a *fatwa* (religious opinion) delivered by a *mufti* is binding on all Muslims in the state once it is gazetted.[28] The *Yang di-Pertuan Agong* officially appoints the *mufti* upon the advice of the minister in charge of religious affairs, who should first consult the Islamic Religious Council before delivering his advice. However, with the growth of *dakwah* organizations, deviations from the state's approved brand or interpretation became inevitable. It was also inevitable that such organizations would command a following (including that of a political nature), threatening to split the Malay-Muslim community's political allegiances.[29]

This brings us to the second point: from a political perspective, the country's ruling elites – led by the multiethnic Barisan Nasional (BN) coalition – began to face serious challenges to its political dominance, particularly within its core support base, i.e., the Malay-Muslim electorate. Its main competitor in this respect was the Islamic party, PAS, who rose to become the United National Malays Organization's (UMNO's) main competitor for Malay votes, especially in the Malay heartlands such as Kedah, Kelantan and Terengganu. UMNO has traditionally galvanized support on the basis that it is the most capable, committed protector of Malay rights and interests. PAS has

---

[26] Gordon P. Means, *Malaysian Politics: The Second Generation* (Singapore: Oxford University Press, 1991), p. 71.
[27] Ibid., p. 72.   [28] See Administration of Islamic Law (Federal Territories) Act 1993, s. 34.
[29] Means, *Malaysian Politics*, p. 72.

campaigned, among others, on the premise that the UMNO-BN government lacked the capacity and motivation to pursue the fundamental principles of Islam. To be sure, PAS was a prominent Malay opposition party established decades before the Islamic revival movement in Malaysia. Its establishment in the 1950s actually had its roots in UMNO's political strategy. UMNO, at that time, sought to expand its Malay support base in the villages and rural areas by attracting the local *ulama*.[30] UMNO thus created its own Islamist camp within the party, but relations soon began to sour. Some UMNO members were dissatisfied with the party's commitment to Muslim concerns and the emergence of liberal, Western-oriented personalities within the party (most notably Tunku Abdul Rahman), and they then broke away to form PAS in November 1951.[31] It is therefore unsurprising that in its early days, PAS had also mobilized support by advocating the supremacy of the Malays and Islam.

That PAS became closely allied to some of the *dakwah* groups that emerged from the Islamic revival movement raised concerns within the ruling coalition. One such group was ABIM (the Malaysian Islamic Youth Movement). Formed in the early 1970s, it was driven primarily by the urban Malay, middle-class youth and was particularly influential amongst Malay university students both at home and abroad.[32] ABIM espoused anti-Western and anti-secularist positions, but aside from campaigning on Islamic-related issues such as alcohol consumption, it was also vocal on the civil liberties front, opposing, in particular, the Internal Security Act (which allowed detention without trial) and the Universities and University College Act (which restricted student involvement in party politics).[33] Another group, which was perceived as associated with PAS, was the Al-Arqam movement. Founded by Ashaari Muhammad, a member of PAS, the Al-Arqam operated as an independent community in a suburb of Kuala Lumpur. It denounced secularism and adopted strict Islamic principles.[34] Its followers were largely middle-class

---

[30] Farish Noor, *Islam Embedded: The Historical Development of the Pan-Malaysian Islamic Party PAS, 1951–2003*, Volume 1, 2 vols. (Kuala Lumpur: Malaysian Sociological Research Institute, 2004), pp. 66–7 (quoting Baharuddin Abdul Latif, *Islam Memanggil: Rencana-rencana Sekitar Perjuangan PAS, 1951–1987* (*Islam Is Calling: Articles on the Struggle of PAS, 1951–1987*) (Perak: Pustaka Abrar, 1994)).

[31] For a detailed account of the establishment of PAS and the circumstances surrounding it, see Noor, *Islam Embedded*, pp. 66–77.

[32] Means, *Malaysian Politics*, p. 73.   [33] Ibid.

[34] See Abdullah Saeed and Hassan Saeed, *Freedom of Religion, Apostasy, and Islam* (Oxon: Routledge, 2004), pp. 129–30; and Abdullahi Ahmed An-Naim, 'Mediation of Human Rights: The Al-Arqam Case in Malaysia' in Joanne R. Bauer and Daniel K. Bell (eds.), *The East Asian Challenge for Human Rights* (Cambridge: Cambridge University Press, 1999).

Muslim professionals and although it was not directly involved in politics, its influence (and cultlike practices) led to its disbandment by the government in the 1990s.

The rise of Islamic revivalism increased the Malay-Muslim community's scrutiny of individual political elites' knowledge of, and commitment to, Islam. Much like the competition between PAS and UMNO to portray which of the two parties are the true champions of Islamic ideals, the competition to prove one's Islamic credentials swept the Malay community, and the ability to demonstrate one's 'superior Islamic moral rectitude' became important political capital for those seeking electoral support from the Malays.[35] In this respect, the ruling Malay elites, who were largely Western- or English-educated and who were mostly seen as secular, faced the added challenge of fending off attacks on their religious background and outlook.

The elites knew that they had to react if they were to stay competitive within the Malay electorate. In the realms of party politics, efforts to appeal to the Malay-Muslims and the Islamic revival movement led to Dr. Mahathir's recruitment of Anwar Ibrahim to UMNO in 1981. Anwar was the former president of ABIM, and as a charismatic, influential leader amongst his ABIM comrades and the Malay university students, he was an important asset for the government's series of Islamic reform plans. Indeed, he accepted the offer to join UMNO and the government on the understanding that he would spearhead the state's 'Islamization' initiatives.[36] By the time the UMNO General Assembly met in 1982, the change in the government's tone was obvious: Dr. Mahathir spoke of the need to enhance Islamic practices and ensure adherence to Islamic teachings. He also outlined plans to establish an Islamic university and an Islamic banking system.[37] Therefore, much like Indonesia's experience under Soeharto, the emphasis on Islamic symbolism and policies appeared to be a response toward the changing attitudes and opinions within the majority Muslim community.

Over time, religious symbolism has emerged as a regular and powerful aspect of Malaysian politics, but it is also a double-edged sword. On the one hand, it has become a means by which the UMNO-led government could compete with the political rhetoric and demands of PAS and Malay-Muslim pressure groups. On the other hand, has also allowed PAS and such groups to pressure the government to formulate policies in a certain direction – a direction which may or may not be favourable to the development of a vibrant Islamic discourse as well as the interests of religious minorities. In a setting

---

[35] Means, *Malaysian Politics*, p. 74.   [36] Ibid., pp. 99–100.   [37] Ibid., p. 100.

where UMNO is pressed to maintain its dominance amongst the core Malay-Muslim electorate, any accusations that it is failing to protect and uphold Islam could be very damaging to its political survival.

This historical overview is important in understanding the ensuing discussions in this chapter, because much of it remains relevant in Malaysia's current political developments. More than three decades after the revival movement hit Malaysian shores, Islamic nationalism has become 'the new Malay nationalism', created as it were to perpetuate the pre-eminence of Malay political power.[38] One may agree or disagree with such a suggestion, but what is clear is that the protection of Islam goes hand in hand with the protection of the Malays, and the rhetoric on the need to ensure the supremacy of these two elements is a potent source of legitimacy for politicians.

Sri Lanka

The interaction between religion, ethnicity and politics in Sri Lanka bears much resemblance to the dynamics in Malaysia. I have previously alluded to the interdependence of the Sinhalese and Buddhist identities and how both elements form the core tenet of the Sinhalese-Buddhist nationalist consciousness, in which the 'Sinhalese homeland' idea plays a pertinent role. This is similar to Malay nationalist claims that Malaysia is the traditional homeland of the Malays. For Sinhalese-Buddhist nationalists, Sri Lanka is a land ordained for the Sinhalese, who are in turn ennobled to preserve and propagate Theravada Buddhism.[39] Put simply, just as Islam is central to the Malay-focused political mobilization, Buddhism is invoked to propagate a Sinhalese-centric political agenda.

Unlike the Malaysian scenario, there is purported textual religious basis for the Sinhalese-Buddhist nationalists' claims for supremacy. For them, the *Mahavamsa* (the sacred Buddhist chronicle) legitimizes the pre-eminence of Buddhism in Sri Lanka. The *Mahavamsa* also propagates ideas that inspire Sinhalese-Buddhist interest advocacy and the rise of political Buddhism: Sri Lanka is said to be designated by the Buddha as the sacred land for Buddhism, and the Sinhalese, as the 'sons of the soil', are the chosen protectors of Buddhism.[40] Scholars such as DeVotta and De Silva challenge these

---

[38] Interview with a constitutional law scholar in Kuala Lumpur, Malaysia (August 2013).

[39] Neil DeVotta, *Sinhalese Buddhist Nationalist Ideology: Implications for Politics and Conflict Resolution in Sri Lanka*, Policy Studies, No. 40 (Washington, DC: East-West Center, 2007), p. vii.

[40] Ibid., p. 8. In his study, DeVotta provides a summary of the *Mahavamsa* and how it underpins the Sinhalese-Buddhist nationalist movement. See ibid., pp. 6–8 and K. M. De Silva, *A History of Sri Lanka*, 2nd ed. (Colombo: Vijitha Yapa Publications, 2008), p. 7.

Mahavamsa accounts as myths,[41] while others provide different explanations as to when, how and why the Sinhalese-Buddhist consciousness emerged. For example, Tambiah points to the history of colonial mistreatment of Buddhism and economic grievances against foreigners,[42] while De Silva underscores the hostile relations between Buddhists and missionary organizations, where the former resisted efforts by the latter to convert people to Christianity.[43] Some theories have a more psychological undertone, emphasizing that the Sinhalese-Buddhists' 'majority with a minority complex' psyche is conditioned by geopolitical pressures (e.g., Sri Lanka's proximity to India – a Hindu-majority country with a large population of Tamils in the south and the predominance of Muslims in neighbouring states) and insecurities over the survival of the Sinhalese-Buddhist race.[44] Regardless of which of these accounts is true, it would appear that the mobilization of Sinhalese-Buddhist nationalism and the Buddhist revivalist movement are reactive to social and political conditions deemed detrimental to Buddhism.

Buddhist revivalism bears important consequences for Sri Lankan politics, some of which are still significant and visible today. For one, it led to both direct and indirect involvement of *bhikkus* (monks) in the political scene, reviving centuries-old monk participation in politics where they advised kings, provided legitimation to rulers and influenced policymaking exercises.[45] Before independence, the *bhikkus* led confrontations with Christians and missionary organizations.[46] Some joined the leftist Lanka Sama Samaja Party (LSSP) and became active in anti-British mobilization, while others provided support to politicians contesting against Christian candidates and acted as legitimators for major political parties in post-independence elections.[47] The practice of politicians seeking blessings from Buddhist monks is a powerful symbolic exercise that still exists today. The monks' influence in policies perpetuating the Sinhalese-Buddhist nationalist fervour has also been important. They have strongly opposed any talk of entrenching secularism in Sri Lanka and resisted the devolution of power to Tamil areas (which,

---

[41] DeVotta, *Sinhalese Buddhist*, p. 7 and De Silva, *History of Sri Lanka*, ibid.

[42] Stanley Jeyaraja Tambiah, *Buddhism Betrayed? Religion, Politics, and Violence in Sri Lanka* (Chicago: University of Chicago Press, 1992), pp. 5–8. The 'foreigners' were South Indian merchants and Muslim ('Muhammedan') businessmen, who were viewed as prosperous, opportunistic traders, leaving the 'sons of the soil' with an economic disadvantage.

[43] De Silva, *History of Sri Lanka*, pp. 427–8.

[44] Interviews with a leading UNP politician and a political scientist in Colombo, Sri Lanka (June 2013).

[45] DeVotta, *Sinhalese Buddhist*, p. 2. Not all monks, to be sure, have been swayed by the Sinhalese-Buddhist supremacy and anticolonial propaganda. Much also depends on which monastic college the monks come from. See ibid., p. 16.

[46] Tambiah, *Buddhism Betrayed?*, pp. 6–7.   [47] Ibid., pp. 15–19.

for them, could unsettle the pre-eminence of Buddhism in the island).[48]
S. W. R. D. Bandaranaike's Sinhala-only language policy, which became
the platform for his election campaign in 1956, had the backing of influential
monks. Bandaranaike's Sri Lanka Freedom Party (SLFP) went on to win the
elections, but when he attempted to accommodate Tamil language demands,
a monk-led revolt ensued and cost him his life.

   Buddhist revivalism has also penetrated the realms of party politics, forcing
major parties to compete to appease majority Sinhalese-Buddhist sensitivities.
The two biggest Sinhalese parties in this respect are the SLFP and the United
National Party (UNP). The UNP actually began as a party organized along
moderate lines – it sought to be both representative of the majority group
and acceptable to the minorities.[49] D. S. Senanayake (the founder of UNP),
for instance, fought to retain the state's secular character and its religious
neutrality.[50] Over time, all this would prove to be malleable rather than fixed
principles underpinning the party. The SLFP, on the other hand, was set up
in 1951 as a political vehicle for those who resented the UNP's seemingly
unsympathetic stance toward Buddhist aspirations in the religious, linguistic,
cultural and economic spheres.[51] The SLFP and UNP's historical battle for
majority support was most clearly reflected in the language policy debates
in the 1950s. The UNP initially agreed to advance a bilingual (Sinhala and
Tamil) language policy, but it was forced to make a U-turn after the SLFP
adopted the Sinhala-only policy to provide itself with an edge over the UNP.
The UNP leaders then knew that their bilingual platform would fail to garner
popular support, and they too adopted a Sinhala-only policy.[52] This competition for Sinhalese-Buddhist support, as we shall see, still shapes much of the
Sri Lankan political scene today, often with adverse consequences on minority
interests. Indeed, as a UNP parliamentarian affirmed, the party is cognizant of
current political realities in relation to the majority electorate and it has had to
adapt accordingly.[53]

   Over the years, other Sinhalese-Buddhist nationalist political parties have
also emerged. The Jathika Hela Urumaya (JHU, or National Sinhalese Heritage Party) is a party formed and led by Buddhist monks. Its predecessor,
Sinhala Urumaya (SU, or National Heritage Party), formed in 2000, is
described by DeVotta as staunchly anti-minority.[54] The creation of the JHU

---

[48] DeVotta, *Sinhalese Buddhist*, p. 23.   [49] De Silva, *History of Sri Lanka*, p. 602.
[50] Ibid., p. 603.   [51] Ibid., pp. 609–10.   [52] DeVotta, *Sinhalese Buddhist*, p. 17.
[53] Interview with a UNP member of Parliament in Colombo, Sri Lanka (June 2013).
[54] DeVotta, *Sinhalese Buddhist*, p. 26.

was triggered when the SU's political fortunes dwindled after failing to gain convincing electoral support in the 2000 and 2001 national elections. The JHU has continued much of SU's rhetoric by campaigning on the platform that it would protect and enhance Sinhalese-Buddhist interests. For instance, it has fought for the ban on cattle slaughter and it engineered the 2004 anti-conversion bill (the JHU Bill). Although the JHU was part of former President Rajapaksa's SLFP-led ruling coalition, when it first contested in the national elections in 2004, it ran independently and posed a real threat to other majority-oriented parties like the SLFP and the UNP. That the JHU managed to win nine parliamentary seats in its first election demonstrated that it was able to gain significant traction amongst the Sinhalese-Buddhists.

The influence of the Buddhist revival movement is well and alive today, shaping the country's social and political discourse. Some of the recent Bodu Bala Sena (BBS) propaganda against the Muslims, for example, is strikingly similar to those espoused by Anagarika Dharmapala – the man known as the father of modern Sinhalese-Buddhist nationalism.[55] For example, Dharmapala blamed the British for destroying the Sinhalese race by 'poisoning' the Aryan Sinhalese with opium and alcohol.[56] Likewise, the BBS accused a popular Muslim-owned fashion chain of selling garments treated with chemicals that would sterilize Sinhalese women. For some, these claims are absurd and extreme, but the BBS's populist propaganda can often gain grassroots appeal. It would of course be misleading to suggest that all Sinhalese-Buddhists (or all Malay-Muslims, in the case of Malaysia) subscribe to these ethno-religious nationalist ideas. However, they are pervasive enough (DeVotta notes, for example, that the Mahavamsa is widely taught in schools) that politicians have had to embrace the ethno-religious nationalist tide and symbolism if they want to remain in power.

INDONESIA: PRAGMATIC POLITICS AND
THE FIGHT FOR THE CENTRE

Since the fall of Soeharto, political parties in Indonesia have proliferated. No single party is truly dominant, and voter loyalty to a particular party, though once important, has increasingly declined.[57] Indonesia adopts the open-list proportional representation system, which empowers voters to select their

---

[55] Ibid., p. 14.

[56] Ibid., p. 15 (quoting Ananda Guruge, *Return to Righteousness: A Collection of Speeches, Essays and Letters of the Anagarika Dharmapala* (Colombo:The Government Press, 1965), p. 530).

[57] Mujani and Liddle, 'Parties, and Voters', p. 37.

preferred candidates. Candidates thus compete with each other and they are encouraged to use localized appeals to garner electoral support. Patronage politics has survived the fall of the New Order period and, together with the power of money politics and the media, these elements may work in ways that could pose a significant challenge to religious tolerance and Indonesian democracy.

Despite indications that religion remains salient in Indonesian political life, some analysts have continued to question the importance of religious identities and affiliations in shaping voting choices amongst Indonesians. A study of the 2009 Indonesian elections, for instance, found no consistent evidence of voter polarization based on Muslim religiosity or religious orientations.[58] At the same time, as noted earlier, political players and parties still recognize the significance of religious symbolism to appeal to voter sensitivities, while there are others who explicitly manipulate religious issues to gain political mileage and electoral support. Conspicuous attendance at religious events and pre-election visits to prominent *ulamas* and religious organizations such as the NU, are examples of symbolic gestures. In some provinces and constituencies, endorsements by local *ulamas* are pertinent.

Whether these strategies will always yield the desired result (in other words, whether voters respond favourably) is a different question. In the 2009 elections, there were attempts to discredit Boediono (a vice presidential candidate) through the spread of rumours that he practiced Javanese mysticism and that his wife was Catholic, but Mujani and Liddle found no evidence that such smear campaigns influenced orthodox Muslim voters.[59] The same strategy was invoked against Joko Widodo in the 2014 presidential elections, and when Widodo ran for the Jakarta gubernatorial elections in 2012, congregants in some mosques were told not to vote for Widodo because his running mate was a Christian.

How seriously religion affects political calculations and how such calculations then shape policy responses involving religion and minorities can be shown by examining the predispositions of Indonesian political players. The most obvious tendencies revolve around pragmatism and a fight for the centre, but equally important, as we shall see, is the prevalence of personality politics.

Party Politics and Broad-Based Support

When political parties compete at the centre for a broader base of support (beyond their core voting base), they may be discouraged from

---

[58] Ibid.   [59] Ibid.

tackling controversial religious issues affecting minorities. Or, at the very least, they may become cautious in how they respond to such issues to avoid alienating majority sensitivities.

The 'centre' at which political parties have occupied in the past decade or so is a centre that emphasizes and appeals to majority Muslim concerns and interests. Platzdasch characterizes this as a 'pro-Islamic ideological middle-ground'.[60] Large, nationalist political parties have moved to bolster their Islamic appeal. Parties such as Golkar, PDI-P and Partai Demokrat have increasingly distanced themselves from being identified as 'secular-nationalist parties' or as bearers of a 'secular-nationalist' agenda.[61] Partai Demokrat, for example, officially identifies itself as a '*nasionalis-religius*' party. The strengthening of religious overtones does not mean that these political parties would campaign for the establishment of an Islamic state or for the constitutionalization of *Shariah*, as Islamic parties have done in the past, or even to explicitly advocate for Muslim supremacy as UMNO has done in Malaysia. Unlike in Malaysia where debates about the implementation of Islamic criminal punishments (*Hudud*) or policies to protect the sanctity of Islam have often arisen before or during major elections, such issues do not occupy the main discourse in Indonesia's national elections. The three main Islamic political parties – PKS, PPP and PBB – have also, for the most part, steered clear of a *Shariah* agenda at their national-level election campaigns. To insist on a comprehensive state-led enforcement of *Shariah* law in Indonesia would indeed be unpragmatic and unwise, as a significant section of the Muslim majority would oppose it despite growing observance of Islamic rituals and practices.[62] Fidelity to the *Pancasila's* pluralistic ideals remains the central message of all political parties, but they also want to be seen as committed to a variety of Muslim interests or to be identified with mainstream Muslim sentiments.

In PDI-P, for example, the non-Muslim community is one of its core support bases. Its leader, Megawati Soekarnoputri, is widely seen as, at best, uninterested and, at worst, averse to political Islam and orthodox Muslim constituents. Yet, in 2006, in what was regarded as a move to reach out to constituents it previously ignored, PDI-P announced the creation of Baitul

---

[60] Bernhard Platzdasch, 'Down but not out: Islamic political parties did not do well, but Islamic politics are going mainstream', *Inside Indonesia* (Jul.–Sept. 2009), online: www.inside indonesia.org/feature-editions/down-but-not-out.

[61] In an interview, a senior Golkar politician was quick to remind me that Golkar is not a secular-nationalist party, but a nationalist party committed to upholding the *Pancasila*. Interview in Jakarta, Indonesia (January 2014).

[62] Bernhard Platzdasch, *Islamism in Indonesia: Politics in the Emerging Democracy* (Singapore: Institute of Southeast Asian Studies, 2009), p. 333.

Muslimin – a body for Islamic affairs under the party's central leadership board. At the same time, PDI-P moved to appease its core supporters from the minority community through an internal, special team (*Tim Khusus*) tasked to address religious freedom concerns.[63] Several PDI-P lawmakers, to be sure, have been outspoken advocates of religious freedom, urging the executive to ban hard-line organizations like the FPI. It has also embraced religious minorities within its party ranks: a well-known Shia leader, for example, is an elected lawmaker for PDI-P. Although the party has, on many occasions, called the previous Demokrat-led government to account for the lack of protection of religious minorities, as an opposition party it was not able to do much to influence policy-making, aside from pressing the government through the Dewan Perwakilan Rakyat's (DPR's) Commission for Legal Affairs, Human Rights, and Security (*Komisi III*). In the 2004, 2009 and 2014 elections, PDI-P only secured 109, 94 and 109 seats in the 560-seat DPR, respectively. In 2004 and 2009, the then president's party (Partai Demokrat) formed a coalition with several parties, allowing it to control more than half of the seats in the DPR. In the 2014 elections, although Joko Widodo (a PDI-P candidate) was elected president, PDI-P was initially a minority party in the DPR as several parties – led by Golkar and Gerindra – formed a coalition to control the legislature. Golkar later left the coalition it formed with Gerindra and the Islamic party PKS to join the PDI-P-led coalition.

Other parties – driven by pragmatic politics – have also positioned themselves to become broad-based, catch-all parties. Golkar has cleverly embraced a diverse base of electoral support through what Mietzner calls a 'federal party structure'.[64] The party has traditionally been strong outside Java, which includes predominantly Christian areas such as Papua, North Sulawesi and East Nusa Tenggara. In these provinces, Golkar placed Christian politicians and reached out to local churches and missionary organizations.[65] In predominantly Muslim provinces where the party is dominant (such as Banten, West Java, South Sulawesi and Sumatera), its politicians supported pro-Muslim policies and projected an Islam-inspired image.[66] The use of Islamic symbolism and styles of expression has also been important for the party, whose support base includes puritan Muslim organizations like the LDII (Lembaga Dakwah Islam Indonesia).[67] These practices underscore the significance of religious symbolism in mobilizing political support.

---

[63] Interview with a prominent PDI-P politician in Jakarta, Indonesia (January 2014).
[64] Mietzner, 'Comparing Indonesia's Party Systems', p. 445.   [65] Ibid.
[66] Ibid. In the 2004 elections, for example, Golkar emerged as the party that won the most votes in these provinces.
[67] Interview with a senior Golkar politician in Jakarta, Indonesia (January 2014). See also Hefner, 'Where Have the Abangan Gone?', p. 89.

The Golkar system highlights the diverse nature of the party's branches and political representation, but this, according to Mietzner, has also prevented its national leadership from taking decisive, partisan stances on religiously sensitive issues, even if it wanted to do so.[68] Liddle raised similar concerns about the Golkar's direction: he argues that in light of the declining popularity of Islamic political parties, there is a tendency for centrist parties such as Golkar to move to the right in the hopes of gaining the former supporters of Islamic parties.[69] Similar tendencies are observable within the Partai Demokrat, which has prioritized itself as a party that carries aspirations of the majority[70] by appealing to both moderate Muslims and secular voters.[71] Just as Golkar's approach prevents it from taking decisive, partisan stances on controversial issues, Partai Demokrat faces the same dilemma. In this respect, my conversations with party members and political analysts suggest that pragmatic objectives may trump fidelity to pluralistic ideals. A Partai Demokrat official, for instance, admitted that politicians need to face the reality that certain sections of their core constituents may respond to particular religious disputes with considerable hostility.[72] The party and its leadership are thus disinclined from taking sides publicly because politicians 'do not want to be perceived as siding with the minorities'.[73] All this makes Liddle's prediction about the worsening protection of minorities seem more real than imaginary.

In any case, for the Partai Demokrat, resolving longstanding religious freedom issues is simply not at the top of its list of priorities.[74] This could also hold true for all other parties. Surveys have indeed shown that Indonesian voters consider economic growth, general prosperity, national unity, education, healthcare and corruption as urgent issues.[75] As these concerns become some of the prime points on which voters evaluate the electability of candidates, religious freedom issues (especially those implicating minorities) may slip down the pecking order. It is thus unsurprising that there is a lack of incentives to protect and fight the cause of the minorities, especially since issues that have surfaced are perceived – especially within government circles – as small, isolated cases.

If large parties have become catch-all parties who seek to cater to mainstream Muslim concerns and thus are unwilling and/or unable to weigh in on

---

[68] Mietzner, 'Comparing Indonesia's Party Systems', p. 445.

[69] 'Bill Liddle: Saya Khawatir Golkar Semakin ke Kanan' ('Bill Liddle: I Am Concerned That Golkar Is Moving to the Right'), *Suara Pembaruan* (9 February 2013), online: www.suara pembaruan.com/home/bill-liddle-saya-khawatir-golkar-semakin-kanan/30512.

[70] Ibid.   [71] Mietzner, 'Comparing Indonesia's Party Systems', p. 446.

[72] Conversation with a Partai Demokrat official in Jakarta, Indonesia (October 2013). This account has been corroborated by other interviewees, some of whom represent smaller parties and minority groups.

[73] Ibid.   [74] Ibid.   [75] Mujani and Liddle, 'Parties, and Voters', pp. 45–8.

issues affecting religious minorities, smaller parties that compete to maintain or increase their electoral support have also been forced to play the same game. A PKS politician, for instance, suggested that the minorities are, in general, electorally insignificant for Islamic parties. Out of concern that taking partisan stances against religious freedom violations may jeopardize their existing support, such parties have largely chosen to keep mum.[76] In PKS's case, the party is also mindful that 70 per cent of its supporters remain suspicious of non-Muslims[77] and that supporters of hard-line organizations are part of its electoral base.[78] In spite of this, in majority non-Muslim provinces, Islamic parties have not necessarily abandoned efforts to secure electoral support. PKS, for example, sought to appeal to Christian electorates in Papua by fielding Christian candidates for provincial legislatures. In previous elections, it also cooperated with the Partai Damai Sejahtera (PDS, or Prosperous Peace Party), which is a Christian-based party. This dual strategy underscores a point that reverberates throughout our analysis on Indonesia, that is, pragmatism informs much of the parties' political strategies and calculations.

The centrist tendencies of Islamic parties meant that they have abandoned the Islamic state agenda and efforts to constitutionalize *Shariah*. In the 2004 elections, religion was notably absent from PKS's political rhetoric and campaign.[79] Instead, it focused on ridding corruption and developing social and economic programs by projecting itself as a clean and professional party. Ideology, therefore, no longer matters as much as it did for Islamic parties five decades ago. As a party insider admitted, views across the party are not homogenous and they can largely be grouped into those who pursue pragmatic politics and moderation on the one hand, and those who hold a more puritanical approach on the other. The desire to hold ministerial positions and to be represented in the government has also encouraged such parties to coalesce with their nationalist counterparts. In the DPR, such coalitions have cooperated to pass the broadly worded Anti-Pornography Law, aspects of which are deemed inimical to religious freedom.

---

[76] Interview with a PKS politician in Tangerang, Indonesia (October 2012) and Jakarta, Indonesia (March 2016).

[77] Mietzner, 'Comparing Indonesia's Party Systems', p. 450 (quoting a survey done in 2005 by Saiful Mujani). See Saiful Mujani, 'Analisis Parpol: PKS, Tantangan Baru Politik Indonesia' ('Political Party Analysis: PKS, A New Challenge in Indonesian Politics'), *Media Indonesia* (28 July 2005).

[78] Conversation with a PKS politician in Jakarta, Indonesia (March 2016).

[79] Syafiq Hasyim, 'Blending Dakwa and Politics: The Case of PKS (Prosperous Justice Party)' in Darwis Khudori (ed.), *The Rise of Religion-Based Political Movements: A Threat or a Chance for Peace, Security and Development among the Nations?* (Jakarta: Indonesian Conference on Religion and Peace, 2009), p. 157.

Politicians and parties are aware of the diversity of religious and political opinion in the country. The more tolerant, pluralistic and pro-religious freedom sentiments among the elites at the top may not always resonate with views amongst the rank-and-file or voters on the ground. In many of the policies or issues implicating religious freedom, politicians have thus avoided invoking the language of 'religion' or 'rights' to justify the restrictions against minorities or the greater state regulation of religion and religious practice. Instead, they are justified as measures to protect public order and communal harmony.

Two consequences follow. First, by invoking these labels, national leaders have often sought to dust their hands off any responsibility for protecting rights; instead, they direct the attention to regional governments who are responsible for regulating public order issues in their districts. Second, what all this amounts to mirrors Platzdasch's analysis on how majoritarian policies and laws are made to look pluralist-friendly.[80] For the sections of the community who are hostile to religious minorities and their activities, restrictions thereof may be interpreted as measures to protect Muslim interests. For the rest (the professed 'neutrals' or 'moderates'), efforts to protect public order, detrimental though they might be to minorities, may seem worth supporting to reduce activities of hardliners and maintain communal harmony in their area. In my conversations with civil society organizations, there were suggestions that societal support for regulations restricting the religious practices of minorities do not necessarily mean that they condone rights violations or are sympathetic toward hard-line organizations like the FPI. On the contrary, they believe that such regulations would keep the likes of FPI out of their neighbourhoods. For those politicians who realize these dual societal interests, the endorsement of restrictions against the Ahmadiyah and the Shiites, or against minority houses of worship, may well be a practical and politically expedient solution.

Presidential Politics and Coalition Building

Pragmatic strategies to secure broad-based support are also observable at presidential elections. First, it is important to note that a president is elected by an absolute majority. Where there are more than two candidates running for office, the winning candidate must secure 50 per cent plus one of the total votes and obtain at least 20 per cent of the popular votes in at least seventeen of

---

[80] Platzdasch, *Islamism in Indonesia*, pp. 336–41.

the thirty-three provinces in Indonesia. If none of the candidates fulfils these requirements, there will be a second round run-off between the top two candidates from the first round of voting. The territorial distribution requirement provides a mechanism to encourage multiethnic appeals and to ensure that minority votes matter, especially since non-Muslims tend to be territorially concentrated in the islands outside Java. However, only five provinces – Bali, Nusa Tenggara Timur (NTT), Maluku, Papua and North Sulawesi – are majority non-Muslim constituencies, which makes any focus on or explicit support for minority issues in nationwide presidential campaigns appear less attractive. It is also plausible that incentives for minority protection will be much less important when only two candidates compete, as both will seek to secure mainstream support by avoiding sensitive religious issues and by focusing instead on economic policies and bread and butter concerns.

Two other characteristics of presidential politics may disincentivize politicians from fighting the cause of religious minorities in the Indonesian context. The first is the prevalence of personality politics. A candidate's likeability and popularity are important determinants of voter choices.[81] This makes it all the more important for politicians to avoid discussing religiously sensitive issues and taking partisan positions on them. The previous president, Susilo Bambang Yudhoyono (SBY) has been criticized for his tendency to dodge addressing the growing persecution of religious minorities and for being slow in condemning religiously motivated violence. On the other end of the spectrum, hard-line organizations have attacked SBY for failing to ban deviant groups like the Ahmadiyah. Caught in a bind, SBY was reluctant to go beyond issuing statements reminding Indonesians about the values of religious tolerance. Insiders suggested that SBY was personally supportive of pluralism.[82] However, within Indonesian political circles, he was also widely perceived as a person who was very conscious about his popular image.[83] Aside from his unwillingness to risk losing support on the ground, SBY may not have wanted to be drawn into a politically sensitive battle with the *ulamas* who, through the Majelis Ulama Indonesia (MUI), issued a *fatwa* declaring the Ahmadiyah as deviant. Given the growing influence of the MUI in the post-Soeharto period, politicians are cautious not to be seen as publicly defying the MUI. These dynamics might explain why the government-sponsored ministerial decree on the Ahmadiyah, problematic though it might be, falls short of a complete

---

[81] Mujani and Liddle, 'Parties, and Voters', pp. 41–2.
[82] Interview with a Partai Demokrat official in Jakarta, Indonesia (October 2012).
[83] Conversation with a member of Parliament and a party strategist in Jakarta, Indonesia (January 2014).

ban against the group but, at the same time, it prohibits vigilante actions against the Ahmadis. Sticking with mainstream interests and the so-called 'middle-ground', therefore, helped safeguard SBY's popularity and support at the grass-roots level.

The second characteristic is rooted in the mechanics of presidential nomination, which, together with a very fragmented legislature, has made coalition building necessary. The electoral law stipulates that only parties with at least 25 per cent of popular support or parties that control at least 20 per cent of seats in the legislative elections may nominate a candidate. Given the large number of parties contesting in legislative elections, no single party has ever controlled a significant proportion of the vote or seats in the DPR. Coalition building – both for nominating a candidate and for forming a government – is inevitable, and large nationalist parties typically draw in smaller parties for support. SBY's party (Partai Demokrat) along with Islamic parties (PKS and PPP) and Muslim masses-based parties (PAN and PKB) supported SBY's presidential nomination in 2009. Until the legislative elections in April 2014, this group of parties controlled about 56 per cent of the seats in the DPR. After SBY's second inauguration in October 2009, Golkar joined to form a grand coalition, controlling more than 75 per cent of the legislature.[84] The advantage of this, as observers argue, was that SBY had the political resources to govern effectively and carry out his policies and agendas.[85] However, as it turned out, his administration was weak and indecisive, crippled by political horse-trading and infighting. With the presence of Islamic parties in the governing coalition who were conscious not to offend their core support base, SBY felt pressured to yield to their demands and concerns, especially since these parties provided vital support for his candidacy in the 2009 elections. They have also placed influential but deeply conservative members within the corridors of state power. The consequence of all this was that minority interests tended to be sidelined under the SBY administration.

A final point that is worth emphasizing is that all this complex interaction between religion and electoral politics is by no means confined to the realms of national legislative and presidential elections; it also affects the election of office bearers at the regional level (such as governors, district heads or mayors). In such elections, the winning candidates must secure a majority (50 per cent plus one) of the total valid votes cast in the elections.[86]

---

[84] Mujani and Liddle, 'Parties, and Voters', p. 48.   [85] Ibid.

[86] Article 107(1), Law No. 32 of 2004 on Regional Government. These requirements have now changed due to a new set of laws and regulations governing regional elections in 2016.

During elections, candidates need to ensure that they secure strong, mainstream electoral support but once elected, maintaining communal order becomes one of the primary considerations in making policy choices.[87] As such, they might not be able to guarantee the rights and protection of the minorities with as much zeal as they would in an ideal situation.[88] This might explain why the current mayor of Bogor – the city at the centre of the Yasmin church dispute – has suggested that he would pursue a more diplomatic route through mediation, much to the chagrin of rights activists who would have liked to see an unequivocal enforcement of the Supreme Court decision. The mayor also drew flak for officiating Hizbut Tahrir Indonesia's office in Bogor in February 2016. Although his actions might understandably be perceived as an endorsement of HTI, they might also be understood as an exercise of political pragmatism, especially given that HTI members form a significant part of the electorate in the religiously conservative city of Bogor.

Patronage politics is also very strong at the regional level. Some candidates strike agreements with influential local clerics for votes from their followers in exchange for the pledge that if elected, they will pursue particular policies on religion. In the 2013 West Java gubernatorial election, for example, the FPI and a candidate from PKS allegedly entered into an agreement to ban Ahmadiyah activities in return for electoral support. There was a similar politicization of the Shia issue in Sampang, where a mayoral candidate mobilized support by yielding to majority demands who oppose the presence of Shiites in the area.[89] Parties across the board have also endorsed regulations that purport to promote public order and curb immorality by regulating gambling, alcohol consumption and dress codes because support for these are perceived as politically beneficial, especially in the more conservative districts.[90] To appeal to a broader electoral base, these laws and policies are packaged with scant reference to the dominant religion (Islam), although they are colloquially referred to as '*perda bernuansa Shariah*' (*Shariah*-inspired regulations). However, what is more worrying is that these laws – as are *fatwas* – often become the basis for hard-line organizations to mobilize and pursue vigilante justice.

Different regulations apply to the Aceh, Jakarta, Papua and West Papua provinces: where no candidate secures more than 50% of the votes, there will be a second round run-off between the top two candidates from the first round of voting.

[87] Conversation with a Partai Demokrat politician in Jakarta, Indonesia (January 2014).

[88] Ibid.

[89] Interview with a member of the National Human Rights Commission (KOMNAS HAM) in Jakarta, Indonesia (October 2012).

[90] See Platzdasch, *Islamism in Indonesia*, p. 325.

SRI LANKA: MAJORITY-MINORITY POLITICAL
DYNAMICS AND MINORITY ISSUES

We have seen that in Indonesia, the quest to appeal to a broad base of the majority electorate has largely pushed parties toward the centre. To some extent, this has discouraged political players from being more assertive on religious freedom issues. By the same token, a majority-centric approach has also been significant for political actors in Sri Lanka. A study of Sri Lankan political history tells us that the dynamics have always been slanted toward the Sinhalese, but there were differences in degree. The two main Sinhalese parties (the SLFP and the UNP) have, at various points in time, flirted with both extreme and moderate positions on matters involving majority-minority relations.

Until the 2015 elections in Sri Lanka, the UNP and the SLFP were regarded as electoral enemies and 'unlikely allies'.[91] There are twenty-two electoral districts in Sri Lanka, and while multiple parties compete in all districts, most contests are virtually a straight fight between the UNP and SLFP's coalitions.[92] The share of parliamentary seats between the UNP and SLFP, until 2010, was more or less evenly divided. In the 2004 elections, for example, the UNP and SLFP won sixty-three and fifty-six seats, respectively.

As we have seen earlier, scholars posit that strong political competition and intragroup party fragmentation will encourage parties to pool votes from those beyond its own electorate. There appears to be some evidence of this when we consider how parties like the Sri Lanka Muslim Congress (SLMC) have aligned with the UNP's or the SLFP's coalitions in parliamentary elections. The two major parties have also fielded minority candidates under their coalition ticket, which suggests that they do look beyond the Sinhalese-Buddhist electorate for support. By any reckoning, these are supposed to encourage moderation on the part of the Sinhalese parties and inevitably push parties toward the centre. However, as we shall see, the story is not as straightforward.

Presidential Politics and the Turn toward
Monopolizing Majority Support

The slant toward the majority in ethnically divided societies like Sri Lanka is inevitable. Yet, it may also present real dangers to majority-minority relations

---

[91] Donald L. Horowitz, *Ethnic Groups in Conflict*, 2nd ed. (Berkeley: University of California Press, 2011), p. 381.

[92] The third coalition that contested in all constituencies is the Democratic National Alliance led by the Janatha Vimukthi Peramuna (JVP). The JVP is a leftist Sinhalese party. In the 2004 elections, the JVP was part of the UPFA coalition but in 2010, it contested under its own ticket and won about 5% of the total votes nationally.

and the protection of minorities, depending on factors such as the prevailing political culture and political calculations about both majority and minority support, as well as intragroup political competition. We have briefly discussed how the latter shaped the language policy debates in the 1950s. There was also some evidence that major parties, in a competition to strengthen their majoritarian credentials, have gone down the path of adopting pro-Sinhalese Buddhist policies on religious issues. For instance, in the run-up to the 1965 elections, the UNP (although professedly secular in its early days) campaigned for the restoration of Buddhism and subsequently defeated the SLFP.[93] What I want to emphasize here is how the turn toward solidifying Sinhalese support, in its extreme, has adversely affected the protection of minorities.

This point can be made clearest by considering the Rajapaksa administration's political manoeuvres and their subsequent impact on the treatment of religious minorities.[94] In the 2010 elections, Rajapaksa focused on efforts to consolidate his power in the state. Having been credited with ending the war in 2009, the dominance of President Rajapaksa and the SLFP – the most dominant party in the United People Freedom Alliance (UPFA) coalition – was stronger than ever, with the political discourse heavily infused with and shaped by Sinhalese-Buddhist nationalism. The support for Rajapaksa was (and still is) particularly strong in the southern province, where the electorate in districts such as Hambantota, Matara and Galle are overwhelmingly (i.e., more than 90 per cent) Sinhalese. He emerged from the 2010 presidential elections as the clear favourite (i.e., with more than 60 per cent of votes) in twelve of twenty-two districts, and in at least five other districts, he secured more than 50 per cent of the popular vote. The following year, Rajapaksa led SLFP to an unprecedented win by securing 104 parliamentary seats (out of a total of 225 seats), almost exclusively in majority Sinhalese electoral districts.[95] In the Sinhalese-Buddhist heartlands in the south, the UPFA coalition won eighteen out of twenty-five seats with over 65 per cent of votes. The JHU, a Buddhist-oriented party, was also part of the UPFA with three seats in Parliament. The UNP, on the other hand, won just over forty seats. The UPFA's resounding victory signalled to its leadership

---

[93] Arundhati Sharma, 'Religion-Politics Nexus and Security Dynamics in South Asia: The Case of Sri Lanka' (2011) 2 *Scholar's Voice: A New Way of Thinking* 29, 34.

[94] Many observers argue that the position of ethnic and religious minorities have been particularly precarious in the last five years (i.e., during the second half of Rajapaksa's ten-year presidency).

[95] Jayadeva Uyangoda, 'Sri Lanka in 2010: Regime Consolidation in a Post-Civil War Era' (2011) 51 *Asian Survey* 131, 133.

(and to the UNP) that minority support was not essential to secure a majority in parliamentary elections.[96]

For Rajapaksa, the belief that he could ride and rely on Sinhalese-Buddhist support shaped his political strategy and policy decisions in the second term of his administration. Rajapaksa won the 2010 presidential elections with scant support from the minorities. Muslims and Tamils had largely pledged to support the UNP's Sarath Fonseka, who campaigned on the platform of abolishing the executive presidency and restoring democratic rights.[97] Fonseka's defeat indicated that the language of 'rights' may not have struck a chord with the majority Sri Lankan population, who threw their support behind Rajapaksa's promises for political continuity and stability.[98] The realization that the minorities have deserted Rajapaksa could explain why the government focused its attention on the majority community and lacked any urgency to protect minorities. By some accounts, this swing toward the Sinhalese-Buddhists also explains why intolerant forces who intensified attacks against minorities operated with considerable impunity, with overt or covert blessings from some members of the Rajapaksa administration.

Presidential and personality politics are important in Sri Lanka, as they are in Indonesia. The president is directly elected and the winning candidate must secure more than 50 per cent of the popular vote. The need to appeal to the majority Sinhalese-Buddhist electorate is thus pertinent: candidates must appeal to the votes that matter. While some have argued that President Rajapaksa's approach and responses toward minorities in the last few years of his administration reflect his underlying chauvinistic tendencies,[99] this is at best speculative. In fact, according to internal estimates, Rajapaksa previously enjoyed some support from minorities – for instance, prior to the 2015 elections, he had at least 40 per cent of Muslim support nationally.[100] However, the prevailing political dynamics led Rajapaksa to believe that the maintenance of his regime and personal influence hinged on portraying himself as a champion of the Sinhalese-Buddhists. The pro-Sinhalese-Buddhist fervour,

---

[96] Ibid.

[97] Minna Thaheer, 'Why the Proportional Representation System Fails to Promote Minority Interests? A Discussion on Contemporary Politics and the Sri Lanka Muslim Congress' (2010) 1 *Journal of Power, Conflict & Democracy in South & Southeast Asia* 95, 112; and Uyangoda, 'Sri Lanka in 2010', p. 132.

[98] Uyangoda, 'Sri Lanka in 2010', p. 132.

[99] Interviews with a president's counsel and a former government official and advisor to the president in Colombo, Sri Lanka (June 2013).

[100] Interview with an SLFP member of Parliament and the former president's close confidant (October 2016).

to be sure, was not shared by all politicians in the UPFA or by the entire Sinhalese-Buddhist electorate. But there was a strong sense within the ruling coalition that a majoritarian fervour will ultimately safeguard the president's position beyond two terms of the presidency.

The SLFP-UNP Tussle for Majority Support

The UNP was in a relatively weaker position compared to that of the Rajapaksa-led SLFP. Its share of the Sinhalese-Buddhist electorate had been reduced over the years due to weak leadership and the failed peace process with the LTTE during the war. At the grassroots level, the UNP faced a mountainous task. Aside from the fact that the party was in disarray, some viewed the UNP as an elitist party shaped by the so-called Colombo circle, that is, the largely Western-educated and Western-oriented civil society and political actors in Colombo. There have also been allegations about the UNP's ideological and religious links: some still maintain that the party is a Western-funded, Christian-dominated party that has, in the past, side-lined and discriminated against Buddhists.[101] Such beliefs form part of a political propaganda against the UNP, driven as they were by the fact that some senior party members and MPs are devout Christians and by party leader Ranil Wickramesinghe's Christian lineage.[102]

The impact of such characterizations should not be underestimated in view of the strengthening of nationalistic sentiments and triumphalist attitude cultivated amongst the Sinhalese, especially in the post-war context. Further-more, a significant section of the Sinhalese-Buddhist population feels that their existence is continually threatened by some form of 'enemy' ranging from Western imperialists to Christian and Muslim groups. In light of all this, the UNP's ability to strike a chord with the rest of the Sri Lankan population, in a language that is palatable to them, has been called into question.[103] This situation was exacerbated by overt objections of certain party members to the involvement of monks in politics.[104]

In an effort to boost its electoral competitiveness, the UNP has also had to draw the ethnic card to appeal to the Sinhalese-Buddhist majority. According to party insiders, while internally the UNP is committed to a liberal and inclusive political agenda as opposed to one structured along ethnic lines,

[101] Interviews with a civil rights lawyer and a member of the president's counsel in Colombo, Sri Lanka (June 2013).
[102] Interview with a UNP member of Parliament in Colombo, Sri Lanka (June 2013).
[103] Interview with a political economy scholar in Colombo, Sri Lanka (June 2013).
[104] Interview with a senior UNP politician in Colombo, Sri Lanka (June 2013).

political expediency has required the party to make calculated moves and to balance between the interests of the Sinhalese-Buddhist majority and the minorities.[105] Prior to the 2015 elections, the party's internal calculations suggested that they had only secured about 20 per cent of support from the core Sinhalese-Buddhist electorate, but they needed at least 30 per cent to pose a threat to the UPFA's and Rajapaksa's electoral successes.[106] Under such circumstances, the UNP, as party insiders admitted, could not alienate the majority; it understood that it needed to regain Sinhalese support, while the SLFP realized the need to keep its Sinhalese supporters from switching to the UNP.[107]

Two other factors might affect political incentives to protect the minorities. First, in most electoral districts, Muslims and Christians – both of whom have been at the receiving end of most incidents of religious freedom violations – are not part of a significant voting bloc. For instance, in sixteen out of the twenty-two electoral districts in Sri Lanka, Muslims constitute less than 9 per cent of the electorate. The figures are much lower for Christians (of all denominations). Second, the UNP, perhaps, could afford to be complacent in increasing its efforts to appeal to minorities. As a party insider revealed, the UNP knew that it already enjoyed significant support from minorities who – despite realizing the party's weaknesses – were increasingly discontented with the Rajapaksa administration. The UNP could thus focus on building support from the majority by pandering to their religious interests when the situation demanded it.[108] The dilemma that the UNP faces in responding to religious issues was evident when members of Parliament were called to vote on the anti-conversion bill. According to an insider, several UNP parliamentarians had to toe the party decision to vote in favour of the bill out of concern for their main voter base (the Sinhalese-Buddhists). The UNP allegedly barred its MPs from taking a vote of conscience. This is unsurprising when one considers the electoral insignificance of the Protestants in Sri Lanka – with only 1 per cent of the population, it was perhaps not electorally beneficial for the politicians to fight their cause.[109]

[105] Interview with a prominent UNP member of Parliament in Colombo, Sri Lanka (June 2013).
[106] Ibid. Interview with a UNP member of Parliament and cabinet member in Colombo, Sri Lanka (October 2016).
[107] Interviews with a senior UNP politician and a UNP member of Parliament in Colombo, Sri Lanka (June 2013). Another source posits that the UNP cannot afford to be perceived as unsympathetic to Sinhalese-Buddhist interests.
[108] Interviews with a UNP member of Parliament, a civil society organization leader and a former diplomat in Colombo, Sri Lanka (June 2013).
[109] Interview with a senior member of a Christian organization in Colombo, Sri Lanka (June 2013).

A prominent UNP politician, in an interview, summarized the situation in Sri Lanka as follows: 'if one wants to be at the centre of the political stage, one needs to align with the majority both ethnically and religiously'.[110] Indeed, the foregoing analysis indicates that intragroup politics (in particular, the SLFP-UNP battle) has, to some extent, evolved into a race to demonstrate which of the two biggest parties can ultimately be trusted to defend Sinhalese-Buddhist interests. Several UNP cadres, to be sure, have been notable critics of the BBS and the escalation in religious violence over the past two years. Some have, in their personal capacities, vocally backed civil society movements calling for religious tolerance and equality. However, with the UPFA's resounding electoral victory in 2010, built on support from the Sinhalese-Buddhist electorate, the message that major parties do not necessarily have to secure minority support to win elections (with a large margin) is clear. Consequently, there is less incentive to address religious freedom issues implicating the minorities, as we see today.

There is a similar story in Wilkinson's study of the state of Gujarat in India. There, the electoral competition was a straight two-party fight between the Hindu nationalist party, the Bharatiya Janata Party (BJP) and the 'secular' Congress Party. In 1998, surveys showed that the BJP got zero per cent of the Muslim vote.[111] The state, as a result, did little to control and to prevent anti-Muslim riots.[112] To compound the situation, the then chief minister (now prime minister), Narendra Modi, and his government facilitated the violence by instructing security forces not to intervene in the violence and by delaying the deployment of the army at the height of the violence.[113] All these resemble what Sri Lanka has experienced, especially with respect to the anti-Muslim campaign that proliferated in the past five years.

Proportional Representation and Minority Protection

As in Indonesia, Sri Lanka adopts the proportional representation system in its national legislative elections – a system which is supposed to ensure that minority votes matter. It also purportedly provides an incentive for parties to field minority candidates on their party lists in multi-member constituencies. For example, Muslims, who comprise approximately 9 per cent of the population and who are largely concentrated in the eastern province, have been able to vote Muslim representatives into the Parliament. In Tamil-dominated constituencies in the north such as Jaffna, Tamil candidates have contested

---

[110] Interview with a UNP politician in Colombo, Sri Lanka (June 2013).
[111] Wilkinson, *Votes and Violence*, p. 155.   [112] Ibid., p. 157.   [113] Ibid.

under the UPFA ticket through the Eelam People's Democratic Party (EPDP – a Tamil party). Yet, these do not always translate into favourable outcomes for minorities.

One of the most striking factors that have crippled the protection of minority interests is that once minority representatives (or parties) are elected into office, they may cease to become a voice for their constituents; instead, they are pulled into the game of political horse-trading for ministerial positions. My interviews with several members of Parliament, from both the government and opposition coalitions, also revealed that smaller parties representing minorities would join ruling coalitions to reap various social and economic benefits.[114] As such, these politicians may be willing to look beyond ideological differences as well as issues affecting their core constituents to ensure that they are not locked out of power and benefits. But the reverse might also be true: minority representatives may decide to coalesce with major parties to ensure that they have some leverage in fighting for their constituents' interests.

The SLMC is an instructive example. The SLMC held eight seats in the Parliament, six of which were won through the legislative elections in 2010 and two of which were appointed seats on the national list.[115] The SLMC initially contested as part of a coalition with the main opposition party, the UNP. Just months after the elections, however, the SLMC defected and joined the government coalition. Incidentally, with the SLMC in the coalition, the SLFP-led government secured the all-important two-thirds majority in the legislature and Rauff Hakeem, the leader of the SLMC, was appointed the minister of justice. A strong legislative majority is crucial, especially since defections – a common characteristic of Sri Lankan politics – may determine the survival of the government of the day.[116] The SLMC defection, however, was not without precedent. In 2004, for instance, several SLMC members of Parliament crossed the floor to join the ruling UPFA coalition, and they were rewarded with ministerial posts soon after.[117] It should be noted that sometimes these floor-crossings were not solely driven by the lure of rewards; they were carried out to avoid internal party splits that could eventually lead to the

---

[114] Interview with various politicians in Colombo, Sri Lanka (June 2013).

[115] National list members of Parliament are appointed by political parties, rather than elected. There are twenty-nine national list member of Parliament positions and these are allocated to political parties according to their share of votes in the national legislative elections.

[116] See Horowitz, *Ethnic Groups*, p. 382 (providing examples in which governments have fallen due to defections and votes of no-confidence).

[117] For a list of SLMC floor-crosses and the ministerial portfolios they held thereafter, see Thaheer, 'Why the Proportional Representation System Fails', p. 106.

party's demise. There were a number of occasions in which individual SLMC MPs were enticed to cross the floor and join the government coalition, leaving behind other MPs who were not keen to do so. However, to avoid splitting the already-fragile SLMC, those remaining members were left with little choice but to cross over.[118]

With the presence of the SLMC in the government, especially in its capacity to make or break the UPFA's two-thirds majority, one would expect that Muslim support would be considered pivotal and, therefore, the government would have the incentive to protect Muslim interests. Indeed, the SLMC once enjoyed a good working relationship in the early years of the Kumaratunga administration. However, with the rise in anti-Muslim campaigns led by groups such as the BBS, causing damage to houses of worship, businesses and physical attacks on Muslims, many have argued that the SLMC were generally unwilling and unable to do much to protect Muslim interests. In the instances when they spoke out against the rising tide of anti-Muslim incidents, their voices were deemed too insignificant to invoke the government's attention. For example, a source disclosed that an SLMC leader had called for a special cabinet meeting to discuss the growing anti-Muslim activities, but his request was rejected.[119] This was of course not the first time that the concerns and reservations of the SLMC leadership were ignored. In the aftermath of the 2001 anti-Muslim riots in Mawanella, Rauff Hakeem's demand for disciplinary actions against a minister allegedly involved in the riots was disregarded.[120]

From the perspective of the smaller parties, there was little promise beyond the then government coalition, in view of a weak and dysfunctional opposition party hampered by internal disputes.[121] Apart from promises of economic and social benefits, ministerial positions and, sometimes, protection from criminal prosecution, sharing political power with the ruling regime was thought to enable minority representatives to seek support for their constituents' developmental needs.[122] Furthermore, the ruling coalition knew that if it were to lose support from the Muslim party, the entrenched practice of patronage politics meant that it would be able to coax other MPs or parties

---

[118] Ibid., pp. 109–10.   [119] Interview in Colombo, Sri Lanka (June 2013).
[120] Thaheer, 'Why the Proportional Representation System Fails', p. 102. Mawanella is a town in the Kegalle district, where about 85% of the population are Buddhists and 6.6% are Muslims. In the 2000 general elections, the People's Alliance (a coalition led by the SLFP) held five seats in the district, while UNP held four.
[121] Interview with a former government official in Colombo, Sri Lanka (June 2013).
[122] Uyangoda, 'Sri Lanka in 2010', p. 135.

to replace the void left by the SLMC. In such a situation, the SLMC politicians were the ones who stood to lose.[123]

Finally, as a former MP admitted, the SLMC was largely a passive actor within the UPFA coalition, whereas pro-Sinhalese-Buddhist parties like the JHU were dominant and vociferous.[124] President Rajapaksa is said to have felt indebted to the so-called extreme wings within the coalition who stood by him and helped him win the electoral support from the core Sinhalese-Buddhist electorate in the 2010 election.[125] Consequently, Rajapaksa was reluctant to rebuke the actions of such parties as well as an influential group of individuals within his government who patronized the BBS and other like-minded organizations.[126] It is believed, for example, that the former defence secretary (the president's younger brother), endorsed the BBS.[127] The secretary's attendance at the launch of the BBS's Buddhist Leadership Academy in 2013 was seen by many as tacit state support for the organization.[128] The former president, however, continued to maintain that the creation and operation of the BBS was a Western-backed conspiracy against his government.

MALAYSIA: A SHIFT TO THE EXTREME RIGHT?

We have seen how the Rajapaksa regime in Sri Lanka turned toward a strategy of maximizing Sinhalese-Buddhist support. This necessitated taking a majoritarian outlook in order to eliminate its competitors for Sinhalese votes (the UNP). The consequence was the adoption of policies and practices that marginalized the minorities and their interests.

Similar patterns exist in Malaysia, although the exact form and dynamics may differ with the other two countries. As a start, it is worth recollecting the differences in religious demography: whereas Muslims and Buddhists constitute 87 per cent and 70 per cent of the population in Indonesia and Sri Lanka, respectively, Muslims comprise 61 per cent of the population in Malaysia, followed by Buddhists (19 per cent), Christians (9 per cent) and Hindus

---

[123] See Thaheer, 'Why the Proportional Representation System Fails', p. 110. In my interviews, several sources suggested that a key figure within the SLMC faced precisely such threats, having been thus far protected from being pursued for criminal charges. Interviews in Colombo, Sri Lanka (June 2013).

[124] Interview with a UPFA parliamentarian in Colombo, Sri Lanka (June 2013).   [125] Ibid.

[126] Interviews with a National Peace Council representative and a former government official in Colombo, Sri Lanka (June 2013). Despite allegations of political backing for the BBS, informants have suggested that mainstream politicians have distanced themselves from the BBS's rhetoric.

[127] Ibid.   [128] Interview with a prominent lawyer in Colombo, Sri Lanka (June 2013).

(6 per cent).[129] In short, non-Muslims compose almost 40 per cent of the population – the biggest proportion among the three countries under study. The multiethnic ruling coalition in Malaysia is a permanent one, and it has been built (and sustained) on the practice of interethnic bargaining and the spirit of reciprocity, good will and compromise. Particular conditions, such as the existence of heterogeneous constituencies and the split of Malay votes (between UMNO and PAS), meant that vote-pooling between Malay and non-Malay parties has also been crucial.[130] In short, the electoral dynamics has necessitated a complex exercise of calculating the electoral costs and benefits of yielding or rejecting various ethnic demands.

To understand the relationship between electoral politics in Malaysia and policies and practices implicating religion, it is pertinent to recognize two features of Malaysian politics. The first feature is the emerging decline in non-Malay (especially Chinese) support for the multiethnic ruling coalition. The second is the competition between PAS and UMNO for Malay electoral support. Both have implications for religious freedom not just for the minorities, but also for Muslims. For the purposes of this book, I focus on the electoral dynamics in Peninsular Malaysia. The two states in East Malaysia (Sabah and Sarawak) are – for a variety of reasons, including the strength of the BN's political machinery on the ground and the politics of financial patronage – virtually 'fixed deposits' for the ruling coalition, in the sense that they have consistently delivered significant numbers of parliamentary seats to the ruling government.[131]

The Malaysian experience with the 'Allah' issue is a potent case study to demonstrate how these features and elements interact. The prohibition on the word 'Allah', as we have seen, is not new. Chapter 3 shows that there are similar laws in most states banning the use of 'Allah' by non-Muslims, and these laws date back to the 1980s and 1990s. Within that period, there were instances in which the federal authorities strictly enforced import restrictions on Bibles containing words that are deemed exclusive to Muslims;[132] in other cases, there were outright bans on the publication, sale or circulation of Malay-language Bibles, except for use in churches. However, the authorities later relaxed the

---

[129] Malaysian Department of Statistics, *Population Distribution and Basic Demographic Characteristic Report 2010* (2010), online: bit.ly/1uxCQxp.

[130] See Horowitz, *Ethnic Groups*, pp. 424–6.

[131] See Faisal S. Hazis, 'Patronage, Power and Prowess: Barisan Nasional's Equilibrium Dominance in East Malaysia' (2015) 33(2) *Kajian Malaysia* 1. According to Hazis, BN seats in Sabah and Sarawak account for 35% of the total number of seats that the coalition secured in the 2013 general elections.

[132] Means, *Malaysian Politics*, p. 104.

restrictions by permitting the publication of Bibles locally.[133] With respect to the weekly Catholic publication (*The Herald*) at the centre of the latest controversy, the government – having sent a warning letter to the editors – permitted the use of 'Allah' in the publication in 2002. In 2009, the Ministry re-enforced the restrictions upon renewing *The Herald*'s publication permit.

The Declining Support from the Minorities

When the results of the 2008 general elections were announced, it immediately became clear that a pivotal moment in the country's political history was in the making. For the first time since the 1969 elections, the ruling coalition, BN, lost its two-thirds majority in Parliament. Worse still, the BN only secured 51 per cent of the popular vote;[134] it lost control of two states, including a Malay heartland, Kedah; and the Democratic Action Party (DAP) and PAS made inroads in the state of Johor, which is regarded as a BN bastion, by winning four and two parliamentary seats, respectively.[135] Five years later, these losses would be eclipsed by the BN's performance in the 2013 general elections: its popular support fell to 46 per cent, and its share of parliamentary seats plunged further to 133 out of 222 seats. It was the worst result in the coalition's history. Immediately after the results were announced, the prime minister held a press conference, stressing the need for national reconciliation and to reject politics of extremism and racism. Yet, one claim stood out: the BN's electoral deficit was attributable to a 'Chinese tsunami'. On the next day, an UMNO-owned newspaper followed up with a very provocative headline – '*Apa Lagi Cina Mahu?*' ('What More Do the Chinese Want?') – indicating a deep sense of betrayal amongst the coalition's Malay-Muslim partners.

There is some truth to the 'Chinese tsunami' theory when we consider the share of seats won by the Malaysian Chinese Association (MCA) in the 2013 elections, although observers have pointed out that this was not the only reason for the BN's poor performance.[136] Of the thirty-seven parliamentary

---

[133] Ibid.

[134] Meredith Weiss, 'Edging toward a New Politics in Malaysia: Civil Society at the Gate?' (2009) 49 *Asian Survey* 741, 742.

[135] In the 1999 and 2004 elections, BN won all parliamentary seats in the state of Johor. Data on file with author. DAP (a secular, Chinese-dominated party) and PAS (an Islamic party) were part of the (now dissolved) opposition coalition, Pakatan Rakyat.

[136] Clive Kessler, 'Malaysia's GE13: What happened? What now?' *New Mandala* (12 June 2013), online: asiapacific.anu.edu.au/newmandala/2013/06/12/malaysias-ge13-what-happened-what-now-part-1/. Conversation with an opposition coalition parliamentary member in Petaling Jaya, Malaysia (August 2013). MCA is a component party (and one of the three founding parties) of the BN coalition.

seats that the MCA contested, it won only seven – less than half of the number of seats won in the 2008 elections.[137] Twelve out of the thirty-seven contested seats were in majority non-Malay constituencies (all of which were lost to the DAP), while the rest were in heterogeneous constituencies.[138] In the 2004 elections, when the BN performed well, the MCA held thirty-one seats. The signs that the BN was drastically losing support from the Chinese voters had been visible since the 2008 elections when it only managed to gain about 35 per cent of Chinese votes.[139] Going into the 2013 elections, a government member of Parliament noted that the BN was aware that it needed minority votes to win convincingly, but it also knew that Chinese support was virtually a lost cause.[140] To make matters worse, support from the Indian voters had also been declining since 2008. The BN garnered an estimated 48 per cent of Indian support in 2008, compared to 82 per cent in the 2004 elections, and the Malaysian Indian Congress (MIC) secured only three parliamentary seats.[141]

In light of these trends, the UMNO-led BN coalition engineered a shift in strategy in the build up to the 2013 elections: it sought to gain as much support from the Malay electorate as possible, targeting, in particular, the rural Malay voters. Kessler aptly summarized the coalition's tactics:

> The UMNO campaign was simple: 'all is at risk!' There is no protection, it kept hammering away, for you and your family, for all Malays, for the Malay stake in the country, for Islam or for the Malay rulers who are the ultimate bastion of our Malay-Islamic identity and national primacy–other than us here in UMNO.[142]

The 'Allah' Polemic and Electoral Calculations

Interreligious issues such as the 'Allah' case undoubtedly factored into the ruling coalition's broader calculations of the electoral price of its policies

---

[137] In the 2008 elections, the MCA held fifteen parliamentary seats. Data on file with author.

[138] From the twelve majority non-Malay constituencies (i.e., where the non-Malays make up more than 70% of the electorate), eight are overwhelmingly Chinese (i.e., more than 70% of the electorate). MCA lost in all of the majority non-Malay constituencies to its rival, the DAP. All seven of the seats that MCA won, therefore, were from mixed constituencies where no single ethnic group constitutes more than 70% of the electorate; in four of those seats, the Malays comprise between 50–58.4% of the electorate. Data on file with author.

[139] Weiss, 'New Politics in Malaysia', p. 743.

[140] Interview with an UMNO politician in Kuala Lumpur, Malaysia (August 2013).

[141] Weiss, 'New Politics in Malaysia', p. 743. MIC is a component party (and one of the three founding parties) of the BN coalition.

[142] Kessler, 'Malaysia's GE13'.

on religion. These calculations not only required it to assess the opposition's (namely, PAS's) take on the issue, but also the ebb and flow of support for PAS and minority votes. Indications of PAS's growing popularity, as demonstrated in the 2008 elections, combined with the steady loss of non-Malay votes were significant considerations.

To maximize support from the core Malay-Muslim electorate in the lead up to the 2013 election, it was not enough for UMNO-BN to demonstrate its unyielding opposition to demands by minorities in the 'Allah' issue; it also had to ensure that its main rival for Malay support, PAS (whose function within the opposition coalition was to erode UMNO's strength in the Malay heart-lands), was discredited. Several UMNO loyalists, Malay-Muslim organizations and government-owned media played up the threat of Christianization in the country. In May 2011, for instance, *Utusan Malaysia* (a Malay-language newspaper owned by UMNO) ran a front-page report of a plot by Christian groups to turn Malaysia into a Christian state.[143] Amplifying interreligious suspicions and hostility generated the right conditions for UMNO to 'out-Islamize' PAS by portraying to the Malays that it was 'the' only champion of Malay-Muslim causes. I will return to a detailed discussion of UMNO's political considerations, but first I want to highlight the opposition coalition's approach on the 'Allah' issue.

The leadership within the opposition coalition (Pakatan Rakyat, or PR) – which comprised PAS, Parti Keadilan Rakyat (PKR) and the secular, Chinese-dominated party, DAP – adopted a more conciliatory stance. In a joint press conference in early 2013, the president of PAS, Abdul Hadi Awang, declared the consensus within PR: while there is no prohibition on those from other faiths to use the word 'Allah', non-Muslims should nevertheless refrain from abusing the word 'Allah' to confuse Muslims. Presumably, what Abdul Hadi was referring to in the second part of his statement was the use of Allah to proselytize on and convert Muslims to other religions, or the use (or abuse) of the word 'Allah' in a way that may disrupt interreligious harmony in the country.

There were, to be sure, differences in opinion within PAS itself – differences which were not only touted as evidence of indecisiveness and disunity in the party, but also of an internal rift within PR as a whole.[144] According to insiders, a faction within PAS – comprising influential personalities such as

---

[143] Rokiah Abdullah and Mohd Khuzairi Ismail, '*Malaysia Negara Kristian?* (Malaysia A Christian State?)', *Utusan Malaysia* (7 May 2011).

[144] Dr. Dzulkefly Ahmad, a member of PAS' Central Working Committee, has written an academic explanation of the apparent 'disunity' within PAS on the use of 'Allah' by non-Muslims. See Dr. Dzulkefly Ahmad, 'PAS' Ulama "disunited" stance on 'Allah' – 2 sides of the same coin?' (22 January 2010), online: bit.ly/1qI56Ae.

Nasaruddin Hassan (the then PAS youth chief) and the late Dr. Haron Din (who was then deputy spiritual leader of the *Syura* Council) – maintained that 'Allah' is a term exclusive to Muslims. A week after PR's joint statement in 2013, the *Syura* Council (the religious consultative council, which is the highest and most powerful institution in PAS) stated that the term 'Allah' is a special term that cannot be readily (and precisely) translated from or into other languages, including from the terms 'God' or 'Lord' in other holy scriptures. Any actions to that effect, according to the Council, should be prohibited. While some PAS members argued that there is no fundamental difference between the *Syura* Council's decision and PR's resolution,[145] Dzulkefly Ahmad attributes the two seemingly opposing views to the methodological differences in analysing the permissibility of the use of the term by non-Muslims.[146] Regardless of the theoretical and academic disagreements, the view that the use of 'Allah' by Christians is acceptable according to the Quran and Islamic principles was regarded as the mainstream position in PAS.[147]

Although many have criticized PAS's stance as nothing more than an exercise of political expediency (that is, to appease its non-Muslim coalition partners and supporters), those within PAS argued that its position was thoroughly deliberated within theological and academic frameworks.[148] What also drove its position was the consideration of Malaysia's delicate multicultural and multireligious fabric, and on that account, a more tactful approach emerged – one which did not sanction the complete freedom to use 'Allah' but was nevertheless flexible enough to accommodate the non-Muslims' freedom to worship and practice their religion.

The UMNO-led government's approach, on the other hand, seemed to resonate with the more exclusivist opinions in PAS. For some, this reflects a genuine conviction that the use of 'Allah' is impermissible, which could be conditioned both by the perceived threat to the survival of the Malay-Muslims and, as a party insider admitted, by the lack of an objective evaluation of the issue at hand. However, as I explained earlier, the more convincing explanation is grounded in the ruling party's strategic political motives. The declining non-Malay support, the internal divisions within PAS over the 'Allah' issue, and evidence of strong mainstream Malay-Muslim opposition

---

[145] Interview with a prominent PAS lawmaker and member of the Central Working Committee in Petaling Jaya, Malaysia (July 2013).

[146] See Ahmad, 'PAS' Ulama'.

[147] Ibid. Interview with a prominent PAS lawmaker and member of the Central Working Committee in Petaling Jaya, Malaysia (July 2013).

[148] Ibid.

to non-Muslims' demand to use 'Allah' all paved way for UMNO to harden its uncompromising stance on the issue.[149]

There is evidence from individual cases to substantiate UMNO's overarching political strategy of attempting to win over as many swing Malay-Muslim voters as possible. One example was the 2013 electoral contest in Shah Alam, a majority Malay-Muslim constituency and a key battleground between UMNO and PAS. PAS had been riding on the support of non-Malays (who comprise about 30 per cent of the electorate), but it could not win without some Malay support. On the other hand, UMNO, hoping that it would win the seat by mobilizing Malay support away from PAS, fielded an extremely controversial candidate from outside its party ranks: Zulkifli Noordin. Zulkifli was the vice president of Perkasa (the Malay-nationalist organization) and he was previously a member of PAS and a member of Parliament for PKR. He is widely known for his anti-minority views, opposing, in particular, the Christians' right to use 'Allah'. In Zulkifli, therefore, UMNO had a figure who is staunchly pro-Malay and pro-Islam in his outlooks – both of which are qualities that were thought to be important to discredit the PAS candidate, Khalid Samad. During the campaign period, UMNO's propaganda and rhetoric focused on the 'sins' of the incumbent PAS candidate against the interests of the Malay-Muslims in the area. For example, Khalid allegedly guaranteed the continued operation of an alcoholic beverage factory in Shah Alam; he was labelled a traitor for supporting the Christians' right to use 'Allah' and nicknamed *'Khalid Gereja'* ('Church Khalid') amongst the ruling party's loyalists in the area. Khalid ultimately retained his seat in Shah Alam by securing just over 55 per cent of the total votes. Notwithstanding UMNO's defeat, that Khalid lost some Malay support in the election indicated that the party's anti-minority rhetoric resonated with some sections of the Malay electorate.

A longitudinal comparison of the government's approach to the 'Allah' issue may also support arguments on how electoral politics define politicians' responses to religious freedom. Recall our observations earlier that state laws banning the use of 'Allah' by non-Muslims had been in place since the late 1980s and that there were occasions – such as in 2002 – when the federal government relaxed such restrictions. Here, we return to the question of minority support. Before 2008, minority support was crucial to the ruling coalition. In three successive elections – 1995, 1999 and 2004 – the MCA

---

[149] Interview with an UMNO politician in Kuala Lumpur, Malaysia (July 2013). According to the UMNO insider, the government's decision to support the restriction on the use of 'Allah' was largely driven by political considerations.

managed to retain more or less the same number of parliamentary seats, before losing half of them in the 2008 elections.[150]

Minority support for the ruling coalition was particularly important during and after the 1999 general elections. The sacking of Anwar Ibrahim from UMNO and from his ministerial posts in 1998 triggered a bitter political crisis. Anwar, who had an extensive following especially among the young and urban Malays, launched his own political movement, Keadilan (now PKR), threatening UMNO's dominance among the Malay electorate. The Anwar factor, in part, contributed to the BN's poor showing in the 1999 elections: UMNO-BN won only 48.5 per cent of the popular vote and twenty-two out of fifty-two seats in large majority Malay constituencies.[151] Meanwhile, PAS made significant progress in the Malay heartlands and managed to win twenty-seven parliamentary seats.[152] As the Malay ground was no longer safe for the government coalition, compromises with and concessions to the non-Malays were inevitable. This situation stood in stark contrast to that in the 2013 elections.

The 2013 Elections: Outcomes, Bolstering Malay Support and Post-Election Onslaught on PAS

UMNO's efforts to boost its image as the sole protector of Malay-Muslim interests, in part by capitalizing on the 'Allah' issue, seemed to have paid off in the 2013 elections. Its share of seats in Parliament increased to eighty-eight – nine more than it had previously and only one seat short of the total seats held by the opposition coalition. PAS lost two parliamentary seats, but a prominent PR politician conceded that in terms of the number of votes, PAS lost support in part due to the intense politicization of the 'Allah' dispute and the conciliatory stand that it took with its coalition partners.[153] I do not intend to oversimplify the battle between PAS and UMNO and attribute the outcomes solely to religious issues. Indeed, many factors are said to have contributed to the electoral success or failure of these parties, namely, the ability of

---

[150] UMNO won seventy-two parliamentary seats in the 1999 elections – seventeen less than what it had won in 1995. See Meredith Weiss, 'The 1999 Malaysian General Elections: Issues, Insults, and Irregularities' (2000) 40 *Asian Survey* 413 (arguing that in the 1995 and 1999 elections, non-Malay voters largely stayed with the ruling coalition, BN).

[151] Francis Loh, 'Understanding the 2004 election results: Looking beyond the Pak Lah factor', *Aliran Monthly*, Issue 3 (2004), online: aliran.com/archives/monthly/2004a/3g.html.

[152] PAS, Keadilan and the DAP contested under the Barisan Alternatif (Alternative Front) ticket. Most contests were one-to-one battles. See Weiss, '1999 Malaysian General Elections', p. 415.

[153] Interview with a PKR politician in Kuala Lumpur, Malaysia (August 2013).

UMNO-BN to offer various financial handouts to the electorate as well as internal leadership issues within PAS.

Nevertheless, religion has remained and will remain a significant battle point between the two parties. As an UMNO politician admitted, religion is an important tool to gain political mileage for both PAS and UMNO, with the latter being keen to show that it is no less Islamic than PAS.[154] In the 2013 elections, Malays were warned that a vote for PAS was effectively a vote for the DAP and gains by the opposition coalition will move the nation a step closer toward realizing the Christianization agenda. The MCA, desperate to win Chinese support, was equally guilty of drumming up religious sentiments by cautioning non-Malays that a vote for the DAP was a vote for PAS (hence, by implication, a vote for the more conservative and dogmatic varieties of Islam). Such votes, according to MCA's campaign advertisement in several Chinese dailies and radio stations, would be tantamount to support for the prohibition on entertainment and alcohol.

In January 2014, in response to a declaration by a Catholic Church official that Catholic churches will continue to use the word 'Allah' in their worship services, the Selangor-state UMNO division, along with organizations like Perkasa and ISMA, threatened to stage a rally at a church in the city of Klang during Sunday services. In the lead up to the protest, the police assured Catholic officials and churches of security protection. Eyewitnesses confirmed heavy police presence at the Klang church, and a protest that could have turned ugly, given rising tensions at the time, was eventually averted. How all this unfolded is important in substantiating Wilkinson's claims about the link between the provocation or prevention of unrest and electoral incentives. That the PR-led government in Selangor – a government that relies on support from the minorities – moved to foil the events in Klang was significant. In the state of Selangor itself, non-Malays comprise the majority electorate in nine parliamentary constituencies. This includes the Klang constituency, where 67.8 per cent of the electorate are non-Malays. In seven other constituencies, the Malays constitute only a narrow majority (between 50.6 per cent and 57.4 per cent).[155] Unsurprisingly, the PR holds all the seats in these constituencies, bar one.[156] This led party insiders to conclude that PR's victory was not

[154] Interview with an UMNO politician in Kuala Lumpur, Malaysia (July 2013).
[155] In Selangor, as a whole, the Malays comprised 52% of the electorate. Data on file with author.
[156] The Hulu Selangor constituency (56.4% Malays) is held by MIC-BN. All other majority-Malay seats (more than 60%) are held by UMNO-BN, except for Gombak (73.6% Malays) and Shah Alam (69.4% Malays). Overall, BN holds five parliamentary seats while PR holds seventeen. With regard to state seats, PR currently holds forty-four seats, while BN holds twelve. In the

only attributable to a huge swing in non-Malay support in its favour, but also to the shift in support among urban Malays.[157]

The UMNO-led provocation is significant in showing that they were ever ready to respond to any 'threats' to the Malay-Muslim community. To further mobilize Malay-Muslim support, in the months following the 2013 elections, the government turned its attention to the Shia Muslims. I have noted in the previous chapters that some aspects of Islamic affairs are matters under the purview of the state, as opposed to federal, jurisdiction. During the Mahathir administration, however, there were increased efforts to centralize Islamic affairs under the federal government. As a result, the federal government's role in decisions pertaining to Islam is important: it has restricted practices or publications that are not just considered a threat to Islam in general, but also those that are deemed contrary to the state-sanctioned version of Islam that is practiced in the country. The latter puts into perspective the increasing persecution of Shiites in Malaysia, which, according to the government, is justified as a means of maintaining the Sunni-character of the country and preventing disorder and disharmony among the Malay-Muslims. From a political perspective, the attack against the Shiites is seen as another attempt to discredit PAS, as some of PAS' most prominent leaders are known followers of (or at least sympathetic to) Shiism.

POLITICAL DEVELOPMENTS, UNLIKELY ALLIANCES AND THE CONSEQUENCES ON RELIGION

Our discussion has reinforced the message imparted in previous chapters, that is, religion remains socially and politically significant in the three countries under study. I have demonstrated how religion has been used (or abused, as the case may be) to mobilize electoral support from the majority and how it can win or lose votes.

The Sri Lankan experience in the 2015 elections, however, offers a cautionary tale for political actors bent on an extreme majority-centric approach. Faced with a disjointed opposition, Rajapaksa went into the elections confident that he could win another term almost exclusively with

previous election in 2008, PR held thirty-six state seats, while BN held twenty. Note that in the 2008 election, the PR coalition was only formally formed a few weeks after the election. During the election, however, there was an informal pact and seats were divided in such a way that no two opposition parties contested in the same constituency at the same time. Data on file with author.

[157] Interview with an opposition party strategist in Petaling Jaya, Malaysia (June 2013). See also Kessler, 'Malaysia's GE13'.

Sinhalese-Buddhist support. For what he thought was politically expedient, Rajapaksa amplified Sinhalese nationalism and alienated the minorities with his administration's policies in matters involving majority-minority relations. All these backfired. Not only did the minorities virtually alienate Rajapaksa (it was suggested, for example, that Rajapaksa was left with only 2 per cent of Muslim votes),[158] prominent SLFP figures defected as Rajapaksa's Health Minister, Maithripala Sirisena (who was also then secretary-general of the SLFP), was chosen as the joint opposition's common presidential candidate. This previously unlikely alliance between the UNP and the SLFP, along with the defection of the pro-Buddhist party JHU, split the Sinhalese-Buddhist votes. Sirisena's selection as the common candidate was also a calculated move: it was thought that his strong Sinhalese-Buddhist background – coupled with his image as a simple man from a rural farming family in Polonnaruwa – would draw Sinhalese-Buddhist votes away from Rajapaksa. These strategies worked and Rajapaksa, who was expected to retain the presidency, lost the election.

Changing political dynamics, therefore, could well offer hope in an otherwise bleak outlook. However, whether all these will improve state practices implicating religion and religious freedom remains to be seen. While some observers have pointed out the conspicuous absence of BBS activities (in the sort of scale prevalent during the Rajapaksa administration) since the political change in Sri Lanka, a meeting in Parliament between the new justice minister and BBS representatives in November 2016 has set off alarm bells within civil society.

In Indonesia, what Hefner calls the 'triumph of normative Sunnism'[159] at the societal level has penetrated through the realms of electoral politics, with parties now subscribing to mainstream Sunni Islam. However, it is still early to draw conclusions about the Jokowi administration's political calculations in matters involving religion. Some civil society organizations have called out the government for its failure to address various religious freedom issues, particularly at the regional level.[160] However, the manner in which the government intervened in the case of the Ahmadiyah in Bangka tells us that strong political will could pave the way for stronger protection of minorities. Patronage of

---

[158] Interview with an SLFP member of Parliament and the former president's close confidant (October 2016).

[159] Hefner, 'Where Have All the Abangan Gone?', p. 89.

[160] SETARA Institute, *Laporan Kondisi Kebebasan Beragama/Berkeyakinan di Indonesia 2015: Politik Harapan, Minim Pembuktian* (*Report on the Condition of the Freedom of Religion and Conscience in Indonesia 2015: Hope Politics, Minimal Delivery*) (Jakarta: SETARA Institute, 2016).

hard-line organizations like the FPI (that is said to have enjoyed some degree of covert blessings from the SBY administration) appears to be on the wane as the Jokowi government has maintained a more antagonistic relationship with the FPI. The FPI's mobilization against the Jakarta governor, Basuki Tjahaja Purnama or Ahok (who ran for a second term in office in the February 2017 elections) for allegedly blaspheming Islam must also be understood in the broader context of religion and politics in Indonesia.

The developments in Malaysia are equally important, given the results of the 2013 elections and the impending elections in 2017. Many observers have expressed concerns with the direction of the ruling party's political strategies in the build up to and during the 2013 elections. It was once seen as unthinkable that UMNO would go at it alone and form a heavily Malay-centric or an all-Malay government.[161] While it has always been understood that UMNO would steer the BN coalition and that minority demands are dependent on electoral calculations involving the Malays, personality politics helped drive conciliatory policies for minorities. As Horowitz argues, everything was negotiable, often with favourable outcomes for minorities.[162]

The result of the 2013 elections nevertheless seemed to strengthen government's belief that it could remain in power by taking extreme positions in favour of the majority. The proposed tabling of a bill to expand the punitive powers of the *Shariah* courts (dubbed by many as the *Hudud* bill), talks of a political alliance between UMNO and PAS (purportedly to strengthen Malay-Muslim political power), and sometimes obvious tolerance for organizations inciting bigotry, could damage majority-minority relations. The inherent risk in alienating the minorities – as we have seen in Sri Lanka – is that it could spur religious intolerance, increase violations of religious rights and ultimately drive tensions toward violent outcomes. Numbers may also play an important factor. It is undeniable that the minorities are increasingly unhappy with the protection of their rights and interests. Some have opted to migrate abroad and statistics show that these numbers have increased in recent years. In short, there is a possibility that the proportion of non-Malays in the country will continue to decrease in the future and, if this is indeed the case (coupled with the continuing belief that the ruling government can win on Malay votes), then there will be much less incentive for the government to adopt conciliatory policies on religion and protect religious freedom.

---

[161] Horowitz, *Ethnic Groups*, pp. 415–16.   [162] Ibid., p. 418.

8

Conclusion

Constitutions may be designed with the hope that they will bind a divided polity, reflect broader national aspirations (which might not necessarily be unequivocally shared but at least agreed upon through mutual bargaining) and safeguard the rights and interests of different (and competing) groups. The Indonesian, Malaysian and Sri Lankan experiences – at least with regard to the arrangements on religion – demonstrate similar motivations at the stage of design. As it turns out, however, the very provisions designed to mitigate conflict have become tools to reify divisions and discriminate against minorities.

The point to emphasize here in relation to the role of constitutions is not that they do not matter, or that they are worthless. Instead, the operation of constitutions and their effects are unpredictable. No matter how carefully drafted and innocently intended – to avoid, as it were, bigger problems such as a complete political deadlock, the escalation of intergroup tensions or the disintegration of a polity – constitutional arrangements, under certain conditions, can produce unintended consequences. This possibility is magnified in divided societies like Indonesia, Malaysia and Sri Lanka, because contests implicating ideology, identity or foundational issues like religion are fundamentally personal and political. Therefore, if there is a single takeaway point to be had from the preceding chapters, it is that politics matters.

In other words, although constitutions establish legal and political structures of government institutions, set the rules of the game and provide tools for the protection of minorities, they do not operate in a vacuum, divorced from the games of power and the political realities surrounding them. Even in the process of constitution-making and/or constitutional amendment, as we have seen, political bargains and negotiations were central to forming a consensus on divisive issues and averting a deadlock.

This study is about how constitutions operate and evolve, not merely on how existing arrangements are lived and applied in practice. For this reason,

I began with a look at constitutional history by examining the constitution-making process. Instead of evaluating the procedural aspects of constitution-making – for example, the type of constitution-making body, the degree of participation and the openness or transparency of the process – I focused on the substance, i.e., the debates and negotiations that drove the process and shaped the outcomes. In doing so, we could see how intergroup conflicts on ethnicity and/or religion played out in the constitution-making arena and understand how they shape subsequent disputes and constitutional practices.

CONSTITUTION-MAKING: STRATEGIES, APPROACHES AND PATHS

As I have demonstrated, the circumstances in which constitution-making took place in Indonesia, Malaysia and Sri Lanka were precarious. We have seen that there was a strong insistence on the part of those purporting to represent the majority community to ensure that the dominant religion is given special constitutional recognition. In Indonesia, the Islamic faction fought to establish an Islamic state in the 1945 constitution-making process. In Malaysia, the Alliance (led by UMNO) responded to opinions on the ground that Islam should be established as the state religion (some demands went even further, by seeking to establish a theocratic state based on the Quran and *Sunnah*). In Sri Lanka, there were demands to restore Buddhism to its 'rightful place' in the constitutional order. In the face of competing demands from different groups regarding the question on religion, these countries faced different kinds of risks should the reaching of an agreement fall through.

In Indonesia's pre-independence constitution-making process, an eleventh-hour threat of secession by nationalists from the eastern islands necessitated the removal of the 'seven words' which would have constitutionalized the implementation of *Shariah* for Muslims. In the post-Soeharto constitutional amendment process, parties that fought for the re-inclusion of the 'seven words' into article 29 eventually relented.[1] It was recognized that article 29 was crucial to the integration of the nation and that after a process that stretched over four years, it was important to avoid a deadlock and to end the amendments through consensus decision-making. In Malaysia, not only was independence made conditional upon the coming together of different ethnic groups on fundamental issues, electoral considerations meant that different

---

[1] See Chapter 2.

ethnic parties needed to rely on each other for electoral, financial and patronage advantage. Thus, reaching an arrangement that was acceptable to all parties was pertinent. In Sri Lanka, the unmistakably Sinhalese and Buddhist balance of political forces that surrounded the constitution-making process in 1970 facilitated the introduction of the Buddhism clause. There was no getting around this – despite objections from the Tamils – as there was wide support for the clause in the Constituent Assembly.

The fragmented and divisive nature of the constitution-making process meant that there needed to be some form of intergroup bargaining, compromise and assurances. The deletion of the 'seven words' in 1945 was facilitated by a skilled negotiator in the form of Mohammad Hatta. In 2002, the decision to retain article 29 in its original form, as we have seen, was also made possible by a process of bargaining and compromise between competing factions. In Malaysia, a consensus was born, in part, out of Tunku Abdul Rahman's assurance that the establishment of Islam will not create a theocratic state, nor will it infringe on non-Muslims' rights and freedoms. In Sri Lanka, faced with demands for a stronger constitutional recognition of Buddhism versus calls for a secular state, Dr. Colvin De Silva engineered what he thought was a 'balanced' provision. He avoided any unequivocal choice between entrenching Buddhism as the state religion on the one hand, and establishing a secular state on the other. He appealed against any changes to the provision – ambiguous though it may be – for he feared deeper polarization between the majority and minority communities.

The wealth of information on the constitution-making debates on religion presented in this book could provide broader lessons for constitution-making in deeply divided societies, particularly in cases where – as Lerner notes in her study of Israel, India and Ireland – there are serious conflicting visions about the foundational aspects of the state.[2] What are the possible options available to constitution-makers? What strategies should they adopt given the conditions and contexts that they face? What kinds of accommodation should be made amongst the fragmented elite? All this information presents a potential for theorizing – as a subsequent study – the approaches and strategies undertaken in the three constitution-making experiences. As a starting point, it may be worth considering whether the approaches in any or all of the three case studies could, for example, reflect the incrementalist approach to constitution-making.

---

[2] Hanna Lerner, *Making Constitutions in Deeply Divided Societies* (Cambridge: Cambridge University Press, 2011).

The three case studies focused on religion, but their experiences may well be instructive in other fundamental constitutional questions where competing visions exist. Consider Sri Lanka, which, as this book is written, is undergoing a process of constitutional reforms. As of December 2016 at least, insiders suggested that debates on a possible revamping of the religion clause will not be taken any further. There seems to be an element of pragmatism in this, generated by the concern that such debates will open the floodgates of arguments for and against the Buddhism provision. Not only would this unsettle influential sections of the Sinhalese-Buddhist majority, it could deepen divisions in a violently polarized society and lead to a possible deadlock. However, what appears to be more of an immediate concern are debates about federalism and the 'unitary' character of the Sri Lankan state. These debates implicate crucial questions about the constitutional recognition – on equal terms – of minorities in the polity. At the time of writing, it remains to be seen what kinds of approaches, bargains or negotiations have taken place or are taking place with regard to these fundamental issues.

CHOICES AND CONSEQUENCES

A key argument presented in this book is that the constitution-makers in Indonesia, Malaysia and Sri Lanka chose three distinct paths in constitutionalizing religion, despite facing more or less similar (though certainly not identical) problems during the constitution-making process. The Indonesians rejected the explicit privileging of Islam and, instead, constitutionalized the pan-religious principle of the 'belief in the one and only God'; the Malaysians established Islam as the religion of the Federation, with the guarantee that this shall not affect the right to religious freedom of non-Muslims; and the Sri Lankan arrangement obligates the state to protect and foster the Buddha Sasana, while ensuring all other religions their religious rights guaranteed in the constitution. The constitution-makers believed, at that time, that these would be the best arrangements to protect the plural character of their respective countries and to ensure the protection of the rights and interests of all.

However, as I pointed out earlier, these arrangements have produced unpredictable and unintended consequences. The religion provisions in the Indonesian, Malaysian and Sri Lankan constitutions – drafted to guarantee religious freedom in spite of pressures to accord stronger and special protection to the majority religion – have been invoked to justify restrictions on religious freedom or even to inspire discrimination and social persecution of minorities. In some cases, such restrictions are also secured through an ever-expansive interpretation of rights limitation clauses or through a peculiar conception of what the right to religious freedom entails. All these examples may challenge normative accounts on the importance of constitutional guarantees in ensuring religious freedom.

A related question that could be considered in subsequent analyses thus concerns the issue of choices and the consequences of choices. In assessing options and making choices, constitution-makers could be moved by historical considerations as well as contemporary causes, but often there is an impulse to look at possible arrangements elsewhere. In the Malaysian constitution-making debates, for instance, state-religion arrangements in Ireland and Burma were brought up as examples. In the Sri Lankan debates, the Malaysian arrangement was raised as a potential model. Another – more nuanced – way of deciding between possible choices rests in the approach that constitution-makers opt for. This again brings to attention Lerner's theory of incrementalist approach to constitution-making. This evolutionary approach entails deferring constitutional choices on divisive, fundamental issues to the future by avoiding clear-cut decisions on such issues, using ambiguous legal language or inserting contradictory provisions in the constitution.[3]

Consider the Buddhism clause in Sri Lanka as an example. Its articulation of the state's duty to protect and foster the Buddha Sasana while assuring the rights of other religions not only appears ambiguous, but also contradictory. In light of how this provision has been expansively interpreted in many different directions,[4] including the notion that religious freedom cannot be exercised at the expense of Buddhism,[5] one does wonder if a less ambiguous and less contradictory provision at the outset might avert the kinds of conflicts and constitutional contestations about the role of the state vis-à-vis Buddhism that have emerged throughout Sri Lanka's constitutional history. The *Menzingen*

---

[3] Ibid., p. 39.

[4] In Chapter 5, I discussed several constitutional cases that the Sri Lankan court has adjudicated in the early 2000s. However, Schonthal's work goes further back in history. He has traced how the Buddhism clause has been utilized by different Buddhist actors to advocate particular visions of the state's role vis-à-vis Buddhism and to activate 'a culture of Buddhist-interest litigation'. They include the notion that the state should intervene to protect Buddhist orthodoxy. See Benjamin Schonthal, 'Securing the Sasana through Law: Buddhist Constitutionalism and Buddhist-interest Litigation in Sri Lanka' (2016) 50(6) *Modern Asian Studies* 1966. In another case, there was an argument that the state's constitutional duties toward Buddhism involved an obligation to deny monks the right to drive legally. See Benjamin Schonthal, 'What Is Buddhist Constitutionalism?' Paper presented at the Harvard Law School's Institute for Global Law and Policy (IGLP) Asian Regional Workshop (Bangkok, 6–10 January 2017), p. 12.

[5] See the discussion on the *Menzingen* case in Chapter 5, as well as the arguments put forth by proponents of the JHU Bill.

case, for instance, illustrates the danger that De Silva's 'balanced' solution to the demands for Buddhist privileges and the protection of religious rights can be easily perverted to produce unbalancing results.[6] Suppose the Sri Lanka constitution-makers had adopted an explicit provision that the state's duty to protect and foster the Buddha Sasana shall not supersede fundamental rights protections guaranteed in the constitution or the rights and interests of other groups. Could we then have avoided a *Menzingen*-like judgment, or claims that the interests of Buddhists and Buddhism – as the religion of the majority – outweigh those of other religions? It is conceivable that the latter claim could arise, say, in a challenge against the practice of animal slaughter, which, is seen as contrary to Buddhist precepts.

These are all, of course, counterfactuals but the Malaysian experience – to some extent – presents a concrete instance where even a more clear-cut provision can produce unintended consequences. Article 3, as we have seen, provides that Islam is the religion of the Federation, but all other religions may be practiced in peace and harmony. A separate sub-provision, article 3(4) states that the establishment of Islam shall not override other provisions of the constitution. As scholars have noted, this means that such establishment cannot trump fundamental rights guarantees. Despite this clearer expression of the limits of the establishment of Islam as the state religion,[7] some of the cases examined in Chapter 5 show that fundamental rights can be made to defer to the special constitutional position of Islam. More significant is the political declaration of Malaysia as an Islamic state. Although this might have started as an exercise of political rhetoric, the idea has become ingrained in the collective psyche of the majority and, in some ways, it has also forced the state to fulfil the Islamic state rhetoric in its policymaking initiatives.

One way to read these consequences, as I have emphasized in the preceding chapters, is to understand them simply as changing conceptions of constitutional commitments over time. A more cynical – though perhaps more accurate – reading of this evolution suggests the emergence of a perversion of constitutional provisions. Admittedly, there is great variance in the extent to which the conceptions have changed, how those changes are reflected in state policies and practices and how these, in turn, affect religious freedom.

---

[6]   See Chapter 5.

[7]   There are contradictory provisions. Despite the establishment of Islam in article 3(1) and the limits of such establishment expressed in article 3(4), the religious freedom clause in the constitution contains a sub-provision that allows state legislatures to regulate the propagation of other religions among Muslims (article 11(4)).

In Indonesia, the founding fathers settled for a pluralistic conception of religious life in the country through the *Pancasila*. For this reason, the 'belief in the one and only God' in the constitution's preamble was sutured with the guarantee of the freedom of worship according to one's religion or beliefs, producing article 29. In practice, restrictions on religion and religious freedom have increased over the years. Soeharto's cunning interpretation and application of the *Pancasila* forced Indonesians to adhere to one of the 'official' religions and the disciplining hand of Ministry of Religious Affairs (MORA) ensured that non-mainstream religious or traditional belief groups conform to standardized versions of a religion, especially Islam. Regulations on houses of worship, the criminalization of blasphemy and the purported religiously inspired local regulations are all packaged as laws regulating public order, but the lack of consistent and fair enforcement across the board has raised suspicions that the minorities are being targeted to bear the burden of such policies.

To the extent that the founding fathers envisioned a country where all religions are given an equal footing, this idea has now been betrayed by the increasing favouritism for the dominant religion. Soekarno, for example, would have disapproved the persecution of the Ahmadis, which, as the *Blasphemy Law* decision shows, can be traced back to the court's peculiar understanding of article 29.[8] He would have also certainly rejected the manner in which Soeharto used the *Pancasila* and article 29 as the bases for his religious 'building up' program. As a strong advocate for rationalism and intellectualism in religious (in this case, Islam) interpretation, Soekarno desired a kind of Islamic discourse in Indonesia that was free from the influence of rigid religious authorities.[9]

Similarly, in Sri Lanka, shifting conceptions on the Buddhism provision (from what De Silva had originally imagined) was manifested in the 1978 revision that bolstered the position of Buddhism in the constitutional order. Concerns about aggressive proselytism and conversion and their effect on Buddhism inspired the drafting of the anti-conversion bill in 2004. Courts seem equally conscious about protecting Buddhism and the need to avoid

---

[8] See 'I Don't Believe Mirza Ghulam Ahmad Is a Prophet', in Soekarno, *Under the Banner of Revolution: Vol. I* (Djakarta: Publication Committee, 1966), pp. 329–31. Soekarno emphasized that although he disagrees with some aspects of the Ahmadiyah teaching, he nevertheless appreciated their 'rational, modern, broadminded, and logical writings'. He then stressed, 'I am just a student of religion who is not conservative, nor a mere blind follower of the traditional interpretations.'

[9] See 'Rejuvenating Our Concepts of Islam', in Soekarno, *Under the Banner of Revolution*, pp. 353–85.

alienating Buddhist supporters, lest they dared to unequivocally declare that fundamental rights outweighed Buddhist prerogatives.[10]

FORCES AND COUNTERFORCES

To understand how and why constitutions operate the way they do, it is pertinent to understand the forces and counterforces that might affect their operation. In the earlier chapters, I have alluded to some of the causal elements that shape the implementation and enforcement of constitutional commitments on religion. Here, I will attempt to produce a richer account of such elements.

I have already mentioned the existence of an underlying motivation of sorts to protect the dominant religion or to appease the sensitivities of the majority. This is especially obvious in the partial attitudes of the states – both by commission and omission – in dealing with competing majority-minority claims on religious freedom. It is also quite clear that regulations that appear neutral on paper – in the sense that they do not explicitly seek to single out any particular religion for special treatment – are not always applied neutrally. In the cases of Malaysia and Sri Lanka, all this can be traced to the intimate relationship between religion and ethnicity, and the preservation of the majority identity in the polity.[11] The anti-Muslim campaign in Sri Lanka, for example, has not only targeted Muslim practices that are deemed offensive to Buddhist principles and values, but there are fears that the Muslims' population growth and the building of mosques will eventually displace the country's Sinhalese-Buddhist character.[12] In Malaysia, the interrelatedness of the Malay and Islamic identities – bolstered by the constitutional provision that defines a Malay as a person who professes Islam – have led to concerns that the failure to protect Islam would eventually lead to the decline of the Malays

---

[10]   This is illustrated in the Supreme Court's determination on the constitutionality of the JHU's Anti-Conversion Bill. See Chapter 5. See also Benjamin Schonthal, 'Constitutionalizing Religion: The Pyrrhic Success of Religious Rights in Postcolonial Sri Lanka' (2014) 29(3) *Journal of Law and Religion* 470, 487–8.

[11]   Hirschl adds a third element – nationality – and argues that the interplay among all three facets of identity provides states with '[a]n embedded interest in preserving or promoting a viable state religion to the extent that this religion provides meaning to the national metanarratives that constitute the nation as such'. See Ran Hirschl, *Constitutional Theocracy* (Cambridge, Mass.: Harvard University Press, 2010), p. 31.

[12]   See Center for Policy Alternatives (CPA), 'Attacks on Places of Religious Worship in Post-War Sri Lanka', *Centre for Policy Alternatives* (March 2013), p. 60, online: www.cpalanka.org/attacks-on-places-of-religious-worship-in-post-war-sri-lanka.

in their homeland. Ethno-religious nationalist supremacy and preservation, therefore, take precedence over religious rights.

At this juncture, it is worth underscoring the point about religious nationalism. Of late, there has been a lot of attention on the rise of religious nationalism around the world. However, in the context of deeply divided societies like Indonesia, Malaysia and Sri Lanka, where religion is highly salient socially and politically, the impact of religious nationalism on constitutional law and policymaking has received very limited attention.

The conflation of religion and nationalist sentiments in these countries has generated a peculiar conception of religion. As I have explained in Chapter 2, the Buddhist revivalist movement that began in the late nineteenth century in Sri Lanka provided much of the impetus for a stronger role for Buddhism in the state, and it has been credited with transforming and shaping Sri Lanka's history.[13] In the 1978 constitution-making process, a bipartisan Select Committee engineered the substitution of the word 'Buddhism' with 'Buddha Sasana', having sought input from various organizations, including militant Sinhalese-Buddhist organizations. The quest to restore the glory of Buddhism mandated the stirring of Buddhist grievances against colonialism and against the spread of Christianity. As Chapter 7 demonstrates, there has been much effort by political parties like the United National Party (UNP) and the Sri Lanka Freedom Party (SLFP) to move toward a discourse which sought to address, if not to manipulate, the outrage among Buddhists at the injustices and discrimination against their religion under colonial rule. The establishment of the Jathika Hela Urumaya (JHU) as well as organizations like the Bodu Bala Sena (BBS) within the past decade or so is also significant as these two actors have undoubtedly been influential in pushing for pro-Sinhalese-Buddhist agendas.

In Muslim-majority countries like Malaysia and Indonesia, the Iranian revolution spurred revivalist movements in the late 1970s and 1980s. The politicians responded. Soeharto, who was incredibly suspicious of political Islam as a challenge to his power and authority, began to pander to Islamic interests. In Malaysia, political elites engaged in a contest to appeal to the groundswell of Islamic nationalism. Under the Mahathir administration, the government pursued many policies, including in the legal, education and economic spheres, to demonstrate the commitment to an Islamic outlook.[14] The separation of the civil and *Shariah* jurisdictions through a constitutional

---

[13] Stanley Jeyaraja Tambiah, *Buddhism Betrayed? Religion, Politics, and Violence in Sri Lanka* (Chicago: University of Chicago Press, 1992), p. 3.

[14] One example is the establishment of the International Islamic University of Malaysia.

amendment in 1988 is particularly significant[15] because the radical shift in the conception of article 3 has been facilitated, in part, by the jurisdictional problems that arise from the amendment. Although the jurisdiction of the *Shariah* courts is limited to certain issues, there is an unresolved loophole in the system where a contested issue lies at the intersection of the civil and *Shariah* jurisdictions. For instance, state-enacted Islamic laws that criminalize non-mainstream religious groups, while falling properly within the *Shariah* jurisdiction to regulate offences against the precepts of Islam, are also inconsistent with the constitutional right to religious freedom. In the face of such jurisdictional overlap, the civil courts have tended to side-step their role as enforcers of constitutional rights guarantees as they are generally cautious about adjudicating controversial matters involving Islam. The right to religious freedom thus takes a back seat against policies and practices that purportedly protect the sanctity of Islam in the country.

The ways in which religious nationalism shapes constitution-making and constitutional change is thus a topic deserving of focused scholarly analysis. A related point that is equally worth exploring in tandem with the issue of religious nationalism is the role of non-state actors in shaping states' constitutional practices and discourse. In this respect, Indonesia provides a fertile example. Hard-line organizations (most notably the Front Pembela Islam) that emerged in the wake of Soeharto's fall have utilized the more open and democratic political space to express their views and mobilize supporters in ways that would have been unimaginable during the New Order era.[16] In the final months of 2016, FPI's activities in the public sphere were particularly marked, as it led rallies and protests (one of which turned violent) against the then Jakarta governor (Basuki Tjahaja Purnama, or Ahok) for allegedly insulting Islam. Amidst increasing public pressure – no doubt generated by the FPI-led protests to demand Ahok's prosecution – the governor was officially named a suspect in a blasphemy investigation in just a little over two months after his purportedly blasphemous remarks. His trial began in the first week of December and he was convicted in May 2017. The swiftness with which Ahok's blasphemy case proceeded may be remarkable by Indonesia's standards, but it might also be attributable to the high-profile nature of the case, Ahok's gubernatorial candidacy and the prevailing political

---

[15] Article 121 (1A), Federal Constitution of Malaysia.

[16] In fact, several founding members of FPI were imprisoned during the Soeharto administration for engaging in *dakwah* (religious teaching) with anti–New Order undertones. See Ismail Hasani and Bonar Tigor Naipospos, *The Faces of Islam 'Defenders'* (Jakarta: Pustaka Masyarakat Setara, 2010), p. 133.

circumstances. The real test for Indonesia's rule of law, however, rests in the authorities' responses toward blasphemy allegations against Rizieq Shihab, the FPI leader. In one case, a Catholic student organization reported Rizieq to the police for allegedly blaspheming Christianity. Since reports surfaced that Rizieq was under investigation for various offences including blasphemy, hate speech and violations of the Anti-Pornography Law, pressure groups and organizations (including the FPI) have begun a campaign to 'defend the *ulama*'.

For the most part, especially during SBY's administration, groups like the FPI have enjoyed considerable impunity. However, the Ahok and Rizieq cases are significant not least because they will be revealing of the course of Indonesia's constitutionalism. This will be reflected in the ways in which the state seeks to manage fundamental rights (of free speech and religious freedom) and its constitutional commitments in an environment of hostile religious nationalism and politicization of religion. Indonesia, however, is not alone in its predicament. In Sri Lanka, the BBS has also emerged as a vocal and visible pressure group, largely immune from the full force of the law. In previous chapters, I have highlighted the social and political complexities in pursuing the BBS monks for their involvement in incidents of violence.[17] In the aftermath of the Aluthgama riots, Rauff Hakeem (the leader of the SLMC who was then the justice minister in the Rajapaksa administration) stated in an interview with a local newspaper that he was ashamed of the government's continuous disregard of the plight of Muslims and the threats posed by the BBS.[18] Hakeem also revealed that a Buddhist monk who had been a strong critic of the BBS was attacked and left to bleed by the roadside. In another incident, two police officers tasked to guard a magistrate who refused a meeting permit for the BBS were subjected to an acid attack.[19] What was particularly revealing in the interview, however, was Hakeem's suggestion that his efforts to control the Buddhist-Muslim violence had fallen on deaf ears, partly because the 'BBS has the patronage of some quarters of the government in taking forward the religious campaign against the Muslims'.[20]

All these accounts underscore the important roles of the judiciary and political calculations in shaping constitutional practices in matters implicating

---

[17] A former cabinet member in the Rajapaksa administration revealed that President Rajapaksa was ready to instruct the investigation of the BBS monks involved in the violent Aluthgama riots and to call them to account for their actions. However, he later heeded calls by several cabinet members to refrain from doing so. Conversation with a former minister in Colombo, Sri Lanka (October 2016).

[18] Sulochana Ramiah Mohan, 'Sri Lanka becoming a banana republic', *Ceylon Today* (22 June 2014).

[19] Ibid.   [20] Ibid.

religion. In this book, I have also attempted to challenge – using empirical evidence from Indonesia, Malaysia and Sri Lanka – both the normative claim that bills of rights are crucial counter-majoritarian safeguards, as well as the judiciary's counter-majoritarian role. Judges are not immune from majoritarian passions and the political exigencies surrounding them. Structural independence of the judiciary matters, but as the case studies show, they are not always determinative. Nonetheless, the experiences of the three countries may encourage further studies on the design of judicial institutions and its relationship to the protection of rights, or on how to strengthen judicial power to enforce constitutional limitations against state actions that deny religious freedom.

Finally, this book stresses the significance of electoral politics in shaping state policies and practices on religion and religious freedom. The focus on electoral politics helps bring attention to a crucial but understudied dynamic in fundamental rights protection in countries like Indonesia, Malaysia and Sri Lanka. One question that would perhaps be of interest is whether particular types of regime and electoral systems would affect the degree of religious freedom violations across all three countries. Malaysia inherited the Westminster parliamentary system from Britain, whereas Indonesia and Sri Lanka adopted the presidential and semi-presidential systems, respectively. As I have explained in Chapter 7, the Indonesian presidential election system requires a successful candidate to win a majority of votes and to satisfy the territorial distribution requirement, i.e., by securing a majority of votes in at least seventeen of the country's thirty-three provinces.[21] In Sri Lanka, the president is elected through a single–round system of preferential voting (a voter lists up to three preferences on the ballot). The winning candidate must secure more than 50 per cent of the votes from the first preferences cast on the ballot. These variations do not appear to affect the *existence* of religious freedom violations, but we have seen that religious violence has been more prevalent in Sri Lanka and Indonesia. This raises the question of whether the prevalence of violence has any relation to a country's regime type.

As a starting point, an analysis of the system of direct election of the president could provide some useful insights. Take the 2014 presidential elections in Indonesia as an example. Religion or religious issues appeared to have played a more prominent role during the presidential elections than during the legislative elections. The coalition of political parties that supported the

---

[21] This applies to the first round of voting, where there are more than two candidates contesting. If no candidate meets the requirements, then a second round run-off is held between the top two candidates from the first round.

candidacy of Prabowo Subianto openly associated itself with the FPI.[22] In
a campaign in Yogyakarta – a city known to have embraced the values of
pluralism and tolerance, but was recently shocked by a series of religiously
motivated attacks – the Prabowo team was greeted by several leaders of
hard-line organizations who had been actively campaigning against religious
minorities such as the Shiites and Ahmadis.[23] In light of all this, it is unsurprising that one of Prabowo's election manifestos highlighted his commitment
to 'religious purification'. This suggests that had Prabowo won the election,
he would have to make good on the promise of 'purification', which would
inevitably affect Muslim minorities such as the Ahmadiyah and the Shia.

In light of the continuing (and increasing) salience of religion in public life,
there are still great avenues for studies on the interaction between constitutions, religion and politics. In the meantime, however, this book provides – for
the first time – a comprehensive comparative analysis of such interaction
in three relatively understudied jurisdictions. What I have illustrated is that
constitution-making and the subsequent operation and implementation of
constitutional commitments – particularly on questions implicating religion,
and especially in divided societies like Indonesia, Malaysia and Sri Lanka –
cannot be separated from the political dynamics surrounding them. Under
conditions of weak rule of law and intense politicization of religion, not only
are constitutional commitments and provisions proving to be malleable; they
may also produce unintended and perverse consequences.

---

[22] Six political parties officially supported Prabowo's candidacy: Gerindra, Golkar, Partai Amanat
Negara (PAN), Partai Keadilan Sejahtera (PKS), Partai Persatuan Pembangunan (PPP) and
Partai Bulan Bintang (PBB).

[23] Bambang Muryanto and Slamet Susanto, 'Hardline leaders greet Prabowo in Yogyakarta',
The Jakarta Post (2 July 2014), online: www.thejakartapost.com/news/2014/07/02/hard-line-
leaders-greet-prabowo-yogyakarta.html.

Bibliography

'50 stage protest against cross on new church', *The Star* (20 April 2015), online: www.thestar.com.my/news/nation/2015/04/20/50-stage-protest-against-cross-on-new-church/

Abas, Mohamed Salleh bin, *Selected Articles & Speeches on Constitution, Law & Judiciary* (Malaysian Law Publishers, 1984)

Abdul, Irfan, 'Mahfud MD Bantah Legalkan Ateisme dan Komunisme' ('Mahfud MD rejects the legalization of atheism and Communism'), *Tempo.co* (12 July 2012), online: www.tempo.co/read/news/2012/07/12/173416582/Mahfud-Md-Bantah-Legalkan-Ateisme-dan-Komunisme

Abdullah, Nurjannah, 'Legislating Faith in Malaysia' (2007) *Singapore Journal of Legal Studies* 264

Abdullah, Rokiah, and Ismail, Mohd Khuzairi, '*Malaysia Negara Kristian?* (Malaysia A Christian State?)', *Utusan Malaysia* (7 May 2011)

Abeyratne, Rehan, 'Rethinking Judicial Independence in India and Sri Lanka' (2015) 10 *Asian Journal of Comparative Law* 99

Adnan, Z., 'Islamic Religion: Yes, Islamic Ideology: No! Islam and the State in Indonesia' in Arief Budiman (ed.), *State and Civil Society in Indonesia* (Victoria, Australia: Centre of Southeast Asian Studies, Monash University, 1990)

Ahmad, Dr. Dzulkefly, 'PAS' ulama "disunited" stance on "Allah" – 2 sides of the same coin?', (22 January 2010), online: bit.ly/1qI56Ae

'Ahmadiyah can worship, Kalla says', *The Jakarta Post* (11 June 2008), online: www.thejakartapost.com/news/2008/06/11/ahmadiyah-can-worship-kalla-says.html

Alatas, Syed Farid, 'Salafism and the persecution of Shi'ites in Malaysia', *Middle East Institute* (30 July 2014), online: www.mei.edu/content/map/salafism-and-persecution-shi'ites-malaysia

Allen, Pam, 'Challenging Diversity?: Indonesia's Anti-Pornography Bill' (2007) 31 *Asian Studies Review* 101

An-Naim, Abdullahi Ahmed, 'Mediation of Human Rights: The Al-Arqam Case in Malaysia' in Joanne R. Bauer and Daniel K. Bell (eds.), *The East Asian Challenge for Human Rights* (Cambridge: Cambridge University Press, 1999)

Anshari, Endang S., *Piagam Jakarta, 22 Juni 1945 dan Sejarah Konsensus Nasional Antara Nasionalis Islamis dan Nasionalis Sekuler Tentang Dasar Negara Republik*

Indonesia, 1945–1959 (*The Jakarta Charter of 22 June 1945 and the History of National Consensus between Islamist Nationalists and Secular Nationalists on the Foundation of the Republic of Indonesia*) (Pustaka Perpustakaan Salman ITB, 1981)

Anshori, Ibnu, 'Mustafa Kemal and Sukarno: A Comparsion of Views Regarding Relations between State and Religion', unpublished M.A. thesis, McGill University (1994)

'Arab Spring adds to global restrictions on religion', *Pew Research Center: Religion and Public Life* (20 June 2013), online: www.pewforum.org/2013/06/20/arab-spring-restrictions-on-religion-findings/#linegraph

Aritonang, Jan Sihar, and Steenbrink, Karel, *A History of Christianity in Indonesia* (Leiden: Brill, 2008)

Assyaukanie, Luthfi, 'Fatwa and Violence in Indonesia' (2009) 11 *Journal of Religion and Society* 1

Assyaukanie, Luthfi, 'Muslim Discourse of Liberal Democracy in Indonesia' in Luthfi Assyaukanie, Robert W. Hefner, and Azyumardi Azra (eds.), *Muslim Politics and Democratisation in Indonesia* (Clayton, Vic.: Monash Asia Institute, 2008)

Assyaukanie, Luthfi, *Islam and the Secular State in Indonesia* (Singapore: Institute of Southeast Asian Studies, 2009)

Aziz, Shamrahayu A., 'Islam as the Religion of the Malaysian Federation: The Scope and Implications' (2006) 14(1) *International Islamic University Malaysia Law Journal* 33

Azra, Azyumardi, 'Bali and Southeast Asian Islam: Debunking the Myths' in Kumar Ramakrishna and See Seng Tan, (eds.), *After Bali: The Threat of Terrorism in Southeast Asia* (Singapore: World Scientific, 2003)

Bagir, Zainal Abidin, 'Advocacy for Religious Freedom in Democratizing Indonesia' (2014) 12(4) *Review of Faith and International Affairs* 27

Bakar, Osman, 'Islam and Politics in Malaysia' in Shahram Akbarzaden and Abdullah Saeed (eds.), *Islam and Political Legitimacy* (Abingdon, Oxon and New York: Routledge Curzon, 2003)

Balasubramaniam, Ratna Rueben, 'Has Rule by Law Killed the Rule of Law in Malaysia?' (2008) 8 *Oxford University Commonwealth Law Journal* 211

Bari, Abdul Aziz, *Islam dalam Perlembagaan Malaysia* (*Islam in the Malaysian Constitution*) (Petaling Jaya, Malaysia: Intel Multimedia and Publications, 2005)

Bartholomeusz, Tessa, 'First among Equals: Buddhism and the Sri Lankan State' in Ian Harris (ed.), *Buddhism and Politics in Twentieth-Century Asia* (London: Pinter, 1999)

'Bill Liddle: Saya Khawatir Golkar Semakin ke Kanan' ('Bill Liddle: I am concerned that Golkar is moving to the right'), *Suara Pembaruan* (9 February 2013), online: www.suarapembaruan.com/home/bill-liddle-saya-khawatir-golkar-semakin-kanan/30512

Blount, Justin, Elkins, Zachary, and Ginsburg, Tom, 'Does the Process of Constitution-Making Matter?' in Tom Ginsburg (ed.), *Comparative Constitutional Design* (Cambridge: Cambridge University Press, 2012)

Boland, B. J., *The Struggle of Islam in Modern Indonesia* (The Hague: Martinus Nijhoff, 1971)

Brinks, Daniel M., '"Faithful Servants of the Regime": The Brazilian Constitutional Court's Role under the 1988 Constitution' in Gretchen Helmke and Julio Rios-Figueroa (eds.), *Courts in Latin America* (Cambridge: Cambridge University Press, 2011)

Bruinessen, Martin van, (ed.), *Contemporary Developments in Indonesian Islam: Explaining the Conservative Turn* (Singapore: Institute of Southeast Asian Studies, 2013)

Buch, Dr. M. N., 'India, Sri Lanka – The Tamil question', *Vivekananda International Foundation* (29 March 2013), online: www.vifindia.org/article/2013/march/29/india-sri-lanka-the-tamil-question

Budianto, Lilian, 'Indonesia's judicial system rated worst in Asia: Survey', *The Jakarta Post* (15 September 2008), online: www.thejakartapost.com/news/2008/09/15/indonesia 039s-judicial-system-rated-worst-asia-survey.html

Butt, Simon, 'Indonesia's Constitutional Court: Conservative Activist or Strategic Operator?' in Bjorn Dressel (ed.), *The Judicialization of Politics in Asia* (Oxon: Routledge, 2013)

Butt, Simon, 'Islam, the State and the Constitutional Court in Indonesia', *Sydney Law School Legal Studies Research Paper No. 10/70*, (July 2010)

Butt, Simon, 'Islam, the State, and the Constitutional Court in Indonesia' (2010) 19 *Pacific Rim Law & Policy Journal* 279

Butt, Simon, *Corruption and the Law in Indonesia* (Oxon: Routledge, 2011)

Butt, Simon, *The Constitutional Court and Democracy in Indonesia* (Leiden: Brill Nijihoff, 2015)

Butt, Simon, and Lindsey, Tim, *The Constitution of Indonesia: A Contextual Analysis* (Oxford and Portland, OR: Hart Publishing, 2012)

Casanova, José, *Public Religions in the Modern World* (Chicago and London: University of Chicago Press, 1994)

Center for Policy Alternatives (CPA), 'Attacks on Places of Religious Worship in Post-War Sri Lanka'. *Centre for Policy Alternatives* (March 2013), online: www.cpalanka.org/attacks-on-places-of-religious-worship-in-post-war-sri-lanka/

Chen, Albert H. Y., 'The Achievement of Constitutionalism in Asia: Moving Beyond "Constitutions without Constitutionalism"' (2015) University of Hong Kong Faculty of Law Research Paper No. 2015/002

Christian Solidarity Worldwide, 'Universal periodic review – 14th session: CSW – stakeholder submission – Sri Lanka', *Office of the United Nations High Commissioner for Human Rights* (April 2012), online: lib.ohchr.org/HRBodies/UPR/Documents/Session14/LK/CSW_UPR_LKA_S14_2012_ChristianSolidarityNetwork_E.pdf

Coca, Nithin. 'Is political Islam rising in Indonesia?', *Al Jazeera* (12 May 2014), online: www.aljazeera.com/indepth/features/2014/04/political-islam-rising-indonesia-20144 2913253417235.html

Commission of Enquiry on the Video Clip Recording of Images of a Person Purported to be an Advocate and Solicitor Speaking on the Telephone on Matters Regarding the Appointment of Judges: The Report, Vol. 1 (Putrajaya: BHEUU, May 2008)

Cooray, Joseph A. L., *Constitutional Government and Human Rights in a Developing Society* (Colombo: Colombo Apothecaries' Company, 1969)

Cottrell, Jill, and Ghai, Yash, 'Constitution Making and Democratization in Kenya' (February 2007) 14 (1) *Democratization* 1

'Court Hands Two Muslim Killers Light Sentences', *South China Morning Post* (29 July 2011), A10

Couso, Javier, and Hillbink, Lisa, 'From Quietism to Incipient Activism: The Institutional and Ideological Roots of Rights Adjudication in Chile' in Gretchen Helmke and Julio Rios-Figueroa (eds.), *Courts in Latin America* (Cambridge University Press, 2011)

Cross, Frank B., *Constitutions and Religious Freedom* (Cambridge: Cambridge University Press, 2015)

Crouch, Melissa, 'Implementing the Regulation on Places of Worship in Indonesia: New Problems, Local Politics and Court Action' (2010) 34 *Asian Studies Review* 403

Crouch, Melissa, 'Preface' to Ihsan Ali Fauzi et al., *Disputed Churches in Jakarta*, Tim Lindsey and Melissa Crouch (eds.), Rebecca Lunnon (trans.) (Asian Law Centre and the Centre for Islamic Law and Society at the University of Melbourne, The Paramadina Foundation (Jakarta) and the Center for Religious and Cross-cultural Studies (CRCS), Postgraduate School, Gadjah Mada University (Yogyakarta), 2011)

Crouch, Melissa, *Law and Religion in Indonesia: Conflict and the Courts in West Java* (Abingdon, Oxon and New York: Routledge, 2014)

De Lange, Roel, 'The European Public Order, Constitutional Principles and Fundamental Rights' (2007) 1 *Erasmus Law Review* 3

De Silva, Colvin R., *Safeguards for the Minorities in the 1972 Constitution* (Colombo: Young Socialist Publication, 1987)

De Silva, K. M., *A History of Sri Lanka*, rev. ed., (London: Penguin Books, 2005)

De Silva, K. M., *A History of Sri Lanka*, 2nd edn (Colombo: Vijitha Yapa Publications, 2008)

De Silva, K. M., *Religion, Nationalism, and the State in Modern Sri Lanka* (Tampa, FL: Dept. of Religious Studies, University of South Florida, 1986)

De Silva, K. M., and Wriggins, William Howard, *J. R. Jayewardene of Sri Lanka: A Political Biography*, Volume 1: 1906–1956, 2 vols. (Honolulu: University of Hawaii Press, 1988), Vol. 1

de Silva, Manohara, 'Proposed Legislation on Unethical Conversions' in A. R. B. Amerasinghe and S. S. Wijeratne (eds.), *Human Rights: Theory to Practice: Essays in Honour of Deshamaya R. K. W. Goonasekere* (Colombo: Legal Aid Commission and Human Rights Commission of Sri Lanka, 2005)

De Silava, Viveka S., *An Assessment of the Contribution of the Judiciary towards Good Governance: A Study of the Role of the Supreme Court of Sri Lanka* (Colombo: Sri Lanka Foundation/Friedrich Ebert Stiftung, 2005)

DeVotta, Neil, 'Sri Lanka's Ongoing Shift to Authoritarianism', *East West Center Asia Pacific Bulletin*, No. 201 (22 February 2013)

DeVotta, Neil, *Sinhalese Buddhist Nationalist Ideology: Implications for Politics and Conflict Resolution in Sri Lanka*, No. 40, *Policy Studies* (Washington, DC: East-West Center, 2007)

Deegalle, Mahinda, '"Foremost among Religions": Theravada Buddhism's Affairs with the Modern Sri Lankan State' in John Whalen-Bridge and Pattana Kitiarsa (eds.),

Buddhism, Modernity, and the State in Asia: Forms of Engagement (New York: Palgrave Macmillan, 2013)

Deegalle, Mahinda, 'The Politics of the Jathika Hela Urumaya Monks: Buddhism and Ethnicity in Contemporary Sri Lanka' (2004) 5(2) *Contemporary Buddhism* 83

Department of City and Rural Planning of Peninsula Malaysia, 'Planning Guidelines for Temples, Gurdwaras, and Churches' (March 2011)

Department of City and Rural Planning of Peninsula Malaysia, 'Planning Guidelines for Mosques and Suraus' (February 2011)

Department of Peacekeeping Operations and the Office of the High Commissioner for Human Rights, *The United Nations Rule of Law Indicators: Implementation Guide and Project Tools 4*. 1st ed. (United Nations, 2011) www.un.org/en/events/peacekeepersday/2011/publications/un_rule_of_law_indicators.pdf

'Deputy minister: Zakir Naik "voice of moderation" needed to fix tarnished Islam', *The Malaymail Online* (19 April 2016), online: www.themalaymailonline.com/malaysia/article/deputy-minister-zakir-naik-voice-of-moderation-needed-to-fix-tarnished-isla

Dewasiri, Nirmal Ranjith, *New Buddhist Extremism and the Challenges to Ethno-Religious Coexistence in Sri Lanka* (Colombo: International Centre for Ethnic Studies, November 2016)

Dicey, A. V., *Introduction to the Study of the Law of the Constitution*, 5th ed., (London: Macmillan, 1897)

Dressel, Bjorn, and Mietzner, Marcus, 'A Tale of Two Courts: The Judicialization of Electoral Politics in Asia' (2012) 25 *Governance: An Intenational Journal of Policy, Administration, and Institutions* 391

Effendi, Djohan, 'Jaminan Konstitusional Bagi Kebebasan Beragama Di Indonesia' ('Constitutional Guarantees for Religious Freedom in Indonesia') in Komaruddin Hidayat and Ahmad Gaus A. F. (eds.), *Passing Over: Melintasi Batas Agama (Passing Over: Crossing Religious Boundaries)* (Penerbit PT Gramedia Pustaka Utama in cooperation with Yayasan Wakaf Paramadina, 1998)

Ellis, Eric, 'The monks' army', *The Global Mail* (undated), online: tgm-archive.github.io/sri-lanka/monks-army.html

Elson, R. E., 'Another Look at the Jakarta Charter Controversy of 1945' (2009) 88 *Indonesia* 105

Elster, Jon, 'Forces and Mechanisms in the Constitution-Making Process' (1995) 45 *Duke Law Journal* 364

Faruqi, Shad Saleem, 'Freedom of religion under the constitution', *The Sun* (18 May 2006), online: www.sun2surf.com/article.cfm?id=14147

Faruqi, Shad Saleem, *Document of Destiny: The Constitution of the Federation of Malaysia* (Petaling Jaya: Star Publications, 2008)

Feener, R. Michael, *Muslim Legal Thought in Modern Indonesia* (Cambridge: Cambridge University Press, 2007)

Fernando, Joseph M., 'The Position of Islam in the Constitution of Malaysia' (2006) 37 *Journal of Southeast Asian Studies* 249

Fernando, Joseph M., *The Making of the Malayan Constitution* (Kuala Lumpur: Malaysian Branch of the Royal Asiatic Society, 2001)

Fox, Jonathan and Flores, Deborah, 'Religion, Constitutions, and the State: A Cross-National Study' (2009) 71(4) *The Journal of Politics* 1499

'Full text of Najib's speech at 2013 Umno General Assembly', *New Straits Times* (7 December 2013), online: www.nst.com.my/latest/full-text-of-najib-s-speech-at-2013-umno-general-assembly-1.425244

Galih, Bayu, and Fadila Fikriani Armadita, 'SBY: Indonesia Bukan Negara Sekuler' ('SBY: Indonesia is not a secular country'), *Vivanews* (1 June 2011), online: http://us.nasional.news.viva.co.id/news/read/224041-sby-96indonesia-bukan-negara-sekuler

Geertz, Clifford, *The Religion of Java* (Chicago and London: University of Chicago Press, 1976)

Ghai, Yash, 'A Journey around Constitution: Reflections on Contemporary Constitutions' (2005) *African Law Journal* 122

Ginsburg, Tom, *Judicial Review in New Democracies: Constitutional Courts in Asian Cases* (Cambridge: Cambridge University Press, 2003)

Ginsburg, Tom and Moustafa, Tamir (eds.), *Rule by Law: The Politics of Courts in Authoritarian Regimes* (Cambridge: Cambridge University Press, 2008)

Gunatilleke, Gehan, *The Chronic and the Acute: Post-War Religious Violence in Sri Lanka* (Colombo: ICES and Equitas, 2015)

Guneratne, Jayantha de Almeida, Pinto-Jayawardena, Kishali, and Gunatilleke, Gehan, *The Judicial Mind in Sri Lanka: Responding to the Protection of Minority Rights* (Colombo: Law and Society Trust, 2014)

Guruge, Ananda, *Return to Righteousness: A Collection of Speeches, Essays and Letters of the Anagarika Dharmapala* (Colombo: The Government Press, 1965)

Hamoudi, Haider Ala, *Negotiating in Civil Conflict: Constitutional Construction and Imperfect Bargaining in Iraq* (Chicago: Chicago University Press, 2013)

Haniffa, Farzana, 'Conflicted Solidarities? Muslims and the Constitution-Making Process of 1970–72' in Asanga Welikala (ed.), *The Sri Lankan Republic at 40: Reflections on Constitutional History, Theory and Practice* (Colombo: Centre for Policy Alternatives, 2012)

Haniffa, Farzana, et al., *Where Have All the Neighbours Gone? Aluthgama Riots and Its Aftermath: A Fact Finding Mission to Aluthgama, Dharga Town, Valipanna and Beruwela* (Colombo: Law and Society Trust, 2014)

Harding, Andrew, 'Sharia and National Law in Malaysia' in Jan Michiel Otto (ed.), *Sharia Incorporated: A Comparative Overview of the Legal Systems of Twelve Muslim Countries in Past and Present* (Leiden: Leiden University Press, 2010)

Harding, Andrew, *Law, Government and the Constitution in Malaysia* (The Hague and London: Kluwer Law International, 1996)

Hart, Vivien, 'Democratic Constitution Making'. Special Report, No. 107, *United States Institute of Peace (USIP)*, Washington, DC (July 2003)

Hasani, Ismail, and Naipospos, Bonar Tigor, *The Faces of Islam 'Defenders'* (Jakarta: Pustaka Masyarakat Setara, 2010)

Hasyim, Syafiq, 'Blending Dakwa and Politics: The Case of PKS (Prosperous Justice Party)' in Darwis Khudori (ed.), *The Rise of Religion-Based Political Movements: A Threat or A Chance for Peace, Security and Development among the Nations?* (Jakarta: Indonesian Conference on Religion and Peace, 2009)

Hatta, Mohammad, *Sekitar Proklamasi 17 Agustus 1945 (About the Proclamation of 17 August 1945)* (Jakarta: Tintamas, 1969)

Hazis, Faisal S., 'Patronage, Power and Prowess: Barisan Nasional's Equilibrium Dominance in East Malaysia' (2015) 33(2) *Kajian Malaysia* 1

Hefner, Robert W., 'Muslim Democrats and Islamist Violence in Post-Soeharto Indonesia' in Robert W. Hefner (ed.), *Remaking Muslim Politics: Pluralism, Contestation, and Democratization* (Princeton: Princeton University Press, 2004)

Hefner, Robert W., 'Where Have All the Abangan Gone? Religionization and the Decline of Non-Standard Islam in Contemporary Indonesia' in Michel Picard and Rémy Madinier (eds.), *Politics of Religion in Indonesia: Syncretism, Orthodoxy, and Religious Convention in Java and Bali* (Oxon: Routledge, 2011)

Helmke, Gretchen, and Rios-Figueroa, Julio, 'Introduction: Courts in Latin America' in Gretchen Helmke and Julio Rios-Figueroa (eds.), *Courts in Latin America* (Cambridge: Cambridge University Press, 2011)

Helmke, Gretchen, and Rios-Figueroa, Julio, (eds.), *Courts in Latin America* (Cambridge: Cambridge University Press, 2011)

Helmke, Gretchen, and Rosenbluth, Frances, 'Regimes and the Rule of Law: Judicial Independence in Comparative Perspective' (2009) 12 *Annual Review of Political Science* 345

Helmke, Gretchen, and Staton, Jeffrey K., 'The Puzzling Judicial Politics of Latin America: A Theory of Litigation, Judicial Decisions, and Interbranch Conflict' in Gretchen Helmke and Julio Rios-Figueroa (eds.), *Courts in Latin America* (Cambridge: Cambridge University Press, 2011)

Hering, Bob, *Soekarno: Founding Father of Indonesia, A Biography*, Vol. 1. (Indonesia: Hasta Mitra, 2003)

Hesko, Tracy, 'Rights Rhetoric as an Instrument of Religious Oppression in Sri Lanka' (2006) 29(1) *Boston College International and Comparative Law Review* 123

Hirschl, Ran, *Constitutional Theocracy* (Cambridge, Mass.: Harvard University Press, 2010)

Horowitz, Donald L., *Ethnic Groups in Conflict*, 2nd ed. (Berkeley: University of California Press, 2011)

Horowitz, Donald L., *Constitutional Change and Democracy in Indonesia* (Cambridge: Cambridge University Press, 2013)

Horowitz, Donald L., 'Democracy in Divided Societies' (1993) 4 *Journal of Democracy* 18

Hosen, Nadirsyah, 'Behind the Scenes: Fatwas of Majelis Ulama Indonesia (1975–1998)' (2004) 15 *Journal of Islamic Studies* 147

Hosen, Nadirsyah, 'Religion and the Indonesian Constitution: A Recent Debate' (2005) 26 *Journal of Southeast Asian Studies* 419

Hosen, Nadirsyah, *Shari'a & Constitutional Reform in Indonesia* (Singapore: Institute of Southeast Asian Studies, 2007)

Hosen, Nadirsyah, 'The Constitutional Court and "Islamic" Judges in Indonesia' (2016) 16 (3) *Australian Journal of Asian Law* Article 4

'Hotel managers arrested over "Nirvana style" dinner event', *The Sunday Times* (27 January 2013), online: www.sundaytimes.lk/130127/news/hotel-managers-arrested-over-nirvana-style-dinner-event-30406.html

Howard, A. E. Dick, 'The Essence of Constitutionalism' in Kenneth W. Thompson and Rett T. Ludwikowski, (eds.), *Constitutionalism and Human Rights: America, Poland, and France* (Lanham, MD: University Press of America, 1991)

Hume, Tim, '"Fascists" in saffron robes? The rise of Sri Lanka's Buddhist ultra-nationalists', *CNN* (18 July 2014), online: edition.cnn.com/2014/07/17/world/asia/sri-lanka-bodu-bala-sena-profile/

Ibrahim, Ahmad, 'The Position of Islam in the Constitution of Malaysia' in Tan Sri
    Mohamed Suffian, H. P. Lee, and F. A. Trindade (eds.), *The Constitution of
    Malaya: Its Development: 1957–1977* (Oxford: Oxford University Press, 1978)
Ichwan, Moch Nur, 'Towards a Puritanical Moderate Islam: The Majelis Ulama
    Indonesia and the Politics of Religious Orthodoxy' in Martin van Bruinessen (ed.),
    Contemporary Developments in Indonesian Islam: Explaining the Conservative Turn
    (Singapore: Institute of Southeast Asian Studies, 2013)
Ikatan Muslimin Malaysia, *Buku Pengenalan Ikatan Muslimin Malaysia* (*Intro-
    ductory Book of the Malaysian Muslim Solidarity*), online: isma.org.my/v2/buku-
    pengenalan/
Imam, Mohamed, 'Freedom of Religion under the Federal Constitution of Malaysia –
    A Reappraisal' (1994) 2 *Current Law Journal* lvii
Imtiyaz, A. R. M., 'The Politicization of Buddhism and Electoral Politics in Sri Lanka'
    in Ali Riaz (ed.), *Religion and Politics in South Asia* (Oxon: Routledge, 2010)
Indonesian Center for Law and Policies Studies, 'The Re-Election of Constitutional
    Judges as a Momentum in Reorganizing the Public Officials Elections', *Indonesia
    Law Reform Weekly Digest*, 35th ed. (October 2013)
Indonesian Survey Institute, 'Trend Dukungan Nilai Islamis versus Nilai Sekular
    di Indonesia' ('Trends of support for Islamist values versus secular values in Indo-
    nesia'), *Lembaga Survei Indonesia* (October 2007), online: www.lsi.or.id/riset/310/
    trend-dukungan-nilai-islamis-versus-nilai-sekular
Indrayana, Denny, *Indonesian Constitutional Reform 1999–2002: An Evaluation of
    Constitution-making in Transition* (Jakarta: Kompas, 2008)
Intan, Benyamin Fleming, '*Public Religion' and the Pancasila-Based State of Indo-
    nesia: An Ethical and Sociological Analysis* (New York: Peter Lang, 2006)
International Bar Association (IBA), 'Justice in Retreat: A Report on the Independence
    of the Legal Profession and the Rule of Law in Sri Lanka', *IBA Human Rights
    Institute Report* (London: IBA, 2009)
International Bar Association (IBA), 'Sri Lanka: Failing to Protect the Rule of Law and
    Independence of the Judiciary', *IBA Human Rights Institute Report* (London: IBA,
    November 2001)
International Crisis Group, 'Sri Lanka's authoritarian turn: The need for international
    action', *Asia Report*, No. 243 (20 February 2013), online: www.crisisgroup.org/~/
    media/Files/asia/south-asia/sri-lanka/243-sri-lankas-authoritarian-turn-the-need-for-
    international-action.pdf
International Crisis Group, 'Sri Lanka's Judiciary: Politicised Courts, Compromised
    Rights', *Asia Report*, No. 172 (30 June 2009)
Jayawickrama, Nihal, 'Reflections on the Making and Content of the 1972 Consti-
    tution: An Insider's Perspective' in Asanga Welikala (ed.), *The Sri Lankan Republic
    at 40: Reflections on Constitutional History, Theory and Practice* (Colombo: Centre
    for Policy Alternatives, 2012)
Jayawickrama, Nihal, 'The Judiciary under the 1978 Constitution' in Asanga Welikala
    (ed.), *Reforming Sri Lankan Presidentialism: Provenance, Problems and Prospects*,
    Vol. I (Colombo: Centre for Policy Alternatives, 2015)
Juergensmeyer, Mark, *Terror in the Mind of God: The Global Rise of Religious Violence*,
    3rd ed. (Berkeley, Los Angeles, and London: University of California Press, 2001)

Kanagasabai, Chandra, 'Malaysia: Limited and Intermittent Judicialization of Politics' in Bjorn Dressel (ed.), *The Judicialization of Politics in Asia* (Oxon: Routledge, 2013)

Keith, Linda Camp, 'Judicial Independence and Human Rights Protection Around the World' (2000) 85 *Judicature* 195

Kessler, Clive, 'Malaysia's GE13: What happened? What now?', *New Mandala* (12 June 2013), online: asiapacific.anu.edu.au/newmandala/2013/06/12/malaysias-ge13-what-happened-what-now-part-1/

Khoo Boo Teik. 'Between Law and Politics: The Malaysian Judiciary since Independence' in Kanishka Jayasuriya (ed.), *Law, Capitalism and Power in Asia* (London: Routledge, 1999)

Khouw, Ida Indawati, '3 years on, GKI Yasmin Church remains victim of absence of the state', *The Jakarta Post* (4 December 2011), online: www.thejakartapost.com/news/2011/12/24/3-years-gki-yasmin-church-remains-victim-absence-state.html

Kim, Hyung-Jun, 'The Changing Interpretation of Religious Freedom in Indonesia' (1998) 29(2) *Journal of Southeast Asian Studies* 357

'Kisah Kang Jalal Soal Syiah Indonesia' ('Kang Jalal's story on Indonesian Shiites'), *Tempo* (3 September 2012), online: www.tempo.co/read/news/2012/09/03/173427066/Kisah-Kang-Jalal-Soal-Syiah-di-IndonesiaBagian-2

'Kisruh di Sidang MK, Akumulasi Kekecewaan Publik' ('Chaos in Constitutional Court, accumulation of public frustration'), *Kompas* (16 November 2013), online: nasional.kompas.com/read/2013/11/16/1441030/Kisruh.di.Sidang.MK.Akumulasi.Keke cewaan.Publik

Kusrin, Zuliza Mohd et al., 'Legal Provisions and Restrictions on the Propagation of Non-Islamic Religions among Muslims in Malaysia' (2013) 31(2) *Kajian Malaysia* 1

Kusuma, RM A. B., *Lahirnya Undang-undang Dasar 1945 (Memuat Salinan Dokumen Otentik Badan Oentoek Menyelidiki Oesaha-oesaha Persiapan Kemerdekaan) (The Birth of the 1945 Constitution (Containing Copies of Authentic Documents of the Investigating Committee for Preparatory Work for Indonesian Independence))*, rev. ed., (Jakarta: University of Indonesia Law Faculty Publishers, 2009)

'Latest trends in religious restrictions and hostilities', *Pew Research Center: Religious and Public Life* (26 February 2015), online: www.pewforum.org/2015/02/26/religious-hostilities/

Latif, Baharuddin Abdul, *Islam Memanggil: Rencana-rencana Sekitar Perjuangan PAS, 1951–1987 (Islam Is Calling: Articles on the Struggle of PAS, 1951–1987)* (Perak: Pustaka Abrar, 1994)

Lerner, Hanna, *Making Constitutions in Deeply Divided Societies* (Cambridge: Cambridge University Press, 2011)

Liddle, R. William, 'New Patterns of Islamic Politics in Democratic Indonesia', *Asia Program Special Report*, No. 110 (Washington: Woodrow Wilson Center, 2003)

Liddle, R. William, 'The Islamic Turn in Indonesia: A Political Explanation' (1996) 55 *Journal of Asian Studies* 613

'Light Cikeusik sentencing highlights legal discrimination: Rights group', *The Jakarta Post* (29 July 2011), online: www.thejakartapost.com/news/2011/07/29/light-cikeusik-sentencing-highlight-legal-discrimination-rights-group.html

Lindsey, Tim, 'Indonesia: Devaluing Asian Values, Rewriting Rule of Law' in Randall Peerenboom (ed.), *Asian Discourses of Rule of Law: Theories and Implementation of Rule of Law in Twelve Asian Countries, France and the U.S.* (Oxon: Routledge, 2004)

Lindsey, Tim, 'Indonesian Constitutional Reform: Muddling towards Democracy' (2002) 6 *Singapore Journal of International and Comparative Law* 244

Lindsey, Tim, and Pausacker, Helen, (eds.), *Religion, Law and Intolerance in Indonesia* (Oxon: Routledge, 2016)

Liow, Joseph Chinyong, *Piety and Politics: Islamism in Contemporary Malaysia* (New York: Oxford University Press, 2009)

Ljiphart, Arend, 'Constitutional Design in Divided Societies' (2004) 2 *Journal of Democracy* 15

Loh, Francis, 'Understanding the 2004 election results: Looking beyond the Pak Lah factor', *Aliran Monthly*, Issue 3 (2004), online: aliran.com/archives/monthly/2004a/3g.html

Madison, James, 'The Structure of the Government Must Furnish the Proper Checks and Balances between the Different Departments', *The Federalist Papers* (6 February 1788), No. 51

'Main functions', *Ministry of Buddha Sasana and Religious Affairs*, online: mbra.gov.lk/en/about-us/main-functions

'Malaysia not secular state, says Najib', *Bernama* (17 July 2007), online: www.bernama.com/bernama/v3/printable.php?id=273699

Malaysian Department of Statistics, *Population Distribution and Basic Demographic Characteristic Report 2010* (2010), online: bit.ly/1uxCQxp

Marga Institute, *The Social Image of the Judicial System in Sri Lanka* (Colombo: Marga Press, 2004)

Matthews, Bruce, 'Christian Evangelical Conversions and the Politics of Sri Lanka' (2007) 80(3) *Pacific Affairs* 455

Means, Gordon P., *Malaysian Politics: The Second Generation* (Singapore: Oxford University Press, 1991)

Mietzner, Marcus, 'Comparing Indonesia's Party Systems of the 1950s and the Post-Suharto Era: From Centrifugal to Centripetal Inter-Party Competition' (2008) 39 *Journal of Southeast Asian Studies* 431

Mietzner, Marcus, 'Political Conflict Resolution and Democratic Consolidation in Indonesia: The Role of the Constitutional Court' (2010) 10 *Journal of East Asian Studies* 397

Millie, Julian, 'One year after the Cikeusik tragedy', *Inside Indonesia*, Edition 107 (January–March 2012), online: www.insideindonesia.org/weekly-articles/one-year-after-the-cikeusik-tragedy

'MK Legowo Sambut UU Baru' ('Constitutional Court accepts the new law'), *Hukumonline* (22 June 2011), online: www.hukumonline.com/berita/baca/lt4e0173 27806e1/mk-legowo-sambut-uu-baru

Moh Mahfud M.D., 'Kebebasan Agama dalam Perspektif Konstitusi' ('Religious freedom in constitutional perspective'), presented at the Conference of Religious Leaders of the ICRP: Strengthening Religious Freedom in Indonesia, Demanding Commitment from Elected President and Vice President (5 October 2009), online: www.mahfudmd.com/index.php?page=web.MakalahWeb&id=3&aw=1&ak=8

Mohamad, Maznah, 'The Ascendance of Bureaucratic Islam and the Secularization of the Sharia in Malaysia' (2010) 83(3) *Pacific Affairs* 505

Mohan, Sulochana Ramiah, 'Sri Lanka Becoming a Banana Republic', *Ceylon Today* (22 June 2014)

Moustafa, Tamir, 'Judging in God's Name: State Power, Secularism, and the Politics of Islamic Law in Malaysia' (2014) 3(1) *Oxford Journal of Law and Religion* 152

Moustafa, Tamir, 'Liberal Rights versus Islamic Law? The Construction of a Binary in Malaysian Politics' (2013) 47(4) *Law and Society Review* 771

Moustafa, Tamir, 'The Politics of Religious Freedom in Malaysia' (2014) 29 *Maryland Journal of International Law* 481

Muhammad, Djibril, 'Pemerintah Persulit Pembangunan Masjid Al-Munawar' ('Authorities complicate building of Al-Munawar Mosque'), *Republika* (15 March 2013), online: www.republika.co.id/berita/dunia-islam/islam-nusantara/13/03/15/mjpg22-pemerintah-persulit-imb-pembangunan-masjid-al-munawar

Mujani, Saiful, Analisis Parpol: PKS, Tantangan Baru Politik Indonesia ('Political Party Analysis: PKS, A New Challenge in Indonesian Politics'), *Media Indonesia* (28 July 2005)

Mujani, Saiful, and Liddle, R. William, 'Personalities, Parties, and Voters' (2010) 21 *Journal of Democracy* 35

Musa, Mohd Faizal, 'The Malaysian Shi'a: A Preliminary Study of Their History, Oppression, and Denied Rights' (2013) 6(4) *Journal of Shi'a Islamic Studies* 411

Mydans, Seth, 'Churches attacked in Malaysian "Allah" dispute', *The New York Times* (8 January 2010), online: www.nytimes.com/2010/01/09/world/asia/09malaysia.html

Naskah Komprehensif Perubahan Undang-undang Dasar Negara Republik Indonesia Tahun 1945: Latar Belakang, Proses, dan Hasil Pembahasan 1999–2002, Buku VIII Warga Negara dan Penduduk, Hak Asasi Manusia dan Agama (*Comprehensive Manuscript of Amendments of the 1945 Constitution of the Republic of Indonesia: Background, Process, and Discussion Results, 1999–2002, Book VIII on Citizens and Residents, Human Rights and Religion*) (Jakarta: Sekretariat Jenderal dan Kepaniteraan Mahkamah Konstitusi, 2010) 529–31

Nasution, Adnan Buyong, *The Aspiration for Constitutional Government in Indonesia: A Socio-legal Study of the Indonesian Konstituante 1956–1959* (Jakarta: Pustaka Sinar Harapan, 1992)

Neo, Jaclyn, 'What's in a Name? Malaysia's Allah Controversy and the Judicial Intertwining of Islam and Ethnic Identity' (2014) 12 *International Journal of Constitutional Law* 751

Noer, Deliar, *The Modernist Muslim Movement in Indonesia, 1900–1942* (Singapore: Oxford University Press, 1973)

Noor, Farish, *Islam Embedded: The Historical Development of the Pan-Malaysian Islamic Party PAS, 1951–2003*, Vol. 1, 2 vols. (Kuala Lumpur: Malaysian Sociological Research Institute, 2004)

Office of the High Commissioner for Human Rights, *General Comment No. 22: Article 18 (Freedom of Thought, Conscience, and Religion)*, para. 9, CCPR/C/21/Rev.1/Add.4 (30 July 1993), online: www.unhchr.ch/tbs/doc.nsf/(Symbol)/9a30112 c27d1167cc12563ed004d8f15?Opendocument

Othman, Norani, 'Islamization and Democratization in Malaysia' in Ariel Heryanto and Sumit K. Mandal (eds.), *Challenging Authoritarianism in Southeast Asia* (London and New York: RoutledgeCurzon, 2003)

Panggabean Rizal, and Ali-Fauzi, Ihsan, *Pemolisian Konflik Keagamaan di Indonesia (Policing Religious Conflict in Indonesia)* (Jakarta: PUSAD Paramadina, 2014)

Parker, M. Todd, 'The Freedom to Manifest Religious Belief: An Analysis of the Necessity Clauses of the ICCPR and the ECHR', (2006) 17 *Duke Journal of International & Comparative Law* 91

Parkinson, Charles O. H., *Bills of Rights and Decolonization: The Emergence of Domestic Human Rights Instruments in Britain's Overseas Territories* (Oxford: Oxford University Press, 2007)

Perera, Jehan, 'Inter-Religious Empathy That Waits to Be Harnessed', *National Peace Council of Sri Lanka Newsletter* (2014)

'Perkasa admits getting aid from Putrajaya', *The Malaysian Insider* (25 December 2013), online: www.themalaysianinsider.com/malaysia/article/perkasa-admits-getting-aid-from-putrajaya

Perlez, Jane, 'Once Muslim, now Christian and caught in the courts', *The New York Times* (24 August 2006), online: www.nytimes.com/2006/08/24/world/asia/24malaysia .html?_r=0

'Rising tide of restrictions on religion', *Pew Research Center: Religion and Public Life*, (20 September 2012), online: www.pewforum.org/2012/09/20/rising-tide-of-restric tions-on-religion-findings/

'Rising restrictions on religion – One-third of the world's population experiences an increase', *Pew Research Center: Religion and Public Life*, (9 August 2011), online: www.pewforum.org/2011/08/09/rising-restrictions-on-religion2/

Pinto-Jayawardena, Kishali, 'Protecting the Independence of the Judiciary: A Critical Analysis of the Sri Lankan Law' in *Sri Lanka: State of Human Rights 1999* (Colombo: Law & Society Trust, 1999)

Pinto-Jayawardena, Kishali, and Weliamuna, J. C., 'Corruption in Sri Lanka's Judiciary' in Transparency International, *Global Corruption Report 2007*: Corruption in Judicial Systems (Cambridge: Cambridge University Press, 2007)

Platzdasch, Bernhard, 'Down but not out: Islamic political parties did not do well, but Islamic politics are going mainstream', *Inside Indonesia* (Jul.–Sept. 2009), online: www.insideindonesia.org/feature-editions/down-but-not-out

Platzdasch, Bernhard, *Islamism in Indonesia: Politics in the Emerging Democracy* (Singapore: Institute of Southeast Asian Studies, 2009)

Pompe, Sebastiaan, *The Indonesian Supreme Court: A Study of Institutional Collapse* (Ithaca, NY: Cornell Southeast Asia Program Publications, 2005)

Posner, Richard A., *How Judges Think* (Cambridge, Mass.: Harvard University Press, 2010)

'PTUN Batalkan Keppres Pengangkatan Patrialis Akbar' ('Administrative Court invalidates presidential decree appointing Patrialis Akbar'), *Kompas* (23 December 2013), online: nasional.kompas.com/read/2013/12/23/1818029/PTUN.Batalkan.Keppres .Pengangkatan.Patrialis.Akbar

Public Representations Committee on Constitutional Reform, 'Report on Public Representations Committee on Constitutional Reform', (May 2016), online: www.yourconstitution.lk/PRCRpt/PRC_english_report-A4.pdf

Raillon, Francois, 'The Return of Pancasila: Secular vs. Islamic Norms, Another Look at the Struggle for State Dominance in Indonesia' in Michel Picard and Rémy Madinier (eds.), *Politics of Religion in Indonesia: Syncretism, Orthodoxy, and Religious Contention in Java and Bali* (Abingdon, Oxon and New York: Routledge, 2011)

Ramanayake, Wasantha, 'SC to communicate determination of anti conversion Bill to President and Speaker', *Daily News* (11 August 2004), online: archives.dailynews .lk/2004/08/11/new12.html

Ramseyer, J. Mark, 'The Puzzling (In)dependence of Courts: A Comparative Approach' (1994) 23 *The Journal of Legal Studies* 721

Reilly, Benjamin, *Democracy in Divided Societies: Electoral Engineering for Conflict Management* (Cambridge: Cambridge University Press, 2001)

'Report of the Buddha Sasana Presidential Commission: Summary of conclusions and recommendations', *Lankaweb* (1 May 2012), online: www.lankaweb.com/news/ items/2012/05/01/report-of-the-buddha-sasana-presidential-commission-2002-summary-of-conclusions-and-recommendations

Reynolds, Andrew, (ed.), *The Architecture of Democracy: Constitutional Design, Conflict Management, and Democracy* (New York: Oxford University Press, 2002)

Ricklefs, M. C., *A History of Modern Indonesia since C. 1200*, 4th ed., (Stanford: Stanford University Press, 2008)

Rios-Figueroa, Julio, 'Institutions for Constitutional Justice in Latin America' in Gretchen Helmke and Julio Rios-Figueroa (eds.), *Courts in Latin America* (Cambridge: Cambridge University Press, 2011)

Saeed, Abdullah, and Saeed, Hassan, *Freedom of Religion, Apostasy, and Islam* (Oxon: Routledge, 2004)

Salim, Arskal, *Challenging the Secular State: The Islamization of Law in Modern Indonesia* (Honolulu: University of Hawai'i Press, 2008)

Sartori, Giovanni, 'Constitutionalism: A Preliminary Discussion' (1962) 56 *American Political Science Review* 853

Schonthal, Benjamin, 'Buddhism and the Constitution: The Historiography and Postcolonial Politics of Section 6' in Asanga Welikala (ed.), *The Sri Lankan Republic at 40: Reflections on Constitutional History, Theory and Practice* (Colombo: Centre for Policy Alternatives, 2012)

Schonthal, Benjamin, 'Constitutionalizing Religion: The Pyrrhic Success of Religious Rights in Post-Colonial Sri Lanka' (2014) 29 *Journal of Law and Religion* 470

Schonthal, Benjamin, 'Environments of Law: Islam, Buddhism, and the State in Contemporary Sri Lanka' (2016) 75(1) *The Journal of Asian Studies* 137

Schonthal, Benjamin, 'Securing the Sasana through Law: Buddhist Constitutionalism and Buddhist-interest Litigation in Sri Lanka' (2016) 50(6) *Modern Asian Studies* 1996

Schonthal, Benjamin, 'The Legal Regulation of Buddhism in Contemporary Sri Lanka' in Rebecca Redwood French and Mark A. Nathan (eds.), *Buddhism and Law: An Introduction* (Cambridge: Cambridge University Press, 2014)

Schonthal, Benjamin, 'What Is Buddhist Constitutionalism?' Paper presented at the Harvard Law School's Institute for Global Law and Policy (IGLP) Asian Regional Workshop (Bangkok, 6–10 January 2017)

Schonthal, Benjamin, *Buddhism, Politics, and the Limits of Law* (Cambridge: Cambridge University Press, 2016)

Schonthal, Benjamin and Welikala, Asanga, 'Buddhism and the Regulation of Religion in the New Constitution: Past Debates, Present Challenges, and Future
Options', No. 3, *CPA Working Papers on Constitutional Reform* (July 2016)

Scolnicov, Anat, *The Right to Religious Freedom in International Law: Between Group
Rights and Individual Rights* (Abingdon, Oxon and New York: Routledge, 2011)

Seah, Datuk George, 'Crisis in the judiciary: The hidden story', *The Malaysian Bar*
(1 May 2004), online: www.malaysianbar.org.my/administration_of_justice/crisis_in_
the_judiciary.html

Secretariat for Muslims, *Violations of Muslim' Civil & Political Rights in Sri Lanka*.
Report submitted to the UN Human Rights Committee (9 September 2014)

SETARA Institute, *Berpihak dan Bertindak Intoleran: Laporan Kondisi Kebebasan
Beragama/Berkeyakinan di Indonesia 2008* (*Siding and Acting Intolerantly: Report
on the Freedom of Religion and Belief in Indonesia 2008*) (Jakarta: SETARA Institute,
2009)

SETARA Institute, *Kepimpinan Tanpa Prakarsa: Laporan Kondisi Kebebasan
Beragama/Berkeyakinan di Indonesia 2012* (*Leadership without Initiative: Report on
the Freedom of Religion and Belief in Indonesia 2012*) (Jakarta: SETARA Institute
2013)

SETARA Institute, *Laporan Kondisi Kebebasan Beragama/Berkeyakinan di Indonesia
2015: Politik Harapan, Minim Pembuktian* (*Report on the Condition of the Freedom
of Religion and Conscience in Indonesia 2015: Hope Politics, Minimal Delivery*)
(Jakarta: SETARA Institute, 2016)

SETARA Institute, *Negara Harus Bersikap: Tiga Tahun Laporan Kondisi Kebebasan
Beragama/Berkeyakinan di Indonesia 2007–2009* (*The State Should Take Action:
Three Years Report on the Freedom of Religion and Belief in Indonesia 2007–2009*)
(Jakarta: SETARA Institute, 2009)

SETARA Institute, *Negara Menyangkal: Kondisi Kebebasan Beragama/Berkeyakinan
di Indonesia 2010* (*Denial by the State: Report on the Freedom of Religion and Belief
in Indonesia 2010*) (Jakarta: SETARA Institute, 2010)

SETARA Institute, *Politik Diskriminasi Rezim SBY: Laporan Kondisi Kebebasan
Beragama/Berkeyakinan di Indonesia 2011* (*Political Discrimination by the SBY
Regime: Report on the Freedom of Religion and Belief in Indonesia 2011*) (Jakarta:
SETARA Institute, 2012)

SETARA Institute, *Tunduk Pada Penghakiman Massa: Laporan Kebebasan Beragama
dan Berkeyakinan di Indonesia 2007* (*Bowing to Public Pressure: Report on the
Freedom of Religion and Belief in Indonesia 2007*) (2009)

Sharma, Arundhati, 'Religion-Politics Nexus and Security Dynamics in South Asia:
The Case of Sri Lanka' (2011) 2 *Scholar's Voice: A New Way of Thinking* 29

Sheridan, L. A., and Groves, Harry. E., *The Constitution of Malaysia*, 4th ed.
(Singapore: Malayan Law Journal, 1987)

Shuaib, F. S., 'Malaysian Judicial Appointment Process: An Overview of the Reform'
(2011) 7 *Journal of Applied Sciences Research* 2273

Simanjuntak, Hotli, and Parlina, Ina, 'Aceh fully enforces Sharia', *The Jakarta Post*
(7 February 2014), online: www.thejakartapost.com/news/2014/02/07/aceh-fully-
enforces-Sharia.html

Sirisena, Priyalal, 'Bill to establish Christian institution challenged in SC', *The Island*
(18 January 2003), online: www.island.lk/2003/01/18/news10.html

'Sistem Hukum di Indonesia Itu Religius, Bukan Sekuler' ('The legal system in Indonesia is religious, not secular'), *Suara Pembaruan* (29 November 2013), online: www.suarapembaruan.com/home/sistem-hukum-di-indonesia-itu-religius-bukan-sekuler/45730

Soekarno, *Under the Banner of Revolution: Vol. I* (Publication Committee, 1966)

Soesilo, Daud, 'Translating the Names of God: Recent Experience from Indonesian and Malaysia' (2001) 52(4) *The Bible Translator* 414

Special Rapporteur of the Sub-Commission on Prevention of Discrimination and Protection of Minorities, *Study of Discrimination in the Matter of Religious Rights and Practices*, UN Doc. E/CN.4/Sub.2/200/Rev.1 (1960) (by Arcot Krishnaswami)

Special Rapporteur of the Sub-Commission on Prevention of Discrimination and Protection of Minorities, *Elimination of All Forms of Intolerance and Discrimination Based on Religion or Belief*, UN Doc. E/CN.4/Sub.2/1984/28 (3 August 1984)

'Speech by the prime minister at the 57th National Quran Recitation Ceremony', *Prime Minister's Office* (13 May 2014), online: www.pmo.gov.my/?menu=speech&page=1676&news_id=716&speech_cat=2

'Sri Lanka: Appointment of new chief justice undermines rule of law', *International Commission of Jurists Press Release* (15 January 2013), online: www.icj.org/sri-lanka-newly-appointed-chief-justices-long-record-of-blocking-justice/

Suaedy, Ahmad, et al., *Islam, the Constitution, and Human Rights: The Problematics of Religious Freedom in Indonesia* (Jakarta: Wahid Institute, 2010)

Suara Rakyat Malaysia (SUARAM), *Malaysia: Human Rights Report 2004* (2005)

Suara Rakyat Malaysia (SUARAM), *Malaysia: Human Rights Report 2005* (2006)

Suara Rakyat Malaysia (SUARAM), *Malaysia: Human Rights Report 2009* (2010)

Sunstein, Cass R., 'Constitutionalism, Prosperity, Democracy: Transition in Eastern Europe' (1991) 2 *Constitutional Political Economy* 371

Sunstein, Cass R., *Designing Democracy: What Constitutions Do* (New York: Oxford University Press, 2001)

Tamanaha, Brian Z., 'The History and Elements of the Rule of Law' (2012) *Singapore Journal of Legal Studies* 232

Tambiah, Stanley Jeyaraja, *Buddhism Betrayed? Religion, Politics, and Violence in Sri Lanka* (Chicago: University of Chicago Press, 1992)

Tan, Roger, 'Religion and the law', *The Star* (12 January 2014), online: www.thestar.com.my/Opinion/Columnists/Legally-Speaking/Profile/Articles/2014/01/12/Religion-and-the-law/

Thaheer, Minna, 'Why the Proportional Representation System Fails to Promote Minority Interests? A Discussion on Contemporary Politics and the Sri Lanka Muslim Congress' (2010) 1 *Journal of Power, Conflict & Democracy in South & Southeast Asia* 95

Thomas, Tommy, 'Is Malaysia an Islamic State?' (2006) 4 *Malayan Law Journal* xv–xlvi, xxix

Tie Fatt Hee, 'Constitutional Challenge to Freedom of Religion in Schools in Malaysia' (2008) 13 *Australia & New Zealand Journal of Law & Education* 89

Toh, Terence, 'Court of Appeal: Banning of book "Outrageous, Irrational"', *The Star* (27 July 2012), online: thestar.com.my/news/story.asp?file=/2012/7/27/nation/2012 0727130848&sec=nation

'Transparency in selecting constitutional judges', *Tempo.co* (15 August 2013), online: en.tempo.co/read/news/2013/08/15/080504615/Transparency-in-Selecting-Constitutional-Judges

'Trends in global restrictions on religion, Appendix E: Results by country', *Pew Research Center: Religious and Public Life* (23 June 2016), online: www.pewforum.org/files/2016/06/Restrictions2016appendixE.pdf

Tun Abdul Hamid Mohamad, 'Human Rights from the Perspective of Islamic Traditions and the Malaysian Constitution', National Forum on Human Rights (24 January 2014)

Tun Abdul Razak, Dato' Seri Mohd Najib bin, 'Perutusan Hari Raya Aidiladha 1434h/2013m YAB Perdana Menteri' ('The Prime Minister's Aidilfitri message'), *NajibRazak.com* (7 August 2013), online: www.najibrazak.com/bm/official-addresses/perutusan-perdana-menteri-sempena-hari-raya-aidilfitri-2013/

Tushnet, Mark, 'Constitution-making: An Introduction' (2013) 91 *Texas Law Review* 1983

Udagama, Deepika, 'The Sri Lankan Legal Complex and the Liberal Project: Only Thus Far and No More' in Terence C. Halliday, Lucien Karpik, and Malcolm M. Feeley (eds.), *Fates of Political Liberalism in the British Post-colony: The Politics of the Legal Complex* (New York: Cambridge University Press, 2014)

U.S. Department of State Report, From years 2002–2005, online: www.state.gov/j/drl/rls/irf/index.htm

U.S. Department of State. 'International religious freedom report from years 2003–2012', online: www.state.gov/j/drl/rls/irf/index.htm

U.S. Department of State, 'International religious freedom report for 2003' (2003), online: www.state.gov/j/drl/rls/irf/2003/index.htm

U.S. Department of State, 'International religious freedom report for 2004' (2004), online: www.state.gov/j/drl/rls/irf/2004/index.htm

U.S. Department of State, 'International religious freedom report for 2007' (2007), online: www.state.gov/j/drl/rls/irf/2007/index.htm

U.S. Department of State, 'International religious freedom report for 2008' (2008), online: www.state.gov/j/drl/rls/irf/2008/index.htm

U.S. Department of State, 'July – December 2010 International religious freedom report' (2011), online: www.state.gov/j/drl/rls/irf/2010_5/

Uyangoda, Jayadeva, 'Sri Lanka in 2010: Regime Consolidation in a Post-Civil War Era' (2011) 51 *Asian Survey* 131

Wählisch, Martin, 'ECHR chamber judgment case of *S.A.S. v. France*: Banning of burqas and niqabs legal?' *Cambridge Journal of International and Comparative Law Online* (July 2014), online: cjil.org.uk/2014/07/21/echr-chamber-judgment-case-s-s-v-france-banning-burqas-niqabs-legal/

Warnapala, W. A. Wiswa, 'Sri Lanka's New Constitution' (1980) 20 *Asian Survey* 914

Weiberg-Salzmann, Mirjam, 'The Radicalisation of Buddhism in the Twentieth and Twenty-First Centuries: The Buddha Sangha in Sri Lanka' (2014) 15(2) *Politics, Religion & Ideology* 288

Weiss, Meredith, 'The 1999 Malaysian General Elections: Issues, Insults, and Irregularities' (2000) 40 *Asian Survey* 413

Weiss, Meredith, 'Edging toward a New Politics in Malaysia: Civil Society at the Gate?' (2009) 49 *Asian Survey* 741

Welsh, Bridget, 'Shifting Terrain: Elections in the Mahathir Era' in Bridget Welsh (ed.), *Reflections – The Mahathir Years* (Washington: John Hopkins-SAIS, 2004)

'What are the functions and roles of the Syariah section', *Attorney General's Chambers*, online: www.agc.gov.my/index.php?option=com_content&view=article&id=187%3A what-are-the-functions-and-roles-of-the-syariah-section-attorney-generals-chambers& catid=73%3Aagc-faqs&Itemid=44&lang=en

Whittington, Keith E., 'Legislative Sanctions and the Strategic Environment of Judicial Review' (2003) 1 *International Journal of Constitutional Law* 446

Wickramaratne, Jayampathy, 'Reflections on the Making and Content of the 1972 Constitution: An Insider's Perspective' in Asanga Welikala (ed.), *The Sri Lankan Republic at 40: Reflections on Constitutional History, Theory and Practice* (Colombo: Centre for Policy Alternatives, 2012)

Wickramaratne, Jayampathy, *Fundamental Rights in Sri Lanka*, 2nd ed., (Colombo: Stamford Lake Publication, 2006)

Wickremesinghe, Roshini, 'The Role of Government and Judicial Action in Defining Religious Freedom: A Sri Lankan Perspective' (2009) 2 *International Journal of Religious Freedom* 29

Wilkinson, Steven I., *Votes and Violence: Electoral Competition and Ethnic Riots in India* (Cambridge: Cambridge University Press, 2006)

Willford, Andrew, 'The Letter of the Law and the Reckoning of Justice among Tamils in Malaysia' in Yew-Foong Hui (ed.), *Encountering Islam: The Politics of Religious Identities in Southeast Asia* (Singapore: Institute of Southeast Asian Studies, 2012)

Wilson, A. J., *The Gaullist System in Asia: The Constitution of Sri Lanka* (1978) (London and Basingstoke: Macmillan Press, 1980)

Woodward, Mark R., 'Indonesia, Islam, and the Prospect for Democracy' (2001) 21(2) *SAIS Review* 29

Zakaria, Fareed, 'The Rise of Illiberal Democracy' (1997) 76(6) *Foreign Affairs* 22

Zoelva, Hamdan, 'Negara Hukum dalam Perspektif Pancasila' ('Law state in the perspective of *Pancasila*'), (30 May 2009), online: hamdanzoelva.wordpress.com/ 2009/05/30/negara-hukum-dalam-perspektif-pancasila/

Archival Material

Alliance Party Memorandum to the Reid Commission (27 September 1956), CO889/6

Constitutional Proposals for the Federation of Malaya, Cmnd 210 (Her Majesty's Stationery Office, 1957), para. 59

Correspondence from Alan Lennox-Boyd to Lord Reid (26 September 1957), CO1030/486

Draft Memorandum by Jackson (undated), CO1030/494

Hansard, HC, Vol. 573, col. 713, 12 July 1957

Hearing of the Malayan Christians' Council before the Constitutional Commission (23 August 1956), CO889/6

Himpunan Risalah Sidang-sidang dari Badan Penyelidik Usaha Persiapan Kemerdekaan Indonesia (BPUPKI) (Tanggal 29 Mei 1945 –16 Juli 1945) dan Panitia Persiapan Kemerdekaan Indonesia (PPKI) (Tanggal 18 dan 19 Agustus 1945) Yang Berhubung Dengan Penyusunan Undang-undang Dasar 1945 (A Compilation of the Minutes of Meetings of the Investigating Committee for Preparatory Work for Indonesian Independence (BPUPKI) (29 May 1945–16 July 1945) and the Preparatory Committee for Indonesian Independence (18 and 19 August 1945) relating to the Drafting of the 1945 Constitution) (Djakarta: Sekretariat Negara Republik Indonesia, 1954)

Inward Telegram to the Commonwealth Relations Office from the United Kingdom High Commissioner in Pakistan (4 May 1957), DO35/6282

Jennings, Sir William Ivor, 'Working Drafts', in *Papers of Sir Ivor Jennings*, ICS 125/B/10.2.7 (on file with the Institute of Commonwealth Studies, London)

Meeting of the Alliance Party with the Reid Commission (27 September 1956), CO889/6

Memorandum by Dato' Panglima Kinta Haji Mohammed Eusoff to the Reid Commission (14 July 1956), CO889/6

Minutes of the 19th Meeting of the Working Party of the Constitution of the Federation (17 April 1957), CO941/25

Minutes of the First Meeting of the Working Party of the Constitution of the Federation (22 February 1957), CO941/25

Note on Islam as the Religion of the Federation of Malaya (undated), CO1030/440

Note on Pakistan and the Reid Commission Report, Constitutional Talks in London, May 1957 on the Future of Malaya (10 May 1957), DO35/6278

Official Report of the Federal Legislative Council Debates (1 May 1958)

Record of a Meeting held in the Commonwealth Relations Office (10 May 1957), CO1030/436

Record of a Meeting held in the Commonwealth Relations Office on 10 May 1957 (21 May 1957), CO 1030/436

Report of the Federation of Malaya Constitutional Commission (21 February 1957), DO35/6282

Report of the Federation of Malaya Constitutional Commission, Justice Abdul Hamid's Note of Dissent (21 February 1957), DO35/6282

Risalah Perubahan Undang-undang Dasar Negara Republik Indonesia Tahun 1945: 1999–2012 (Reports of the Amendments of the 1945 Constitution of the Republic of Indonesia: 1999–2012) (Jakarta: Sekretariat Jenderal Majelis Permusyawaratan Rakyat Republik Indonesia, 2002)

Sri Lanka Constituent Assembly Official Report, Debates Vol. 1 (Ceylon Government Press, 1972) (29 March 1971)

Index